President McKinley, War and Empire

American Presidents Series

Alexander Hamilton and the Growth of the New Nation
John C. Miller
With a new introduction by A. Owen Aldridge

Conversations with Lincoln
Compiled, edited, and annotated by Charles M. Segal
With a new preface by the editor and
an introduction by David Donald

Eisenhower and the American Crusades
Herbert S. Parmet

Fathers and Children:
Andrew Jackson and the Subjugation of the American Indian
Michael Paul Rogin

George Bush: The Life of a Lone Star Yankee
Herbert S. Parmet

Herbert H. Humphrey: The Politics of Joy
Charles L. Garrettson III

The Illusion of a Conservative Reagan Revolution
Larry M. Schwab

President McKinley, War and Empire
Richard F. Hamilton

President Roosevelt and the Coming of the War, 1941:
Appearances and Realities
Charles A. Beard
With a new introduction by Campbell Craig

Thomas Jefferson: America's Philosopher-King
Max Lerner
With an introduction by Robert Schmuhl

Woodrow Wilson: A Psychological Study
William Bullitt and Sigmund Freud

President McKinley, War and Empire

Volume 1

President McKinley and the Coming of War, 1898

Richard F. Hamilton

Transaction Publishers
New Brunswick (U.S.A.) and London (U.K.)

Library of Congress Catalog Number: 2005056879
ISBN: 0-7658-0329-1
Printed in the United States of America

Library of Congress Cataloging-in-Publication Data

Hamilton, Richard F.
    President McKinley, war and empire / Richard F. Hamilton.
        p. cm.—(American presidents series)
    Includes bibliographical references and index.
    Contents: v. 1. President McKinley and the coming of war, 1898.
    ISBN 0-7658-0329-1 (cloth : acid-free paper)
        1. Spanish-American War, 1898—Causes. 2. United States—Politics and government—1897-1901. 3. McKinley, William, 1843-1901. 4. United States—Territorial expansion. I. Title. II. Series.

E721.H36   2006
973.8'9—dc22   2005056879

Contents

Preface   *vii*

A Note on Sources   *ix*

Prologue   *xi*

Chapter 1   Power and Policymaking: Who Rules?   1

Chapter 2   William McKinley: From Niles to the White House   43

Chapter 3   The New President Selects His Cabinet   83

Chapter 4   The Decision for War   105

Chapter 5   Cuba and the American Press   149

Chapter 6   A Mobilization of the Masses?   171

Chapter 7   Public Pressures and the Congress   213

Chapter 8   On the Various Readings   239

Index   *255*

Preface

In the mid-nineties, I was working on a book that was entitled *The Major Social Theories*. But as it was getting much too large, I divided it into two volumes, the first of which would review Marxism, Marxist revisionism, and Leninism's focus on imperialism. That volume also grew enormously, with the result that I dropped one of the chapters, "Imperialism: The United States' Experience." I had also written on some American presidents in the post Civil War era, mostly sketches and rough drafts. My thought at the time was to combine these somehow in a book focused on the Spanish-American War and the beginnings of "the American Empire." After a digression for a large and complex volume dealing with the origins of World War I, I returned to work on this volume. The first result of this new effort was a long chapter entitled "Presidents, Bosses, and Businessmen: 1868-1896." That too had reached impressive size and I had not yet discussed Presidents Arthur, Cleveland, and Harrison. It occurred to me that it would be best to drop that chapter.

Several more years of work resulted in a 600-page manuscript (with some 200 pages of notes) entitled *President McKinley, War, and Empire*. I then realized that a division would be appropriate and useful. This volume, the first of two, deals with the origin of the war. The second, still to come, will deal with the outcome, with America's acquisition of a "New Empire."

This work has been supported by the Mershon Center at the Ohio State University. I wish to thank Richard Herrmann, the Center's director, and Mershon's superb staff, most especially Beth Russell, for their support and assistance.

Three good friends, William H. Form, David Trask, and Henry A. Turner, deserve special commendation. They have read and commented on all of the chapters, in some instances doing so for several versions. For all three, I wish to award a summa cum laude. My thanks also to various friends and associates who have provided generously of their time and wisdom—to Edward Bell, Michael Les Benedict, Paul Beck, G. William Domhoff, Hal Durian, Richard Gunther, Peter Hahn, John Higley, Austin Kerr, John H. Kessel, Richard Ned Lebow, Frederick Milford, Carman Miller, Randolph Roth, David Stebenne, and Herbert Weisberg.

Once again, the many contributions of Irene Hamilton are gratefully acknowledged.

A Note on Sources

Several sources have been used with great frequency in the following pages. To simplify their citation, some abbreviations will be used throughout. There are:

Biographical sources:

Dumas Malone, ed., *Dictionary of American Biography* (New York, 1946 [1934]). Abbreviated as DAB, followed by the volume and page numbers, e.g., for John Jacob Astor, we would have DAB, 1:397–399.

John A. Garraty and Mark C. Carnes, eds., *American National Biography* (New York, 1999). Abbreviated as ANB, the listing for Astor, for example, will be ANB, 1:696–699.

In addition, four leading American history textbooks have been cited at many places. They are:

Robert A. Divine, T. H. Breen, George M. Fredrickson, and R. Hal Williams, *America Past and Present*, Vol. 2, fifth edition (New York, 1999).

James A. Henretta, David Brody, Susan Ware, and Marilynn S. Johnson, *America's History*, Vol. 2, fourth edition (Boston, 2000).

Gary B. Nash, Julie Roy Jeffrey, John R. Howe, Peter J. Frederick, Allen F. Davis, and Allan M. Winkler, *The American People*, Vol. 2, fifth edition (New York, 2001).

Mary Beth Norton, David M. Katzman, Paul D. Escott, Howard P. Chudacoff, Thomas G. Paterson, and William M. Tuttle, Jr., *A People and a Nation*, fifth edition (Boston, 1998).

These will be abbreviated throughout as Divine et al., Henretta et al., and so forth.

Prologue

Why do the nations so furiously rage together? Or, put simply, why war? It is an ancient question. An easy formal answer would be that a nation's leaders chose war, seeing it somehow as their best or most appropriate option. To understand such choices, one must address two questions: Which individuals or groups made the decision? and, What were their motives?

In authoritarian regimes, the decision-makers are easily discerned. In 1740, for example, Frederick, the King of Prussia, chose to invade Silesia, then a part of the Austrian empire. Empress Maria Theresa responded in kind, deciding to meet war with war. Frederick's motivation might best be described as territorial aggrandizement. In this case, a twenty-eight-year-old monarch, one who had only recently gained the throne, took his nation to war.

Decisions for war made by individuals, the pure case, seems unlikely. One can easily imagine some larger group, the ruler's advisors, civilian and military, providing some direction or at least offering guidance. In 1914, the first decisions for war were taken by three authoritarian regimes: Austria-Hungary, Russia, and Germany. In all three states, the decision was the work of a small coterie, less than a dozen persons.

All three nations at that point had adopted constitutions, documents that specified the procedures of governance. We ordinarily think of constitutions as embodying liberal principles, as documents specifying limits on the powers of authoritarian rulers. But in this experience, surprisingly, all three constitutions contained clear, unambiguous statements assigning the war powers to the monarch alone.[1] Other "forces" might have been present within those societies—Social Darwinism, nationalism, imperialism, press campaigns, and so forth—but, given the basic governing arrangements, to have any effect on policy those influences would have to impact on the monarch or at least on members of the decision-making coterie.

The United States' Constitution, operative since 1789, stipulates a very different assignment of "the war powers." Article I, Section 8 states that, "The Congress shall have Power . . . To declare War . . . [and] To raise and support Armies." That means, unlike the authoritarian regimes, a decision for war would involve several hundred people.[2] Another clause in the same document specifies one of the powers of the president—Article II, Section 2 declares that: "The

President shall be Commander in Chief of the Army and Navy of the United States, and of the Militia of the several States, when called into the actual Service of the United States . . .''

That division of the powers could become a problem if a president and Congress were not in agreement. That precise problem did occur in the last months of Grover Cleveland's second term of office. Members of the Congress pressured the reluctant president, calling on him to intervene in support of the Cuban insurgents then fighting against oppressive Spanish rule. Cleveland effectively blocked those demands.[3] But within months similar demands were made of his successor, William McKinley. In this case, the demands from Congress were supported—or appeared to be supported—by demands from "the public" calling for American intervention to put an end to the suffering caused by Spanish oppression. That public "clamor" is said to have been generated by "sensational" press reports, by accounts that exaggerated or fabricated stories about the outrages perpetrated by the Spanish forces in Cuba. Under heavy pressure, especially after the sinking of the battleship *Maine*, McKinley conceded and called on Congress to authorize American intervention. This, in brief, was the beginning of the Spanish-American War.

That war-making process is a rare case, possibly unique in human history. It is a far cry from the wars decided by a monarch's decree or those decided by a monarch and his coterie. The hesitant steps toward republican forms of governance in the nineteenth century did allow some limited public influence in decision-making. In the post-Napoleonic era, the efforts of European intellectuals brought several nations to intervene in support of the Greek independence movement, to aid in the struggle against Ottoman rule.

Inflammatory newspaper reports and a popular clamor had some impact in the United States in 1812, those events preceding the declaration of war against Great Britain. The decision was made by 160 members of the Congress, the vote being 98 for and 62 against. Another new factor, partisanship, appeared at this time. A majority of the Republicans approved the declaration; all of the Federalists opposed it. Some public pressures were said to have helped generate the United States' war with Mexico in 1846. Again, the basic decision was taken by the Congress, by its 230 members, this time by an overwhelming majority.

In 1854, public pressures "played a role" in moving the British government to participate in the Crimean War. The actual decision to get involved, however, was made by a small group, by the cabinet. In 1870, Bismarck and Louis Napoleon had to be concerned with "public opinion" in the German states and in France. Decision-making at that point was clearly quite different from the war-making of Frederick or Napoleon Bonaparte. But still, the decisions for war taken in 1870, on both sides, were made by small coteries.

None of those nineteenth-century developments could match the circumstances in the United States in 1898 where public pressures were declared, by many authors, to have been an irresistible "force." That "outraged public" was moved, presumably, by those "sensational" newspaper accounts. And many members of Congress argued vociferously for intervention seeking to generate support. Some members portrayed themselves as responding to the demands made by their constituents. Although clearly reluctant, McKinley ultimately yielded and called on Congress to authorize American engagement. As opposed to the decisions made by monarchs or those made by small coteries, the 1898 decision resulted, supposedly, from the demands made by tens of millions of citizens. Ultimately, following McKinley's call for involvement, the decision for war was made several hundred persons, the members of the Congress.

Another group, big business leaders, should be considered in this connection. Most accounts of the 1896 election report that a coterie of big businessmen made McKinley the nation's president. With that victory, with the defeat of Bryan and "the people," big business was "in power." A curious disjuncture follows. Big business was generally opposed to the prospect of war with Spain, but despite those manifest objections, as of April 1898, the nation was at war. This curious disjunction, business "in power" but losing in an important contest, needs attention, some explanation.

This book reviews the American decision-making in 1898, the events that brought the nation to war. The task, basically, is to inquire about the accuracy of those portrayals, about the behavior of "the masses" with their "irresistible" demands, about the reactions of the Congress, and about McKinley's message to Congress, his call for involvement.

Wars may be divided into three parts, each with different participants, settings, and activities. The activities are: first, those involving the origins, the outbreak of the war; second, those involving the conduct of the war, actual combat; and third, those involving the outcome or settlement. This work reviews the origins of the Spanish-American War. The conduct, the actual fighting—in Manila Bay, at El Caney and San Juan Hill, at Santiago Bay, in Puerto Rico, and elsewhere—has been reviewed in many accounts.[4] The war's outcome was unexpected. The intervention to end the suffering in Cuba and to secure that island's independence ended with the United States' annexation of Puerto Rico, the Philippines, and several islands in the Pacific. That settlement will be the subject of a subsequent volume.

A final observation: This work is based entirely on published primary sources and on secondary works. It does not present new original source material. The aim, instead, is to reassess the uses made of previously published material, of the narrative accounts, biographies, and statistical evidence. It criticizes the key elements of "the economic interpretation" of the McKinley presidency, of the war, and of the subsequent territorial acquisitions. McKinley was not a "chocolate éclair," not a pliable figurehead easily moved by representatives of "the interests." Nor was he the cunning Machiavellian as portrayed in some later revisionist accounts. The war did not result from the competition of two New York City press lords, the proprietors of two low-quality newspapers. Nor was it the result of "irrepressible demands" made by "aroused masses" throughout the nation. Based on those same published sources, this work will provide other more plausible readings of those events.

Notes

1. The Russian constitution of 1906 is generally viewed as a step ahead, a progressive achievement, but the text tells a different story. Article 4 declares that: "To the All-Russian Emperor belongs the Supreme Autocratic Power. To obey his power, not only through fear, but also for the sake of conscience, is commanded by God Himself." With respect to the war powers, Article 13 announces that: "Our Sovereign the Emperor shall declare war and conclude peace as well as treaties with foreign states." See Richard F. Hamilton and Holger H. Herwig, eds., *The Origins of World War I* (New York, 2003), pp. 13–15.
2. For a comprehensive review, see Louis Fisher, *Presidential War Power* (Lawrence, KA, 1995).
3. The opposite experience, a president wishing war but with Congress either opposed or reluctant, is much more frequent. For a critical review and assessment of this experience, see Peter Irons, *War Powers: How the Imperial Presidency Hijacked the Constitution* (New York, 2005).
4. See those listed in chapter 4, note 1.

1

Power and Policymaking: Who Rules?

Much of American history has been written within the framework of the "progressive" tradition. A key work, one that established the new direction, is that of Charles A. Beard and Mary R. Beard, *The Rise of American Civilization*. The two volumes of the first edition appeared in 1927. Many other editions followed: trade versions, college versions, one-volume revisions, and more. Its impact was enormous, one account declaring that until the 1950s "this remarkable history was America's history—it was the touchstone of professional scholarship, it reached a wide public, and it was distilled by the Beards and by others into schoolbooks and read by the nation's children."[1]

Richard Hofstadter, an eminent historian of a later generation, remembered his excitement on first reading *The Rise* when, as he put it, "all American history seemed to dance to Beard's tune." The influence of this work extended far beyond the universities, it being chosen as a Book of the Month Club selection. Thomas Bender provides some of the details, writing that Beard was "this century's most influential scholar of American politics and history, and he was the most prolific as well. He wrote forty-seven books, plus seven more with Mary Beard and twenty-four with other collaborators. . . . When he died, his books had sold more than eleven million copies."[2]

The Beards' account of the Spanish-American War begins effectively with the 1896 presidential election, one depicted as a titanic struggle between "the people" and "the interests." In the decades after the Civil War a "Second American Revolution" had occurred when "big business" came to dominate the nation, replacing the previous leadership group, the "landed aristocracy." In the 1890s, the people—the nation's farmers and workers—were demonstrating, organizing, and taking political action, thus threatening the power of their big business opponents. The struggle culminated in the 1896 presidential campaign, which is introduced as follows: "At this juncture Marcus A. Hanna, a retired businessman, weary of the routine of the counting house and enamored of Warwick's role, entered the lists in full panoply. By a liberal expenditure of money, judicious publicity, and an early management of Negro politicians from the South, he made William McKinley the man of the hour."[3]

The "climax" of the Democratic convention came with the nomination of William Jennings Bryan, who "flung the gage full and fair in the face of the enemy, naming defiantly those for whom he spoke—the wage laborer, the country lawyer, the cross-roads merchant, the farmer, and the miner—Andrew Jackson's farmer-labor cohorts—and summoning them with the zeal of Peter the Hermit to the silver standard, that waved above his head, in a fateful battle against the plutocracy. . . . With the opposing forces sharply aligned, the great battle of 1896 was on. . . . [it was] the most clearly defined struggle of economic groups since the first campaign of Lincoln." McKinley won with a large plurality, Hanna's campaign having "succeeded beyond all calculations . . ."

Under McKinley's direction, the Republicans, described by the Beards simply as "the party of business enterprise," now "gave a new tone to American foreign policy." The authors briefly describe the Cuban struggle, touching on the threats to the property or lives of Americans living there and to American economic investments, mentioning also the damage done by the war. In this connection they refer to "a trade reaching approximately a hundred millions annually." The events leading up to the war are then reviewed, the Hearst-Pulitzer press war, the deLôme letter, and the sinking of the *Maine*. Overwhelmed by the bellicose demands coming from the press, the Congress, his own advisers, and the "public tumult," the weak president "surrendered" and called on Congress to authorize armed intervention.[4]

The Beards' discussion of the outcome—this focused on the annexation of the Philippines—begins with a description of McKinley on his knees praying for divine guidance. The authors then review the salient secular concerns, ending with this quotation: "Of course he was fully alive, as he said on another occasion, to the 'commercial opportunity to which American statesmanship cannot be indifferent. It is just to use every legitimate means for the enlargement of American trade.' "[5]

The Beards' depiction of these events may be summarized with three propositions: First, that the success of the Republicans in the 1896 election was a victory for big business and simultaneously a defeat for "the people." Second, in the 1898 decision for war, one salient concern was the threat to American investments and trade in Cuba. And third, the decision "for empire," specifically for the taking of the Philippines, stemmed largely from a concern with trade. The key foci in later progressive readings of the events of 1896–1900 are "big business" and its commercial interests, specifically the "growing importance" of foreign markets.

With "the party of business enterprise" in power, one would expect a presentation of evidence showing business demands or pressures for intervention in Cuba—but no such evidence appears there. Readily available evidence from 1898 in fact showed "big business" generally opposed to the prospect of a war. One would expect also some evidence showing business demands for expansion, for annexation of those new territories. But that evidence is also missing. Although Marcus Hanna was clearly a leading figure in McKinley's career, even the assumption of his dominant influence, as will be seen, must be qualified.

The Beards' work has had major, long-lasting influence. *The Rise of American Civilization* was the leading textbook in university-level American history courses in the 1930s and 1940s. Two outstanding textbooks of the "next generation," those of Samuel Eliot Morison and Henry Steele Commager and of John D. Hicks, were written within the same general framework.[6] And the leading current American history textbooks also follow in the progressive tradition.[7]

This work will review and assess the elements of the history produced by the Beards and continued in the work of their many successors. Four basic questions will be considered:

First, are the accounts of McKinley's career and of the 1896 presidential campaign accurate?

Second, is the portrait of the McKinley presidency accurate? Were his cabinet members and ambassadors drawn from big business? Were they agents of big business? Or did they represent some other interests?

Third, are the causes of the war with Spain accurately depicted?

Narrative accounts, sequences of factual observations, typically appear within some "guiding" theoretical framework. Knowingly or unknowingly, in order to deal with complex matters, we all need and make use of simplifying logics that are called theories. For their analyses of the McKinley presidency, the coming of the war, and the outcome of the war, progressive historians have made use of a class-dominance theory and a mass society theory. The fourth basic question asks about the adequacy of those theories. An alternative, elite theory, will be proposed and recommended.

Another basic question also needs attention: Is the war's outcome, the acquisition of the "new empire," accurately depicted? Because of the complexities involved, consideration of that question will be postponed. It will be addressed in the second volume of this work.

When nations shift from tyranny or monarchy to some kind of democratic regime, a new and recurrent question appears, namely, who rules? With the coming of representative government this becomes a salient question, one that often has no immediate or obvious answer. Those new regimes eventually arrange for periodic elections in which, by degrees, an ever-larger electorate chooses its representatives. The enlarged participation allows an easy answer to the recurrent question: "The people rule." But that answer evades the issue since "the people" do not make or administer laws. They do not decide policy in everyday affairs and most certainly not in crisis situations.

Charles and Mary Beard, as seen, provided an easy answer to the "who rules" question with their sweeping categorical declaration that in the United States after 1896 it was "the interests." An earlier sweeping declaration of class-dominance, one that would ultimately have "world-historical" influence, appeared in a work of Karl Marx and Friedrich Engels, in *The Communist Manifesto*, published in 1848. They declared that "the bourgeoisie has at last, since the establishment of modern industry and of the world market, conquered for itself in the modern representative state, exclusive political sway. The executive of the modern state is but a committee for managing the common affairs of the whole bourgeoisie."[8] Although a central assumption their position, the authors never undertook the research required to support that key hypothesis, the exclusive sway of the bourgeoisie. At minimum, one would have to show how "the whole bourgeoisie" chose and directed that "executive committee." Some serious research would be needed to demonstrate the "exclusive sway" of the bourgeoisie over Britain's prime ministers then and in later decades. That would include Lord John Russell, Lord Henry Palmerston, Benjamin Disraeli, and William Gladstone, their cabinets, and the houses of Parliament. But no systematic documentation of this bold hypothesis appears in their extensive subsequent writing.[9]

Some accounts have claimed that it is the politicians, the office holders, who actually rule. Others point to political bosses as the real rulers, as the men who choose and direct the office holders. Countering that claim, those arguing class-dominance declare both the politicians and the bosses to be "puppets." The politicians are "serving the interests" of the bourgeoisie with the latter "pulling the strings." Another theatrical image puts the bourgeoisie "offstage," directing affairs from "the wings." Two other clichés provide serviceable wisdom in such matters—"he who pays the piper calls the tune" and the rich are "calling the shots."

Those usages indicate a lack of thought. A cliché is prefabricated language; the user is drawing from a set of stock formulas rather than providing appropriate concepts and accurate depictions of the presumed linkages. The use of metaphor, as with puppets and stage management, points to another difficulty: the absence of pertinent evidence. If the commentator had evidence showing "big business" directing political events ("calling the shots"), it would be presented, clearly and unambiguously. Lacking that evidence, the savvy commentator makes use of the literary device, knowing that a properly trained audience will "resonate" with the image, agreeing that "they" are indeed stage-managing the events. But that resonance is no more than a trained response, a behavior showing no greater intelligence than the salivation of Pavlov's dogs on hearing the bell. In common parlance, it is called gullibility.

Inquiry and research are always useful, two efforts that are always to be recommended.[10] There is a substantial historical record with respect to most major events in the modern era, a record most likely to be available in democratic regimes. One can often discover answers to that familiar question: Who rules? And one can also address and answer two important related questions: How do "they" rule? and, What are the consequences of that rule?[11]

Governance involves a wide range of activities, many of them dealing with routine affairs, some with exceptional or unique events. Some efforts allow years of prior discussion and planning. Some allow time also for subsequent adjustment or correction, as with public school systems, welfare systems, internal improvements, canals, railways, highways, and so forth. The same holds for government financing, for the formulation of tax policies. But some events, catastrophes of all kinds, famine, floods, fires, plagues, and wars, require rapid responses. For them another kind of governance is both likely and appropriate, this involving fewer persons and different procedures.

Given the variety and unique character of those catastrophes, general explanations prove difficult if not impossible. A war might begin with a surprise attack, one requiring an immediate response. Or, there might be a long build up, one allowing some months for discussion, negotiation, and planning. There would be little room for public "input" in the former case, much room in the latter. The "who rules" question, accordingly, would have markedly different answers.[12]

The monarchs of the seventeenth and eighteenth centuries made the decisions about war and peace, usually aided by a coterie of civilian ministers and military leaders, all of whom were chosen by the ruler. Louis XIV and Frederick the Great made those decisions with little or no concern for any public opinion. Beginning in the early nineteenth century, however, some very limited public interventions were made and, surprisingly, some conservative governments responded. When Greek insurgents sought to throw off Ottoman rule, they gained the support of classically educated intellectuals in Britain, France, the German states, and elsewhere who pressed their governments to support this early independence movement. The leaders of the major powers were opposed to intervention, seeing it as a dangerous precedent. But eventually, over Metternich's objections, Britain, France, and Russia sent naval forces, the aims being to block the resupply of the Ottoman forces and to impose a compromise. But the plan went astray and a four-hour naval battle followed. That battle, Navarino Bay, 20 October 1823, was the central event in the struggle. Overcoming the opposition of the established leaders, those intellectuals brought about the intervention that made Greek independence possible. It was Europe's first successful national liberation struggle in the nineteenth century.[13]

Public opinion figured with much greater prominence at mid-century when the British press, reporting and commenting on events in the Near East, generated public support for an otherwise unlikely intervention, a war with Russia, the Crimean War of 1853–1856.[14] Bismarck made use of "public opinion" in 1870 with a cunning use of the Ems dispatch to lead an opponent, Louis Napoleon, to declare war, thus providing "justification" for Prussia's response.[15] At the end of the century, public opinion was an important factor, in Britain and on the continent, in the origins and conduct of the Boer War (1899–1902). And some commentators have claimed that public opinion was the primary cause of the war to be considered here, the Spanish-American War of 1898.

The decision-making involved in the origins of wars changed considerably in the course of the nineteenth century. Bismarck's direction of affairs was very different from that of Frederick the Great or of Maria Theresa. With many more "actors" involved, the process was now much more complicated, the most elusive factor being that thing called public opinion. That public might consist, as in the Greek struggle, of several hundred west European intellectuals. Later in the century it might mean a limited electorate, perhaps some five or ten percent of a nation's adult citizens. The notion of "aroused masses," as if a movement of the vast majority, is the favorite image of the mass society theory. That, however, as will be seen, is a most unlikely hypothesis. Establishing such claims is difficult, the key problems being the estimation of size and the determination of influence of any involved "masses."[16]

One additional complication involves the sources of that mass public arousal. Most accounts focus on internal sources pointing to grievances felt by segments of the citizenry. But in some instances the demands were generated by outsiders, by persons or groups seeking to "stir up" support within the domestic population. This kind of activity, for obvious reasons, is most likely in democratic regimes. In 1793, revolutionary France sent Edmond Charles Genêt, popularly known as Citizen Genêt, as their minister to the United States. He was very well received in his travels by some American leaders and by enthusiastic citizens. His assigned task however was to "strike blows against Spanish and British possessions in North America" and he proceeded to hire secret agents to work for those goals. Less bellicose efforts were undertaken by Louis Kossuth, who sought support for Hungarian independence, and by Giuseppe Garibaldi, who sought and received support in Britain and the United States for Italy's national liberation struggle. Irish Americans agitated for the liberation of their homeland, among other things undertaking the Fenian raids, invasions of Canada in 1866 and 1870. On two occasions, Cuban insurgents established offices in the United States to help gain American support. Efforts of this kind also make the tracing of causes and the assignment of responsibility for policy decisions more difficult than is the case with the old regimes.[17]

The present work, as indicated, will focus on three complex events beginning with William McKinley's presidential campaign in 1896. That campaign was the most portentous since Lincoln's election in 1860. William Jennings Bryan had overwhelmed the conservative forces within the Democratic Party and was arguing the case for "silver" as the solution for the problems of farmers and workers. An aroused business community, it is said, backed McKinley to defeat the inflationist threat. That contest, many specialists have argued, produced a realignment as many voters shifted to the Republican ranks, giving that party a considerable advantage, one that lasted (with a significant interruption during Wilson's presidency) until the advent of Franklin Roosevelt and the coming of the New Deal.

The immediate task facing McKinley on his election was the staffing of his government, beginning with the members of his cabinet. Given the role of "big business" in the nomination and the election, one might expect that influence to be evident here with businessmen (or their representatives) chosen for most of those offices. But that was not the case.

During McKinley's first year in office demands were made for American intervention in support of the Cuban independence movement. McKinley was opposed to intervention but, with considerable reluctance, yielded to those demands and called on Congress for the declaration of war with Spain. The leaders of big business were generally opposed to the prospect of war.[18] That vague passive-voice expression—"demands were made"—clearly requires investigation and elaboration. What groups were making those demands? How is their success to be explained?

The war was fought quickly and expeditiously. John Hay, the Secretary of State, described it as a "splendid little war." In the aftermath, unexpectedly, the United States acquired an empire consisting of Puerto Rico, Hawaii, the Philippine Islands, and an assortment of other Pacific islands. This shift from a long history of continental expansion, much of that driven by small-holding settlers, has sometimes been referred to as "the new imperialism." This choice too has been said to reflect business interests, specifically the need for new markets and investment opportunities. The assortment of Pacific islands, presumably, were "stepping stones" leading to the massive China market, the real goal of the new imperialism. Here too, investigation is useful: Did the new empire "reflect" the demands of big business? Or was it something else? These questions, as indicated, will be considered in the subsequent volume.

An important transition is said to have occurred with the 1896 election. Big business had grown in the previous decades. Its leaders now, so it appeared, took control of the nation's government, replacing the landholders, generals, and politicians who had dominated up to that point. If an accurate depiction, it follows that the other decisions—the formation of the cabinet, the decision for war, and the decision for empire—would somehow "reflect" business interests. But any such inferences would misrepresent the role of "big business" in the three events considered here. The key questions to be addressed here are: How were those decisions made? Which group (or groups) participated? And, what considerations motivated those various decision-makers?

This effort will begin with a depiction of the decision-makers, of the "cast of characters." The key figure in all three episodes, the presidential campaign, the staffing decisions, and the choice of war, was William McKinley. He served commendably in the Union Army during the Civil War. He then studied law and opened a practice in Canton, Ohio. Later he ran for office and served several terms in the Congress. And still later he served two terms as governor of Ohio. In the mid-1890s, McKinley is said to have been chosen by a coterie of businessmen as their candidate for the presidency. The group was directed by Marcus Alonzo Hanna, a tough and resourceful campaign manager. Many accounts portray McKinley as weak-willed and spineless, as Hanna's "willing tool." But those accounts are not accurate, their actual relationship being quite different, a fact that has implications for the class-dominance argument.[19] Some unexpected findings appear also in the second episode, McKinley's selection of cabinet members.

There is a near complete disjunction between the accounts of the 1896–1897 events and those of 1898. The 1896 election was fought, largely, over a single issue: that of "silver." Cuban affairs received very little attention in the months of the campaign. And in the selection of the cabinet, specifically of the men to head the War and Navy departments, the possibility of war was still a distant consideration. Although the Cuban revolution began earlier, in 1895, the account here will focus on the events of 1897 and 1898, on the reports of outrages by Spanish troops in Cuba, then with later events, the de Lôme letter and the sinking of the *Maine*. McKinley did what he could to fend off the conflict, but, overwhelmed by "events," he called for the intervention that led to the war. The key questions here are: Who advocated the war, that is, which persons or groups? How did they operate? What were their aims?

Discussion of the role of persons, of the relevant decision-makers, is a relatively easy task, documents and biographies being in plentiful supply. Discussion of formally organized groups is somewhat more difficult because they were of less interest to later scholars. An additional difficulty is that pressure groups typically claim large memberships and much influence. But both claims, especially the latter, ought to be viewed with caution. A still more difficult task is the assessment of public opinion. Lacking public opinion polls, we do not know if interventionist sentiment was shared by five, twelve, or seventy-two percent of the population.

Moving beyond those empirical inquiries, this work, as indicated, will undertake a fourth task, a review of the theoretical frameworks used in the analysis of these decisions. The aim is to consider the adequacy of some often-invoked theories, or, put differently, to assess their usefulness in dealing with the experience reviewed here.

* * *

Before turning to the three major substantive questions, it is useful to sketch out a typology of elite roles. For this purpose, six categories of actors may be distinguished: the rich, the party leaders (also called the bosses), the politicians (holders of electoral office), the brokers (mentors, sponsors, liaison persons), the press lords, and the appointees (cabinet members, ambassadors, and others).

That first category—the rich—requires some explication. It is easy, because of prior conditioning, to assume that the expression refers to the nation's major financial and industrial leaders, to John Pierpont Morgan, John D. Rockefeller, Andrew Carnegie, and perhaps a dozen or so others. They were undoubtedly rich men, their greatest influence beginning in the last decades of the nineteenth century. Prior to their appearance, throughout the eighteenth and early nineteenth centuries, the richest men in the United States were landowners.

At one point, the richest man in the nation was George Washington. His estate, in 1799, was estimated to be worth $530,000. He owned land in Virginia, Maryland, New York, Kentucky, the city of Washington, and elsewhere. All of the states had their major landholding families. The Virginia experience is perhaps the most familiar with, in addition to Washington, those other "first families," the Byrds, Carters, Harrisons, Jeffersons, and Randolphs. Members of the last five families formed the Virginia Land Company that undertook settlement in Ohio, southern Indiana, and Illinois. Among the original landed families of New York one found the Beekmans, DeLancys, Johnsons, Livingstons, Schuylers, Stuyvesants, Van Cortlandts, and van Rensselaers. Like the Virginians, they too were actively engaged in land speculation, looking out for further opportunities to expand their holdings.[20]

For much of the nineteenth century, the richest men in the nation were the Astors, John Jacob (1763–1848) and his son William Backhouse (1792–1879).[21] The father was the proprietor of the American Fur Company whose activities reached into the Midwest and beyond. The company was simultaneously engaged in real estate, Astor's agents founding Milwaukee, Madison, Fond du Lac, Prairie du Chien, LaCrosse, and Oshkosh. In Iowa they founded Davenport (named for an Astor agent) and Keokuk (named for an Indian chief who dealt with the Astors). Astor was also engaged in New York City real

estate, properties he acquired when foreclosing mortgages in the downturn of
business cycles.

Every major city and every growing region was essentially a giant real estate
operation. Cincinnati, for a time, was the largest city west of the Appalachians. Nicholas Longworth, the city's major landholder, was one of the richest
men in America.[22] Moses Cleaveland, the founder of another Ohio city, gave
"500 pounds New York currency, two beef cattle, and 100 gallons of whiskey"
in exchange for Indian claims to all lands east of the Cuyahoga River.[23]
William Blount was one of the largest holders in Tennessee. Another entrepreneur engaged in the same business there was Andrew Jackson.[24] Much of
this activity was conducted with borrowed money, that is, on credit. It followed, like the night the day, that banks and bankers would figure prominently
in this history.

Prior to the coming of industrialization, in short, the history of the United
States was the history of land speculation. That land, by itself, was not worth
much. If intended as farmland, it had first to be cleared then cultivated; someone had to undertake immense backbreaking labor. That effort might yield subsistence, but again, by itself the land would bring no money, no profits. To
obtain such benefits, the crop had to be brought to a market where it could be
sold. Roads could be built to bring produce to nearby villages or towns. One
could transport goods with boats on navigable rivers. Other rivers could be
dredged to make them navigable or, another alternative, one could build canals.
Steamboats enhanced the opportunities. Robert Fulton was married to a Liv-
ingston who owned Hudson River properties. His first steamboat, the *Cler-
mont*, was named for one of the family's estates. The Great Lakes provided
another important option with grain being moved across to Buffalo, then over
the Erie Canal for export to European markets. Later on, railroads would bring
most of the farm produce to the distant markets. Those railroads, at the same
time, dramatically increased the value of those landholdings, urban and rural,
located along the main line.

In American history textbooks, this subject comes under the heading of
"internal improvements." In modern-day economics textbooks, it is referred
to as infrastructure. Ultimately, the builders of those internal improvements
would replace the landholders as "the richest men in American." The Astors
were replaced by another father-son team, by the Vanderbilts, Cornelius
(1794–1877) and William H. (1821–1885), the proprietors of the New York
Central, a rail line connecting New York to Chicago.[25] There were many other
railway fortunes, those of Jay Gould and Jim Fisk, Henry Villard, Collis P.
Huntington, James J. Hill, Edward H. Harriman, and Leland Stanford.

The railroad connections "made" cities and benefited towns, villages, and
farms along a mainline. The railroads themselves, it should be noted, were

major real estate operations. Many of them received immense grants of land, most from the Congress.[26] Some were given a fifty-mile swath of land, 25 miles on both sides of the throughway. It was "in the cards" also that telegraph lines and still later telephone lines would be strung along those same throughways. The railroad magnates would gain also by participation in those enterprises.

The real estate and railway activities did not disappear with "the growth of industry." Steel, oil, automobiles, machine tools, clothing, and furniture manufacture were added to the ongoing business efforts. The steel industry grew with the immense demand for rails and bridges. Automobiles brought new demands, for sheet steel, rubber, and gasoline. Automobiles also brought substantial changes in land usage, providing still new opportunities for the speculators.[27]

Some merchants also gained considerable wealth, joining the ranks of "the rich." Among them we have two leading department store proprietors, John Wanamaker in Philadelphia and Marshall Field in Chicago. Another was Alexander T. Stewart, New York City's leading merchant, who had an eight-floor establishment located at Broadway and Tenth Street. His 1860 income has been estimated at two million dollars.[28]

In the years immediately after the Civil War, "the rich" would have consisted of landholders (real estate speculators), railroad magnates, and dry goods merchants. Only toward the end of the century did major industrialists appear as leading figures among the rich. These men, it should be noted, joined the rank; they did not displace their predecessors. There was no conflict, no dialectical struggle as between landed- and industrial-wealth. One could, moreover, easily diversify one's holdings. Or, one could shift base entirely. Henry M. Flagler, one of the original Standard Oil partners, became nervous about the further growth of the industry. He sold his holdings in the company, left Cleveland, and turned to the development of Florida real estate.[29]

Some of the new industrialists became national figures, men with wide-ranging interests. Many of them came to be based in New York where some could develop ties with Wall Street bankers. John D. Rockefeller, for example, began in Cleveland, Andrew Carnegie and Henry Clay Frick in Pittsburgh, but later moved to New York. An exclusive focus on the New York leaders however would be seriously misleading since many important business leaders were located elsewhere. The coterie that backed McKinley was located in the Midwest with its center in Cleveland and some members in Pittsburgh and Chicago.

These men, with rare exception, were "new rich," the founders of the firms. That means, again with rare exception, their time was occupied, first and foremost, with the requirements of those enterprises. They put in long hours managing the firms' affairs and, as a consequence, had little time remaining for direct and active political involvement. They did, of course, have political interests, most of them understandably wanting policies favorable to their firm (or firms). And they also shared some general interests, wishing a proper "climate" for the flourishing of business. Because of their heavy full-time commitments, however, the major political decisions were made by others, by other elites. One might think of those others, the de facto political leaders, as agents, as if subordinates in a hierarchy, but another option is possible, that of independence or autonomy. As opposed to the either-or dichotomy, there were (and are) many other possibilities, such as discussion, negotiation, and compromise.

The categorical usage comes easily—the idea that "big business" thought and acted as a single cohesive group. But businessmen and their firms typically compete with one another. Vanderbilt's New York Central competed with the Erie and Pennsylvania railroads. Rockefeller's Standard Oil, originally based in Cleveland, used that fact to its advantage and demanded rate advantages.[30] Both the New York Central and Pennsylvania, at one point, began construction of lines parallel to those of the other. In this case, J. P. Morgan, the leading investment banker, intervened and brought an end to the "destructive competition." Ruthless businessmen, those engaging in questionable practices, such as Jim Fisk and Jay Gould, the proprietors of the Erie Railroad, were generally disliked and, when possible, were excluded from "inner circle" affairs. Thomas Edison learned business practice from Jay Gould. Subsequently his use of Gould's methods led to his quiet removal from a very important firm, one based on his inventions, General Electric.[31] Edward H. Harriman was generally disliked. His railroad ventures brought him into serious conflict with several major lines, ones supported by J. P. Morgan and his banking house. The result was a struggle of "the titans" (described just below).[32]

The shorthand expression, "big business," is clearly misleading. It avoids consideration of the leading individuals, of the various sectors and firms, and of their relative importance. The unqualified use of that expression suggests a uniformity of outlook and a cohesiveness that is not justified. Other shorthand expressions, "the banks," "finance capital," and "Wall Street," present the same problem, also overlooking a wide range of complexities.

Philip H. Burch, Jr. has provided an overview with lists of the fifteen largest industrial firms and fifteen largest railroads plus a discussion of the large financial institutions as of 1913.[33] That portrait differs in some respects from the arrangements as of 1898. The largest industrials in 1913 (measured by assets) were the United States Steel Corporation ($1,635.9 millions), American Telephone & Telegraph ($656.0 millions), and Standard Oil Company of New Jersey ($357 millions). The Steel Corporation was a Morgan creation formed in 1901, an amalgamation of several predecessors, the largest of which was Carnegie Steel. Although created by others, A.T. & T. had Morgan financing, the first connection dating from 1902. And Standard of New Jersey, the most important Rockefeller firm, had assets of $357 millions in 1913, a figure well below the $860 millions held in 1911 when the original Standard Oil firm was broken up following its loss in the government's antitrust suit. The "lost" assets were now with other Standard Oil firms, those of New York, Ohio, Indiana, and California. The next industrials on the list are both smaller and less well-known, Amalgamated Copper (later Anaconda), International Mercantile Marine, American Smelting & Refining (a Guggenheim property), and the United States Rubber Company (Harvey Firestone).

Accounts that treat "industry" and "industrialization" as the dominant facts at the turn of the century are misleading. As of 1913, U.S. Steel was the nation's largest firm. But the next seven firms on Burch's lists were railroads headed by the Pennsylvania ($940.1 millions), Union Pacific ($902.7 millions), and Southern Pacific ($892.1 millions). The ninth largest firm was A.T. & T., which was then followed by eight more railroads. If assets were viewed as equivalent to power, one would have to focus on the railroads.

Burch reports further that the assets of the nation's financial institutions were "considerably smaller than either the railroad or industrial concerns." Three of the four largest financials, moreover, were insurance companies, New York Life Insurance (roughly $720 millions), Mutual Life Insurance (assets roughly $600 millions), the Equitable Life Assurance Society, the fourth being a bank, the National City Bank of New York. In this connection Burch has a paragraph on "the legendary" J. P. Morgan, who is described as "the most influential" of the investment and commercial bankers and "probably the most powerful banker ever to grace the national economic scene." Together with George F. Baker, his "close friend and business associate," the longtime president of the First National Bank of New York, Morgan "fashioned "an enormous network of economic power, which understandably revolved primarily around his own firm of J. P. Morgan & Co. Eight other financial institutions were said to be part of this network, these including Mutual Life and the First National Bank.

Another financial group, also based in New York City, is referred to as the Stillman-Rockefeller complex. Burch reports that the "bulk" of this money came from "the highly lucrative" Standard Oil Company, which was then placed in the "Rockefeller-dominated" National City Bank, which, as just seen, was the largest of nation's banks. William Rockefeller, the brother of John, was involved there along with James Stillman, the bank's longtime head. This bank too had a larger network (Burch cites three other banks with total assets in 1913 of $330 millions). This group also had "close links" to other capitalists, ones not in the "Morgan camp," the most important of them being the railroad magnate, Edward H. Harriman, and the banker, Jacob Schiff. The relationship between the Morgan group and the Rockefeller-Stillman group, according to Burch, was one of "deep-seated hostility."[34]

Because of the heavy emphasis on moneymaking, on the sedulous drive for "profits," many discussions overlook the "cultural" divisions within business ranks. Some prominent businessmen did not care for John D. Rockefeller, objecting to his business practices. Some found his "straight-laced" morals not to their liking. Jim Fisk, known for, among other things, his loose morals, offended his upright peers. There was another source of division: Some businessmen were anti-Catholic, some were anti-Semitic. Facing the latter sentiment, a prominent banker, August Belmont, affiliated with and ultimately led the "other" party, that is, the Democrats.[35]

Those cultural divisions made possible some otherwise unexpected linkages. Edward H. Harriman, an excluded railroad magnate, worked with Jacob Schiff, an investment banker who happened to be Jewish. In 1901, Harriman, aided by Schiff and Stillman, attempted to gain control of James Jerome Hill's Northern Pacific Railroad. Hill, allied with Morgan, only narrowly avoided the takeover.[36] Harriman and Schiff both sat on the board of the Rockefeller-Stillman National City Bank.

Morgan's attitude toward the rival group appeared in the course of some discussions in 1904 about a possible merger with the British banking house of Barings. That bank's representative, Lord Revelstoke, reported Morgan's sentiments as follows: "He inveighed bitterly against the growing power of the Jews and of the Rockefeller crowd, and said more than once that our firm and his were the only two composed of white men in New York." The two firms, Chernow adds, "had long identified with each other as the leading Protestant houses in their respective cities."[37]

In a later period, another shunned magnate, William Randolph Hearst, a Democrat, joined with Joseph Kennedy, a very wealthy speculator (in several fields), a Democrat and a Catholic, and also with Louis B. Mayer, a leading motion picture executive who was Jewish. Those who were excluded, Protestants, Catholics, and Jews, formed what might be called coalitions of outsiders. The evident divisions did not necessarily mean open conflict since on occasion the contending groups had to work together. "The strain of anti-Semitism running through the Morgan story," Chernow comments, "is fascinating precisely because it had to be so carefully suppressed."[38]

This review indicates that the near-automatic assumption of big business unity and cohesion should be viewed with skepticism. The use of those all-embracing terms such as "Wall Street" or "the interests" can be seriously misleading. That is not the only or even the most obvious hypothesis; division and fragmentation were, and are, easy alternatives.

The second elite group, the party bosses, was especially important in this period. These were the men who ran the local and state political machines and who contested for influence in the national government. We have been trained to think of political machines as urban, as big city institutions. It is best, however, to recognize their presence in all communities, including villages and rural counties. At the turn of the century, the most important bosses headed machines based in states: Thomas Platt in New York, Nelson Aldrich in Rhode Island, Henry Cabot Lodge in Massachusetts, Matthew Quay in Pennsylvania, and Mark Hanna in Ohio. There were many others. These men were full-time political leaders, all of them United States senators. That office gave them a fair amount of free time for political management. Membership in that "club" also facilitated negotiation with one's peers.[39] These men undertook the basic organizational tasks of their party—choosing candidates, managing elections, and attempting to direct government policies. The bosses also, understandably, engaged in related private business activities.[40]

Although routinely portrayed as "powerful," the bosses faced threats from two quarters. There were competing or aspiring contenders, other bosses, some of them local, some based elsewhere, within the county or state. The bosses, moreover, engaged in rather dubious activities, many of them being recipients of honest and not-so-honest graft. Those misdeeds stimulated the occasional reform movement. Both threats meant that bosses were vulnerable. Possibly the most often mentioned of the nineteenth-century bosses was William Marcy Tweed, the Democratic Party leader in New York City. But that "powerful" boss was deposed by a reform movement, his career ending with disgrace, exile, and jail.[41]

Roscoe Conkling was the "powerful" Republican boss of New York State. But in 1880 he suffered a series of humiliating reverses. His candidate for the presidency, Ulysses S. Grant, sought a third term but was defeated in the convention by James A. Garfield. Disgruntled and vindictive, Conkling threatened to withhold support in pivotal New York but later, in quiet negotiations, an understanding was reached, one involving subsequent appointments. But then, the president-elect named James G. Blaine, who was hated by Conkling, to be his Secretary of State. This posed serious problems for the other cabinet appointments, particularly for Treasury, Conkling's chief interest. After several months of contention, that position went to Senator Windom of Minnesota.

New York's postmaster, Thomas James, a Conkling associate, was named as Postmaster General but the boss, not assuaged, was "angry and abusive." In May 1881 he lost another struggle when Garfield named Conkling's "most virulent enemy in the state" to a very important patronage position, collector of the Port of New York. Conkling's reaction was astonishing—he resigned his Senate seat. One interpretation is that he expected vindication, that a docile state legislature would rename him. But the legislature did not reappoint him and Conkling's political career was suddenly ended. Another interpretation of his move, one that seems more plausible, is that Conkling intended that outcome. The political career provided rather limited financial returns; his "retirement" allowed him to pursue a much more profitable legal career.[42]

A third category of elites consists of the candidates for elected offices, national, state, and local, the top executive positions in government. Their career lines are markedly different from those of the business leaders and the bosses. They were (and are), in effect, political entrepreneurs, working their way up from minor, to middling, and finally, to major offices. They were, typically, less affluent than the other actors. Although not averse to business activity and ordinarily not without talent, the choice of a political career usually meant the sacrifice of much income. Losses, of course, are all relative. Successful candidates might end their careers with fortunes in the hundreds of thousands. But if they had continued full-time in business, they could easily have made millions.[43]

The candidates, typically, were ambitious, hardworking men who had demonstrated evident capacity. Those observations would scarcely need mention except for a persistent tendency to assert some opposite claims. Candidates are, of course, ambitious—otherwise they would never seek such demanding, chance-ridden, and, in terms of income, relatively unrewarding careers. For the political bosses, one important criterion in the selection of a candidate, almost of necessity, was some evident capacity. General Ulysses S. Grant had demonstrated his ability to manage the Union armies in what at that time was the largest war in the nation's experience. His successors, Hayes, Garfield, Harrison, and McKinley, had all shown similar although less prominent administrative capacities. Grover Cleveland did not serve in the Civil War but demonstrated his capacities as mayor of Buffalo and then as governor of New York, in both instances, providing "clean government" and taking some steps toward "reform" (civil service, reducing the extent of the spoils system).[44]

The fourth category of elites, a rather diverse collection, might be termed brokers, sponsors, or mentors. They were neither big businessmen nor political bosses. Many of them were publishers of influential newspapers or magazines, an occupation that allowed the development of extensive social contacts. These men were basically advocates: They found potential candidates and supported their careers. They also performed important liaison tasks, bringing candidates together with party bosses and, on occasion, with industrial and financial leaders. Horace Greeley, who founded the *New York Tribune* in 1841, was an important and very active broker. Originally a Whig, in the mid-1850s he helped to organize the Republican Party and was then active in the selection of its presidential candidates. Later, in 1872, a curious set of events led to his nomination, first as a Liberal Republican, then as the Democratic Party's candidate in 1872, as a reformer to oppose corruption in Grant's administration.[45]

Whitelaw Reid, another important broker, was a journalist and early Republican activist, originally based in southern Ohio. After the Civil War, in 1868, he became the lead editorial writer for the *New York Tribune*. The following year he became managing editor and then, in 1872, following the death of Greeley, he became the paper's principal owner and editor-in-chief. From this base, the nation's leading Republican journal, he influenced the direction of the party and supported its candidates.

Some sense of this broker's "resources" may be seen in a description of Reid's relationship with a close friend, Congressman James A. Garfield. The latter recognized Reid's "unique position" as a man who "controlled the news and editorial columns of a great newspaper in a doubtful state." By virtue of Reid's position "at the center of an information net made up of regular reporters and scores of contributors [he] had privileged access to nationwide wire services. [Garfield] respected Reid's judgment, his knowledge of men, and above all his relative disinterest in appointive office or political payoff."[46]

William C. Whitney, a lifelong Democrat, was another important broker in this period. He began his career as a Democratic reformer, as a prosecutor of the Tweed Ring. As New York City's corporation counsel from 1872–1882 he defended the city against lawsuits stemming from Tammany mismanagement. He also had a business career involving New York City street railways and various public utilities. In 1882 he became a full-time political broker and organized Grover Cleveland's gubernatorial campaign in 1882. Two years later, he organized Cleveland's presidential campaign. The newly elected president twice called on Whitney to serve as his Secretary of the Navy. Taking that position meant a considerable loss of income but Whitney, responding to his wife's wishes, ultimately accepted. He returned to business in 1889 following the Democrats' defeat. In 1892, Whitney was again working for Cleveland.[47]

Edwin L. Godkin, editor of *The Nation* (and later of the New York *Evening Post*), was an influential intellectual in the post-Civil War period. He was also a broker, but one with a rather distinct procedure. A quarrelsome advocate, he was, among other things, a leader of the Mugwumps, a reform group active in the eighties. The popular vote in some states divided almost fifty-fifty, which meant a small number of "swing votes" could determine the outcome. Some "good government" reformers saw this circumstance as an opportunity. Rising above party, they could support reform candidates and penalize the spoilsmen, whether Republicans or Democrats. In 1884, they supported Cleveland against spoilsman Blaine. Republican stalwarts hated them. In 1887, a young just-defeated Republican candidate, Theodore Roosevelt, was "yearning to take a hack at the estimable Godkin." Wishing to "give the Mugwumps something to howl over," he wrote, "I am for war to the knife with the whole crew."[48]

The sponsors, like the candidates, also sacrificed income. William C. Whitney had a business career that promised "surpassing wealth and power." But, "pressed by his wife," he agreed, with considerable reluctance, to serve in Cleveland's cabinet as Secretary of the Navy. His wife, Flora, was the daughter of Henry B. Payne, a very wealthy man, a United States senator (from Ohio), and a presidential aspirant. It was the father's money that made possible Flora's career as a Washington social leader.[49] Whitelaw Reid's career, as just seen, was also aided substantially by his father-in-law's support. John Hay, another important sponsor, and later McKinley's Secretary of State, was aided by his father-in-law, Amasa Stone, a wealthy Cleveland bridge builder.

Two "press lords," our fifth elite category, were notorious in the period being considered, these being Joseph Pulitzer, publisher of the *World*, and William Randolph Hearst, publisher of the *Journal*. Their operations were centered, primarily, in New York City. They are listed separately from the brokers because at this point they were not engaged in candidate selection or liaison tasks. The two were fighting a circulation war, one that, among other things, led to the production of "sensational" accounts of events in Cuba, accounts that allegedly had significant effects on public opinion. Most accounts of the war focus on those two journals, but another newspaper, the New York *Sun*, with the city's third largest circulation, engaged in the same kind of endeavor. The New York *Herald* was once the nation's largest circulation daily. In 1896, it was New York's fourth largest and it too was "sensational" in tone.

Some words of caution are appropriate. First, those mass-circulation newspapers, as is well known, were of very low quality. Their readers, presumably, would be persons with limited political influence. And most political leaders would probably have discounted any demands coming by way of such questionable sources. A second caution involves the depiction of those journals, most accounts emphasizing their "sensational" character. But the *World* and *Journal* shared another distinctive trait: They were both Democratic. Until it defected in the 1896 election, the *Sun* had also been staunchly Democratic. The *Herald* had been Democratic earlier but now was said to be thoroughly "mugwump." All four papers had correspondents in Cuba.[50] The regular focus on the "sensational" press and the alleged response among "the masses" hides an important fact, that the effort had a partisan character. The questions of content and impact—of likely impacts—will be reviewed in later chapters.

The sixth category of actors, the most diverse of them all, consists of the appointees. Until the passage of the Civil Service Act (often called the Pendleton Act) in 1883, an incoming president could remove almost all office-holders, from cabinet members to postal clerks, and replace them with an army of party loyalists. The Pendleton Act, an important step toward "modern bureaucracy," covered only one-tenth of government positions. It did allow the president to increase the proportion that were "classified," that is, were given job security. But at the turn of the century, three-fifths of the positions were still unclassified, still available as patronage to reward the party faithful.[51]

The cabinet appointments are generally viewed as the most important of the lot. There were eight positions in 1897 when McKinley took office. State and Treasury were the most important, those charged with the most far-reaching policy implications. The Treasury Department held some important patronage positions, notably the collectors of revenue in the major ports. The New York collector's post, mentioned just above, was easily the most important of these positions, one of the most sought-after in the government.

From 1865 to 1876, the War Department had a very important task, it being charged with the enforcement of reconstruction policies, with the occupation and administration of the states of the former Confederacy. Thereafter, the War Department was of much less importance, its principal task being to "keep the peace" in the frontier regions. The army was small and generally neglected until 1898. The navy also was small and generally neglected. Some improvements were initiated in the 1880s but in 1898, compared to the world's major powers, the development was clearly laggard.[52]

The Postmaster General position was important for patronage, almost half of the government's employees being named by this office holder. The Attorney General was charged with an important oversight function, maintaining the law or, put differently, prosecuting suspected wrongdoers. The most important concern for the Secretary of the Interior in this period involved what was termed "Indian affairs." The eighth position, probably the least important of the lot, was that of Secretary of Agriculture. The many positions as ministers (later ambassadors) to foreign countries were generally treated as having less importance, providing little opportunity for patronage. These were largely honorific positions, basically rewards for a party's wealthy supporters.[53]

The cabinet appointees came from diverse backgrounds, so diverse as to make generalization difficult. They were not, on the whole, drawn from the ranks of the very rich (either commercial, industrial, or financial), nor were they chosen from among the political bosses. There was a shared understanding, however, about "the rules" governing appointments, an informal agreement that lasted well beyond the period in question. It was understood that the bosses, many of them senators, were entitled to name people for their "fair share" of the available offices. They would supply the names and the president was expected to respond and make the appointments.

The amount of benefit granted would depend on the importance of the constituency (New York for example getting more than Delaware) and also on the support the political leader had provided. The procedure had a name, senatorial privilege, which for several years even had some limited legal backing in the Tenure of Office Act (1867). Aimed at Andrew Johnson, that law declared that appointees could not be removed from office without senatorial approval. President Grant resisted that demand and had some success in restoring presidential privilege.

These six "roles" should not be thought of as separate and distinct. People could and did shift from one role to another following interest and circumstances. Elihu Washburne was an important congressional leader and a leading supporter of an eminent constituent, Ulysses S. Grant, for both his military and political careers. Washburne was later chosen, by Grant, to serve as the nation's minister to France. Daniel Manning played an important role in Grover Cleveland's career. He was a banker, a newspaper proprietor, the boss of the party machine in Albany, and also chairman of New York State's Democratic Party. Cleveland named Manning to be his Secretary of the Treasury.[54] William C. Whitney too, as seen, was a prosperous businessman who sponsored a candidate for two high offices and later served as a cabinet member. Mark Hanna gave up full-time involvement in his coal and iron firm to devote himself to politics, as a sponsor of presidential candidates, then as national chairman of the Republican Party and as a United States senator from Ohio.

To this point we have been delineating various kinds of activities or behaviors. It is tempting to read motives into those efforts, seeing those efforts as narrowly self-interested, aiming "to maximize profit." But, clearly, there was another option: For many, it was a matter of personal honor and pride. For some sponsors and some candidates the aim appears to have been furtherance of the common welfare. For many office holders, as indicated, political service meant a considerable loss of income. Diplomatic and consular positions, as noted, were largely honorific positions, ones typically given out late in life to persons who had performed meritorious service. These office holders had to be willing to pay considerable sums out of their own private funds. One requirement, accordingly, was a substantial private fortune, these men in effect subsidizing the government. Unlike the conventional image of businessmen and bosses, they were clearly not seeking to "maximize profits."

With infrequent exceptions, the appointments made in this period are peculiar in that little attention was paid to the professional or technical training of those named to office, a practice sometimes referred to as amateurism. Decision-makers, in short, were strikingly indifferent to the requirements and expectations of bureaucratic rule. The lack of specific technical knowledge or of experience obviously meant little to those elites who assumed a wide-ranging general competence on the part of successful businessman, lawyers, and politicians. The abilities demonstrated in the creation or management of a firm or in the direction of a government agency could, presumably, be easily transferred and applied in another setting.

Lincoln's (and Johnson's) Secretary of State, William H. Seward, for example, had no prior experience with foreign affairs. Lincoln's first Secretary of
War, Simon Cameron, had no prior military experience. Lincoln appointed
Salmon P. Chase as Secretary of the Treasury in his first cabinet. Chase, who
would be responsible for the nation's finances in the imminent war, "had never
studied economics, had never even read a book on the subject. His ideas of
finance, he boasted, were entirely intuitive."[55] Grant's Secretary of State, Hamilton Fish, also had no foreign affairs experience. Grant appointed Donald
Cameron (Simon's son) for a brief term as his Secretary of War, although like his
father, he too was without military experience. Grant appointed two men to the
Navy department, neither with any naval experience. President Hayes appointed
Indiana's Richard Thompson to head the Navy department "even though he had
never been aboard any vessel larger than a rowboat." On his first tour of a warship, Thompson expressed his surprise—"Why, the durned thing's hollow!"[56]

When Cleveland's first Secretary of State died in office, he appointed his
Attorney General, Richard Olney, to that position. At that point, one writer
reports, Olney "knew nothing about foreign affairs." When Elihu Root was
appointed as Secretary of War in 1899, he "knew almost nothing about the
army." President Taft chose Philander C. Knox, a corporation lawyer, to be
his Secretary of State. One source reports "he had no experience in foreign
affairs."[57] The assumption, clearly, was that capable men would learn quickly.

In addition to considering those various leadership groups, the elites, some
attention must also be given to the political parties and to the character of the
party struggle in the post-Civil War period. The principal contenders were the
Republicans and the Democrats. The former was the successor to the prewar
Whig Party that, in turn, was the successor to the Federalists. The Democrats
had greater organizational continuity beginning as the anti-Federalists, later
called the Republicans, the party of Jefferson, Madison, and Monroe. Throughout American history, both were classic liberal parties, that is to say, opposed
to old-regime privilege, to inherited rank and benefits. If judged from the per-
spectives of the later twentieth-century liberalism, however, both parties at that
early point would have to be counted as conservative. Prior to the New Deal,
neither party called for radical social transformations. Neither advocated a welfare state or called for public support of the poor. The major issues in the post-
Civil War period were reconstruction, the tariff, the currency question, and
"good government," that is, restricting the power of the bosses, eliminating
patronage appointments and substituting a civil service system. Later there
were demands for the control of monopolies and these brought regulation of
railroad rates and the passage of an antitrust law.

Reconstruction was abandoned as an issue with the 1877 settlement that
withdrew federal troops and returned power to the planter elites in the former

Confederate states, those frequently referred to as the Bourbon Democrats. Republicans generally favored high tariffs and "hard money," the two leading issues of the period. Following in the Hamiltonian tradition, the Republicans generally preferred that political initiatives and direction be centered in a strong national government.

The Democrats were not quite an opposite party with respect to these issues. With its support strongest in the South and in the border states, a bloc called "the solid South," the party opposed, either by force or indifference, any moves for the amelioration of the black population. The Democrats generally favored low tariffs. And, following the Jeffersonian tradition, now reinforced by the wartime experience and Reconstruction, the Democrats wished the state governments be dominant, that is to say they favored "states' rights."

Prior to the 1896 upheaval, the Democrats in most states were conservative, showing more sympathy for local banks and commercial interests than for poor farmers, workers, or the dispossessed. Like the Republicans, they too favored "hard money," a position that, especially in bad times, posed a problem given the inflationary (or "soft money") preferences of indebted farmers. This threat appeared with the Greenback Party in the 1870s and again, in much more serious form, with the Populists in the 1890s. In 1896, the inflationists won their great victory, defeating the conservative Democrats and naming their candidate, William Jennings Bryan, as the party's presidential candidate.

A few paragraphs cannot begin to describe the complexities involved in these issues. On the tariff question, for example, the extreme positions would be high prohibitive tariffs versus completely free trade. But there were many other options: tariffs for revenue only, free trade for goods not produced in the United States, reciprocity with other countries, plus several thousand other possibilities, that is, different rates for each product.

On the currency question, too, there was a range of options: an exclusive Gold Standard, the use of gold and silver (with limited or unlimited coinage of the latter), plus the printing of Greenbacks, this too in various quantities. There were complexities also with respect to the "good government" reforms, such as limiting the "taxation" of government workers for campaign funds, prohibiting the use of their services in campaigns, the demand for education and/or technical training, and, finally, some guarantee of job security. The linkages of parties and issues reviewed here are best seen as general tendencies. There was some diversity, that is, some non-conforming cases in both parties. Prior to 1896, as will be seen, William McKinley had been "soft" on the currency question.[58]

The Republicans dominated the presidency in the period from 1868 to 1892, winning five of the seven presidential elections. That dominance, however, is deceptive, since it resulted largely from victories in the electoral college. The popular vote totals were generally close to a fifty-fifty division.[59] In 1876, the famous—or infamous—disputed election, Samuel J. Tilden, the Democrat, won the popular vote (by 254,000 out of the 8,323,000 two-party total) but lost the presidency to Rutherford B. Hayes by a single vote in the electoral college.[60] Grover Cleveland won the presidency in 1884, the first Democratic victory since 1856, by a very slim margin (25,700 votes out of a 9,724,000 total). In 1888, Cleveland again won the popular vote, this time by a 90,000-vote margin—but Harrison won the presidency in the electoral college with 233 votes to 168.

In the "classical" view of democratic politics, candidates and parties spell out their positions on the issues and voters choose those most adequately representing their preferences. In another reading, the mass society view, demagogic candidates or parties gull the voters, hiding their issue positions and/or offering distractive themes.[61] Both of those options, campaigns based on issues and those on distraction, would presumably produce a highly volatile electorate with major changes occurring from one campaign to the next. But the relative constancy of the voting patterns, overall and in the various states, shows those assumptions to be mistaken.

Some electoral specialists, however, have provided another reading of voter behavior, one more in accord with the evidence just reviewed. They argue that most voters learn their politics from their parents, a process called primary political socialization, and that most of them subsequently maintain that direction.[62] Instead of volatility, their evidence shows continuity or relative stability. Most of the states in the post-Civil War period had easily discerned voting patterns, each showing an equilibrium level that varied little from one election to the next. The southern states, those of the former Confederacy, and the border states showed substantial Democratic majorities in the post-1876 elections. Most of the northern states along with most in the west were regularly Republican.[63]

Five states, however, New York, Indiana, California, Connecticut, and Nevada, had near fifty-fifty divisions between the major parties and the outcomes there could easily shift from one election to the next. The outcomes in two of those states, New York and Indiana, those with the largest number of electoral votes, effectively determined which party won the presidency. The two "went Democratic" in 1876, 1884, and 1892. Had the two remained Republican in 1876, there would have been no "disputed election." Hayes would have been the undisputed winner.

One result of this distinctive pattern was that New York and Indiana were favored in the naming of candidates. Of the fourteen major party candidates presented in those seven elections, six were New Yorkers and two were Hoosiers (this counts Cleveland on three occasions and Harrison twice). The same tendency appeared also in the choice of vice-presidential candidates, with four New Yorkers and four Hoosiers. On four occasions, the parties presented

Yorker-Hoosier combinations. Cleveland's slim victory in 1884 was one of these with Thomas Hendricks of Indiana as his running mate.[64]

The implications of the near fifty-fifty equilibrium levels are best seen in a comparison of the 1880 and 1884 elections. In 1880, Garfield won with an overall margin of fewer than 2,000 popular votes. In the electoral college, however, the division was 214 to 155 in his favor. Four years later, Cleveland won with an overall popular vote margin of some 29,000. But the decisive factor was the small shifts of popular votes in New York and Indiana. The winning popular vote margins in those states were 1,047 and 6,523 respectively. Allan Nevins claimed a sweeping public reaction, a mass rejection of Blaine because of questionable behavior in public office, but the minuscule vote shift makes that claim untenable.[65]

The selection of Grover Cleveland, New York's "favorite son," might have changed some votes. The Mugwumps, led by Godkin, recommended against Blaine, but the number of voters moved by that group was probably small. Some voters, possibly, were moved by bigotry, a prominent Blaine supporter having tagged the Democrats as the party of "Rum, Romanism, and Rebellion." A more important factor, probably, was the presence of a new third party, the Prohibitionists, whose candidate took 18,403 votes, most of them likely to have come from the Republicans.

There was still another factor: Roscoe Conkling, the resentful and vindictive ex-boss, detested Blaine. He is said to have "passed the word among his friends in Utica to support the Democratic candidate." Perhaps moved by the former boss, a group of Republican Stalwarts in Oneida County, Conkling's original home base, came out for Cleveland. In 1880 that county had supported Garfield by a margin of 2,053 votes. In 1884, it supported Cleveland by, depending on the source, a margin of either 19 or 33 votes.[66] In 1888, with minor shifts in the popular vote, New York and Indiana were again Republican. And that put Indiana's Benjamin Harrison in the White House.

The post-Civil War equilibrium was dramatically altered in 1890s. Many accounts focus on the 1896 election, portraying the "titanic" Bryan versus McKinley contest as the source of the realignment, a struggle that pitted the representatives of "the people" against those favoring "the interests." Many accounts argue that it was Hanna's skillful demagogic campaign, aided by generous funding from alarmed businessmen, that caused many voters to rethink and to change their party loyalties. Hanna's campaign against Bryan and "silver," in short, drove many Democratic voters into the Republican ranks and thus blocked, or at least postponed, the imminent progressive tendency. A new period of Republican dominance began at that point, one that would last, with one significant interruption, through to the 1930s. The Republicans now had a fair-sized popular majority and New York and Indiana were no longer pivotal states. The next realignment would come in the 1930s, in the midst of a major economic crisis. That Democratic resurgence brought the election of Franklin D. Roosevelt and, with time, saw the institution of new and markedly different progressive policies.

V. O. Key's groundbreaking article contains a brief paragraph suggesting an alternative hypothesis, namely, that the 1890s realignment occurred first in 1894 and resulted from a strikingly different set of causal factors. An account of the 1896 election, he wrote, must include consideration of the panic of 1893—"Bank failures, railroad receiverships, unemployment, strikes, Democratic championship of deflation and of the gold standard, and related matters created the setting for a Democratic setback in 1894." Key presented some limited evidence (for the New England states) on the outcome of that election. His tentative conclusion reads: "The luckless William Jennings Bryan and the free-silver heresy perhaps did not contribute as much as is generally supposed to the decline . . . in Democratic strength." In 1892, the Democrats had shown remarkable strength, electing 218 Representatives to the House (versus 127 Republicans). In the 1894 election they suffered immense losses, falling to 105 while the Republicans rose to 244. The Democrats remained the minority party in the House until the 1910 election. Although many accounts continue to focus on 1896, other studies provide unambiguous support for Key's alternative, that the realignment came first in 1894. Bryan's "dramatic" campaign came after the sizable changes that had occurred two and three years earlier. Rather than causing the realignment, the 1896 campaign probably reinforced the judgments many voters had drawn earlier.[67]

One important specification should be noted. The accounts of the 1896 election typically focus on the farm question and, accordingly, emphasize developments in the South and the West. But the major political change in 1894 came elsewhere. One historian, Samuel T. McSeveney, summarizes as follows:

> . . . if we are to understand the lasting significance of the political upheaval of the 1890s, we must view the period from a different perspective. To begin with, political discontent was by no means confined to the South and West. On the contrary, fully two-thirds of the congressional districts that changed hands during the 1890s lay to the north and east of the regions of acute agrarian discontent. Similarly, the decisive shifts toward the Democrats in the electoral vote in 1892 and toward the Republicans in that of 1896 occurred east of the Mississippi River and north of the Ohio River and Mason and Dixon's Line. Within this populous area where the fortunes of the major parties shifted so decisively, Democratic gains at the beginning of the decade were reversed with a vengeance by the Republicans following the onset of the economic depression in 1893. Though the presidency changed party hands in 1892 and 1896, the congressional political pendulum swung to its furthest extremes in the midterm elections of 1890 and 1894, neither of which has received its due attention from historians.

McSeveney presents a table showing the distribution of House seats in the New England, Middle Atlantic, and East North Central states. The Democrats and Republicans were fairly evenly divided from 1888 through to 1892. In that latter year, the respective numbers were 88 and 89. In 1894, the year of the shift, the distribution was 9 and 168. The Democrats made a limited recovery in 1896 but the distribution was still a lopsided 27 and 150.[68]

* * *

The concern with the "who rules" questions in 1896–1900 might be viewed as "narrow" empirical issues. But our knowledge, most of it, comes in some "larger" contexts. That knowledge is aided or guided by theoretical frameworks that, presumably, help us to organize and manage a welter of information. Many of those theories provide general answers to the question of who rules. The detailed findings to be presented here allow consideration of the utility of those general theories. Some of the major current theories used to analyze the modern world have appeared, in one way or another, in the preceding pages. A brief sketch of some of those theories follows.

For Marxism, both in its original formulation and in all later variants, the answer to the question of who rules is simple: In the capitalist era, the capitalists rule. Those who have economic power, so it is said, have political power. This conclusion appears also in the work of non-Marxist commentators, some in the American progressive tradition and some "critical" liberals. This position, the argument of business-dominance, is open to serious question.

Various arguments about imperialism must also be considered. For much of the twentieth century, V. I. Lenin's position on this question was the "canonical" formulation, the argument being that expansion was needed for the survival of advanced capitalism. His specific claim was that "finance capital" needed new opportunities for investment. That hardly seems likely in the case of the "new American Empire," the scatter of newly acquired islands providing few such opportunities.

Many American historians have argued a need for new markets, this presumably driving the American effort. Those new 1898–1899 acquisitions, by themselves, seem implausible targets but here, it is said, there was a larger target, namely "the China market." If that were the case, the impetus for the new empire would have come from business elites. But this argument also, as will be seen in a subsequent volume, has little plausible support. Some other explanations, accordingly, must be considered. Some other groups and other motives appear to have been dominant.[69]

The mass society theory is another frequently invoked framework. In this case, we have two principal variants, the original formulation put forward by conservative commentators, and a later one favored by leftists and left-liberals.[70] The conservative mass society position, one that originated in the eighteenth and nineteenth centuries, views the mobilization of "the masses" with considerable alarm. Cunning demagogues could easily mislead the masses, promising benefits that could not possibly be achieved. The end result, it was declared, would be disaster, destruction, and death—as was seen in the French Revolution. Put simply, the rule of the demagogues would make things worse.

The left mass society view also centers on the easily-moved masses. But in this case the demagogy is the work of those in power, the established rich, big business, the bourgeoisie. The mass media, the newspapers, motion pictures, radio, and television are the principal instruments used. The manipulative effort in this case is intended to pacify or divert the masses. The intent, basically, is to maintain "class rule." For Marxists this argument provides an explanation for the failure of the key prediction, the absence of the proletarian revolution.

The mass society argument appears in many contexts. For conservatives, William Jennings Bryan was the threatening demagogue in 1896. For the populists, progressives, and leftist critics, Mark Hanna was the master manipulator. He organized the campaign, generated the immense sums from the nation's alarmed capitalists, and, through astute use of the media, deflected the Bryan threat and thus stabilized "the system." The argument is easily invoked because, typically, no serious evidence is available to support the claims made about the masses and their motives.

A simple question: What effect did the 1896 campaign have on the American electorate? Did voters shift to the Republicans because of Hanna's demagogy? Or did they shift because Bryan's key issue, inflated currency, would reduce their real earnings? Or, had most of those who changed party done so already in 1894? And, another question: Was the Spanish-American War the result of a press war? Did it stem from the Hearst-Pulitzer demagogy or did it result from some other causes?

Another theory, one that figures somewhat less directly in discussion of the events in this period, is the technocratic or bureaucratic argument.[71] American government up to this point—and beyond—was notoriously non-bureaucratic. It was essentially a highly personalized arrangement with staffing and promotion depending on friends and favors. One of the key issues of the day was civil service reform, essentially, removing government positions from the "free hand" of politicians and party bosses. Although rarely called bureaucratization, these were steps in that general process, one anticipated by Max Weber and many others.

How one evaluates that process is a separate question. One should, however, be wary of a persistent bias, of the tendency to depict "bureaucracy" as a bad thing, as an "iron cage," as something limiting our freedom. Would we be better off with non-bureaucratic education systems, social security, or armies? All of the administrations touched on here, from Grant to McKinley, were non-bureaucratic in character. Would the anti-bureaucratic critic wish to see a reversion to that "free" or easygoing style?

The new democratic regimes provided freedom of speech and of association. Those freedoms allowed like-thinking individuals to come together in voluntary associations for the realization of their interests. The pluralist theory focuses on these associations and their implications. A challenge to the mass society view, this theory pointed to the presence and importance of intermediary groups, agencies mediating between individuals and the government. Given the multiplicity of interests and groups, this theory argues multiple centers of power. As opposed to both Marxism and the mass society views, its proponents claimed accuracy (or realism)—this was how democracy actually worked.[72]

Possibly the most important voluntary association in this period was the G.A.R., the Grand Army of the Republic, an organization representing veterans of the Union armies. It was closely aligned with the Republican Party, effectively a support group for the party. It also, understandably, agitated for veterans' benefits. Later in the period, another important association, one furthering the populist insurgency, was the Farmers' Alliance. As with all theories, one must consider the questions of adequacy or appropriateness. The sweeping formulations come easily. The provision of evidence in support of those claims of influence and impact is much more difficult.

The framework to be used here reworks elements of both the pluralist and the elitist approaches. It is clear from the foregoing that multiple centers of power are assumed, each of those elite coteries having its own base of power, each having some degree of independence or autonomy. As opposed to a "ruling class" or a "power elite" said to be cohesive and in possession of "the power," the diverse elite coteries are contenders in decision-making, in struggles for power. Other contenders will also appear in those struggles, voluntary associations (also called pressure groups), the option signaled and argued in "classical" pluralist theory.

The "specific form" of those pressure groups and the character of their activities in the struggle for power that led to the Spanish-American War differ from the accounts found in most sources. They portray those organizations as emanating from "the grass roots." They are agencies formed in response to the needs or grievances of otherwise powerless individuals within "the underlying population." But the agitation for intervention in Cuba was begun by the insurgents themselves. They formed a pressure group with offices in New York City and Washington and support groups in other cities. Their efforts were similar to but more advanced than the outside interventions mentioned earlier, those of the Irish, Hungarian, and Italian liberation struggles. The Cuban group, called the Junta, generated support from some American newspapers, from some members of the Protestant clergy, from Congressional expansionists, and, last not least, from a unique coterie, a group best described as intellectuals in government. The character of this coalition, one that ultimately succeeded, is not anticipated in any of our received theories.

Classical "elitism" sees modern societies as having a range of specialized institutions led by separate and distinct leadership cadres.[73] Those leadership groups might contain several hundred persons such as all of the nation's big businessmen or all of the top officials in the federal government. But the three events reviewed here, the presidential campaign, the staffing of the executive branch, and the decision for war, were ultimately directed by a few persons, hence the focus on coteries, on small groups containing six, eight, or ten persons. All the antecedent causes, whether sensational newspaper accounts, pressure group influences, or clamorous masses, would converge in one way or another on those decision-makers. Borrowing the familiar metaphor, they were the last, the decisive link in the causal chain.[74]

Another cautionary note: Intellectuals, many of them, have a distinct preference for "big" themes, for the "dramatic" event, for the "sweeping" changes. Widespread moral outrage, for example, is an acceptable cause; the action of a rejected and vengeful rejected boss in an upstate county is not. Demagogic themes, events that move "the masses," are acceptable; equilibria or minimal change are not. The big-theme bias means preference will be given to class dominance and mass society theories. And, avoiding the empirical task, it means either indifference or disdain for the "little" facts of political socialization and intergenerational continuity. That bias means "structures" will be "privileged" causes, always preferable to arguments showing signs of "contingency," another term for "small causes." In an analysis focusing on coteries, however, those small, accidental, or contingent factors will always be present. If that is "the way it is," nothing would be gained by imposing inappropriate theoretical frameworks. Explanatory schemes should accord with available evidence; they should guide our understanding of that evidence. Nothing useful is gained by the imposition of, by the read-in of a "powerful" but misleading theory.

Most of the questions broached here may be addressed with evidence. Where available, that evidence should be sifted and winnowed and the appropriate lessons drawn. That is the task of this book. At the outset in any investigation, it is useful to consider a wide range of hypotheses.[75] If the received wisdom, the business-dominance claim for example, has no solid foundation, if based on nothing more than newspaper cartoons (e.g. the fat businessman with dollar signs on his vest), it ought to be viewed as "mere" hypothesis, on the same level as any other *a priori* claim. Class-dominance and mass society theories portray "the ruling classes" as very knowledgeable; they operate with a high awareness and understanding of "events." One should, however, consider other possibilities, such as limited interest, indifference, and/or ignorance. Manufacturers of cotton goods for the American market might not have known or cared about the needs of other businesses. And most of them probably knew next to nothing about market conditions in Latin America or Asia. Capable elites, like all other groups, moreover, can also act on the basis of misinformation. Put differently, they too can make mistakes.

A cautionary note: The exercise of power in 1896–1900 tells us nothing about power relations at other times in the American experience. The most useful lesson contained in the heritage of ancient Greek is a sentence by Heraclitus—"All is flux, nothing is stationary." The "causal dynamics" would be different in the presidencies of Theodore Roosevelt, Woodrow Wilson, Franklin Roosevelt, Dwight Eisenhower, Ronald Reagan, and George W. Bush.[76]

Notes

1. Charles A. Beard and Mary R. Beard, *The Rise of American Civilization,* two volumes (New York, 1927). A single volume edition, revised and enlarged, came out in 1933.

   The quotation marks in the opening sentence are intended to signal a need for caution. The unqualified use of the term progressive gives an *a priori* positive evaluation to the movement and its advocates. Progressives did advocate many good things—shorter work weeks, better working conditions, ending child labor, women's suffrage, and so on. They opposed "the interests," advocated railroad regulation, the breakup of "the trusts," and an income tax. The accounts, unfortunately, often present "the sides" in stark categorical terms with the progressives championed and their opponents depicted as "the bad guys." But the evaluation of movements and persons should not be done by labeling but rather by evidence, by consideration of the actual or likely consequences of their programs. The principal element of William Jennings Bryan's 1896 presidential campaign, the free coinage of silver, for example, would have hurt millions of wage and salary workers, hardly a progressive accomplishment.

2. The quotations are from Thomas Bender, "Beard," *ANB,* 2:401–406. For more on his impact, see Richard Hofstadter, *The Progressive Historians: Turner, Beard, Parrington* (New York, 1969), p. 209. See also Howard K. Beale, ed., *Charles A. Beard: An Appraisal* (Lexington, KY, 1954); Lee Benson, *Turner and Beard: American Historical Writing Reconsidered* (New York, 1960); and Ellen Nore, *Charles A. Beard: An Intellectual Biography* (Carbondale, IL, 1983). There were serious criticisms of Beard's writings, but these, on the whole, had very limited impact. For an overview, see Forrest McDonald, *Recovering the Past: A Historian's Memoir* (Lawrence, KA, 2004).

3. Beard and Beard, *Rise,* Vol. 2, pp. 337–341, includes also the quotations in the following paragraph.

4. Ibid., pp. 370–372.

5. Ibid., p. 376.
6. Samuel Eliot Morison, Henry Steele Commager, and William E. Leuchtenburg, *The Growth of the American Republic*, two volumes, seventh edition (New York, 1980 [first edition, 1930]); and John D. Hicks, George E. Mowry, and Robert E. Burke, *The American Nation: A History of the United States from 1865 to the Present*, fifth edition (Boston, 1971 [first edition, 1941]).
7. Four leading American history textbooks will be referred to throughout this work. They are: Divine et al.; Henretta et al.; Nash et al.; and Norton et al. The full references are given in the Note on the Sources.

   A sizable monographic literature provides more detail, elaboration, and support for the basic progressive viewpoint. Possibly the most important later work in this tradition is that of William Appleman Williams, *The Tragedy of American Diplomacy*, second edition (New York, 1972 [first edition 1959]). The revised version was reprinted in 1988 and, as of 2005, was still in print. It contains almost no documentation and therefore is perhaps best described as an interpretative analysis. Much of the same ground is covered, with extensive documentation, in Williams' *The Roots of the Modern American Empire: A Study of the Growth and Shaping of Social Consciousness in a Marketplace Society* (New York, 1969). An autobiographical sketch telling of Williams's background and his influence as leader of "the Wisconsin School" appears there in a prefatory statement, pp. ix–xxiv. Works in this tradition will be referred to here as the Williams school.

   For more extended discussions see Lloyd C. Gardner, ed., *Redefining the Past: Essays in Diplomatic History in Honor of William Appleman Williams* (Corvallis, OR, 1986) and Paul M. Buhle and Edward Rice-Maximin, *William Appleman Williams: The Tragedy of Empire* (New York, 1995). Walter LaFeber, a student of Williams, is the most important subsequent writer in this tradition. Among his many works, see especially the following: *The New Empire: An Interpretation of American Expansion, 1860–1898* (Ithaca, 1963) and *The American Search for Opportunity, 1865–1913* (New York, 1993). See also, Thomas J. McCormick, *China Market: America's Quest for Informal Empire, 1893–1901* (Chicago, 1967); Lloyd C. Gardner, *Imperial America: American Foreign Policy Since 1898* (New York, 1976); and Lloyd C. Gardner, Walter F. LaFeber, and Thomas J. McCormick, *Creation of the American Empire*, two volumes, second edition (Chicago, 1976).

   For a brief comprehensive review of works in this tradition, see Emily S. Rosenberg, "Economic Interest and United States Foreign Policy," ch. 3 of Gordon Martel, ed., *American Foreign Relations Reconsidered, 1890–1993* (London, 1994).
8. Marx and Engels, *Collected Works*, Vol. 6 (New York, 1976), pp. 476–519 (quotation, p. 486). Although sharing a common assumption with regard to "the rulers," the Beards and the Marxists differ in their predictions with regards to outcomes, the former anticipating rule by disinterested technocrats, the latter expecting revolution and subsequent rule by the proletariat.
9. The fifty volumes of the *Collected Works* contain hundreds of comments about British, French, and German political leaders, most of them either assuming or declaring support for the authors' basic claim. But typically those comments lack supporting evidence. For a review of the bourgeois revolution thesis, see Richard F. Hamilton, *The Bourgeois Epoch: Marx and Engels on Britain, France, and Germany* (Chapel Hill, 1991).
10. An extensive research effort began in the 1950s, this stimulated by Floyd Hunter who, with evidence based on Atlanta, argued the dominance of top business leaders, in

32 President McKinley, War and Empire

his *Community Power Structure* (Chapel Hill, 1953). An important countering case, with evidence from New Haven, argued a dispersion of power. See Robert Dahl, *Who Governs? Democracy and Power in an American City* (New Haven, 1961). William Domhoff later reviewed the New Haven experience covering a wide range of documentary evidence and found substantial support for the business-dominance position. See his *Who Really Rules? New Haven and Community Power Reexamined* (Santa Monica, CA, 1978). For comprehensive general reviews covering American national politics, see Domhoff, *The Power Elite and the State* (New York, 1990) and *Who Rules America? Power and Politics*, fourth edition (Boston, 2002). See also Jeff Manza, Fay Lomax Cook, and Benjamin I. Page, eds., *Navigating Public Opinion: Polls, Policy and the Future of American Democracy* (New York, 2002).

11. The leaders of democratic regimes also, on occasion, attempt to hide or distort the historical record. The president and premier of France made a trip to St. Petersburg in July of 1914, just prior to the outbreak of the war. But we have no adequate account of their discussions with the Russian leaders. The minutes of those meetings, those of both sides, are not available, an extensive search proving "almost entirely fruitless." From Luigi Albertini, *The Origins of the War of 1914*, Vol. II (London, 1953), p. 189. For a more general review, see Holger H. Herwig, "The Use and Abuse of History and the Great War," pp. 299–330 of Geoffrey Parker and Mary R. Habeck, eds., *The Great War and the Twentieth Century* (New Haven, 2000). The text statement is one of probability, documentation being more likely in the democratic than in the authoritarian regimes.

12. For a review and analysis of the 1914–1917 decisions for war in thirteen nations, see Richard F. Hamilton and Holger H. Herwig, eds., *The Origins of World War I* (New York, 2003). The decision-making coteries were smallest in the authoritarian regimes, Austria-Hungary, Germany, and Russia. Elsewhere, in France, Britain, and the United States, the participation was somewhat larger and definitely more complicated.

13. David Brewer, *The Greek War of Independence* (Woodstock, NY, 2001), pp. 329–336. Most accounts focus on the role of the literati with the poet Byron in the forefront. But the painters also joined in the effort. Delacroix produced two graphic paintings depicting Turkish outrages in Greece. A Paris salon exhibited twenty-one works by Delacroix and others dealing with Greek themes. A radical art critic wrote that the "Salon is as political as the elections; the brush and the chisel are party tools just as much as the pen" (Brewer, p. 287). On the poet, see Elizabeth Longford, *Byron* (London, 1976), ch. 9.

14. Norman Rich, *Why the Crimean War? A Cautionary Tale* (New York, 1991), pp. 10–11. France, then with an authoritarian regime, also participated but the public response to newspaper agitation there was quite different. Rich provides some suggestive explanations to account for the disparity.

15. Gordon A. Craig, *Germany, 1866–1945* (New York, 1978), pp. 22–27.

16. This means any sweeping claims about mass involvement should be viewed with extreme skepticism and evidence should be demanded. The first and most dramatic "crowd event" of the modern era was the taking of the Bastille on 14 July 1789. William Doyle reports massive involvement, declaring that on the twelfth, "the whole city" was "frantically trying to arm itself." Then, once armed, "the populace did not hesitate to act." No estimate of the numbers is given, only that the "impatient crowds" forced their way into the Bastille, this from *The Oxford History of the French Revolution* (Oxford, 1989), pp. 109–110.

Simon Schama provides the appropriate figure, reporting the number of attackers to have been "about nine hundred." In *Citizens* (New York, 1989), pp. 400–410. There was an official record: The "sacred nine hundred" received a *brevet de vainqueur* certifying their involvement (p. 410). The population of Paris at that time was about 600,000. If one assumes the potential combatants, those who might have joined the struggle, to consist of males of ages eighteen to fifty, that would have meant an "eligible population" of roughly 100,000 persons. The *vainqueurs*, at best, were one in a hundred among those eligible. The other ninety-nine, clearly, were doing something else. The most likely hypotheses: They were either at work or at home engaged in household tasks. For another account finding serious misrepresentation of "mass" involvement, see Mark Traugott, *Armies of the Poor: Determinants of Working-Class Participation in the Parisian Insurrection of June 1848* (Princeton, 1985).

17. For a brief review of Genêt's activities, see Ron Chernow, *Alexander Hamilton* (New York, 2004), pp. 437–447. For Kossuth's efforts in the United States, Great Britain, France, and Italy, see Istvan Deak, *The Lawful Revolution* (New York, 1979), pp. 342–346. For more detail see Arthur James May, *Contemporary American Opinion of the Mid-Century Revolutions in Central Europe* (Philadelphia, 1927); John Komlos, *Louis Kossuth in America, 1851–1852* (Buffalo, NY, 1973); and Donald S. Spencer, *Louis Kossuth and Young America: A Study of Sectionalism and Foreign Polity 1848–1852* (Columbia, MO, 1977).

Kossuth's efforts stimulated some reactions from the political parties. Northern Democrats favored initiatives in support of Hungary's aspirations, some arguing for a break with Austria. The Whigs, led by Millard Fillmore and his Secretary of State Daniel Webster, opposed any such intervention. Southern Democrats were strongly opposed to any such move seeing intervention in support of "liberation" as a serious threat to their interests. The recognition of partisan advantage (or disadvantage) in such efforts would appear again in the mid-1890s in connection with the Cuban insurgency.

For Garibaldi's efforts, see Jasper Ridley, *Garibaldi* (London, 2001 [1974]), pp. 143, 298, 375–377, 391, 456–458. On the Irish efforts, Brian Jenkins, *Fenians and Anglo-American Relations during Reconstruction* (Ithaca, 1969). Parnell traveled through the United States in 1880 seeking support among Irish-Americans. He addressed meetings in sixty-two cities and also a joint session of Congress (p. 319).

There were other attempts: In the 1820s, American Philhellenics, like their European counterparts, sought support for the Greek independence movement. Germans in Philadelphia formed the "American Revolutionary League for Europe" in 1852 to overthrow the monarchies of Europe. Mexico's General Santa Anna visited the United States in 1866 to seek support for his effort to overthrow Emperor Maximilian's rule there. On these cases, see Myrtle A. Cline, *American Attitude toward the Greek War of Independence, 1821–1828* (Atlanta, 1930); Komlos, pp. 131–132; and Glyndon G. Van Deusen, *William Henry Seward* (New York, 1967), p. 493.

18. That conclusion was presented, with evidence, in Julius W. Pratt's *Expansionists of 1898* (Baltimore, 1936), ch. 7. His work will be reviewed and discussed in chapter 4.

19. On this theme, see Richard F. Hamilton, "McKinley's Backbone," *Presidential Studies Quarterly*, forthcoming.

20. Gustavus Myers, *History of the Great American Fortunes* (New York, 1936); Jackson T. Main, *The Social Structure of Revolutionary America* (Princeton, 1965); Stephen Hess, *America's Political Dynasties* (Garden City, NY, 1966). On the

Virginia families, Charles S. Snyder, *Gentlemen Freeholders* (Chapel Hill, 1952) and Kenneth P. Bailey, *The Ohio Company of Virginia and the Westward Movement: 1748–1792* (Glendale, CA, 1939). See also Paul Wallace Gates, *The Jeffersonian Dream: Studies in the History of American Land Policy and Development* (Albuquerque, 1996), especially ch. 1, "The Role of the Land Speculator in Western Development." The Turner thesis has obvious relevance for this discussion. For a comprehensive overview complete with extensive documentation see Ray Allen Billington, *The American Frontier Thesis: Attack and Defense* (Washington, D.C., 1971).

21. Axel Madsen, *John Jacob Astor: America's First Multimillionaire* (New York, 2001).

22. There is no book-length biography of Longworth, but see the brief entry in ANB, 13:898–899. See also Richard C. Wade, *The Urban Frontier: The Rise of Western Cities, 1790–1830* (Cambridge, 1959).

23. William Ganson Rose, *Cleveland: The Making of a City* (Cleveland, 1950), p. 25. See also Lois Scharf, " 'I Would Go Wherever Fortune Would Direct': Hannah Huntington and the Frontier of the Western Reserve," *Ohio History*, 97 (1980):5–28.

24. Thomas Perkins Abernathy, *From Frontier to Plantation in Tennessee* (Chapel Hill, 1932).

25. Arthur T. Vanderbilt, *Fortune's Children: The Fall of the House of Vanderbilt* (New York, 1989).

     It is easy to assume that great wealth would be carried over from one generation to the next but this author reports an opposite experience—when "120 of the Commodore's descendents gathered at Vanderbilt University in 1973 for the first family reunion, there was not a millionaire among them" (p. ix).

26. States and communities also supported railroad development. For a study of one important line, see Paul Wallace Gates, *The Illinois Central Railroad and Its Colonization Work* (Cambridge, 1934). Abraham Lincoln represented this railroad, a north-south line connecting Chicago and Mobile, in an important tax case. For the details, see Albert A. Woldman, *Lawyer Lincoln* (Boston, 1936), especially ch. 15, "Railroad and Big Business Lawyer." Stephen A. Douglas also performed various services for the Illinois Central, Woldman, p. 160. For still more, see John W. Starr, Jr., *Lincoln and the Railroads* (New York, 1927).

27. For an overview, see Edward C. Kirkland, *Industry Comes of Age: Business, Labor, and Public Policy, 1860–1897* (New York, 1961).

28. DAB, 18:3–5; ANB, 20:740–742; and, Harry E. Resseguie, "Alexander Turney Stewart and the Development of the Department Store, 1823–1876," *Business History Review*, 29 (1965):301–322.

29. Edward N. Akin, *Flagler, Rockefeller Partner and Florida Baron* (Kent, OH, 1988).

30. Allan Nevins, *Study in Power: John D. Rockefeller*, Vol. 1 (New York, 1953), pp. 60–64; 231–249.

31. Robert E. Conot, *A Streak of Luck* (New York, 1979). On the Gould connection, pp. 65–66, 69–70, 75, 84, and 183; on General Electric, pp. 301–302, and 304. There was another major consideration: Edison stubbornly insisted that GE should operate with direct current, which was much more costly than alternating. That choice put GE at a considerable disadvantage vis-à-vis a major competitor, George Westinghouse. Edison's preference was the condition for the success of the latter's firm. On this, see pp. 253–255, 301.

32. Maury Klein, *The Life and Legend of E. H. Harriman* (Chapel Hill, N.C., 2000), ch. 15.
33. Philip H. Burch, Jr., *Elites in American History*, Vol. 2, *The Civil War to the New Deal* (New York, 1981), pp. 131–136.
34. Morgan created the United States Steel Company in 1901, the largest component, by far, being Carnegie Steel. The Rockefellers owned two other components, the Mesabi iron ore deposits in Minnesota and a fleet of Great Lakes ore carriers. Ron Chernow describes the attitudes of the principals as follows: "Pierpont considered [Carnegie and Rockefeller] too crude for his stuffily refined tastes; they saw him as pompous and overbearing. The prudish Carnegie also disapproved of Pierpont's adulterous escapades," from *The House of Morgan* (New York, 1990), pp. 83–84.
35. Irving Katz, *August Belmont: A Political Biography* (New York, 1968). Horace Greeley, a leading Republican and publisher of the *New York Tribune*, was an anti-Semite, on this see pp. 19–20, 29, and 39. The *New York Times* also shared the tendency, one editorial complaining of Belmont and his use of "Jew gold" (i.e., Rothschild) to influence American elections (p. 19). The *Chicago Tribune* declared the "key question before the country" in the 1864 election to be whether the nation would have "a dishonorable peace, in order to enrich Belmont, the Rothschilds, and the whole tribe of Jews who have been buying up Confederate bonds" or an honorable peace won by Grant and Sherman (p. 144).
36. This struggle caused the Panic of 1901, which brought ruin to many brokerage houses. For overviews, see Chernow, *House of Morgan*, pp. 90–93; Vincent P. Carosso, *The Morgans: Private International Bankers, 1954–1913* (Cambridge, 1987), pp. 474–479; and Jean Strouse, *Morgan: American Financier* (New York, 1999), pp. 418–427, 431–434. Harriman, it should be noted, controlled the Union Pacific and Southern Pacific Railroads, numbers 2 and 3 on Burch's list; Hill controlled the Northern Pacific and the Great Northern, numbers 7 and 9 on that list.

    Given the routine equation of money and power, one should note the relative standing of three leading capitalists. Excluding his artworks, the net value of Morgan's estate was estimated at "some $68.3 million." His art works were judged to be worth roughly $50 million. Carosso (p. 644) comments that Morgan "left a relatively modest estate" compared to those of Rockefeller and Carnegie. Of Morgan, Carnegie is reported to have said, "And to think he was not a rich man." Carnegie had sold his steel company in 1901 for $480 million.
37. Chernow, *House of Morgan*, pp. 103–104.
38. Ibid., p. 90. Businessmen also divided over wage and benefits issues, some being "hard liners," some compromise-oriented moderates. On these divisions, see James Weinstein, *The Corporate Ideal in the Liberal State: 1900–1918* (Boston, 1968), especially pp. 8–11. The moderate leaders formed an advocacy group, the Civic Federation, that brought together business and labor leaders. Its first president was Marcus Alonzo Hanna.
39. For an analysis of the Senate in this period, see David J. Rothman, *Politics and Power: The United States Senate, 1869–1901* (Cambridge, MA, 1966).
40. For an overview, see Ernest S. Griffith, *A History of American City Government: The Conspicuous Failure, 1870–1900* (New York, 1974). For a classic case study, see Harold F. Gosnell, *Machine Politics: Chicago Model*, second edition (Chicago, 1967 [1937]). And for analysis of subsequent changes in that case, see Thomas M. Guterbock, *Machine Politics in Transition* (Chicago, 1980). For comprehensive accounts, see Charles R. Adrian and Charles Press, *Governing Urban America*, fifth

edition (New York, 1977) and Edward C. Banfield and James Q. Wilson, *City Politics* (Cambridge, MA, 1963). Big city affairs are more "dramatic" than those of smaller communities, a view shared by academics and journalists alike, a reading that leads to very selected (or biased) sampling. For a useful study of a village political machine and its "dynamics," see Arthur J. Vidich and Joseph Bensman, *Small Town in Mass Society* (Princeton, 1958).

41. Seymour J. Mandelbaum, *Boss Tweed's New York* (New York, 1965), chs. 7 and 8.
42. David M. Jordan, *Roscoe Conkling of New York* (Ithaca, N.Y., 1971, chs. 25 and 26. For Conkling's motives, his "thinking of getting out," see pp. 394–395, 398, and 400.

    Following the death of Garfield, who was killed by a "disappointed office-seeker," a Conkling lieutenant, Chester A. Arthur, became president. The one-time boss had a long visit with the new president and, still seeking vindication, asked that he discharge the New York collector. But Arthur refused, a decision that "destroyed an old friendship," pp. 414–415.

    Many discussions of the "powerful" bosses are selective, failing to report their losses or outright failures. On occasion, to undercut the threat of a reform movement, a boss would present a "clean" candidate. In 1910, the Democratic party leader of New Jersey, James Smith, Jr., chose a clean candidate, Woodrow Wilson, the president of Princeton University, to be his party's candidate for governor. A few weeks after taking office, Wilson broke with the boss, blocked his election to the United States Senate, and took control of the New Jersey party organization. For this, see Arthur S. Link, *Woodrow Wilson and the Progressive Era, 1910–1917* (New York, 1954), pp. 9–10.

43. With only rare exceptions, political careers meant some sacrifice of income. Roscoe Conkling agreed to manage Garfield's presidential campaign. Before he could begin working for Garfield, however, he had to wind up his law practice, which meant that Conkling "had to return some $18,000 worth of retainers already paid." This "must have hurt, because the senator was not wealthy," Jordan, *Conkling*, p. 355. Those income losses did not begin in the so-called Gilded Age. They were there from the beginning of the republic. Alexander Hamilton lost the considerable income gained from a successful law practice when he agreed to serve as the nation's first Secretary of the Treasury. His losses while in government service are reviewed in Chernow, *Alexander Hamilton*, pp. 287, 483, 501, 509, 526, 563, 584, and 596.

44. One can readily cite opposite examples. Warren Gamaliel Harding was definitely not hardworking and had not demonstrated much capacity. And he knew his limits. In 1916, concerned about talk of him as a candidate for the presidency, the newly chosen senator wrote a confidant that he was "unsuited" for that position. He added that: "I do not desire it and most sincerely want to escape the responsibilities that candidacy and the office would bring." But for the party bosses, faced with a deadlocked convention in 1920, Harding's personal attractiveness and demonstrated vote-getting ability seemed a solution to the immediate problem. See Francis Russell, *The Shadow of Blooming Grove* (New York, 1968), pp. 269 and 333.

45. Glyndon G. Van Deusen, *Horace Greeley* (Philadelphia, 1953), ch. 25.

    Brokers sponsored people; they also sought to block others. Greeley tried to prevent Lincoln's renomination in 1864. He tried to prevent Garfield from being named to head the House Ways and Means committee, see Allan Peskin, *Garfield* (Kent, OH, 1978), pp. 178–179, and 320.

46. Bingham Duncan, *Whitelaw Reid* (Athens, GA, 1975), p. 82.

The *Tribune* was in serious difficulty when Greeley died, having lost circulation and revenues as a result of his curious 1872 campaign for the presidency. To acquire control of the *Tribune* after Greeley's death, Reid borrowed money from several prominent people, one of these being Jay Gould. This was public knowledge—Charles Dana's New York *Sun* denounced him as "Jay Gould's stool pigeon." In 1881 Reid married the daughter of Ogden Mills, one of the nation's wealthiest men. Members of the Mills family then acquired Gould's shares. On these matters, see Duncan, pp. 48–49, and Richard Kluger, *The Paper: The Life and Death of the New York Herald Tribune* (New York, 1986), pp. 133–135.

Later, Reid actively sought some important offices. President Harrison named him as minister to France (1889–1892). He was Harrison's vice-presidential candidate in the 1892 election, which the Republicans lost. He sought some important positions in McKinley's administration but with no success. McKinley did appoint him, in 1898, to the American Peace Commission to negotiate the settlement of the war with Spain. In 1905, Theodore Roosevelt appointed him as ambassador to Great Britain.

47. Mark D. Hirsch, *William C. Whitney: Modern Warwick* (New York, 1948), chs. 9 and 13 and W. A. Swanberg, *Whitney Father, Whitney Heiress*, (New York, 1980), pp. 8–13, 72–75, and 95–103.

Many accounts portray Mark Hanna as a unique figure, as the master-organizer of a candidate's presidential campaign but Whitney obviously preceded him in this line of work. Hirsch's subtitle, it will be noted, makes the comparison with Warwick, the same that the Beards used with respect to Hanna.

48. Henry F. Pringle, *Theodore Roosevelt* (New York, 1931), p. 116. For more, see Edmund Morris, *The Rise of Theodore Roosevelt* (New York, 1979), 279–282 and H. W. Brands, *T.R.: The Last Romantic* (New York, 1997), pp. 175–178.

In a later period, George Harvey, the editor of *Harper's Weekly* and of the *North American Review*, an important intellectual journal, also worked as a broker. Described by Arthur Link as an "old booster" of Woodrow Wilson, he planned the initial steps of the university president's new career, first as governor of New Jersey. Harvey was the man who convinced boss James Smith that Wilson "could be used to head off a growing progressive revolt within the party" (described in note 42 above). Later, when Wilson moved in a "progressive" direction, he and Harvey had a falling out. Wilson felt that Harvey's ties with some business leaders, with J. P. Morgan among others, would hurt his effort. Harvey was asked to withdraw his support and their relationship effectively ended. Later, the two differed on some major issues, most importantly, about the League of Nations.

Harvey subsequently changed party and played an important role in the nomination of Warren Harding. His biographer states that Harvey was "second to nobody" in the nomination proceedings at Chicago and that "his rooms at the Blackstone Hotel formed the real center of the Convention." Harding offered Harvey the post of Secretary of State but, as a newcomer to the party, he "unhesitatingly" declined. Harding wanted Harvey's help in the selection of the Cabinet but this request was also declined. Subsequently, Harding named him as ambassador to the Court of St. James. See Arthur Link, *Woodrow Wilson*, p. 10. For a brief biography of Harvey, see ANB, 10:276–277 and Willis Fletcher Johnson, *George Harvey* (Boston, 1929), pp. 282–283. Also, for Harvey's connections with J. P. Morgan, see Strouse, *Morgan*, pp. 365–367, 665–666 and John Milton Cooper, Jr., *The Warrior and the Priest* (Cambridge, 1983), pp. 121, 178–179, 181.

49. Hirsch, *Whitney*, pp. 1, 253. For Flora's transformation of Washington's social life, see pp. 302–304, 312–313. In their four years there it is estimated the couple entertained more than 60,000 guests. Whitney began the revival of the badly deteriorated navy. One of his achievements was the construction of modern battleships, among them the *Maine*.

50. Frank Luther Mott, *American Journalism: A History: 1690–1960*, third edition (New York, 1962), pp. 421, 528.

51. Morton Keller, *Affairs of State: Public Life in Late Nineteenth Century America* (Cambridge, 1977) and Stephen Skowronek, *Building a New American State: The Expansion of National Administrative Capacities, 1877–1920* (Cambridge, U.K, 1982), ch. 3.

52. Helmut Pemsel, *Atlas of Naval Warfare*, G.D.G. Smith, trans. (London, 1977), appendix 3, pp. 156–157.

53. For an account of one diplomat's activities, in France and later in Great Britain, see Duncan, *Whitelaw Reid*, chs. 9–11, 15, and 16.

54. Allan Nevins, *Grover Cleveland: A Study in Courage* (New York, 1933), chs. 10 and 11.

55. Peskin, *Garfield*, p. 154. Cameron's management of the War Department in the first months of the Civil War left much to be desired and Lincoln had to remove him. In January 1862, "to be rid of him," he was appointed as minister to Russia. See ANB, 4:259–260.

56. Peskin, *Garfield*, p. 517. On Don Cameron, see ANB, 4:257–258.

57. On Olney, see Karl Schriftgiesser, *The Gentleman from Massachusetts: Henry Cabot Lodge* (Boston, 1945), p. 24; on Root, see Richard W. Leopold, *Elihu Root and the Conservative Tradition* (Boston, 1954), p. 24; and for Knox, Charles Vevier, *The United States and China, 1906–1913* (New Brunswick, 1955), p. 89. For more on the Knox appointment, see George Harvey, *Henry Clay Frick: The Man* (New York, 1928), p. 292. The appointments of Root and Knox will be discussed further in chapter 3. For more examples of such indifference to training and background, see Charles S. Campbell, *The Transformation of American Foreign Relations 1865–1900* (New York, 1976), pp. 77–78, 87, 91–92, and 97.

58. For some sense of the complexities, see H. Wayne Morgan, *William McKinley and His America*, revised edition (Kent, OH, 2003 [1963]), pp. 45–47.

59. All of the election statistics, both the popular and electoral votes, cited in this chapter are from Carolyn Goldinger, ed., *Presidential Elections Since 1789*, fourth edition (Washington, D.C., 1987). The Republicans were also generally dominant in the United States' Senate. In the period from 1868 to 1894 there were fourteen senatorial bodies, the 41st to the 54th Congresses. Twelve were ruled by the Republicans. The House reflected more closely the popular vote where the Republicans were dominant in only six of the fourteen sessions. For the Senate results, see: http://www.senate.gov/learning/stat_13.html. And for the House, see: http://clerkweb.house.gov/histrecs/househis/lists/divisionh.htm.

60. The Republicans disputed the 1876 popular vote tallies in Florida, South Carolina, and Louisiana. An Electoral Commission was formed to resolve the matter. By strict party votes, eight to seven, Republicans were declared the winners in all three states, those decisions making Hayes the president. For this history see C. Vann Woodward, *Reunion and Reaction*, revised edition (Garden City, NY, 1956). See also, for later comment, Allan Peskin, "Was There a Compromise of 1877?" *Journal of American History*, 60 (1973): 63–75; Michael Les Benedict, "Southern

Democrats in the Crisis of 1876–1877: A Reconsideration of *Reunion and Reaction*," *Journal of Southern History*, 46 (1980): 489–524; and George C. Rable, "Southern Interests and the Election of 1876: A Reappraisal," *Civil War History*, 26 (1980): 347–361.

61. For a more extended discussion, see Richard F. Hamilton, *Class and Politics in the United States* (New York, 1972), ch. 1.

62. The focus on political socialization and the corresponding radical discounting of issue orientations appeared in sociology and in political science with the following major works: Bernard R. Berelson, Paul F. Lazarsfeld, and William N. McPhee, *Voting: A Study of Opinion Formation in a Presidential Campaign* (Chicago, 1954) and Angus Campbell, Philip E. Converse, Warren E. Miller, and Donald E. Stokes, *The American Voter* (New York, 1960). For some comparative evidence showing the primacy of political socialization as a determinant of party preferences see Ronald Inglehart, *The Silent Revolution* (Chapel Hill, 1977), pp. 246–249. Parents' party was by far the strongest predictor of the respondent's party identification in their American sample, the Beta (partial relationship) being .409, that followed by religious denomination, .190. The Beta weights for a much-discussed trio of presumed powerful factors—race, class (here occupation of family head), and gender, were: .175, .102, and .060 (from p. 248).

63. The work in this tradition begins with V. O. Key, "A Theory of Critical Elections," *Journal of Politics*, 17 (1955):3–18. See also, William Nisbet Chambers and Walter Dean Burnham, eds., *The American Party Systems: States of Political Development* (New York, 1967); Walter Dean Burnham, *Critical Elections and the Mainsprings of American Politics* (New York, 1970); and James L. Sundquist, *Dynamics of the Party System* (Washington, D.C., 1983). The literature in this tradition is extensive. For a recent review and criticism, see David R. Mayhew, *Electoral Realignments: A Critique of an American Genre* (New Haven, 2002).

64. For an overview, see Samuel T. McSeveney, *The Politics of Depression: Political Behavior in the Northeast, 1893–1896* (New York, 1972), ch. 1. And for a brief discussion of Indiana's centrality and of the consequent focus there, see Keller, *Affairs of State*, pp. 537.

    One might think that New York was favored because it had the largest number of electoral votes. By that argument, Pennsylvania, with the second largest number of electoral votes, should also have been favored. But it was safely Republican and, accordingly, only one Pennsylvanian, Winfield Scott Hancock in 1880, received a call. He was a career army officer with very limited ties to his home state. His running mate was a Hoosier.

    There were two further implications: Vote buying would be concentrated in those two states. For comment on Indiana, see Jordan, *Conkling*, pp. 349, 358, and 375. And those competitive states would also have very high levels of participation. In the 1884 election, Allan Nevins reports that "in Massachusetts 45 per cent of the voting population remained at home; in Illinois 21 percent; but in Indiana, only 7 percent," *Grover Cleveland* (New York, 1933), pp. 177–178.

65. Ibid., ch. 11. On the New York election outcome, see Lee Benson, "Research Problems in American Political Historiography," in Mirra Komarovsky, ed., *Common Frontiers in the Social Sciences* (Glencoe, IL, 1957), pp. 123–146.

66. Jordan, *Conkling*, pp. 420–421. Asked to speak on behalf of Blaine in the 1884 election, Conkling replied: "No, thank you, I don't engage in criminal practice." See also Duncan, *Reid*, p. 103. The figures given are from Jordan, who does not

give his source. Dean Burnham's compendious volume gives slightly different numbers but the Conkling-effect argument is still clearly supported. Oneida County produced a Republican majority in all but one of the presidential elections from 1856 to 1892. The Republican margins in 1880 and 1888 were 1,964 and 1,965 respectively. But in 1884, they lost the county by 33 votes. None of the neighboring upstate counties showed that deviation. See Dean Burnham, *Presidential Ballots 1836–1892* (Baltimore, 1955), pp. 632–646.

Nevins reports (pp. 171, 173–174) that some anti-Cleveland Democrats, among them some "Tammany elements," supported Ben Butler, a third party candidate running as a Greenbacker, the aim being to defeat their own party's candidate. These efforts were also "abetted by the Republicans." Charles A. Dana, publisher of the normally Democratic New York *Sun*, detested Cleveland and "lifted the Butler banner," a choice that for him came "at almost ruinous cost." The paper lost nearly half of its circulation in a few months. Nevins and Benson mention still another factor, a more prosaic one: rain in upstate New York on election day. The reduced turnout probably hurt the Republicans.

67. Key, "Critical Elections," pp. 12–13 and Congressional Quarterly, *Members of Congress since 1789*, third edition (Washington, D.C., 1985), p. 182.

For studies showing the 1894 realignment, see, Paul Kleppner, *The Cross of Culture: A Social Analysis of Midwestern Politics, 1850–1900* (New York, 1970); Samuel T. McSeveney, *The Politics of Depression: Political Behavior in the Northeast, 1893–1896* (New York, 1972), especially ch. 4; Morton Keller, *Affairs of State: Public Life in Late Nineteenth Century America* (Cambridge, 1977), ch. 15; Richard L. McCormick, *From Realignment to Reform: Political Change in New York State, 1893–1910* (Ithaca, 1981), ch. 2; Paul Kleppner, *Continuity and Change in Electoral Politics, 1893–1928* (New York, 1987), chs. 2–4; and David W. Brady, *Critical Elections and Congressional Policy Making* (Stanford, 1988), ch. 3.

Many accounts are based on the results of presidential elections, thus missing the lesson of the 1894 Congressional contests. Brady's Tables 3.1 and 3.2 (pp. 58–59) show results from 1884 to 1900 for the nation, for the nation with the South excluded, and for seven major regions. In the non-South states the percentages for the key years were:

Year	Republican	Democrat
1892	45.8	47.5
1894	52.5	37.9
1896	54.2	41.7

For the Democrats, 1894 was clearly the year of disaster. They regained some strength in 1896 but the Republicans gained also at that time (both clearly at the expense of the minor parties).

68. McSeveney, *Politics of Depression*, pp. x–xi. Among the four leading American history textbooks, Devine et al., pp. 628–629, provide the clearest statement of the 1894 election and its importance, reporting the extent of the shift and its significance, that it ended the "deadlock" existing since the 1870s. Norton et al. (pp. 591–592) report that the Populists "made good showings" in 1894 but otherwise have nothing on this election. Nash et al. (p. 624) have a sentence reporting that in 1894 "voters abandoned the Democrats in droves, giving both Populists and Republicans high hopes for 1896." That is followed by a heading: "The Crucial Election of 1896." The "landslide Republican victory" in that year "broke the stalemate . . ."

(p. 629). Henretta et al. pass over the earlier election, mentioning it only in a comment of the 1896 result—McKinley "kept the Republican ground that had been regained in the 1894 midterm elections . . ." They also report that the "party stalemate" was broken in 1896 (p. 593). At best, these textbooks give only a couple of sentences to the 1894 election. They all give four or five pages to the "dramatic" 1896 contest.

69. For expositions of Marxism and its principal variants together with empirical assessments of their major claims, see Richard F. Hamilton, *Marxism, Revisionism, and Leninism* (Westport, CT, 2000).

70. For expositions and assessments, see Richard F. Hamilton, *Mass Society, Pluralism, and Bureaucracy* (Westport, CT, 2001), ch. 1.

71. Ibid, ch. 3.

72. Ibid, ch. 2. For a discussion of business organizations, with evidence, see Hamilton, *Restraining Myths* (New York, 1975), ch. 7.

73. For an overview, see Lowell Field and John Higley, *Elitism* (London, 1980); Eva Etzioni-Halevy, *The Elite Connection* (New York, 1993); Etzioni-Halevy, ed., *Classes and Elites in Democracy and Democratization* (New York, 1997); and Etzioni-Halevy, ed., special edition of *International Review of Sociology*, Vol. 9, 2 (July 1999).

74. For analysis and evidence on coterie decision-making, see the case studies in Hamilton and Herwig, *Origins of World War I*.

75. For the definitive statement, see T. C. Chamberlin, "The Method of Multiple Working Hypotheses," *Science* 148 (1965): 754–759. Originally published in *Science* in 1890, it has been reprinted there on four subsequent occasions.

76. For discussion and evidence on later twentieth-century experience, see the works of William Domhoff cited in note 10 above. For a compendious inventory, one reviewing the many styles of rule, see Frederic Cople Jaher, ed., *The Rich, the Well Born, and the Powerful: Elites and Upper Classes in History* (Secaucus, N.J., 1975).

It is easy to assume intergenerational continuity but again research is useful. E. Digby Baltzell published two outstanding studies documenting the power and privilege of an American elite group, his *Philadelphia Gentlemen: The Making of a National Upper Class* (Glencoe, IL, 1958) and *The Protestant Establishment: Aristocracy and Caste in America* (New York, 1964). Twelve years after this last work, Baltzell published an article describing the collapse of that privileged group, his conclusion: ". . .the Protestant establishment has been watered down beyond recognition," in "The Protestant Establishment Revisited," *American Scholar*, 45 (1976):499–518.

2

William McKinley:
From Niles to the White House

William McKinley, like the other post-Civil War presidents, was not from a privileged background. His father was a founder, the owner, and manager of charcoal blast furnaces that produced pig iron, one of them located in Niles, Ohio. The future president was born there in 1843, the seventh child of the family. The family was "neither rich nor poor . . . never prosperous in a large way." The McKinleys were neither "established rich" nor "old line gentry."[1]

Although not well-educated themselves, the father and mother clearly valued learning and, at some cost, moved to Poland, Ohio, which had an academy (the predecessor of the later high school). McKinley was "always studying. . . . It was seldom that his head was not in a book." He was also active in the school's debating society. And, still another formative influence, he joined and was active in the Methodist church. In September 1860, at age seventeen, he enrolled in Allegheny College, located a short distance away. His mother and a sister loaned him "their savings" to make this possible, Mother McKinley hoping he would enter the clergy. But his higher education ended that winter when an illness forced him to withdraw and return home.[2]

At that point, the family's "already severe economy" was followed by financial disaster when the father incurred responsibility for the debts of a brother (who was also his business partner). The disaster prevented the son's return to college. McKinley worked, briefly, as a clerk in the Poland post office. But then, a local school district announced an opening. Teaching at that point "required no special study" and the eighteen-year-old McKinley applied. He was given the position, one he held until the onset of the Civil War.[3]

In June 1861, McKinley volunteered, serving in Ohio's 23d Regiment. The lieutenant colonel of the regiment was a prominent Cincinnati lawyer, Rutherford B. Hayes. Leech says that Hayes was "particularly impressed by the lad's unusual executive ability" and, a year later, made McKinley the commissary sergeant, in charge of supplies during the Maryland campaign. In the autumn of

1862, he was promoted to lieutenant and now was "closely associated with Hayes," serving as an aide-de-camp. McKinley distinguished himself in battle, most especially in a heroic action at Antietam. He was promoted to captain in 1864, saw further combat, and served "on the staffs of various generals." He was mustered out in 1865, at age twenty-two, with a brevet commission of major.[4]

McKinley had developed political ambitions and recognized that legal training was a necessary prerequisite. He read law in the office of a "rising" attorney in his home area and then, aided financially by his eldest sister and a friend, attended law school in Albany, New York. He wrote Hayes in the autumn of 1866 telling him of his intentions. Hayes replied saying that with his business capacity and experience he should have gone into railroading or some commercial business. "A man in any of our Western towns with half your wit," he continued, "ought to be independent at forty in business." Hayes argued that, "As a lawyer, a man sacrifices independence to ambition. . . ." He saw it as "a bad bargain at best." But McKinley, Leech writes, had "none of the shrewd and imaginative drive for profit that makes for business success. . . . The accumulation of wealth held no interest for him at all."[5] Unmoved by Hayes' advice, McKinley moved to Canton, the seat of Stark County, and opened a law office.[6]

McKinley achieved a fair success in the law. And he had early success in local politics. In 1867, he spoke on behalf of Hayes, who was then running for governor. In 1868 he worked for Grant, organizing local clubs and speaking on his behalf. Shortly thereafter he was made chairman of the Republican Central Committee for Stark County, charged with organizing throughout the area. In 1869, he sought and won his first elective office, prosecuting attorney for Stark Country. But the Republicans and Democrats were fairly evenly matched in the area and in the subsequent election, in 1871, he lost the position.

McKinley was a social success in Canton, joining and active in the Methodist church, working also with the Masons and the YMCA. In January 1871, he married Ida Saxton, a daughter of Canton's most prominent family. Her father, James Saxton, gave them a house, one that would figure prominently in McKinley's "front porch campaign" for the presidency in 1896. Other members of the Saxton family owned the local newspaper, the Canton *Repository*, which supported McKinley throughout his career.[7]

The steps in McKinley's political career are easily summarized. It began, as just seen, with the contest for the office of county prosecuting attorney. In 1876 he ran for Congress and was elected. He was reelected to that office in six subsequent contests. These were not easy struggles, the parties in the district being roughly evenly divided. McKinley also faced gerrymandering in 1878 and again in 1884 but on both occasions bested his opponents.[8] One indication of McKinley's abilities, at least as judged by his Republican Party peers, may be seen by his committee assignments in the Congress. Early in 1880, in his second term, he was appointed to the House Ways and Means Committee. In 1889, he was named as chairman of that body, easily the most important committee in the House. Morgan describes the initial appointment as follows: "Early in 1880, the Ohio legislature elected his friend James A. Garfield to the United States Senate, creating a vacancy on the House Ways and Means Committee. McKinley wished to sit there, since the committee dealt with tariff legislation. Speaker Randall told Garfield that he would appoint whomever he chose and Garfield chose McKinley."[9]

The Constitution stipulates that all tax measures originate in the House of Representatives and there such matters are assigned initially to the Ways and Means Committee. Most federal government revenues at that point were generated by tariffs on imported goods. McKinley wrote the tariff measure that bears his name and saw its successful passage in the fall of 1890. It would provide the basis for his national reputation. McKinley's defeat in the subsequent election was a consequence of another gerrymander, the legislature having cut a district with a fair-sized Democratic majority.[10] But the following year Ohio's Republicans chose McKinley as their gubernatorial candidate and in November he was elected. He was reelected in 1893.[11]

The familiar stereotypic accounts portray McKinley as a conservative Republican, as a man aligned with "the capitalists" and working diligently in defense of their interests. One episode in McKinley's biography, however, provides an important challenge to that view and accordingly deserves special emphasis. In 1876, coal miners in the Massillon district, a dozen miles west of Canton, went on strike to fight cutbacks and wage reductions that followed the Panic of 1873. One of the mine owners brought in strikebreakers and a violent clash followed, with severe injuries on both sides and one company official nearly killed. The sheriff asked Governor Hayes to send troops and, reluctantly, he sent a company of the militia. The strikers set two mines afire and the militia subsequently arrested "twenty-three half-starved proletarians."[12]

Opinion ran strongly against those arrested and no local attorneys could be found willing to defend them. But McKinley, Leech reports, "was in sympathy with the workers' grievances" and, despite the objections of his friends, took the case. His efforts brought the release of all but one of the defendants. Friends of the workers "made up a purse" to pay his fee but "McKinley refused to accept payment from the impoverished strikers." That effort had some important consequences, Leech reporting that his "good offices redounded to his political advantage by winning him the loyal friendship of labor in Stark County." And, the effort also brought him to the attention of the mine owners, one of them being Marcus Alonzo Hanna, the head of the mine operators' association. One of the men representing the mine owners was a Canton lawyer, later a judge, William R. Day. He and McKinley became close friends and, two decades later, McKinley chose him to be the Assistant Secretary of State and, less than two years later, to be Secretary of State.[13]

The move to Washington as congressman was a costly one. It brought a smaller income than the Canton law practice and much larger expenses. Leech declares that he "deliberately chose to exchange an annual income of $10,000 from his law practice for the congressman's salary of half that amount."[14] McKinley, as seen, had opted for a smaller income with his choice of law rather than business. With the choice of politics over law he was again sacrificing income. McKinley, clearly, was not in it for the money.

McKinley worked for Grant's election to the presidency in 1868 and 1872, for Hayes in 1876, for Garfield in 1880, and for Blaine in 1884. In 1888 he supported the candidacy of Ohio's favorite son, Senator John Sherman and, later that year, worked for the Republican nominee, Benjamin Harrison. McKinley's support for all of these candidates meant that party loyalty was a primary factor in his judgment. He could easily support Hayes, a friend and a man of "fine moral character." But the absence of such virtue in Blaine was no impediment to similar support. That loyal support earned him obligations on the part of those aided. In those years McKinley enlarged his circle of friends and acquaintances and some people, politicians and sponsors, recognizing his potential for higher office sought him out.

Marcus Alonzo Hanna (1837–1904) was easily the most important of McKinley's friends and sponsors. He was, effectively, the general manager of the large and complex operation that led to the presidency. Hanna was born in New Lisbon, Ohio, a village in northeastern Ohio (since 1895, called Lisbon). Recognizing the limited opportunities there, the family moved to Cleveland in 1852 where the father and his sons developed a "great wholesale grocery and shipping business." Apart from a brief term of military service late in the war, Hanna continued his business activities without interruption. He branched out after the war, investing in an oil refinery and a lake steamer but both projects failed (fire destroyed the refinery; the steamer collided and sank). He then entered the firm of Rhodes & Company, owned by his father-in-law, Daniel P. Rhodes, a prosperous Cleveland coal and iron dealer.[15] In a subsequent reorganization, Hanna became the proprietor and the firm was renamed, becoming M. A. Hanna and Company. It was the second or third largest coal and iron firm in the Great Lakes region. Hanna was also the director of a street railway firm, president of a bank, involved in a shipbuilding company, partner in three rolling-mills, the owner of a newspaper, and also of the Euclid Avenue Opera House.[16]

Politically, Morgan reports, Hanna was an "ardent Republican, high protectionist, [and] gold-standard advocate." He was not, however, contrary to the stereotype, a hard-hearted capitalist. "Admired by his workers," Hanna was "fair to men who were fair to him [and] established a reputation for equitable dealing with labor that put him far in advance of his fellow entrepreneurs." Later, in 1900, Hanna served as the first president of the National Civic Federation, described as "the most important single organization of the socially conscious big businessmen and their academic and political theorists."[17]

Myron Herrick (1854–1929), probably the second most important of McKinley's sponsors, was a lawyer, a banker, and later a diplomat of some considerable importance. Like McKinley and Hanna, he too was from a modest background, his father being a farmer in Lorain County, Ohio. Obviously talented, he pursued his education, somewhat erratically, and tried several careers before turning to business. In 1875, then based in Cleveland, he turned to the law. As his law practice developed, he branched out in several other areas, one of these involving politics.[18]

Early in his career, Herrick and some friends decided to try their hand at reform politics and challenged Cleveland's Sixth Ward boss, one Billy King. This gentleman was in the insurance business and used his political base to bring him "practically all the City Hall insurance contracts." As a point of more than passing interest, Herrick notes that King's political existence was an indication of the indifference of the "best people," the city's upper class, who were strongly represented in that ward. King made the usual threatening response that successfully frightened off the first line of insurgents. But Herrick and several other amateurs stuck to it and he was elected to the city council.[19]

Herrick and a few other successful reformers were then put on "absurd committees," ones that "never met and were never expected to meet, [the politicians] keeping the important or profitable things for themselves." Upon exploration, however, the reformers discovered that these "absurd" committees had rather formidable investigatory powers that they proceeded to use. With the help of willing newspapers, they wreaked havoc on the operations of the "established" politicos. The "powerful" machine proved to be a very flimsy affair. Herrick drew an important lesson from this experience: "I would not accept any public office that required [me] to give most of [my] day to it until [I] was financially independent." He could and did serve in less demanding positions.

Herrick was a delegate to the Republican national convention in 1888. Hanna at the time "was the old war-horse of [the] congressional district and . . . had always dominated the district primaries." Hanna intended to be the first delegate and had someone in mind for the second. But Herrick's friends were so successful that he was elected as first delegate putting Hanna in as second. The latter, however, did not bear a grudge and this was the beginning of their joint political efforts.[20]

The largest bank in Cleveland at that time was the Society for Savings. The head of the bank was in his seventies and clearly due for retirement. The secretary of that Society was the heir apparent but Hanna wanted that man to head one of his own enterprises, a shipbuilding firm. The bank's directors were understandably perturbed but in subsequent discussions Hanna proposed a substitute, Herrick, who was made secretary and treasurer of the Society in 1886. Later, in 1894, he became its president.[21]

Charles G. Dawes (1865–1951) was by far the youngest member of McKinley's active sponsors. He was born in Marietta, Ohio, the son of Rufus Dawes, an eminent Civil War general who later prospered in the lumber business and served a term in Congress. Dawes received what for that age was an exceptional formal education, gaining a B.A. and an M.A. from Marietta College and a law degree from the Cincinnati Law School. In 1887 he settled in Lincoln, Nebraska, began a law practice there, and invested in real estate. In 1894 he extended his interests, investing in gas works in La Crosse, Wisconsin, Evanston, Illinois, and later in Akron, Ohio. He and his family took up residence in the Evanston. Dawes had known McKinley through his extensive Ohio family connections. McKinley's campaign for the nomination, as will be seen, had two main headquarters, one in Chicago, the other in New York. Dawes managed the Chicago office, directing campaign operations in Illinois but also overseeing operations throughout the Midwest and Western states.[22]

Hanna, Herrick, and Dawes were the leading members of McKinley's group of sponsors. Eventually, theirs would be a full-time commitment although, to be sure, they still found time for their diverse business affairs. Several less prominent figures also deserve some consideration. One of these was Will Osborne, McKinley's cousin. Friends from boyhood, the two enlisted together in the army in 1861. Decades later, Colonel Osborne moved to Boston where, for a time, he served as police commissioner and was active in Republican politics. McKinley visited him there in the summer of 1892 and spoke before prominent Republicans at several lunches arranged by his cousin. At a later point Osborne began working full-time for the campaign. He was engaged in money raising and was among those who worked out the gold statement in the party's 1896 platform. He also served as secretary to the Republican National Committee, the body headed by Hanna.[23]

Joseph P. Smith, a newspaperman, was one of McKinley's "most loyal and loving friends." When governor, McKinley chose him to be the state librarian. Charles Dick was another close friend and active aide. He was chairman of the Ohio Republican committee and in charge of all statewide campaigns. McKinley's brother, Abner, was also an active worker, traveling extensively and negotiating on William's behalf. And there were some unanticipated free-lance efforts. Addison Porter, a young and ambitious newspaper proprietor in

Hartford, formed the first "McKinley for President Club" in Connecticut and invited the candidate to speak there. The opportunity to campaign in New England, in Congressman Reed's territory, was most welcome and McKinley of course accepted.[24]

John Hay (1838–1905), a latecomer in the McKinley circle, would subsequently have considerable importance. Beginning first in law, in Springfield, Illinois, he then took a much more important position, serving for four years as a secretary to President Lincoln. He later held several State Department appointments, serving in Paris, Vienna, and Madrid, and in 1878 was appointed to be Assistant Secretary of State. He had a brief career as a journalist, as editorial writer and night editor of the New York *Tribune*, this under Whitelaw Reid who, as seen earlier, was another important Republican sponsor. His marriage to Clara Stone, the daughter of a rich Cleveland industrialist, a builder of railroad bridges, allowed him to retire from these activities and to pursue his literary interests. He was a recognized author, of poems, short stories, a novel, and, with John Nicolay, of a ten-volume biography of Lincoln. Hay undertook "political errands" on McKinley's behalf in the mid-nineties and also "made a generous contribution" to the candidate's personal expenses.[25]

Herman Henry Kohlsaat (1853–1924), an important member of the group is better described as a part-timer, one who appeared or contributed when the need arose. He was born and raised in small-town Illinois, in Albion and Galena, the child of recent German immigrants. He later settled in Chicago where he made a fortune with a wholesale baking concern and a chain of low-priced lunchrooms. Like Hanna, he also embarked on a political career, basically as a sponsor. He appeared, as an alternate, at the Republican convention in 1888, where he and McKinley renewed their acquaintance. The part owner of a newspaper, the *Daily Inter-Ocean* from 1891 to 1894, he provided support for the Republicans and in this period became "a devoted admirer" of McKinley, Kohlsaat reporting that they "came in contact very often." His first work for McKinley's nomination came at a meeting following the 1892 convention, in a discussion with Hanna and the prospective candidate. In 1895, Kohlsaat became the editor and publisher of the *Chicago Times-Herald*, using it to advocate a protective tariff and the gold standard. Initially, it was the only Chicago newspaper that supported McKinley.[26]

Bellamy Storer (1847–1922) was another supporter but like Kohlsaat one best described as an occasional worker. His career differed substantially from those of the men described to this point. Storer was born and raised in a large city, in Cincinnati, Ohio.[27] He came from a very well-educated family, and, keeping with that tradition, received an A.B. from Harvard in 1867 and later was graduated from the law school of Cincinnati College. He practiced law in his home city and also served as assistant attorney for the southern federal district. He was "well placed" in the city's affairs, working with Charles P. Taft, at that point the most prominent member of one of city's leading families. In 1886, Storer married Maria Nichols, a widow, who was from the city's wealthiest family, the Longworths. Storer served two terms in Congress in the early 1890s although without producing any major achievements. He admired McKinley and helped with his gubernatorial campaigns and in 1896 with the presidential campaign. The Storers, husband and wife, were social leaders rather than leaders in business or politics. They preferred the company of educated persons, of Henry Cabot Lodge and Theodore Roosevelt among others, rather than association with "crass" businessmen.[28]

Some sense of the McKinley campaign effort may be gained from entries in Dawes's journal. That of 29 March 1896 reads:

> Arrived Cleveland. Joe Smith came in and took me to Hanna's with John Goodnow. Governor and Mrs. McKinley, Leonard Hanna and his wife, Miss Phelps, Joe Smith, John Goodnow and I were the guests. Governor McKinley went over fully the proposition made to him by Cullom through Federal Judge Grosscup to withdraw as a Presidential candidate upon certain concessions. The Governor would not make these concessions, and told me he proposed to take the place, if it came to him, unmortgaged. Had a long conference over the Illinois situation with McKinley, Hanna and Smith. Everybody is breathing the air of confidence—and it is not to be wondered at with such fine reports of progress in every section of the country.[29]

A brief review of the recent political history may prove helpful. From 1885 to 1888, Hanna was managing the candidacy of Senator John Sherman for the Republican presidential nomination. Hanna became a member of the Republican National Committee in the latter year and was named, by its chairman, Matthew S. Quay, the powerful Pennsylvania senator, to its Resolutions Committee mainly because of his knowledge of tariff questions. The Sherman candidacy failed in the convention that year and the nomination went to Benjamin Harrison. At one point during the convention, some enthusiastic supporters began a movement to name McKinley, who was chairing the gathering, as the party's candidate. But in an impressive gesture of loyalty, McKinley refused all support and the delegates chose Harrison, a Civil War general, lawyer, governor of Indiana, and later senator. The Democrats renominated Grover Cleveland, who announced a strong anti-protectionist campaign. The Republicans responded with a demand for a higher tariff. Harrison won the election.[30]

Hanna actively supported Harrison's candidacy, his principal task being to solicit financial contributions from businessmen, especially those who stood to benefit from tariff protection. He was assigned the northern Ohio territory, one he knew well. An important change in party financing was occurring at this time. With the decline of support from government workers, with civil service laws reducing the possibility of forced exactions, the parties had to find other sources and businesses, big, medium, and small, were the most obvious alternative.[31]

In October 1890 the Republican high-tariff program, the McKinley Tariff, became the law of the land. In the November elections, the Republicans suffered serious reverses in the House and some commentators blamed the new tariff. McKinley was unseated in this election but, as seen above, the decisive factor was a gerrymander.[32] The two losses threatened the "larger plans" of McKinley and Hanna. But fortunately, a saving opportunity appeared when Governor Joseph Foraker refused to run again for governor, hoping instead to be named to the Senate. Hanna's first major political task in 1891 was to manage McKinley's campaign for governor. A second task proved more difficult, ensuring that John Sherman would be renamed to the Senate (which would frustrate Foraker's purpose). Hanna succeeded in both efforts. McKinley won the gubernatorial election by an unusually large margin, thereby dispelling any doubts about his political viability. In an unusual move, Hanna solicited financial support from out-of-state sources, from his contacts in Chicago and Pittsburgh.[33]

In 1892, Harrison declared for a second term, leaving little that Hanna (or anyone else) could do with respect to alternative candidates. The election brought a serious defeat for the Republicans. Cleveland regained the presidency, the Democrats continued to control the House, and now, for the first time in a decade, they gained control of the Senate. It was the Democrats' greatest victory since the Civil War. The tariff was a major theme in the elections. Again, many commentators saw the McKinley Tariff as the cause of the debacle.[34]

The new Democratic regime quickly enacted a low tariff measure, the Wilson-Gorman Act. But then, in 1893, the nation experienced a major economic crisis that began with the stock market collapse on 3 May, an event that had wide-ranging consequences. McKinley ran for a second term as governor that fall and was reelected with a substantial majority, the party's largest since 1865. Cleveland and his party were held responsible for the economic collapse and in the 1894 the Democrats, as seen in chapter 1, experienced major losses.

Throughout this period, McKinley and Hanna continued their work for the presidential nomination. During Harrison's 1892 campaign, "special efforts" were undertaken to "make Mr. McKinley conspicuous on the stump." An extended speaking tour was arranged by Hanna and the head of the Republican National Committee, a tour that took McKinley to Colorado, Iowa, Minnesota, Maine, and "all the important intervening states." His secretary reported the receipt of 1,500 invitations to speak. The most important engagement, possibly, was a speech on protection before a large audience in Carnegie Hall.[35]

After the Congressional victories in 1894, to allow more time for the campaign, Hanna retired from active direction of his firm leaving business matters to his brother Leonard. As of 1 January 1895, he was free to devote himself to politics. One of his first tasks was to rent a house in Thomasville, Georgia as a base for his efforts to secure the support of Southern delegates to the forthcoming convention.[36] McKinley was a frequent guest there, greeting the potential supporters and asking for their assistance.[37] This early and sustained effort meant that McKinley entered the convention with a large bloc of assured votes.

Many accounts place considerable emphasis on Hanna's role as if he commanded the entire operation with McKinley, as in a frequent metaphor, the easily directed puppet. But Croly, Hanna's first and best biographer, declares that, "to a large extent," McKinley "had been his own general manager." He adds some further details: "No account of the promotion of his candidacy would be correct which understated the essential part played by Mr. McKinley himself. He had many friends and acquaintances among the Republican leaders in all parts of the Union, and he, himself, had established certain alliances which were of utmost value to his personal cause. No important step was taken without consulting him, and his counsel and cooperation were indispensable to the success of the enterprise."[38]

It would also be a mistake to conclude that McKinley was deferential or subservient in his relationships with his business sponsors. For those raised on the Hearst image of Hanna, one shared by the Populists and later by various progressives, as a cynical manipulator, it will come as a surprise to learn that Hanna "treated McKinley with conspicuous deference." William Allen White thought Hanna was the better man of the two but felt that Hanna was "just a shade obsequious in McKinley's presence." Charles G. Dawes wrote that McKinley gave the orders and Hanna obeyed without question. Kohlsaat thought Hanna's attitude toward McKinley to be that of "a big, bashful boy toward the girl he loves."[39] McKinley joked about Hanna, for example, encouraging him to sing at their Sunday evening gatherings. Hanna was without appreciable talent in this area and McKinley would praise him as a "sweet tenor." The relationship was one of good-hearted comradeship. In its details, however, the relationship was not symmetrical. Hanna appeared to look up to McKinley; McKinley in turn was grateful and loyal to the man.[40] A *New York Times* journalist who knew both men declared that, "contrary to a too-general belief," McKinley "was the master and Hanna the faithful lieutenant."[41] John Hay held the same opinion— "there are idiots who think Mark Hanna will run him!"[42]

The character differences are also striking. McKinley had a kind of idealism, including conceptions of duty, patriotism, and public service that were not strong in Hanna. The latter was, as Leech puts it, a "frank, profane, cheerfully ignoble realist." Hanna, a man with an extraordinary pragmatic outlook, curiously enough, admired McKinley's idealism. In some ways it was an ideal fit. Hanna undertook all of the crass social engineering. McKinley, by himself, could have done little of the necessary organizational work. Morgan says he showed "a curious lack of talent" for such matters. But McKinley provided an attractive and virtuous character, the figure around whom the entire episode, the "making of a president," was focused. Leech has a lengthy paragraph describing McKinley's closest friends. The opening sentence reports that he "was naturally attracted to men of mental refinement, moral rectitude, and deep religious feeling." The next paragraph opens with the statement that Hanna "was outside this circle of intimacy."[43]

In 1893 a catastrophe threatened the entire plan. Robert L. Walker, a respected banker and manufacturer, was an early McKinley benefactor and an old friend from his Poland days. Walker had loaned money for McKinley's Albany law school education and also had helped to finance his early congressional campaigns. Out of gratitude, and not-too-wise trust, McKinley had endorsed Walker's notes, actions that made him liable for payment should the original signator default. Walker's default came with the financial crash of 1893. McKinley eventually found himself with a total debt of $130,000 and facing imminent bankruptcy.[44]

The news reached McKinley in Buffalo while en route to New York for a speaking engagement. He returned immediately to Ohio, first to Youngstown for a meeting with the distraught Walker and then to Cleveland where he stayed for a week at Myron Herrick's home. Herman Kohlsaat arrived shortly thereafter and Hanna, who had been away on business, joined them and took control. The three businessmen arranged for payment of the most pressing demands. Herrick describes the event as follows: "In ordinary times we could have cleared the affair up without much difficulty, but the panic of the early '90's was on . . . even M. A. Hanna . . . with all his great interests, was fighting for his life at that moment. However, we all got busy, and the same night twenty-five men had put up enough money to pay off all the notes that McKinley had endorsed." Herrick, Kohlsaat, and William R. Day, now a judge in Canton, were appointed to act as trustees for their friend while Hanna acted on behalf of Mrs. McKinley.[45]

But then more notes were discovered and more solicitation was necessary. Bellamy Storer telegraphed an offer of a $10,000 contribution. Another friend, Philander C. Knox, now a successful Pittsburgh corporation lawyer, made a contribution. Many large donations "were secured on the basis of the Governor's importance to the Republican party." Contributions came from John Hay (who would later serve as ambassador to Great Britain and, still later, would be Day's successor as Secretary of State), from Charles P. Taft (the brother and financial supporter of William H. Taft), from Henry Clay Frick in Pittsburgh, and from George Pullman and Philip Armour in Chicago. The contributions paid off the debt and allowed the return of all properties of both McKinleys.[46]

With the disaster behind them, McKinley and his coterie began working for his election to a second term as governor.[47]

This episode provides insight into "the dynamics" of Hanna's activities. It also shows the limited reach of McKinley's circle of supporters. Most of them were based in Cleveland. The rest were from three other "heartland" cities, Cincinnati, Pittsburgh, and Chicago. The circle contained no New Yorkers, no one from "the East."[48] Except for Frick (and perhaps Carnegie) the list of contributors does not include any of the nation's leading capitalists.[49] There are no major railroad magnates, no Rockefellers, and no Wall Street bankers.

The accounts of Hanna and his political activity make few references to Rockefeller and Standard Oil. This is surprising since the Rockefellers lived and worked in Cleveland for some three decades. John and his younger brother William attended its Central High School where the former met and became a friend of Mark Hanna. The Standard Oil Company was founded in Cleveland and was based there for many years. But only a few brief references to Rockefeller appear in Croly's biography of Hanna. At one point, a syndicate, a group of prominent Clevelanders, took over the *Herald*, a floundering Republican newspaper. Rockefeller and Hanna were both members of the group. But the paper continued to lose money and the "weary millionaires" withdrew, leaving it to Hanna. He stayed with the enterprise for five years, it costing him "a good deal of money," but he finally decided to quit. Apart from the high school connection, this is the only linkage of the two men reported by Croly during their Cleveland years.[50]

Allan Nevins' two-volume biography of Rockefeller contains only a few references to Hanna.[51] Early in his first volume, Nevins reports the high school contact. The next mention, well into the second volume, reports a Hanna letter, from 1891, addressed to "my dear John" expressing concern over Rockefeller's recent severe illness. Another mention appears, this involving some 1890 events. Ohio's attorney general undertook an antitrust action against Standard Oil. Hanna "was deeply disturbed to find a Republican official taking such a course" and wrote him "an impassioned letter." The officers of the company, he declared, are "some of the best and strongest men in the country. They are pretty much all Republicans and have been most liberal in their contributions to the party, as I personally know, Mr. Rockefeller always quietly doing his share." But the attorney general, Nevins reports, "did not flinch."[52]

Mott's biography of Herrick contains a single passing reference to Rockefeller's firm. Early in his career Herrick was offered a position with Standard Oil. He was enthusiastic about the possibility but, following his wife's advice, declined the offer. "You could not be your own master," she said, adding that she did not "think it worth that sacrifice" and he concurred. Looking back later, Herrick said he "never had any regrets."[53]

The previous chapter touched on the presence of "cultural" divisions within the upper class. One such factor appears to have been operating here: John D. Rockefeller and his wife were ascetic Protestants, a commitment that put serious constraints on their social life. They had "seats at the philharmonic" but theater and opera were counted as "too racy." "Shying away from social situations that weren't safely predictable," a biographer writes, "they socialized only within a small circle of family members, business associates, and church friends and never went to clubs or dinner parties." "Club life did not appeal to me," Rockefeller said. Apart from his family, he "especially enjoyed the company of ministers whose genial, homiletic style matched his own." The family led a remarkably insular existence. Rockefeller kept his children "hermetically cut off from the world. . . . Aside from church, they never engaged in outside social or civic functions." Those constraints reflected "a very Baptist fear of worldly entertainments." The Rockefellers, husband and wife, were "deeply involved in temperance work." They "avoided the very presence of liquor," a choice that "severely cramped their social activities."[54]

The absence of the Rockefellers from the McKinley history in the last decade of the century has a simple explanation: Rockefeller moved Standard Oil's headquarters to New York City in the early 1880s. All of the firm's top leaders were now based in "the East." Standard Oil was unquestionably active in politics, especially when, following Rockefeller's retirement, the firm was directed by John D. Archbold. Standard Oil's political ties in Ohio, however, were with another faction of the state's Republicans, one led by Hanna's competitor, Senator Joseph B. Foraker. That connection, ultimately, would have disastrous consequences for Foraker and many other politicians.[55]

Allan Nevins provided a useful summary of Standard Oil's political affairs this in an appendix entitled "Politics, Lobbyists, and the Standard." The opening paragraph reads:

> The governmental relations of the Standard, and its exposure to attack by investigating commissions and prosecuting agencies, gave it necessarily a constant interest in political affairs. On this head four generalizations may be stated with confidence: that its interest in politics was primarily defensive—the Standard looked to the avoidance of inquiry and attack, not to the gaining of subsidies, tariff favors, or other special privileges; that down to 1900 it took far more interest in state than Federal politics; that its preferred method was to gain trusty agents in the principal legislatures who would help it get action out of "unfriendly" into "friendly" hands; and that while much political action was reported to Rockefeller by subordinates, he seldom appears as an active agent.[56]

A focus on the Rockefeller-Hanna relationship would be misleading in any case. Hanna was an Ohio party leader beginning in the 1880s but, as seen, he was first named to the Senate in 1896. Prior to that time, Standard Oil operated through other channels. In the 1880s, the Ohio legislature was referred to as the "Coal-oil Legislature" in recognition of its "obeisance to Standard Oil." In 1884, that legislature chose Henry B. Payne to represent Ohio in the U.S. Senate. His son, Oliver H. Payne, who managed his father's campaign, was a partner in Standard Oil. Charges of bribery in that campaign brought "a firestorm of abuse" against the company.[57]

Another linkage that one might expect, especially given the heavy rhetoric directed against "Eastern bankers," is missing from the McKinley and Hanna biographies. Those sources have little to say about John Pierpont Morgan, New York's leading investment banker. This is curious, since we have a document, the Herrick biography, first published in 1919, that reports a contact and an extended political discussion. At some point prior to the 1896 convention Herrick made a trip to New York. Before leaving, he had "a long talk" with McKinley in which the banker reviewed the question of "free silver" versus gold. In the next sentence, without any words of explanation, Herrick reports that: "When I got to New York I went down to Wall Street to see J. Pierpont Morgan and we discussed the matter of the nomination, and especially McKinley's candidacy, in every detail." Olcott provides some words of explanation writing that "McKinley commissioned his friend Herrick to go to the East and explain his position privately to certain leaders and prominent business men." Olcott reports that McKinley provided the direction; he reviewed the currency question and argued the need, for political purposes, of avoiding "a declaration in favor of gold now."[58]

Herrick reports that Mr. Morgan "was rather violent in expressing his views. The monetary repudiation which the adoption of the 'free silver' standard involved was nauseating to him; he feared McKinley has a 'backbone of jelly'; he ought to come out and meet the issue squarely, etc. [Herrick] pointed out that the question was not altogether one that bankers could decide—politics and the politicians also had to be considered."[59] McKinley's equivocal position, Herrick argued, was advantageous in that it would not split the party at the convention or ensure the defeat of the party as would be the case with such "gold-bugs" as Thomas B. Reed or Levi P. Morton. "Any Republican who comes out now," Herrick reasoned, "for either gold or silver will not get the nomination. Let McKinley stay where he is. He is the only man you can both nominate and elect, and once he is nominated we can take care of gold in the platform. I feel perfectly confident of that and I would not work for McKinley's nomination if I had any doubt on the subject. You must have the votes of Western men in the convention and their support afterward in the election. Old party ties are powerful, and once McKinley is nominated they will support the candidate, gold or no gold."[60]

Morgan abruptly ended the discussion of the issue and the candidate and announced, "I have never met Hanna." Herrick reported that he was in the city. Morgan asked if they could have dinner with him that evening. The dinner was arranged (they met on Morgan's private yacht, the *Corsair*) and the three men covered much of the same ground reviewed by Herrick that morning. Herrick stressed the mutual education involved: Hanna learned "what the gold standard meant to our country's business" and Morgan "learned a few things about how Presidents are nominated."[61]

That meeting, one might think, would have been the start of a long and fruitful relationship. But one leading account reports otherwise—it "failed to alter Morgan's distaste for politics and politicians. Hanna continued to call on Morgan for contributions, but their friendship remained a purely formal one, as were most of Morgan's other political relationships. Politics and politicians never commanded much of his attention." The dynamics of Hanna's relationship with "the bankers" came up in a discussion some years later, in 1904. One banker, evidently exasperated, said: "To think that we sent this man [Hanna] to Washington to look out for us!" His partner in the conversation was J. P. Morgan, who responded as follows: "We did nothing of the kind, he sent himself. We did not know how to spell his name in '96."[62]

Hanna's plan for the convention was straightforward. The first task, winning those southern delegates, proved relatively easy and largely uncontested. Gaining delegates in the major northern states, where the group had to work with the party bosses and respond somehow to their interests, proved more complicated. For this purpose Hanna arranged a secret conference with "the great national leaders," the group meeting at the Fifth Avenue Hotel in New York. Present were Senators Nelson W. Aldrich, Thomas C. Platt, Matthew S. Quay, Joseph H. Manley, David B. Henderson, and possibly some others. At that time Hanna "had not done much in politics outside of Ohio" and this was his first meeting to discuss McKinley's candidacy with the leading Republican bosses. At the meeting, Herrick reports, Hanna "succeeded in convincing them that McKinley was the strongest candidate." Hanna returned to Cleveland in a good mood sensing that they had the nomination in hand. McKinley, however, on learning of their demands for control of patronage, rejected the arrangement. Kohlsaat, who was present on this occasion, quotes McKinley as follows: "If I cannot be President without promising to make Tom Platt Secretary of the Treasury, I will never be President." Hanna accepted that decision and agreed to a second strategy, a struggle against the bosses. McKinley suggested the slogan—"The Bosses Against the People"—which later, Herrick reports, "became the campaign battle cry."[63]

The bosses now faced a serious problem. Their solution was to run "favorite sons" in their respective bailiwicks in the hope that together they could block an early McKinley victory, thus forcing the hoped-for negotiation, the trade of delegate votes for the promise of patronage. But here, too, as in the South, Hanna adopted a new procedure. Violating the informal understandings, he and Dawes ran active and largely successful campaigns against those "favorite sons."[64]

The Republican convention took place in St. Louis, beginning on 16 June 1896. The Platform Committee met and submitted its statement that was subsequently adopted by the entire body. The nomination of candidates followed with Senator Foraker, an outstanding orator, giving the speech for McKinley. Several favorite sons were nominated but the outcome was hardly in doubt. McKinley won on the first ballot with 661½ votes. Maine's congressman, Thomas Reed, came in as a distant second with 84½ votes. There was a scatter of votes for several others. A motion for acclamation was made and carried. It was an impressive victory.[65] And it was achieved without any serious obligations to "the bosses," a fact that would have implications later when the president-elect began the selection of his cabinet.

Garret A. Hobart was chosen to be the vice presidential candidate. Leech describes him as a "rich corporation lawyer and businessman, scarcely known to the country but influential in the Republican party in his state"—New Jersey—adding that he was "Mark Hanna's choice." Another source declares that the New Jersey delegation "led the movement" for his nomination. Hobart had directed the party's gubernatorial campaign there the previous year, a campaign that elected the first Republican governor in thirty years. Regional balance plus the need to carry an uncertain state appear to have been the two key considerations leading to the choice. Leech reports that McKinley and Hobart became "devoted friends." He was to be influential in both appointments and policymaking.[66]

Before choosing the candidate, the platform committee, as noted, had convened to write the party's program. McKinley had supplied an outline indicating his wishes. Various others contributed and some adjustments were made. McKinley preferred that the campaign center on the tariff, his area of competence and achievement. But the currency question, whether gold or bimetallism, had to be addressed.

McKinley's most important legislative achievement as head of Ways and Means, as mentioned, was the 1890 tariff act that bears his name. The rates were lowered subsequently, in 1893, by the Democrats' Wilson-Gorman Act. McKinley and the Republicans now argued again for increases, this, they said, being the key to the nation's prosperity (another slogan advertised him as the "Advance Agent of Prosperity"). Increased rates would have benefited the producers of several hundred products. Given a multiplicity of producers in most fields, those changes would presumably create several thousand grateful industrialists. Although protective tariffs are often presented as "serving business interests," that being the reading of Bryan and the Populists, they had some appeal also for many salaried employees and blue-collar workers. The high tariffs, it was said, protected their jobs from low-wage foreign competition. Low tariffs, Republicans argued, brought a flood of cheap foreign goods with shutdowns and mass unemployment the obvious consequences. Business and workers, it was argued, had a common interest with respect to this issue.[67]

The currency question could not be bypassed and the platform committee, after some discussion, produced a document that spoke of the need to protect "the existing gold standard." That "small event" was to have major implications for the subsequent campaign. Many people subsequently claimed credit for the writing of that phrase. A negative finding should be noted here: One leading banker did *not* influence the writing of the statement. Whitelaw Reid, Jones reports, stopped in Canton and "took away a copy of McKinley's draft, which he submitted to J. P. Morgan. On the basis of conversations with Morgan, Reid developed a memorandum summarizing his own and Morgan's ideas about the currency plank, which he mailed to McKinley on 13 June. Reid's memorandum came too late; before it was mailed the McKinley-Hanna organization had framed the financial plank which the convention would adopt."[68]

The Democrats faced very serious problems in their choice of a candidate. The nation was in the worst depression in its history. President Cleveland's leadership in this crisis proved to be seriously deficient. "Soft money" advocates argued that an increase in the money supply was the solution, their specific proposal now being silver rather than greenbacks. The conservative Democrats, the advocates of "hard money," suffered a series of defeats in state conventions. The national convention met in Chicago early in July. William Jennings Bryan delivered his famous "cross of gold" speech and, shortly thereafter, was chosen as the party's candidate.[69]

Bryan was also nominated by the People's Party, usually called the Populists. That party had hoped to displace the Democrats, having won, a first step, more than a million votes in the 1892 presidential election and twenty-two electoral votes. Their increasing appeal was indicated in the 1894 congressional elections where they received some 1,500,000 votes. The Populists planned their 1896 convention to follow that of the Democrats who were expected to name a "hard-money" candidate. But the nomination of Bryan and the Democrats' adoption of "silver" in their program left the Populists in a difficult position, the choices being continued independence or "fusion." They chose the latter course and named Bryan as their candidate. The Democrats had nominated Arthur M. Sewall of Maine as their vice-presidential candidate. Although an advocate of free silver, he was also a "well-to-do bank president, railway director, and shipbuilder," which did not appeal to the Populists. They accordingly chose their own candidate, Georgia's Thomas Watson.[70]

The Democratic and Populist party agendas differed in focus and emphasis. Both platforms called for the free and unlimited coinage of silver in a 16 to 1 ratio with gold. But the Populists, addressing farm problems, also called for government ownership and operation of railroads and the telegraph. They wanted changes in federal land grant policies and direct legislation through the initiative and referendum.[71]

Paying little attention to the latter issues, Bryan put "the silver question" at the top of his agenda. Both the Democratic and Populist programs signaled intense opposition to "the interests." If implemented, however, their basic plan would have brought an enormous subsidy to a single "special interest," to the producers of silver. The "silver interests," understandably, were "only too happy to lend their assistance" in this educational effort. They had created pressure groups to advance their cause, the American Bimetallic League in 1889 and later, in 1893, the Pan-American Bimetallic League.[72] John D. Hicks reported that "the silver states supported the Populist ticket enthusiastically. . . . [But the] silver states were not interested in Populism, they were interested in *silver*, and they supported the Populist ticket solely because of this one item in the Populist creed. Had the Populist program not included free coinage it could hardly have appealed seriously to any of the mountain states."[73] C. Vann Woodward, in an unusually strong statement, declared that it was "the Western Populists," those from the silver producing states, "who planned and led the movement to sell out the party to the Silverites."[74]

The addition of silver to a nation's money supply would bring some degree of inflation, the extent depending on the amount added. A similar effect occurred when, as an emergency measure, "greenbacks" were circulated during the Civil War. That expedient helped to pay the costs of the war and brought the automatic side effect, some inflation. For debtors with a regular source of income, as with farm produce, inflation was (and is) a good thing, allowing easier payment of obligations than would otherwise be the case. In a parallel case, in the early 1920s Germany solved its then current problems through massive issue of paper money that brought the enormous inflation. If one were carrying a mortgage of say 20,000 Reichmarks, that debt could be paid off in 1923 with inflated currency worth only a fraction of the original sum.[75] Farmers, most especially those producing foodstuffs, were favored by that development since "everyone has to eat." Creditors of course, bankers and many others, would be major losers, being the receivers of depreciated currency. The lenders, Republicans and Democrats alike, emphatically opposed the inflationary "scheme," which they saw, in plain terms, as theft—the creditor borrowed a dollar and settled the debt with fifty cents, all of this, presumably, a completely legal procedure.

Although often formulated in sharp categorical terms (farm versus city, West versus East), the nation's farmers probably had diverse reactions to the inflation proposal. Heavily indebted farmers might be beneficiaries. But debt-free farmers might sense no gains at all. Except for the rare subsistence farmer, all farm families made some purchases—some foodstuffs, farm implements, and supplies, some clothing, medicine, and so forth. All of those purchases would become more difficult with the inflated currency (one might have to sell twice as much wheat or cotton to pay for a horse). Although not well documented, it seems likely that farm indebtedness increased as one moved from East to West, the latter being the most recent arrivals, those who had just purchased "everything."[76]

Although Populists often spoke of the imminent union of farmers and workers (also a frequent theme in the Beards' *Rise of American Civilization*), that would be an unlikely expectation. Persons on fixed incomes, effectively all wage and salary workers (and all retirees) stand to lose in a general inflation. For "the workers," Bryan's promise to inflate the currency could easily, and appropriately, be seen as a policy that would reduce their real incomes.[77]

Understanding the relationship between a voter's personal interests and the appropriate choices with respect to the tariff and currency issues, a rational choice, in other words, was no easy task. Much discussion of "the tariff" is formulated in simple dichotomous terms, high versus low. The reality however consisted of a thousand or so schedules together with a "free list." There were, moreover, frequent changes, the McKinley Tariff of 1890, as indicated, being replaced by the low-tariff Wilson-Gorman Act of 1893. One consequence of an imminent tariff reduction was that importers, anticipating the new legislation, stopped buying foreign goods. And that brought a decline in the government's revenues and also, given the smaller supply of remaining goods, it brought an increase in domestic prices. To make up for the expected loss of revenue, the Wilson-Gorman Act contained a significant innovation: It provided for an income tax, albeit at a very modest rate.

All legislation affecting tariffs and currency required compromise. The "price" for support of a high tariff bill was agreement to another proposal, one calling for the government to purchase more silver. Senator John Sherman, a hard-money man, with some misgiving, had agreed to sponsor the Silver Purchase Act that bears his name, a measure passed in the same year as the McKinley tariff. The resulting silver purchases brought some hoarding of gold and, a more serious problem, a loss of gold reserves to other nations. To stem that loss, a desperate President Cleveland sought the assistance of Wall Street bankers, of J. P. Morgan and August Belmont. The generous compensation allowed for their services provided material for later Populist complaint. An "informed voter" would have to collect information on these diverse issues (often from unreliable sources), sort out the implications, and finally decide which candidate or party best served his interests.[78]

The near-exclusive focus on those two questions, moreover, assumes that "other factors" were not important, a conclusion that would be unjustified at any time. For voters in the "solid South"—which meant the solid white South—"the race question" was always a factor, one that impinged on any purely economic calculation. Religion had some impacts and also ethnicity, the recently arrived groups showing diverse reactions to the options presented.[79]

The Republican and Democratic campaign efforts in 1896 might both be described as issue-oriented, both centering on currency questions and the tariff. But that said, it should also be noted that their campaign "styles" differed markedly. Bryan and his supporters made heavy use of moralistic themes in the course of the campaign. Richard Jensen sees this as a tactic, one that allowed the Democrats to avoid the complexities of the key issue. On the defensive, never quite able to explain how their monetary policy would help farmers and workers, the silverites "changed the thrust of their rhetoric from economics to virtue after Bryan's nomination." The "root issue" was to be "whether the financial interests of the East and Europe would overpower the people . . . [and] totally corrupt the democratic foundations of American politics." Bryan's tours, Jensen reports, "were continuous revivals, often likened to Methodist camp meetings of the old times." Bryan's words "were all about good and evil, the righteous and the wicked, the common people and their oppressors, salvation and damnation . . . bimetallism would be the means of redemption."[80] The Republicans also made generous use of invective, but their efforts, on balance, gave greater attention to logic and evidence, their focus being the fallacies of the pro-silver arguments.

Many accounts of the campaign focus on Hanna's role, on his management of McKinley's campaign. For many, it is a history of "the Republican boss" mobilizing the support of "rich capitalists." Hanna did collect funds; he did call on "the capitalists" for contributions, some of them based in Wall Street. Initially, those efforts proved unexpectedly difficult. As indicated, Hanna was not well known New York and the men he met were evasive and reluctant. In early August he wrote Dawes reporting only "moderate success in getting funds." Then, by "a stroke of luck," Hanna met "an old acquaintance," James Jerome Hill, the railroad magnate (and a Democrat), who "took him by the arm and led him through the great commercial houses, vouching for his integrity and ability." William Rockefeller made some telephone calls. Cornelius Bliss, a businessman and also the treasurer of the Republican National Committee, helped with the introductions and the volume of contributions increased enormously.[81]

Ultimately, the Republicans spent about $3,500,000, twice the sum expended for Harrison's campaign in 1892. It was the largest campaign budget ever up to that point, one that would not be exceeded until the 1920 election, which had a much larger electorate resulting from women's suffrage. That figure was stated first in Croly—"a little less than $3,500,000, and some of this was not spent." He reported "a little over $3,000,000 came from New York and its vicinity" adding that the money raised there "was spent chiefly in Chicago." Dawes' *Journal* contains a very detailed statement giving total expenditures as $3,562,325.59. Other sources have provided much higher figures. Croly mentions estimates as high as $12,000,000, but those, he adds, were "quoted only by the yellow journals and irresponsible politicians." Coletta thinks the total national and local expenditures "may have approached $16,000,000."[82]

A large part of the campaign money was used for the printing and distribution of articles and pamphlets dealing with the currency question. Dawes "assembled a team of writers who turned out campaign pamphlets in a dozen languages." In all, he sent out over 200 million pamphlets while the New York headquarters sent out 20 million in the Northeast, all that for a grand total of 15 million voters. Some 275 different pamphlets were produced, nearly all "tailored to a specific voting group and locale." Five years earlier, Andrew Carnegie had published an essay entitled "ABC of Money." The Republicans reprinted it and circulated more than five million copies. The principal aim of this vast effort was to educate voters on the fallacies of "the silver question."[83]

Much attention has been given to a new and widely publicized innovation, to McKinley's "front porch" campaign. Groups of supporters were brought to Canton by special trains (with subsidized rates). They then walked from the station to the McKinley's house on Market Street where the candidate greeted them, listened to their statements of support, and responded with a speech and some commentary. The hundreds of thousands who came to Canton to see and hear McKinley were probably convinced Republicans. But his comments were then published the following day in Republican newspapers across the land thus reaching millions of voters, many of them perhaps wavering, undecided, and open to the alternatives.[84]

Another factor, one regularly overlooked, was the newspaper support. The press, heavily Republican at the outset, was now joined by many Democratic newspapers, those that were devoted to "hard money." Four major New York newspapers defected, leaving only the *Journal* to support Bryan. The important Democratic newspapers of New England, of Philadelphia and Baltimore, defected. A single defection in Chicago left the Democrats without any major newspaper support there. And there were important losses in large cities of the South. Coletta reports that "about half of the Democratic and Independent press" opposed Bryan. James J. Hill bought the St. Paul *Globe*, "the only Democratic newspaper in the Upper Mississippi Valley and made it a gold organ." One source reported 503 of 581 German-language newspapers as opposed to Bryan. Hanna's organization delivered "boilerplate" stories (preset material) to newspapers throughout the nation.[85]

Hanna organized a speakers' bureau that employed the services of some 1,400 persons. The published material and speakers obviously would reach a large audience, many of them, unlike the visitors to Canton, uncertain about both the issues and their party loyalties. The Republican campaign also benefited, it has been said, from efforts of coercion. There were reports of workers blacklisted or threatened with firing. Some, allegedly, were told not to report back for work the next day if Bryan won. Farmers, too, it is said, were threatened. Banks would not extend credit, would not renew loans, or would demand immediate payment of outstanding loans. Evidence in support of these claims is limited and difficult to assess. Most of it comes from newspapers that supported Bryan; some came from the candidate himself. Another difficulty: Unless repeated in subsequent elections, coercion would have had a short-term impact. But for many voters the change appears to have been long lasting, suggesting a conversion rather than a response to immediate pressures.[86]

The Democratic campaign, in contrast, was largely personal, with Bryan undertaking an extended speaking tour, the first of its kind in American electoral history. The crowds were large and enthusiastic. He is said to have given 570 speeches during the campaign and to have been heard by two or three million persons. Bryan's speeches, as indicated, made heavy use of emotional appeals, providing depictions of good-versus-bad forces with accompanying lessons of sectionalism ("West" versus "East," of "farm" versus "city") and of class ("the people" versus "the rich"). But this campaign plan, Hollingsworth reports, was flawed—Bryan's "energies and nerves were eventually strained to the breaking point. For over four months Bryan had undergone an endurance test that would be difficult to match. . . . As he ran out of steam, his arguments became caustic and bitter. To make matters worse, only the most undesirable aspects of his appearances were reported in the press."[87] The word "speech" in this connection is misleading, suggesting a presentation of perhaps an hour or more. But Jensen points up one implication of the basic numbers—"the candidate spoke only briefly; he could not stay more than five minutes, for there were ten or twenty or even thirty more stops on the day's itinerary."[88]

The two campaigns obviously differed in their financial resources, Jones describing the contrast as a turn from "riches to poverty." Hanna's organizational efforts have been described repeatedly. But few of the subsequent accounts provide comparable reports of the Democrats' efforts. The leading account describes the contrasting efforts as "meticulous organization" versus "motley confusion." Heading the Democratic campaign was Senator James K. Jones of Arkansas, an "able man" but one with "no experience in managing a national campaign." The organization and campaign plan had to be extemporized and even in mid-August these matters had not been developed. Bryan appears to have been indifferent to these questions, his prime concern being with the planning of his speaking tour. Bryan "expected that he alone, carrying to the people the message of free silver, would win the election for his party." But that single-minded attention to "the silver issue" worked to Bryan's disadvantage, making it easy for the Republicans to plan countering tactics.[89]

McKinley and the Republicans won the election with a margin of victory greater than that of any election since Grant's defeat of Greeley in 1872. Given the differences in organization and "resources," it is impressive that Bryan did so well, gaining 46.7 percent of the total vote. One frequent contention, Hollingsworth calls it a commonplace, is the argument of a trend: If the election had been held a week after the "Cross of Gold" speech, Bryan "would have swept the country." Hollingsworth provides an appropriate comment about this claim: "No one will ever know."[90]

The detailed results indicate the serious flaws in the arguments of "sectionalism" and the related one of "farm support" for Bryan. A long-standing usage developed by the Bureau of the Census groups the states into nine regions, New England, Middle Atlantic, East North Central, and so forth. In 1900, 35 percent of the nation's 76 million persons were located in the Midwest, in the East North Central and West North Central regions, extending from Ohio to the Dakotas. A third of the population lived in the South. If "the West" referred to the Mountain and Pacific states, it contained one-twentieth of the nation's population (5.4 percent) with most of them in the Pacific states.[91] The Bryan forces were clearly including much of the Midwest, certainly the West North Central region, in their definition of "the West."

As for the farm versus city dichotomy, the Census has an easy division, with incorporated places of 2,500 or more defined as "urban" and all other places classified as "rural." By that definition, three-fifths of the nation was rural. The nation at that point had roughly 30 million farmers, the majority of whom lived in the South and Midwest. The West (Mountain and Pacific states) had only four percent of that total, most of them in the three Pacific states. Approximately one-sixth of the nation lived in towns or villages, urban places of less than 50,000. If city referred to places of 250,000 or more, one is referring one-seventh of the total, 14.4 percent of the population. There were fifteen such cities in 1900, eight of them located west of Pittsburgh—Cleveland, Cincinnati, Detroit, Chicago, Milwaukee, St. Louis, New Orleans, and San Francisco.

The Mountain and Pacific states did go, overwhelmingly, for Bryan—but given the small populations there, the impact in the electoral college was small, a fact evident well before the onset of the campaign. It would be a mistake to assume that the vote in those western states stemmed from the grievances of farmers. Half of the region's farmers were located in California and Oregon. Both of those states, by small margins, went for McKinley. South Dakota, a farm state, went Democratic but with a close, near fifty-fifty division. North Dakota, another farm state, supported McKinley with a fair-sized margin. For many of those western states, the "silver interest" was probably decisive, that referring both to the mine owners and the far more numerous silver miners. The silver producing states, Colorado, Idaho, Montana, Nevada, and Utah, all cast roughly four-fifths of their votes for Bryan.[92]

The South remained solidly Democratic, some of those states providing margins even greater than before.[93] The East remained solidly Republican. In some settings there, notably in New England and New York, the cities actually provided higher percentages for Bryan than the rural counties. The outcome of the election depended largely on the Midwest. Only four of those states, South Dakota, Nebraska, Kansas, and Missouri, went to the Democrats, one by "a hair," two by small margins. The rest, all states from Ohio to Minnesota and North Dakota, went to the Republicans.[94]

Sundquist's summary of the election results in the Midwestern states amply demonstrates the limited impact of Bryan's appeals to "the farmers." "Not a single county," he writes, "in Illinois, Indiana, Iowa, or Wisconsin showed a gain in its 1896 Democratic percentage over the combined Democratic-Populist strength of 1892. Bryan carried only three counties in all of Wisconsin. He lost ground in North Dakota and even in his home state of Nebraska as against the 1892 showing of the two parties."[95]

Two results deserve special emphasis, both involving the realignment said to have been produced by the McKinley-Bryan contest. First, large numbers of workers in the great cities, as seen, abandoned the Democrats. Bryan's program, which would have reduced their purchasing power, had a lasting impact, one that continued through to the next realignment, that of the 1930s. Samuel Gompers, head of the American Federation of Labor, came out against him. Bryan's most famous speech, Sundquist points out, "set rural against urban" when he spoke of "*your* cities" and "*our* farms" and in doing so "cast out of his circle not just urban capital but urban labor too." The choice, as indicated previously, was probably a reinforcement effect, a confirmation of a decision reached already in 1894.[96]

Secondly, the character of the party struggle was also changed. "After 1896," Sundquist writes, "states that had been evenly divided between the parties— Connecticut, New York, New Jersey, Indiana, California—and even the Democratic states of Delaware and West Virginia became predominantly Republican." Others that had leaned to the Republican side "became virtual one-party domains." The previously pivotal states, New York and Indiana, now voted Republican, with only a single exception, in all elections from 1896 to 1928.

The exception, in both cases, was the 1912 election when Theodore Roosevelt split the Republican vote.[97]

* * *

Analyses of historical events, as noted in chapter 1, make use of interpretative frameworks, these to simplify, or give some order to, a large array of events. Class analysis is one such framework, clearly the case in the progressive literature and even more prominent in the Marxist literature that subsequently gained much influence in American intellectual circles. In those frameworks, rich capitalists—the bourgeoisie—are said to dominate, to be all-powerful in the direction of the nation's affairs. Politicians are depicted as "agents," as men willingly accepting the direction provided by those powerful bankers and industrialists. The aim of the capitalists, it is said, is "profit maximization." Their collective aim, their "class interest," is to arrange matters so as to serve that purpose.

The McKinley-Hanna history reviewed here indicates the need for significant modifications of that imagery. Hanna, the businessman, was not the dominant figure in the coterie. As attested by several sources, McKinley "gave the orders" and Hanna, the businessman, assented. The businessmen active in the McKinley-Hanna coterie, moreover, were not the leaders of the nation's largest railroads, manufacturing firms, or banks. The members of the coterie were leaders of sizable enterprises, most of these located in the Midwest, many of them in the city of Cleveland. The "biggest names" in banking and industry from the period appear only in secondary roles. J. P. Morgan was consulted about the choice of McKinley, but even this came after the fact, after the basic work for the nomination had been done. Carnegie, Rockefeller, and J. J. Hill also appear but again in ancillary roles. The McKinley-Hanna group operated with remarkable independence, giving little attention to the concerns of those "top level" capitalists. Systematic contact was made only when campaign funds were needed. And the leading capitalists responded generously, along with their less prominent peers across the land.

Revision is needed also in the accounts of the McKinley-Bryan contest, those too reporting a sharp confrontation, a struggle of the classes. But analyses of the voting results indicate considerable working-class support for McKinley with many former Democrats defecting. McKinley could plausibly be presented as "a friend of the worker" beginning with the Massillon episode. The same argument could and was made with respect to his advocacy of high tariffs and as an opponent of soft money. Bryan's leading theme was used for the same purpose. For blue-collar workers a vote for McKinley was a realistic, issue-oriented decision, the aim to prevent the threatened loss of real income.

The argument of sectionalism, most especially the East-versus-West version, is hopelessly inadequate. It neglects "the South" entirely. And it fails to note the decisive importance of "the Midwest," much of which supported McKinley. The farm-versus-city image, the third pair of "dialectical opposites," is also inadequate, a seriously misleading depiction of the struggle and its outcome.

Revision is needed, finally, with respect to the question of motivation: What moved the members of McKinley's coterie? In this connection, most importantly, one must reconsider the focus on "profit maximization." Politicians generally, McKinley among them, sacrificed income as a result of their career choices. Hanna, as seen, retired from the firm, reducing his subsequent income, so as to allow more time for his political activities. Herrick and Dawes also "settled for less" rather than seeking to maximize. This evidence points up an easy alternative, one best termed sufficiency, having "enough" money for one's purposes.

The "profit maximization" notion is clearly inappropriate with respect to McKinley. As opposed to a concern with economic interests, a focus on early family influence seems more appropriate. Leech writes of his relationship with his mother, of his "dutiful acceptance" of her "precepts of a righteous life, the sanctity of the home, and the veneration due to womanhood." He also "inherited his mother's deeply religious nature."[98] Such depictions of "motive," it should be noted, even when well documented, are treated as somehow inappropriate in much of the scholarly literature. Some motivations, the drive for money and/or power, are acceptable. But these "soft" concerns are viewed as questionable, as having dubious merit.

A basic question was stated early in the title of the first chapter: Who rules? The evidence reviewed in this chapter allows answers with respect to two contests. In the first, the McKinley-Hanna coterie won the Republican presidential nomination in 1896, defeating the other contenders, those favored by the coalition of political bosses. And the coterie won the second contest, the struggle for the presidency. The group was led by McKinley, the politician-candidate, and his business sponsors, the principal members being Hanna, Herrick, and Dawes. Simplifying somewhat, this evidence indicates a kind of business dominance, that of the Cleveland-based faction. The coterie won both contests.

One last observation: Foreign affairs received little attention in the course of the presidential contest. The Republican Party platform declared, rather vaguely, that "our foreign policy should be at all times firm, vigorous and dignified. . . ." The United States should control the Hawaiian Islands; it should build, own, and operate the Nicaragua Canal; and it should purchase the Danish Islands as a "much needed Naval station." The massacres in Armenia were condemned. The Monroe Doctrine was reaffirmed. A large paragraph reviewed the recent Cuban experience. The people of the United States, it was declared, "watch with deep and abiding interest the heroic battles of the Cuban patriots against cruelty and oppression, and best hopes go out for the full success of their determined contest for liberty." The government of the United States should "actively use its influence and good offices to restore peace and give independence to the Island."[99]

The Democratic platform had even less on foreign affairs. A single sentence reaffirmed the Monroe doctrine. That was followed by another sentence—"We extend our sympathy to the people of Cuba in their heroic struggle for liberty and independence."[100] The Populists also tendered "deepest sympathy" for the struggling Cubans; their program called on the United States to recognize Cuba as an independent state.

The nation's press had been carrying reports of Spanish oppression of the Cubans for several years. The stories continued to appear throughout 1896, a regular accompaniment to reports on the election. But those events did not appear as topics for discussion in the presidential campaign.[101]

The narratives and commentaries on the McKinley-Bryan campaign, most of them, are peculiarly incomplete. Bryan's candidacy is regularly portrayed as providing a serious positive option for America's farmers and workers. Bryan's defeat by the candidate of "big business," accordingly, is portrayed as something of a tragedy, the suggestion being that good things—benefits for the masses—would have followed a Bryan victory. The suggestion gives no consideration to an obvious "what if" question: What if Bryan had won the election?

At thirty-six years of age, Bryan was the youngest candidate ever presented by one of the major parties. He had worked as a small town lawyer and had served a term in Congress. But he had never held an important executive position and, obviously, had no serious organizational experience. Bryan's conduct of his most important administrative task up to that point, his presidential campaign, did not bode well for his management of the federal government. The first major task facing any successful presidential candidate is the selection of a cabinet. How would he have fared in that effort? Who would he have named as Secretary of the Treasury? Would Bryan and his supporters have proceeded with the unlimited coinage of silver? And if so, what would have been the consequences? And who would Bryan have named as his Secretary of State? How would he and his cabinet have dealt with the Cuba agitation? And, perhaps the most important question, would the nation have gone to war? How would that have been managed? And, what outcomes would have been likely?

The person in the best position to answer those counterfactual questions was the candidate himself—William Jennings Bryan. In one of Coletta's footnotes one learns that "his defeat brought a great sense of relief to Bryan." He admitted that he "had no administrative experience and viewed the Presidency with no pleasurable anticipation." Years later, a follower told Bryan of his disappointment following the 1896 defeat. Bryan told him that "the news of my defeat was a relief. Before the news came I literally and sincerely prayed, 'O, Lord, let this responsibility be averted. . . .' When the news came I went to bed happy."[102] The lesson contained there deserves more than a brief footnote.

Notes

1. Charles S. Olcott, *The Life of William McKinley*, two volumes (Boston, 1916), Vol. I, pp. 4–5; Margaret Leech, *In the Days of McKinley* (New York, 1959), pp. 4–5; and H. Wayne Morgan, *William McKinley and His America*, revised edition (Kent, OH, 2003), pp. 3–11.

   Olcott writes that "the duties of the manager included the chopping of wood, the burning of the charcoal, the mining of the ore, and all the details of the manufacture. . ." (p. 4). Leech states that the father "followed the trade of mining and manufacturing pig iron." At various times, he "bought or rented two or three small furnaces in the Mahoning Valley, and another, in partnership with his younger brother Benjamin, in Pennsylvania" (p. 4).

2. Olcott, I, ch. 2; the quotations, from Morgan, pp. 8–11. The significance of the debating societies, in academies, high schools, and colleges, has gone largely unrecognized. Members were trained in rhetoric, in logic, and public speaking, that being ideal training for later careers in public service. Social life in those institutions was centered in those societies with the students attending, discussing, and assessing those intellectual performances. Subsequently, with the appearance of organized sport, the debating societies were eclipsed and attention shifted to other things.

3. Morgan, pp. 11–12. A small detail—Olcott reverses the job sequence, the clerkship following the teaching (I, p. 21).

4. Olcott, I, ch. 3; Leech, pp. 6–7 (quotations); Morgan, pp. 13–27.

5. Olcott, I, ch. 4; Leech, p. 9 (quotations).

6. Niles, then a very small community, is located northwest of Youngstown. Poland, then even smaller, lies south of that city. Canton, then a community of some 5,000, is located about forty miles west of Poland and some fifty miles south of Cleveland. McKinley's "base," as a child, young man, and adult, was in the northeast corner of Ohio, not ordinarily seen as a center of national power and influence.

7. Olcott, I, chs. 5 and 6; Leech, pp. 10–17; Morgan, pp. 31–37.

8. On the gerrymanders, see Olcott, I, pp. 82–85. Legislatures could redraw the districts at any time, not just following the decennial census. In 1882, in his third contest for the House, McKinley was declared the winner by an eight-vote margin and took his seat. But the result was subsequently contested and late in the term, in May 1884, by a strict party vote, he was unseated, Morgan, pp. 56–58; and, for more details, Olcott, I, pp. 229–232.

9. On his appointment to Ways and Means, see Morgan, p. 55; and for his naming as chairman, see p. 126. Democrats controlled the House from 1883 to 1889. That meant 1889 was the first opportunity for him to be chairman.

10. Olcott, I, ch. 9; Leech, ch. 2; Morgan, ch. 8. Olcott (p. 266) reports a Republican plurality of 9,490 votes statewide in the 1890 congressional elections. But, due to the artful construction of the districts, the Republicans gained only seven seats as opposed to the fourteen won by the Democrats.

11. Olcott, I, ch. 14; Leech, pp. 24–28, 50–55; Morgan, ch. 9.

12· Herbert Croly, *Marcus Alonzo Hanna* (Hamden, CT, 1965 [1912]), pp. 93–94; Thomas Beer, *Hanna* (New York, 1929), pp. 78–80; Olcott, I, pp. 78–80; Leech, p. 12; Morgan, pp. 40–42. Morgan reports that Hayes too "sympathized with the miners" and knew it would be "folly to identify the Republican state administration with the mine operators," especially in an election year (p. 40).

13. On Day, see ANB, 6:276–77. During his term as prosecuting attorney, McKinley conducted a "war" on the illicit sale of liquor. In one case, a Mount Union college student, Philander C. Knox, provided testimony in support of his case. Knox later became "one of the biggest lawyers in Pittsburgh" and, still later, as will be seen, he too served in McKinley's cabinet, Leech, p. 13.

14. Leech, p. 17, and pp. 21–22; see also, Morgan, pp. 60, 68–69.

15. Croly, chs. 5–7; Beer, pp. 12, 54–55. Rhodes was an active Democrat. He was a cousin of Lincoln's opponent, Stephen Douglas. His daughter Charlotte married Hanna even though Rhodes, initially, was strongly opposed to the union. A son, James Ford Rhodes, Hanna's brother-in-law, was an eminent historian, the author of a nine-volume history of the United States, one of which deals with the period under review—*The McKinley and Roosevelt Administrations, 1897–1909* (New York, 1922).

16·. Croly, ch. 8; Beer, pp. 112–113.

17. Morgan, pp. 42–43; Croly, ch. 9; and James Weinstein, *The Corporate Ideal in the Liberal State: 1900–1918* (Boston, 1968), ch. 1, quotation, p. 6.

18. This information is from the DAB, 8:587–589; NAB, 10:664–665; and T. Bentley Mott, *Myron T. Herrick: Friend of France* (Garden City, NY, 1929). Herrick was "born in a log cabin built by his grandfather." Also, like McKinley, he too had a brief teaching career—"when about sixteen he was appointed teacher of a district school" (DAB, p. 587 and Mott, pp. 2–3).

19. Mott, ch. 4, contains also the quotations in the following text paragraph.

20. Ibid., p. 35.

21. Herrick, it will be noted, was the head of Cleveland's largest bank at age forty. Mott describes Herrick's business activities as follows: He "went in for railroading extensively, organized the Illuminating Company of Cleveland, took a leading part in various building associations, helped organize the Carbon Company (now [1929] the Union Carbide and Carbon Corporation), took a hand in the Quaker Oats Company, and all the time presided over the destinies of the Society for Savings. Everybody was making money and Mr. Herrick was getting his share." In 1901, he was elected president of the American Bankers' Association. Later, Herrick shifted from business to politics becoming governor of Ohio in 1903. In February 1912, President Taft appointed him as ambassador to France, service that continued into the Wilson administration. He was named to that position a second time, again by an Ohioan, Harding, this service lasting from April 1921 until his death in March 1929.

22. ANB, 6:249–250; Leech, pp. 73–74; and Morgan, pp. 156–158. For more detail, probably the best day-to-day account of McKinley's presidential campaign, see Charles G. Dawes, *A Journal of the McKinley Years* (Chicago, 1950); also, John E. Pixton, Jr., "Charles G. Dawes and the McKinley Campaign," *Journal of the Illinois State Historical Society*, 48 (1955):283–306. Dawes held several important appointive positions, in World War I, in the 1920s, and the early 1930s.

The age factor is often overlooked in discussions of "power" and "its" dynamics. Hanna, the senior member of the coterie, was six years older than McKinley. Herrick was eleven years younger than the candidate. Dawes, born in 1865, was considerably younger. Earlier Hanna and McKinley had both supported Senator John Sherman (born, 1823) for the presidency but the 1888 convention would be his last opportunity.

23. Leech, pp. 57 and 75.
24. On Smith, Leech, pp. 26, 62, 64, 68, and 73; on Porter, Leech, p. 63.
25. DAB, 7:430–436; ANB, 10:367–371; Leech, pp. 59, 68, 71, and (the quotations), 95. For more, William Roscoe Thayer, *Life and Letters of John Hay*, two volumes (Boston, 1915).
26. DAB, 10:489–490; Leech, pp. 56–57; and Morgan, p. 157. For more detail, H. H. Kohlsaat, *From McKinley to Harding: Personal Recollections of Our Presidents* (New York, 1923), pp. 1–9. Kohlsaat was not a central figure in McKinley's support group. Dawes portrays him as problematic, putting the interests of his newspaper ahead of those of McKinley's candidacy. In May 1896 Kohlsaat spoke to Dawes about investing in the *Times-Herald*. Dawes replied that it was "out of the question." Kohlsaat later opposed consideration of Dawes for a position in McKinley's cabinet. Dawes, *Journal*, pp. 66–68, 83, and 110.
27. In 1860, Cincinnati had 161,044 inhabitants; it was the largest city west of the Appalachians. Chicago then had 112,172 and Cleveland a mere 43,417. The Civil War cut off the north-south commercial traffic. The war, railroads, Great Lakes shipping, and industrialization all greatly enlarged the east-west trade. Cincinnati was surpassed by Chicago in the subsequent decade, the respective figures for 1870 being 216,239 and 298,997. Cincinnati was overtaken by Cleveland in the 1900 census (325,902 and 381,768 respectively). At that point Chicago had close to 1.7 million persons. See Campbell Gibson, *Population of the 100 Largest Cities and Other Urban Places in the United States: 1790–1990*, microform (Washington, D.C., 1998).
28. Nicholas Longworth (1782–1863), the family founder, began his career in Cincinnati as a lawyer. His fortune, however, stemmed from real estate. One account declares that by mid-century he "was paying more real estate tax than any other American except William B. Astor." ANB, 13:898–899. Maria (Longworth) Storer was an aunt of a later Nicholas Longworth (1868–1931) who served in Congress for many years and ultimately become speaker of the House. An even greater claim to fame, perhaps, was his marriage to Theodore Roosevelt's daughter, Alice Lee. On the role of the Storers, see Edmund Morris, *The Rise of Theodore Roosevelt* (New York, 1979), pp. 543–545.
29. Dawes, *Journal*, p. 74. Dawes made a remarkable number of trips at this time, journeys that took him to Cincinnati and Marietta to visit relatives, to Akron on business, and to Columbus, Canton, and Cleveland for visits with McKinley, Hanna, Herrick, and others. Few people in the twenty-first century are likely to know about the extensive railway links of the prior age. The first regular passenger train service between Columbus and Cincinnati began in 1850. Later, Columbus was the hub of seven trunk lines, which each day brought some seventy passenger trains to and from the city. For an overview, see George E. Condon, *Yesterday's Columbus* (Miami, 1977). For the railroads, see p. 19.
30. Olcott, I, pp. 260–263; Leech, pp. 40–42; Morgan, pp. 90–94; Croly, ch. 12.
31. Croly, pp. 145–149.

32. Ibid., pp. 150–151.
33. Ibid., pp. 158–161. The Hanna-Foraker split had its origins in 1888, in connection with the nomination for the presidency. See Leech, pp. 40–43.
34. Croly, pp. 165–167; Leech, pp. 57–58; Morgan, pp. 125–129.
35. Croly, p. 167. The most comprehensive account of the 1896 campaign is by Stanley L. Jones, *The Presidential Election of 1896* (Madison, 1964). On the early organization of McKinley's campaign, see his ch. 8.
36. Croly, pp. 173–174; Morgan, pp. 143–144; Jones, *Election of 1896*, pp. 112–113, 129. For more on their efforts in the South, see Jones, ch. 10.
37. Croly, pp. 175–176; Leech, pp. 62–63; Morgan, p. 147.
38. Croly, pp. 174–175; for further detail and confirmation, see Jones, *Election of 1898*, pp. 103–106. Jones reviews the beginnings of the McKinley-as-puppet myth on pp. 176–177.
39. Leech, p. 67.
40. Kohlsaat, *McKinley to Harding*, p. 96. Later, in 1904, Dawes referred to Kohlsaat as "a monumental egotist." The two had become estranged, Dawes reports, "because McKinley would not allow Kohlsaat to dictate to him." Even then, Dawes writes, Kohlsaat "constantly refers to McKinley in a way which assumes that when the two were together he (Kohlsaat) dominated, whereas he broke with McKinley because this was not so. The man did not live who dominated William McKinley" (*Journal*, pp. 367–368). Decades later, a leading authority concurred with that judgment—"No man, not even Marcus A. Hanna, dominated him," this from Paolo E. Coletta, ed., *Threshold to American Internationalism: Essays on the Foreign Policies of William McKinley* (New York, 1970), p. 12.
41. Charles Willis Thompson, *Presidents I've Known and Two Near Presidents* (Indianapolis, 1929), p. 18. See also the discussion of Henry C. Payne in the next chapter.
42. Leech, p. 95. See also R. Hal Williams, *Years of Decision: American Politics in the 1890s* (New York, 1978), pp. 100–101.
43. Morgan, pp. 141–142; Leech, pp. 68–69.
44. Olcott, I, pp. 288–292; Cowly, p. 170; Kohlsaat, *McKinley to Harding*, pp. 10–17; Mott, *Herrick*, pp. 48–55; Leech, pp. 58–60; Morgan, pp. 129–133; and Jones, *Election of 1896*, pp. 107–108.
45. Herrick, p. 49; Leech, p. 59.
46. This summary is based on Leech (her quotation, p. 59). Both Leech and Croly (p. 170) list Andrew Carnegie as a contributor. Morgan, citing a Hanna letter to Herrick, does not (p. 133). Two recent Carnegie biographies have nothing on the Walker question, those of Joseph Frazier Wall, *Andrew Carnegie* (Pittsburgh, 1989 [1970]); and Peter Krass, *Carnegie* (Hoboken, NJ, 2002).
47. Some sense of McKinley's feelings about that saving effort is indicated by his behavior following the state convention. After a late night adjournment, he caught the two o'clock train to Cleveland and was waiting for Herrick at the bank early that morning. "Myron," he said, "I just came up to tell you that I know that without your prompt action last April I could never have been renominated for governor. I am going back to Columbus on the eleven o'clock train, but I wanted you to understand how I feel about it" (Mott, p. 50). It was an unusual gesture on McKinley's part. Leech portrays him as an unusually self-contained person. "The inner minds of few public men," she wrote, "have been so well concealed. He left almost no personal papers. He rarely wrote a private letter" (p. 36).

48. Croly (p. 170) has the most complete list of contributors. He lists sixteen people and indicates "many others." Smaller contributions were received from a large number of well-wishers but these were all returned.

    Samuel Mather and James S. Pickands, two prominent Cleveland contributors, were the proprietors of an iron-mining operation with iron ore holdings in the Mesabi region, coal mines in Pennsylvania and West Virginia, and a fleet of forty-nine lake freighters transporting goods east and west. Mather was married to Flora Stone, the sister of Clara, John Hay's wife. Pickands was married to Savilla Hanna, Mark's sister. Mather was active in a wide range of philanthropic activities. At his death in 1931 he was the richest man in Ohio. For more, see ANB, 14:693–695.

    One source, reviewing the limits of Hanna's influence (as of 1888), provides this comment: He was "a lord of the Great Lakes. . . . But a hundred miles from the edge of the Lakes, Mr. Hanna ceased to be . . . in New York he was unknown. Mr. Adler saw him walk through a crowd of bankers and business men one crowded night at Delmonico's with his youngest brother, Leonard, without getting a nod." Beer, pp. 128–129.

49. It is unlikely that these two men were directly involved in Hanna's efforts to nominate McKinley. The leading Carnegie biography makes no mention of the Walker affair. See Wall, *Andrew Carnegie*.

50. Croly, pp. 66–68.

51. Allan Nevins, *Study in Power: John D. Rockefeller*, two volumes (New York, 1953).

52. Nevins, I, 6; II, 95, and 230–231. That case was prosecuted under state law. The famous national law was passed in the same year. Nevins reports that Hanna "frankly decried the Sherman Act and asserted that any prosecution of trusts would be injurious." II, 237. That law, it will be noted, was the work of Senator John Sherman, a man Hanna had ardently supported. For more on Hanna's intervention, including the text of his letter, see Croly, pp. 266–271.

    A recent biography of the oil magnate also suggests limited contact, Ron Chernow, *Titan: The Life of John D. Rockefeller, Sr.* (New York, 1998). At some point, Hanna actually disparaged his "close chum" from high school, calling Rockefeller "a kind of economic super-clerk, the personification of ledger-keeping" (p. 179, originally from Beer, p. 249). In June 1903, Hanna's daughter Ruth married Medill McCormick of the famous Chicago family. Many eminent persons were present including President Roosevelt and his daughter Alice. But there were no Rockefellers. George E. Condon, *Yesterday's Cleveland* (Miami, 1976), p. 60.

53. Mott, pp. 43–44.

54. Chernow, *Titan*, pp. 121–122, 124. An entry in Dawes' *Journal* (from 11 May 1896, p. 83) gives some sense of the differences in the lifestyles of the two millionaires. Dawes had just spent two days with the McKinleys in Canton and then, with two associates, went on to Cleveland—"Joe Smith met us and took us to the Union Club where M. A. Hanna gave us an elaborate lunch. Myron Herrick was present. Spent the afternoon with Hanna and Smith. In the evening we had another elaborate repast after which we went to Hanna's Opera House as his guests to see Sarah Bernhardt in 'Izeyl.'"

55. In 1908, some letters were stolen from the Standard Oil Company's offices and given to Hearst, who publicized their contents in speeches and in his newspapers. The senator was being paid by the company and, so it appeared, was attend-

ing to its affairs. Foraker said there was no conflict of interest. Publication of the letters ended his political career. Foraker reviewed the matter in his *Notes of a Busy Life*, two volumess (Cincinnati, 1916), II, ch. 44. See also Everett Walters, *Joseph Benson Foraker* (Columbus, 1948), ch. 19; and Earl R. Beck, "Joseph B. Foraker and the Standard Oil Charges," *Ohio State Archeological and Historical Quarterly*, 56 (1947):154–178.

56. Nevins, II, pp. 467–476. Nevins wrote two editions of his Rockefeller biography, the first entitled *John D. Rockefeller: The Heroic Age of American Enterprise*, two volumes (New York, 1941). Both provide very positive accounts of Rockefeller and Standard Oil. For the negative readings, we have Henry Demarest Lloyd, *Wealth against Commonwealth* (New York, 1894), and Ida Tarbell, *The History of the Standard Oil Company* (New York, 1904). Nevins gives very negative assessments of both these works. But see also the remarkable defense of Lloyd by Chester McA. Destler, "Wealth against Commonwealth, 1894 and 1944," *American Historical Review*, 50 (1944–45):49–72. Nevins wrote a reply, *American Historical Review*, 50 (1944–45):676–689. Destler wrote a response but that, unfortunately, was not published, "A Commentary on the 'Communication' from Allan Nevins," typescript. Destler wrote a biography of the man, *Henry Demarest Lloyd and the Empire of Economic Reform* (Philadelphia, 1963). For a brief review of the Destler-Nevins exchange, see Peter Collier and David Horowitz, *The Rockefellers: An American Dynasty* (New York: 1976), p. 641, n28. For a brief account of Lloyd's effort, see Chernow, *Titan*, pp. 339–342.

57. Payne was a Democrat. Rockefeller, a staunch Republican, denied any connection with the choice. For a brief overview, see Chernow, *Titan*, pp. 289–290. For more details on the allegations and evidence, see the exchange between Destler and Nevins. Standard Oil had another possible link to the Democratic Party. Oliver Payne's brother-in-law was William C. Whitney, a "rich Wall Street lawyer" who, as seen in the previous chapter, was a sponsor of Grover Cleveland. See also, Chernow, pp. 290–291.

58. Olcott, I, pp. 311–312. Herrick was not alone in this effort. Jones, *Election of 1896*, p. 156, reports that "a delegation of McKinley's middle western friends spent several days in New York seeking interviews with the city's business leaders and assuring them that McKinley had no harmful views on money."

59. Mott, pp. 68–69. This episode is reported also in Jean Strouse, *Morgan: American Financier* (New York, 1999), p. 355.

60. Mott, p. 69. The subject under discussion, it will be noted, was issue-avoidance, how to avoid a clear commitment on the key issue coming up in the campaign. An effort at compromise is being recommended; the political broker is arguing for the compromise—as opposed to the clear but self-defeating statement demanded by Morgan.

61. Mott, p. 70.

62. From Vincent P. Carosso, *The Morgans: Private International Bankers 1854–1913* (Cambridge, 1987), p. 293 and Beer, pp. 275–276.

63. Mott, pp. 59–60; Olcott, I, pp. 306–307; Leech, p. 70; Kohlsaat, p. 30; and, for much more detail, Jones, *Election of 1896*, ch. 11, "McKinley Battles the Bosses." The senators listed were from, respectively, Rhode Island, New York, Pennsylvania, Maine, and Iowa.

64. Olcott, I, pp. 305–309; Leech, pp. 72–75. Senator Cullom, Illinois's favorite son, was "furious" about McKinley's "invasion" of his state but could do little about it.

Leech, p. 73; Morgan, p. 157. The McKinley forces "invaded" all of the Midwestern states except Iowa, the home state of Senators Allison and Henderson. They had considerable success in these efforts. For details, see Jones, *Election of 1896*, ch. 8.

65. Olcott, I, pp. 309–318; Leech, pp. 80–84; Morgan, pp. 165–167; and Jones, ch. 12.

66. Leech, pp. 83; DAB, 9:92–93; ANB, 10:892–893; and Morgan, p. 168. Although not explicitly stated in any of the sources reviewed, Hobart must have sacrificed considerable income on taking this position.

67. Olcott provides a useful review of some hundred years of tariff history, I, chs. 7–9. Also, Leech, pp. 36–48, 60–62; Morgan, pp. 48–51, and ch. 8; and Jones, at many points.

   For McKinley, the nation's universities were a source of the problem. He was "alienated from the modern system of higher education by the discovery that 'free trade" ideas had become 'a fashion' in American colleges. 'I would rather have my political economy founded upon the every-day experience of the puddler or the potter than the learning of the professor,' he caustically remarked in 1888. 'Do not permit college ideals to warp you,' he warned the students of Mount Union in 1896," from Leech, p. 24.

68. See Olcott, I, pp. 310–314; Leech, pp. 79–80; Morgan, pp. 161–165; Beer, pp. 143–144; and for a more extended discussion, Croly, pp. 192–205. For Jones' statement, see his p. 167. Bingham Duncan reports this effort, indicating that Reid showed McKinley's draft proposal to J. P. Morgan and to some other New York bankers. But he appears to be mistaken when he writes that McKinley "moved closer" to the single standard forces as a result of Reid's findings. From Duncan, *Whitelaw Reid* (Athens, Georgia, 1975), p. 164.

69. On the events leading up to the Democratic convention, see Jones, *Election of 1896*, chs. 13–17; J. Rogers Hollingsworth, *The Whirligig of Politics* (Chicago, 1963), chs. 2 and 3; Paolo E. Coletta, *William Jennings Bryan*, Vol. 1, *Political Evangelist 1860–1908* (Lincoln, 1964), ch. 7; Paul W. Glad, *McKinley, Bryan, and the People* (Philadelphia, 1964), ch. 6; and Williams, *Years of Decision*, chs. 3–5.

   Several sources state that Bryan was supported by "the silver interests." One author writes: "A former Congressman, Bryan had recently served (mostly *in absentia*) as editor of a major Omaha newspaper, which had been bought by two wealthy silver miners, William Clark and Marcus Daly, with a view to building up this progressive agrarian as a presidential candidate." Philip H. Burch, Jr., *Elites in American History*, Vol. 2 (New York, 1981), p. 184, n20. His source, which lacks documentation, is Charles Morrow Wilson, *The Commoner: William Jennings Bryan* (Garden City, NY, 1970), pp. 195–204. Bryan invested some of his own money in the Omaha *World-Herald* and did work as its editor. Coletta, Bryan's most comprehensive biographer investigated this question; he describes the supposed contribution of the silver mine owners as "apparently a myth," in *Bryan*, Vol. 1, pp. 100–101. A Clark-Daly cooperative effort seems unlikely since the two men were fierce antagonists. For Clark, see ANB, 4:955–957, and for Daly, ANB, 6:41–42.

70. For the history, see John D. Hicks, *The Populist Revolt: A History of the Farmers' Alliance and the People's Party* (Minneapolis, 1931) and Lawrence Goodwyn, *Democratic Promise: The Populist Movement in America* (New York, 1976). On the Populist convention, see Jones, *Election of 1896*, ch. 8. Also C. Vann Woodward, *Thomas Watson: Agrarian Rebel* (New York, 1938), chs. 16 and 17.

71. Kirk H. Porter and Donald Bruce Johnson, *National Party Platforms, 1840–1968* (Urbana, 1970), pp. 97–111.

72. Hollingsworth, *Whirligig*, pp. 37–38. Led by Anaconda's Marcus Daly, the mine owners contributed $289,000 to help elect pro-silver delegates to the Democratic convention, this according to Don C. Seitz, *Joseph Pulitzer: His Life and Letters* (New York, 1924), p. 226 and Oliver Carlson and Ernest Sutherland Bates, *Hearst: Lord of San Simeon* (New York, 1936), pp. 81–82. Their effort began just after the repeal of the Sherman Silver Purchase Act in 1893. For more details, see Jones, *Election of 1896*, chs. 2, 5, 14, and 16.

William Randolph Hearst's father, George Hearst, was an owner of Anaconda (which produced silver and copper) and a friend of Daly. George Hearst was also an owner of Homestake, which produced gold. Hearst's *New York Journal* declared its support for Bryan in July 1896, the only newspaper in the city to do so. But the easy inference is misleading. Hearst "opposed silver" but decided for Bryan "to build up circulation" (Coletta, p. 148). For more detail, see W. A. Swanberg, *Citizen Hearst* (New York, 1961), pp. 84–86; Ben Procter, *William Randolph Hearst: The Early Years, 1863–1910* (New York, 1998), pp. 88–90; David Nasaw, *The Chief: The Life of William Randolph Hearst* (Boston, 2000), pp. 117–119; and, a key primary source, Willis J. Abbot, *Watching the World Go By* (Boston, 1934), ch. 9. Nasaw summarizes as follows: "Though the Hearst family owned silver mines, it had larger investments in gold, which would depreciate significantly if Bryan were elected" (p. 118).

Some sources claim the silver interests gave direct support to Bryan. For his 1892 Congressional campaign (in Nebraska's first district), his campaign manager did collect money, $4,000, from "the silver states," a fact that was hidden at the time. He was "on the stump" in the spring of 1893, giving speeches in the Middle West and South and arguing "the cause" in correspondence and in some newspapers. Coletta says he was working as "a member of the Nebraska State Council of the American Bimetallic League." Bryan's congressional career ended in March 1895 and he again "took to the lecture platform." Several sources allege that the "silver interests" paid for this work. Coletta says Bryan received speaker's fees, $50, then $100 per speech from local sponsors, but "was not, as frequently charged, on the payroll of the Western Silver Miners' Association, and there is no record that he associated with any similar organization" (p. 104). A long footnote there reviews the claims and counterclaims, see also pp. 73, 80, and 108.

73. Hicks, *Populist Revolt*, p. 268.

74. Woodward, in *The Burden of Southern History*, (New York, 1961 [1960]), p. 151.

75. For a brief overview of the German experience, obviously an extreme case, see Gordon A. Craig, *Germany 1866–1945* (New York, 1978), pp. 450–456. Desperate city-dwellers resorted to barter, carrying various household goods to the farms to trade for food. This later brought a sardonic comment about farmers and their circumstances—"even the cows have rugs."

76. For a comprehensive overview, see Allan G. Bogue, *Money at Interest* (Ithaca, 1955). One source describes the situation in Kansas as follows: ". . . after the boom years of the early and mid-eighties gave way to drought and crop failure, 60 percent of Kansas's taxed acres were mortgaged. The state's per capita debt of $347 was four times the national average." From Morton Keller, *Affairs of State: Public Life in Late Nineteenth Century America* (Cambridge, 1977), p. 574.

The Bryan forces claimed the limited money supply was the source of the farmers' problem. Republicans argued supply and demand factors, specifically, overproduction of wheat. Wheat shortages in India, Russia, and Australia that year brought an increase in demand for American wheat and in September and October "a rather sharp advance" in wheat prices followed. For a detailed review, see Gilbert C. Fite, "Republican Strategy and the Farm Vote in the Presidential Campaign of 1896," *American Historical Review*, 65 (1960):787–806. Early in the campaign, a Chicago firm canvassed 4,000 farmers in Illinois, Minnesota, Nebraska, Iowa, and Missouri whose mortgages it held. Fewer than 1,300 replied, but of these, 979 preferred McKinley, only 186 favored Bryan, as reported in James A. Barnes, "Myths of the Bryan Campaign," *Mississippi Valley Historical Review*, 34 (1947):367–404, p. 400, n63.

77. Morton Keller presents results for nine major cities in 1892 and 1896. Seven of these had Democratic margins in 1892; in 1896, the Republicans were the victors all nine. New York City was Democratic by 76,300 votes in 1892. In 1896, by 21,997 votes, it went to the Republicans. From his *Affairs of State*, p. 585.

78. All sources cited in this chapter deal with these matters. On the money question, see Glad, *McKinley, Bryan*, pp. 75–88. For more technical accounts, see Milton Friedman and Anna Jacobson Schwartz, *A Monetary History of the United States 1867–1960* (Princeton, 1963) and Paul Studenski and Herman E. Krooss, *Financial History of the United States*, second edition (New York, 1963), pp. 231–234.

79. See the works of C. Vann Woodward, especially *Origins of the New South, 1877–1913* (Baton Rouge, LA, 1951) and *The Strange Career of Jim Crow* (New York, 1957). The Populists, most of them poor white farmers, were challenging the well-off conservative Democrats and, accordingly, rather tentatively, made overtures to poor black farmers. The Bourbons' response, initially, was violence. Lynchings increased considerably, reaching an all-time high in 1892 with both blacks and whites among the victims. For this history, see Richard F. Hamilton, *Class and Politics in the United States* (New York, 1972), pp. 427–434.

The subsequent Bourbon response, a legal one for more than a half-century, was the Jim Crow laws. Voting restrictions came at the same time: Poor farmers, white and black, were removed from the electorate. On the "electoral demobilization," see Paul Kleppner, *Who Voted? The Dynamics of Electoral Turnout, 1870–1980* (New York, 1982), p. 57. Turnout in the South, he reports, fell from 63.5 percent in the 1876–1892 period to 49.9 percent in the 1896–1900 presidential elections. It would fall still further, to 20.4 percent, in 1920–1924. Even greater declines occurred in the off-year congressional elections, the figures: for 1894–98, 41.0 percent; and for 1922–26, 10.6 percent.

80. Richard J. Jensen, *The Winning of the Midwest* (Chicago, 1971), pp. 270–271, 274, and 277.

81. Morgan, pp. 172–173; Croly, pp. 219–220; Beer, pp. 155–156. James J. Hill was the owner of the Great Northern Railway. Although based in St. Paul, he spent much time in New York, arranging the finances of his many enterprises. A "hard money man," he joined forces with Hanna to counter the Bryan threat. See Michael P. Malone, *James J. Hill: Empire Builder of the Northwest* (Norman, OK, 1996), p. 160. McKinley later named Bliss to be his Secretary of the Interior.

82. Morgan, p. 173; Croly, p. 220; Dawes, p. 106. Although citing both Morgan and Croly, Procter makes no mention of the difficulties and presents those high figures as accurate (in *Hearst*, p. 91). For more details and sources, see Coletta, who again

reviews the question of the silver mine owners' support for Bryan, putting the highest estimate at $228,000 (*Bryan*, pp. 196–198; for the estimate, p. 198, n148). Coletta depended heavily on material published in the Omaha *World-Herald*. Bryan, as noted, had been editor of that newspaper and was also a part owner (p. 100).

Matthew Josephson, without any sources, gives a range of estimates, declaring the size of Hanna's "war chest" as between $10,000,000 and $16,500,000, in *The Politicos 1865–1896* (New York, 1938), p. 699. A footnote reports that: "Joseph Foraker frankly ridiculed Croly's estimate, saying only that Mr. Hanna's war chest was of a size 'which would have made a very popular man out of any distributor of it' (Foraker, *Notes of a Busy Life*, pp. 445–47)." Those pages (in Volume One of Senator Foraker's memoirs) deal with Hanna's efforts in support of Senator Sherman's campaign for the United States Senate several years earlier. The quotation does appear on a later page but the lesson drawn there is quite different. Pointing to conversion of newspapers, half of "the leading Democratic and independent newspapers" were "bolting Bryan," Foraker states that "McKinley's election was assured from the start . . . he would have been successful even if there had not been anything extraordinary done by the National Committee." The point is reiterated in the next paragraph: "In fact, I never had the slightest doubt from the day Bryan was nominated on a free silver platform about his defeat. . ." *Notes of a Busy Life*, two volumes (Cincinnati, 1916), p. 498.

83. Morgan, p. 173. For another useful summary, see Williams, *Years of Decision*, pp. 119–122. For discussion of the Carnegie essay, including Hanna's letter of appreciation, see Wall, *Carnegie*, pp. 467–468.
84. Morgan, ch. 11; Jones, *Election of 1896*, ch. 20.
85. On the defecting press, see Hollingsworth, pp. 70–71. He describes the "change in newspaper sentiment" as "the most widespread shift of party allegiance in the history of presidential elections." He reports that the *Boston Evening Dispatch* was "the only newspaper of any consequence in New England to support Bryan." But it "folded two weeks before the election as the gold men of State Street directed their advertising to papers with saner editorials" (p. 86). For Coletta's account, see *Bryan*, p. 200.
86. On the coercion, see Coletta, *Bryan*, p. 202 and Robert F. Durden, *The Climax of Populism: The Election of 1896* (Lexington, KY, 1965), pp. 138–140.
87. Hollingsworth, *Whirligig*, p. 89. The Chicago *Tribune* commented as follows on Bryan's "Cross of Gold" speech: "The Nebraskan is young in years, but aged in the wiles of the politician and the demagogue, and eloquent as are all his speeches, he never fails to inject into them a sufficient amount of claptrap to capture his hearers." From Lloyd Wendt, *Chicago Tribune: The Rise of a Great American Newspaper* (Chicago, 1979), p. 314.
88. Jensen, p. 275; also, Coletta, p. 184.
89. Jones, *Election of 1896*, pp. 297–301. For comprehensive reviews of the Democratic campaign, see Jones, ch. 21; Hollingsworth, ch. 5; Jensen, ch. 10; and Coletta, ch 9.

The Democrats had nothing like the Republicans' massive publications and delivery procedures. Some pro-silver writings did have large circulation but these were produced independently. William H. Harvey's pro-silver monograph, *Coin's Financial School*, first published in June 1894, was a bestseller in 1896. Richard Hofstadter discussed this work in his introduction to a later reprinting—Hofstadter, ed. (Cambridge, 1963). There were several mass circulation efforts. We have no precise figures but their circulation appears to have been much smaller than that produced by the Republicans. The pro-silver works also stimulated the production of an extensive counter-literature. See Jones, pp. 32–35; Williams, pp. 105–106; and Jensen, pp. 282–283.

Frank Baum's "enduring allegory," *The Wonderful Wizard of Oz*, is sometimes discussed in this connection, but it did not appear until 1900. See Henry Littlefield, "The Wizard of Oz: Parable on Populism," *American Quarterly*, 16 (1964):47–58.

90. Hollingsworth, p. 84. For a bittersweet nostalgic formulation of the steady-erosion argument, see Vachel Lindsay's poem, "Bryan, Bryan, Bryan, Bryan." The argument assumes certain knowledge of voter sentiment as of June-July that year and some monitoring of "the trend" over the subsequent months. Some people, clearly, did share that view, but it could only be a feeling, a guess, one based on small and erratic samples. Charles Dawes was confident, at all points, that McKinley would win. He knew and was friendly with Bryan and met him in the midst of the campaign and they had "quite a talk." His journal entry for that day, 4 September, adds that "Bryan, somehow, imagines he has a chance to be elected President" (p. 96). Andrew Carnegie wrote William Gladstone, on 28 September, that "the forces of Law, Order & Honesty in the Republic are on the eve of a remarkable triumph," from Jones, *Election of 1896*, pp. 336–337. In a later letter, Carnegie reported that his friends thought differently, believing that Bryan would have won if the election had come just after the nomination, Jones, pp. 403–404, n63. Owen Wister asked some friends, Roosevelt, Lodge, and Winthrop Chanler, "if the country had sunk to the possibility of such a wind-bag [Bryan] becoming our President. They thought not, they thought McKinley would win," from *Roosevelt: The Story of a Friendship, 1880–1919* (New York, 1920), p. 50. See also, Foraker's statement in note 82 above.

91. U.S. Bureau of the Census, *Historical Statistics of the United States* (Washington, D.C., 1975), pp. 11, 12, 457, 458.

92. Minnesota, presumably a farm state, gave 56.6 percent of its votes to McKinley, only 40.9 to Bryan. The Bryan percentages for those five Mountain states are: Colorado, 84.9; Idaho, 78.1; Montana, 79.9; Nevada, 81.2; and Utah, 82.7. Wyoming differed from the others in the region, giving Bryan only 51.6 percent. From Carolyn Goldinger, ed., *Presidential Elections Since 1789*, fourth edition (Washington, D.C., 1987), p. 110.

Wyoming's Republicans gained a decisive victory in the 1894 elections, this stemming from the 1893 panic. The Democrats were broken, the Populists a mere "nuisance." The state differed from the others in the region in that it "had no silver mines of its own." Its principal industries, wool, coal, and iron, were protected, which meant that much greater attention would be given to the tariff issue. Some citizens, however, were apparently convinced that the discovery of silver ore was only a question of time. The thin margin for Bryan (he carried the state by 300 votes) appears to have been largely a media effect. Many citizens depended on newspapers from neighboring states, many of which were pro-silver. From the surrounding states residents also received "a shower of pamphlets, editorials, and letters singing the praises of bimetallism." For these details, and much more, see Lewis L. Gould, *Wyoming: A Political History, 1868–1896* (New Haven, 1968), pp. 196–197, 234, and 246.

93. Mississippi cast 69,591 votes in the 1896 election, 91.0 percent of them for Bryan; see Goldinger, *Presidential Elections*, pp. 104–110. A speculation: Given the

exclusion of thousands of small farmers there, both blacks and whites, much of that support must have been given by "Bourbon Democrats," by the "landed interests" rather than by "the people."

94. Ibid., p. 110. For much detail, see William Diamond, "Urban and Rural Voting in 1896," *American Historical Review*, 46 (1941):281–305. For the unexpected reversals in New England and New York, see pp. 287–288; for the vote in the largest cities, pp. 297–298.

95. James L. Sundquist, *Dynamics of the Party System*, revised edition (Washington, D.C.: 1983), p. 166. For other comprehensive reviews, see Jones, pp. 340–348 and Keller, ch. 15.

   Some of the counties in upstate New York would have been rural, predominantly farm. But in only one of the state's counties, Schoharie, did Bryan's vote exceed McKinley's, from Edgar Eugene Robinson, *The Presidential Vote 1896–1932* (Stanford, 1934), pp. 275–280.

96. Sundquist, pp. 162–165. Both McKinley and Hanna "had long been on good terms with labor." Hanna had "attracted widespread attention by cursing George Pullman for his refusal to arbitrate" the 1894 strike, this from Hollingsworth, *Whirligig*, pp. 92–93.

   The Democratic losses were long lasting in most cities; see Sundquist's Table 7–2, p. 163, pp. 147–150. New York and Boston, however, were exceptions, where the Democrats made remarkable recoveries in 1900. The recoveries, apparently, were due to the efforts of political machines, ones supported by substantial Irish constituencies.

97. Sundquist, *Dynamics*, p. 158.

98. Leech, p. 5.

99. Porter and Johnson, *National Party Platforms*, pp. 107–109. The platform also announced the party's "unqualified condemnation" of lynching—but indicated no solution. The last substantive item was a reminder that the party "is mindful of the rights and interests of women, and believes that they should be accorded equal opportunities, equal pay for equal work, and protection of the home." Although no specific measures were indicated—such as the right to vote—the party did "favor the admission of women to wider spheres of usefulness. . ."

100. Ibid., pp. 97–100. The Democratic platform contained nothing on lynching, nothing on women. It contained two sentences on "Civil-Service Laws," one of them indicating opposition to "life tenure." Bryan was to become "the only presidential candidate to campaign actively against the merit system." The Republican platform contained nothing on this subject. Once elected, McKinley "acknowledged that things had gone too far" and subsequently exempted more than 9,000 classified positions from examination, this from Skowronek, *Building a New American State*, p. 73.

101. The New York *World* put out a "thrice-a-week" election edition in 1896. Material on Spain and Cuba appeared there in their issues of 15, 18, and 20 May ("Famine and Flames," and "Weyler's Way"). Several pages contained deprecating comments about McKinley. Two cartoons portray Hanna muzzling the candidate, refusing to allow any discussion of the currency question (15 May, p. 2; 22 May, p. 1).

102. Coletta, *Bryan*, p. 189.

3

The New President Selects His Cabinet

A second decision-making effort, the new president's selection of his cabinet and ambassadors, allows another test of the power and influence of the various elites. The key questions: Which groups sought to influence McKinley? And, which were successful, that is, which gained the sought-for positions?

Many years later, the eminent journalist, William Allen White, declared, with no qualification whatsoever, that Hanna was "the most powerful man on the American continent."[1] Given that "truth," and given the man's role in McKinley's nomination and presidential campaigns, one might expect that Hanna would direct the work of cabinet selection. One might also expect him to have a place in the cabinet so as to allow continuous influence on the president and easy direction of the executive branch of government. But Hanna did neither. He had a limited role in the selection of the cabinet and he refused the position McKinley most insistently offered, that of postmaster general. He preferred instead to be a senator.

If Hanna had been close at hand and was seen to be "pulling the strings," it would have undercut McKinley's credibility, giving support for the Hearst and Democratic Party portraits of the man. The need for some distance was obvious to Hanna and to most others close to the president-elect. John Hay wrote to Whitelaw Reid, publisher of the *New York Tribune*, on "the vital necessity for McKinley of asserting himself at the start and letting all and sundry know who is boss."[2] Another important McKinley supporter, Herman Henry Kohlsaat, claimed that Hanna wanted to be Secretary of the Treasury. But, he reported, McKinley hesitated, "first, because it would look too much like paying a political debt and, second, because he did not think Hanna had the necessary training. He said to me: 'I don't think Mark knows enough about governmental finance to fill the position.'"[3]

One might think, because of the persistent influence of the progressive readings, that businessmen would be prime candidates for cabinet positions but, on the whole, they were not promising choices. For a successful businessman, taking a cabinet position, as seen, would mean loss of income, a move to Washington, and a job with an uncertain future. There was also a question of interest: Would the railroad executive, steelmaker, or manufacturer of farm implements be willing to deal first with hundreds of job seekers? Would he then be willing to negotiate, showing proper deference, of course, with dozens of importuning congressmen?

At this point, there were eight cabinet posts, with State and Treasury by far the most important. The postmaster general held the most political of the cabinet positions. Aided by solicitous congressmen and by state and local office holders, he would dispense some thousands of jobs. The War Department, since 1865, had been largely a minor "caretaker" operation. The Navy Department was somewhat better off, some efforts having been made to modernize the fleet. The attorney general was charged with the enforcement of federal laws, no overwhelming task at that point. Finally, there were the Interior and Agriculture departments. The only department with even an approximate connection to some prior business activity would be Treasury, but even there, as just seen, the president-elect recognized some constraints. Manufacturing farm implements or the smelting iron ore were in no way comparable to overseeing the technicalities of tariff, taxes, and currency. The Congress was a more likely source for cabinet recruits, its members having much more knowledge of government and of its distinctive requirements. McKinley had more personal knowledge of these people than of businessmen, persons employed in other locations and doing other tasks.

For any new president, cabinet selection involved delicate matters of balance. Regional representation was a prime concern at least for those areas where a party was based. Some negotiation with the party leaders was necessary. One had to reward them but, at the same time, the chief executive had to maintain some independence vis-à-vis "the bosses." A close division in the Senate presented an important tactical problem. For McKinley, any Republican removed from the Senate meant a possible problem of control. He would need assurance that the successor, chosen by that state's legislature, would be a reliable Republican.[4]

McKinley's first choice for his Secretary of State was William B. Allison of Iowa, one of the "Big Four" Senate Republican leaders. Leech describes him as politically "an impeccable choice." The two men knew each other, shared viewpoints, and got along well. Allison was the chairman of the Senate Committee on Finance and had proved skillful in financial matters and in Senate diplomacy. Although "inexperienced in foreign affairs" that was not seen as a problem. For capable persons, as seen in chapter 1, professional training, the technocratic concern, was not ordinarily viewed as a requirement. But Allison declined, indicating he did not wish to leave the Senate.[5]

Leech reports that Hanna then suggested John Sherman for the post. The move would create a Senate vacancy that Hanna hoped to fill. Sherman, a financial expert, had served earlier as Hayes' Secretary of the Treasury. Although a member of the Senate Foreign Relations Committee from 1883 and its chairman after 1886, he had not shown "particular distinction" in that area. Also, he had "never been noted for his talents as a diplomat," recently in fact having been "excitable and intemperate in his public references to Spain." There was another consideration: He was nearly seventy-four years old and "no longer in his vigorous prime."[6]

There was another problem with the tactic: It was not certain that Ohio's governor, Asa Bushnell, would appoint Hanna to fill out Sherman's term. Bushnell, a Republican, was affiliated with the Foraker faction of the party, one opposed to Hanna and his aspirations. A six-week stalemate followed Sherman's acceptance and his prompt resignation from the Senate. During that time much pressure was laid on the reluctant governor, including a "respectful" request from Sherman who "claimed the right to a voice in naming his successor." Finally, McKinley made a personal request and, ten days before the inauguration, Bushnell conceded.[7]

Allegations had been made in those intervening weeks, claims that Sherman's mental powers were declining. McKinley, however, received positive firsthand reports from his cousin and confidant, Will Osborne, and from Joseph Medill, publisher of the *Chicago Tribune*. McKinley talked with Sherman during a visit in Canton and was convinced of his "perfect health, physically and mentally." He concluded that the stories about Sherman's "mental decay" were "cheap inventions of sensational writers." But later, while preparing his inaugural address, McKinley asked Sherman for suggestions about Cuba. He received, Leech reports, "a rather inconsistently worded memorandum, stating that intervention was . . . inevitable." McKinley edited this recommendation, dropped the conclusion, and finally discarded the memorandum entirely.[8]

McKinley chose his good friend, William R. Day, to be Assistant Secretary of State. It was Day who, among other things, had conveyed McKinley's wishes with respect to Hanna's appointment to Governor Bushnell. Day insisted that he did not want the assistant secretary position but McKinley's insistence had greater weight. Day, who "had no special knowledge of international law, and was entirely untrained in diplomacy," became effectively the acting Secretary of State in the following two years. Morgan has some positive words about this "quiet, legalistic judge"—"his country-lawyer's bearing hid a sharp acumen and common sense." Morgan also indicates the subsequent importance of Day's appointment, noting that Sherman's position "became intolerable with the outbreak of war. His hearing and memory all but failed, and subordinates conducted the department's business. McKinley and Assistant Secretary Day were in fact Secretary of State. Day attended cabinet meetings and was close to the president, facts that never escaped the touchy Sherman."[9]

McKinley's first definite decision with respect to the cabinet involved the Treasury. At that point, prior to any thought of war, it was easily the most important of the eight cabinet positions. His first choice was Congressman Nelson Dingley, Jr. of Maine, a member of long-standing on the Ways and Means Committee, an important supporter of McKinley, and a man known for his "mastery of problems of government finance and revenue." Dingley was offered the post and he accepted. But then, toward the end of January, he wrote McKinley that his doctor and family had advised him to decline—he would not live two years if he took it.[10] Dingley would continue instead as chairman of the Ways and Means Committee where he was busy writing the new tariff bill. Several politicians endorsed Senator Shelby Cullom of Illinois for the position. Cullom had been a contender for the 1896 nomination and, as a consequence, this recommendation did not sit well with some of McKinley's political friends. There was an additional difficulty: He "knew little of finance."[11]

The informal understanding with regard to patronage, to regional representation, led two Republican Senators, George Frisbie Hoar and Henry Cabot Lodge, to recommend Thomas Jefferson Coolidge for the "Massachusetts place." Coolidge, a prominent Boston businessman with wide-ranging interests (he had served briefly as minister to France), would appear qualified for the Treasury position. But McKinley disregarded the senators' wishes. He had already filled the state's "place" by naming John Davis Long as Secretary of the Navy. One biographer writes that Hoar "was conciliated by a warm and lengthy handclasp; Lodge, with the appointment of his Harvard classmate, Theodore Roosevelt as Long's assistant." Coolidge was not troubled by the outcome. He wrote that "I do not regret the loss of the place, for the labour is excessive and the responsibility very great. . ."[12]

Several advisors, Dawes, Kohlsaat, and Hanna, spoke on behalf of Lyman J. Gage, the president of First National Bank of Chicago. He was knowledgeable in financial affairs (Grover Cleveland had offered him the position four years earlier) and was well known in banking circles, where he was regarded as "an able and cautious" financier.[13] Gaining his consent, however, proved rather difficult. Kohlsaat made the first inquiries but the banker "was obdurate." "I have no political ambition," he said. Kohlsaat pursued the matter that evening at a social gathering, enlisting the support of Mrs. Gage—"She was greatly interested as I drew a picture of a cabinet officer's social position." The next day, Kohlsaat urged reconsideration but the banker again objected: "Why should I give up a perfectly easy job with $25,000 salary to accept one at

$8,000 and spend three times my salary to live in Washington?" Further discussions followed. When the banker weakened, Kohlsaat "rang up" McKinley at Canton to tell him, "I have a Secretary of the Treasury for you."[14] Charles Dawes, McKinley's supporter, friend, and confidant, interviewed Gage. Gage then traveled to Canton and spoke at length with the president-elect. McKinley offered the position and Gage accepted. This was to be one of McKinley's "happiest selections."[15]

For Secretary of War, McKinley chose Russell A. Alger. His career included military service in the Civil War, ending with the rank of brevet general. He was later elected to be commander-in-chief of the G.A.R. Alger was a successful businessman whose activities centered primarily in lumbering with mills and large tracts of timber in northern Michigan and in Canada. He subsequently moved into politics to become Michigan's governor and, at the same time, a leader in Republican national affairs. He was a favorite son candidate for the presidential nomination in 1888 and 1892. Morgan describes him as a "genial McKinleyite."

Alger actively sought to head the War Department and in this effort had strong backing from the G.A.R and the support of several friends, notably from the Republican bosses of several important states, Tom Platt, Matthew Quay, and Joseph Foraker. McKinley was "showered with requests" to give this office to Alger. The peacetime army, Gould writes, with its twenty-five thousand officers and men "had only a modest military role." Its civilian responsibilities included "exploration, flood relief, and construction or rivers and harbors," which meant that Alger's business experience would prove useful.[16]

There were, however, some problems. Leech describes the "handsome and affable" Alger as "a lightweight, pleasant and rather evasive." Some questions had been raised about his political actions and some also about his business activities. McKinley "made careful inquiries" about the latter and found the result "entirely reassuring." In 1892 allegations had been made in the New York *Sun* about Alger's military service, casting doubt on his record as "a gallant cavalry officer." McKinley sent his confidential clerk to Washington to investigate. Checking War Department records, the report vindicated Alger. McKinley checked also with an old friend, Senator Julius Caesar Burrows of Michigan, who provided the same conclusion. Wishing no further difficulty on this account McKinley sought additional assurance. Burrows spoke with Tom Platt who, in turn, spoke with the publisher of the *Sun*, Charles A. Dana, who promised "no unfriendly action." Alger's appointment soon followed.[17]

There was, however, still another difficulty, the question of Alger's physical capacity. Leech reports that he had "grown quite frail," aged and shaken possibly by the scandal over his military record. The War Department had been rather inactive (Leech says "somnolent") since 1865, its major tasks being

Indian wars plus routine work on the nation's rivers and harbors. Hanna had "suggested" to Alger that this was "the only Cabinet seat for which a busy man could spare the time from his own affairs."[18]

Alger's appointment was to prove McKinley's worst mistake. Morgan describes Alger as "rich, addicted to ease, often indolent because of his bad heart as well as his nature. Alger's appointment had little to recommend it except politics." Morgan reports also that Alger "knew little if anything about the War Department, and unlike his colleague Long in the Navy Department, he did little in the year given him before the war to prepare for the conflict." Gould writes that "Alger was not an utter disaster as secretary of war, but he was over his head when the Spanish-American War came."[19]

Graham A. Cosmas, a leading authority on the U.S. military of this period, provides a page of comment on Alger's virtues and failings. On the latter, he writes:

> For all his combat experience in the Civil War, he had no real training in large-scale military administration, never having commanded a body of troops larger than a brigade and that only briefly. He was not well informed about the changes in weapons and tactics that were revolutionizing the conduct of war. Except for his work in veterans' organizations, his one term as governor of Michigan, and his unsuccessful campaign for the Presidency, he possessed little background in politics and government—certainly nothing to fit him for management of a major federal department in wartime. Defects of temperament annoyed and bewildered his colleagues. . . .[20]

John Davis Long was the only serious candidate for the Department of the Navy. He had been governor of Massachusetts for three terms and later served in Congress where he met McKinley and became a close friend. A Harvard-educated lawyer, he was "a gentle and scrupulous man of limited means and scholarly tastes." Like Alger, he too had "no special aptitude or training" for this position. And, as with Sherman and Alger, there were some grounds for concern—Leech reports that he "was in poor health." He had, moreover, "recently retired from law practice and had taken no part in the presidential campaign because of nervous prostration." Morgan, however, credits Long with "surprising energy, quickness of mind, and willingness to experiment," factors that "made his department one of the best in the new administration."[21]

An impressive and diverse group of Republican notables supported Theodore Roosevelt for the position of Assistant Secretary of the Navy. Henry Cabot Lodge traveled to Canton for this purpose. The effort was supported by John Hay, William Howard Taft, Thomas B. Reed, the Storers, Myron Herrick, and even Mark Hanna. New York's Republican boss, Tom Platt, hated Roosevelt and was happy to see him removed from the New York scene, his only concern being that the appointment not be charged to his patronage account. Secretary Long "was persuaded to agree" to the appointment.[22] McKinley knew the hazards, Roosevelt was a "militant-minded expansionist [who] hankered for war with Spain." To Mrs. Storer he said, "I am afraid he is too pugnacious." Senator Chandler of New Hampshire showed some doubts, recognizing that Roosevelt "might be uneasy and troublesome" as an assistant. Roosevelt was "not inclined" to go to Canton, saying, "I don't wish to appear the supplicant." But his friends succeeded in their efforts, Platt "capitulated," and McKinley offered the appointment.[23]

Early on, McKinley offered Hanna the postmaster general position, which was an obvious, a logical choice. But Hanna, as indicated, preferred the Senate. Still hoping, McKinley held the position open until mid-February and accordingly it was one of the last to be filled. Hanna and "a host of other influential Republicans" demanded the position for Henry Clay Payne, a party leader in Wisconsin, one who had been especially active in securing McKinley's nomination. But here too there were grounds for concern. Payne was an anti-union employer and a politician with questionable ties to "the corporations." McKinley consulted with Wisconsin's Robert La Follette, a friend and one-time colleague on the Ways and Means Committee, who objected that the man was "a railroad lobbyist" and was "anathema to Wisconsin's progressive element." McKinley told La Follette that Hanna had made a very urgent appeal for Payne but that he, McKinley, had replied saying he could not put a known lobbyist in his cabinet. Eventually James A. Gary, a Baltimore textile manufacturer and Republican activist, was appointed to that position.[24]

For Secretary of the Interior, Leech reports, McKinley's "thoughts turned to" California's Joseph McKenna, a man he had known earlier on the Ways and Means Committee. McKenna was now a judge, a "prominent lawyer and jurist." He was a reluctant candidate because of "financial reasons"—the job would mean a cut in salary and he turned down the initial offer. A visit by Harrison Gray Otis, publisher of the very Republican *Los Angeles Times*, followed and Otis "talked long and earnestly about his duty and the willingness of friends to help him out." McKenna agreed to visit Canton for further discussion. Early in his conversation with McKinley, the candidate pointed out a possible difficulty: "I am a Roman Catholic, and the Protestants will never permit a Catholic to have charge of the Indian Missions." McKinley promptly "corrected" an apparent error, saying he wanted him not for Interior but for attorney general. It was certainly a more plausible "fit" given his manifest talents. McKenna promptly accepted.[25]

That passive-voice statement—McKinley's "thoughts turned to" McKenna—needs some additional comment. Myron Herrick, Hanna's associate and key McKinley supporter, was vacationing and politicking in California in 1895 and while there "spent some time" with John Cline, the state's Republican leader. Herrick "told Cline that if he could get the Californian delegation pledged to McKinley and the latter afterward was elected, I would make it my business to see that a cabinet position was given to that state, for I felt sure that McKinley would do it, as being not only good politics but thoroughly deserved." That agreement, presumably, drew McKinley's thoughts to a Californian. Herrick does indicate some ties between the political and economic elites. "In those days," he reports, "California was more or less run by the railroads and it was Cline, I believe, who had much to do with swinging the railroad men and the state politicians to McKinley."[26]

Iowa Republicans wished cabinet representation and, on Allison's advice, James Wilson was recommended to be the Secretary of Agriculture. He too had modest origins, having "plowed his own fields and sheared his own sheep." Later he was employed as a professor of agriculture at Iowa State College, there running the Agricultural Experimental Station. It was the easiest of all McKinley's appointments, the two men getting on very well. Wilson proved to be a useful counselor and he continued in that position under Roosevelt and Taft until 1913. His service, Morgan reports, "was wise if not colorful, and prudent if not spectacular."[27]

The sudden "switch" that made McKenna the attorney general brought some problems given that several other people were being considered for that position. Moreover, at that point New York had not been "rewarded" in any serious way. The state posed some further complication in that three Republican factions fought over "the spoils," each claiming its just deserts. Colonel John J. McCook, a wealthy corporation lawyer, had been under consideration for the attorney general position and overtures had been made. He had no interest at all in the offered substitute, that is, the Interior position. Ultimately, just before the inauguration, another New Yorker, Cornelius Bliss, a dry goods merchant, a member of the Republican National Committee, and the treasurer of the party's National Committee (from 1892 to 1904) agreed in the "interest of party" to take the position.[28]

Counting the president and Vice President Garret Hobart, the cabinet consisted of ten persons.[29] It was not a strong cabinet—Morgan describes it as "not spectacular" and as "an average assembly." The guiding considerations had been political: McKinley was "rewarding the faithful [and] representing the sections," but that, Morgan adds, "was only normal." The most striking characteristic of the cabinet was the high average age and, a more serious problem, the evident frailty of some of its members. Only three of the eight appointees, Gage, Long, and Wilson, would survive in office the events of the next two years. Gould describes the cabinet as "an average, competent group that could easily have handled the anticipated domestic politics of the new government." But when war came, he adds, "McKinley strengthened his official family and grew much more discerning in his choice of subordinates."[30]

McKinley faced another major task, the appointment of representatives to foreign nations, ambassadors to the major powers, ministers to the others. John Hay, McKinley's friend and sponsor, was named as ambassador to Great Britain, to the Court of St. James. General Horace Porter, earlier an aide to General Grant, later a railway executive, was named as ambassador to France. Andrew D. White, an eminent historian, later a cofounder and president of Cornell University, was named to Germany. Charlemagne Tower, a business-man, an active Republican, and a friend of Pennsylvania's Senator Boies Pen-rose, was named to Austria-Hungary. A St. Louis businessman, Ethan Allen Hitchcock, a manufacturer of plate glass, also of iron and steel, was chosen to represent the nation in Russia.[31]

McKinley retained two of Cleveland's appointees in positions that would soon have great importance, Fitzhugh Lee as consul-general to Cuba and Han-nis Taylor as minister to Spain. Lee was a former Confederate cavalry general (a nephew of Robert E. Lee) and recently had been governor of Virginia. He had "no diplomatic experience and could not speak Spanish" but Cleveland and Olney expected him to provide analysis of the military situation. Taylor was "a southern lawyer" who had "steadfastly supported the Democratic Party against Populism." Like Lee, he had no diplomatic experience and could not speak Spanish. In mid-1897, Taylor was replaced by Stewart L. Woodford, a Civil War veteran, New York state politician, and lawyer, who also lacked diplomatic experience and knowledge of the language.[32]

The choice of the minister to China is of special interest given the events of the immediately following years. Anyone contemplating that nation's potential would recognize that the appointee would have to be an exceptionally talented individual, a person of demonstrated ability, and, most important, one with appropriate language knowledge. One man possessing all of those qualifica-tions, William W. Rockhill, was both available and willing. He had been edu-cated in France, was a graduate of St. Cyr, and for a while had served in the Foreign Legion. He subsequently turned to scholarly matters with a focus on East Asia. He traveled extensively in Tibet, became a leading specialist on that region, and published on the subject. Later he served with the United States legation in Peking, developing fluency in Chinese. He then served with the legation in Korea. In the 1890s, during Cleveland's presidency, he served first as the chief clerk of the State Department, later moving up to the assistant sec-retary position. In that capacity, he dealt with both the Venezuelan and the developing Cuban crises.

Following McKinley's election victory, an impressive group of supporters recommended Rockhill to the president-elect for the China position. The group included two close friends of Rockhill's, Theodore Roosevelt and Henry Cabot Lodge, also Senators Allison and Hale. General James Wilson, a "friend since Legation days in Peking," was the "aggressive manager" of the movement, commending the candidate and organizing his supporters. But despite the initial promising prospects, in the end the president-elect appointed Edwin H. Conger, a former Iowa congressman and an "old friend" of McKinley. The reason for the choice, reputedly, was because McKinley "felt he had to appoint a western man." Leech states that prior to his arrival in Peking in the summer of 1898 Conger "had no training in Far Eastern affairs." Once again, "party interest" was the decisive consideration. No "big business" concern about "China" is evident in the efforts to secure that appointment. Another curiosity about this effort should be noted. Successful attempts at influence by Roosevelt, Lodge, and their circle receive much attention but a failure, as in this case, gets little notice.[33]

Conger was minister to China during the Spanish-American War. More importantly, he was there, in the Legation quarter, during the Boxer rising. He would also be the United States' representative during the lengthy negotiations over the resulting settlement. Conger proved a very capable manager during the siege. But at all points during his China service, he lacked one essential qualification, knowledge of the necessary languages—he knew only English. At the Peking Conference representatives of the powers worked out the settlement, a process that lasted a full year. The discussions were conducted in French, which meant that Conger sat through the sessions "without the slightest notion as to what was being said." The Belgian minister translated some for his benefit. Rockhill was returned to China to provide help but since only one representative per nation was allowed at the table he could not participate. On occasion, Conger "voted without knowing what he was voting for." Understandably frustrated, Conger asked for a leave and in February 1901 he was replaced by Rockhill.[34]

A discussion of selection procedures that focused only on the "positive cases" would be incomplete. Some lessons may also be learned from the failures, from the attempts to influence McKinley's choices that were denied. The outcome of the Roosevelt-Lodge effort on behalf of Rockhill is one of many such cases.

A popular biography of Henry Clay Frick, the steel magnate, gives the standard reading on the 1896 election. McKinley, described as the "author of the tariff bill beloved of industrialists," was

> swept into the White House on a high tide of money raised by Mark Hanna, a wealthy Ohio businessman turned politician. Earlier, it is said, in gratitude for past favors, Frick and Carnegie had been among the contributors to the McKinley [Walker] fund. They were to be rewarded by the appointment of their lawyer, Philander C. Knox, as Attorney General. Business was very firmly in the saddle.[35]

There is an obvious difficulty with that conclusion since, as just seen, McKinley chose McKenna as his attorney general and he would be followed by Griggs. Frick (and perhaps Carnegie) had contributed to the Walker fund. They both made substantial contributions to the Republican Party in 1896, far larger than ever before. And both men wrote letters to McKinley in support of Knox but, ignoring their wishes, the president-elect made another choice.[36]

It was later, in 1899, that McKinley first asked Knox to be attorney general but the candidate declined, citing his corporate obligations. Two years later, McKinley asked again and this time Knox accepted, taking office in April of 1901 at the start of the second term. Knox continued in that position under Theodore Roosevelt, serving until 1904. His most famous achievement was the successful conduct of an antitrust suit against the Northern Securities Company, the railroad holding company created by J. P. Morgan. Knox would later be chosen to be a United States senator for Pennsylvania. Still later he served as Secretary of State under President Taft where he was known for his "dollar diplomacy" in respect to Honduras and Nicaragua. In 1916, he was again chosen as senator.[37]

Many accounts, as seen, suggest a chain of command—the business potentates ask, and the newly elected president is obliged to respond. Schreiner, for example, states that the president "owed Frick just about any favor he might ask." But Leech provides a markedly different account of the factors involved in McKinley's choice of Knox. At the end of McKinley's first term, Griggs indicated his wish to leave the cabinet and return to private practice. At that point, Leech reports, McKinley "was thinking of appointing his old friend, Philander C. Knox of Pittsburgh." The two had first met back in the 1870s when Knox, a college student, gave testimony that helped McKinley, then a prosecuting attorney, to secure a conviction. He was impressed by the "lad's honesty and manliness" and the relationship developed in the following decades.[38]

Whitelaw Reid was another disappointed supporter. A friend of McKinley's, an important sponsor, and an assiduous giver of advice, he let it be known that he was "willing" to be Secretary of State. Failing that, he asked John Hay for help to be named as Secretary of the Navy. When that too failed, his next request was to be made ambassador to the United Kingdom, a position he held earlier under President Harrison. But that position went to John Hay. McKinley did name him, in 1898, to be a member of the Paris Peace Commission. McKinley later named him as special ambassador to Queen Victoria's Jubilee.[39]

Bellamy Storer, another McKinley sponsor and a major contributor to the Walker fund, was named as minister to Belgium, but that was a disappointment because Storer and his wife wanted London or Paris, something more glamorous than Brussels. Earlier, he had been offered the position of Assistant

Secretary of State. But, deferring to Senator Foraker's wishes, an "old enemy" of the Storers, the offer was withdrawn and the position was given to Judge Day.[40]

Another unexpected outcome, as seen above, followed Hanna's recommendation of Wisconsin's Henry Clay Payne to be the postmaster general. It was probably the most strongly phrased request Hanna ever put to McKinley. Made in person, it was formulated as follows: "You may wipe out every obligation that you feel toward me, and I'll ask no further favors of you, if you'll only put Henry Payne in the Cabinet." Two senior Wisconsin Republicans traveled to Canton to support Payne's nomination. But, as seen, McKinley, concerned about the man's previous history, rejected the entreaties and instead chose James A. Gary.[41]

* * *

Many accounts have portrayed United States politics, beginning in the 1870s and 1880s, as coming increasingly under the control of the nation's leading capitalists. McKinley's victory in 1896, as seen, is often portrayed as the culmination point, as the victory of "big business" over "the people." Mark Hanna's planning of the nomination and his successful management of the presidential campaign is central to the business-domination thesis. But rather than maintaining close proximity with McKinley so as to exercise his control during the next four years, Hanna steadfastly refused the most obvious positions of power. The "powerful boss" stepped aside, effectively removing himself from the "executive committee of the bourgeoisie."

The power of any "boss" would be demonstrated by his "wins" in struggles with other contenders. But Hanna's record shows several important losses. As just seen, he lost in his plea on behalf of Payne, that he should be named as postmaster general, as the leading dispenser of patronage. Hanna's most serious defeat would come in 1897–1898 over the issue of the war. He strongly opposed the involvement, but there too he lost the contest. Hanna had serious doubts about Theodore Roosevelt, about the man and his political directions. But the "powerful boss" lost that contest also when, in 1900, Roosevelt was chosen as his party's vice presidential candidate.

Another event in Hanna's career deserves attention, one that has been generally overlooked. Governor Asa Bushnell, it will be remembered, with evident reluctance had appointed Hanna to fill out the remainder of Sherman's Senate term. At that time senators were chosen by state legislatures and, accordingly, his appointment for a full term would come two years later. The Ohio legislature, the officiating body, was chosen in the November 1897 election. Hanna was active in the campaign, traveling throughout the state and speaking on behalf of the party faithful, which included the governor. And the party leaders in turn, explicitly or implicitly, indicated their support. The Republicans gained an overall majority of fifteen in the legislature and Hanna's election seemed assured.

But when the legislature convened, in the first week of January 1898, an unexpected coalition indicated that the outcome was not at all certain. A combination of Democrats and independent Republicans (some of them "silver Republicans") joined with Governor Bushnell, who was aligned with the Foraker faction, in a movement to drop Hanna. The anti-Hanna forces settled on Robert E. McKisson, an ambitious young man, as their candidate. McKisson was from Cleveland, Hanna's home city. Surprisingly, especially for those who know Hanna as the "powerful boss," McKisson was the mayor of Cleveland. The vote for senator, it appeared, would be very close and, understandably, several days of intense lobbying, of personal pressures, use of patronage, plus allegations of bribery followed. Hanna won the contest with the precise required minimum. A single defection would have removed "Warwick" from the United States Senate.[42]

McKisson was first elected as mayor of Cleveland in 1895. A "practiced and affable politician," he had asked for Hanna's backing but "the boss" preferred someone else. Nevertheless, McKisson was successful—the city's Republicans chose him as their candidate and made him mayor. Beer draws the lesson: "The truth is that Mark Hanna's control of Cleveland was never so absolute as legend asserts." McKisson proceeded to establish his own machine and was reelected in 1897, at which time he was "very much disliked by the prominent business men of Cleveland." He was renominated by the Republicans in 1899, after a bitter primary struggle, but lost in the following election (to Tom L. Johnson, a "reform" Democrat). Ten years would pass before Cleveland had another Republican mayor. With the election of McKisson in 1895 and a Democrat in 1899, Mark Hanna, the "powerful boss," had twice lost control in his Cleveland base. And in Ohio, his home state, he had to "share power" with the hostile Bushnell-Foraker faction of "his" party. The notion of Hanna as the all-powerful boss, clearly, is a gross misrepresentation.[43]

* * *

This review of McKinley's staffing of the top positions in his government, his first major activity as the newly elected president, allows six conclusions:

First, a conclusion with respect to his "style" or "method"—the president-elect demonstrated his independence in making these decisions. When he found candidates unacceptable, whether recommended by "powerful" politicians or "important" business leaders, some of them his sponsors, they were rejected. McKinley, in short, was not the pliable, deferential man seen in the frequent caricatures. He was, to use a cliché, very much his own man.

The second conclusion addresses a key element of the political rhetoric of the era (much of it carried over in subsequent history textbooks), that being the portrayal of "the East," or of "New York" or, still more precisely, of "Wall Street" as the "villain of the piece." What is striking about McKinley's cabinet selection is the absence of Wall Street influence. No Wall Street personage was named, either in the process or the result. The second conclusion, therefore, is a repeat of a conclusion seen in the previous chapter: The group of political entrepreneurs led by Mark Hanna was based in Cleveland, not New York. A focus on Euclid Avenue, while not entirely accurate, would be more appropriate than the insistent emphasis on either Fifth Avenue or Wall Street. Hanna's group was based in the Midwest, including members from Chicago and Pittsburgh.

McKinley's initial cabinet was not dominated by business elites. That cabinet was divided evenly with five businessman and five politicians. The third conclusion, accordingly, is that a differentiated judgment is required, one recognizing the presence of both political and economic elites in the top decision-making positions. The businessmen, moreover, were a diverse lot—a corporation lawyer and businessman, a Chicago banker, a Michigan timber proprietor, a Baltimore textile manufacturer, and a New York City dry goods merchant. Gage, the Secretary of the Treasury, the hard-money banker, it should be noted, was discovered and recommended by the Chicago-based Herman Kohlsaat, not by any Wall Street potentate. Three of those businessmen, moreover, were gone by the end of 1898. They were replaced by Elihu Root, Charles E. Smith, and Ethan Allen Hitchcock. Root can be described, appropriately, as a "Wall Street lawyer." He was also a very capable manager of American foreign affairs. Smith was a Philadelphia newspaper proprietor. Hitchcock was another McKinley friend who Leech described simply as "an elderly businessman." He was appointed first as minister to Russia then was recalled to take over Interior.

A fourth conclusion is a comment on a major social theory. The decision-making reviewed here shows a striking indifference to technocratic (or bureaucratic) assumptions. People were considered and appointed to positions for which they had no plausible prior training, academic or practical, the most striking instance being the choice of Edwin Conger as minister to China. Clearly another set of rules prevailed in this period, the assumption being that capable people could learn quickly; they could easily master the necessary tasks. In this regard, McKinley proved inconsistent, citing the need for knowledge and experience in some instances, as for example with Hanna and the Treasury position, but neglecting such considerations entirely in other instances.

A specification should be noted with respect to an important later appointment. Russell Alger, as seen, failed miserably in his direction of the War Department and, under heavy fire, on 1 August 1899 he resigned the position. McKinley had already sought out a successor, a man who, without any prior notice, was told that the president wished him to head the War Department. In response, Elihu Root, a successful corporation lawyer, told the emissary to thank the president but also to "say that it is quite absurd, I know nothing about war, I know nothing about the army." The emissary responded that McKinley was "not looking for anyone who knows anything about the army; he has got to have a lawyer to direct the government of these Spanish islands . . ." Not having a Colonial Office, the president was planning an ad hoc redirection of the department. On those grounds, still with some reluctance, Root accepted the position.[44]

A fifth conclusion addresses the lesson of a familiar cliché. Hanna, Reid, Carnegie (possibly), Frick, and the Storers had all "paid the piper" but, as seen, they did not "call the tune." The cliché is obviously misleading. That declaration of importance overlooks all other possibly relevant factors, among which would be partisan obligations, personal ties, reputation, and questions of competence. Still another consideration should be noted: With multiple "payers," unless in complete agreement, it was inevitable—"in the cards"—that in any contest one or more of those rich supporters would lose.

A sixth conclusion, a methodological observation, should be considered, namely the need to be open to alternative hypotheses. An author may, with relative ease, demonstrate the existence of a tie (or a link, or a connection) between two individuals. But a "tie" per se says nothing about either the fact or the direction of influence. This problem, declarations about influence (as opposed to investigations of influence) occur regularly in Burch's work. Ties are indicated—Businessman A is connected (or linked) with Politician B. Then, without further evidence, both the fact and direction of influence are assumed: The businessman directs and the politician, presumably, accepts or conforms. This kind of argument provides the basis for Burch's conclusion, that the "vast majority" of McKinley's cabinet members "had one or more key links with various large economic enterprises, many of which were supplemented by the ties of close kinsmen or trusted associates. Hence it seems fair to say that the McKinley administration was heavily dominated by corporate influence."[45]

Some examples from later experience indicate the difficulty. Michael Straight was from a wealthy and "well-connected" capitalist family, the third child of Willard D. Straight, an investment banker with J.P. Morgan & Company, and Dorothy Payne Whitney Straight, an heiress. As a young man he attended several progressive schools. Then, in 1934, while at Cambridge University, he "socialized with young radical patricians like himself and joined the

Communist Party." At one point he was "a reluctant Soviet agent in New Deal Washington."[46]

Paul M. Sweezy's father was vice president of the First National Bank of New York. Sweezy was educated at Harvard (B.A., 1931, Ph.D., 1937). Then, during a year at the London School of Economics, he chose to become a Marxist. He taught briefly at Harvard but, failing to get tenure, left academia to establish "a serious and authentic American brand of Marxism." An inheritance from his father gave him "enough money to support himself." He was a founder and coeditor of the *Monthly Review*, an independent Marxist journal, and the author of many articles and books reflecting that viewpoint.[47]

We have another similar experience from a later period. Although "connected" to a leading capitalist family, Abby and Peggy Rockefeller "were deeply attracted to the revolutionary ideas and causes of the 1960s." Abby was "drawn to Marxism, became an ardent admirer of Fidel Castro, and joined the Socialist Workers Party for a brief time." This choice is explained as the result of a competing influence—she "met a number of teachers who encouraged her growing disenchantment with 'the inequities of American life.'" A brother, Dave, "rejected the family's traditional Republicanism," preferring instead "a politics that placed more emphasis on protecting the environment, ensuring civil rights . . . and ending the war in Vietnam. In the late 1960s he helped finance a 'vigorously anti-establishment' Boston weekly."[48]

Establishing "links" or "ties" is at best only a first step in defending an argument about influence. That a rich man and a politician "are connected" tells us nothing about either the fact or the direction of influence. Here, too, one must consider and address other possibilities—that they are friends but neither attempts to influence the other, or, that the politician shows independence and rejects the attempts at influence, or, that the politician assigns greater weight to the needs of party than to the needs of his business associate. The Hanna-McKinley "tie" is indisputable. The handed-down claims about Hanna's influence and direction, however, are not sustained.

Notes

1. *The Autobiography of William Allen White* (New York, 1946), p. 280.
2. H. Wayne Morgan, *William McKinley and His America*, revised edition (Kent, OH, 2003), p. 190.
3. Herman Henry Kohlsaat, *From McKinley to Harding: Personal Recollections of Our Presidents* (New York, 1923), p. 56. This is the only source I have found indicating that Hanna wished a cabinet post. Kohlsaat reports this as a fact but one "not generally known."
4. See Morgan, p. 191, for some discussion of these problems. The Senate in the 55th Congress had forty-seven Republicans, thirty-four Democrats, five Populists, and

two independent Silver members, which would seem a safe margin for the president's party. But five members of his party were Silver Republicans. A worst-case situation might mean a minority of only forty-two reliable Republicans. See Congressional Quarterly Inc., *Members of Congress Since 1789*, third edition (Washington, D.C., 1985), p. 182.

5. Margaret Leech, *In the Days of McKinley* (New York, 1959), p. 99 and Morgan, p. 194. See also, Leland L. Sage, *William Boyd Allison* (Iowa City, 1956), pp. 267–268.

6. Leech, p. 100; Lewis L. Gould, *The Presidency of William McKinley* (Lawrence, KA, 1980), pp. 14, 17–18 and Morgan, pp. 194–195. Gould indicates uncertainty on McKinley's part. A second approach to Allison was made, this after Sherman had signaled his willingness.

   The major sources are divided about one aspect of this history, whether Hanna had initiated this offer. Sherman, subsequently, felt resentment about his situation and blamed Hanna for his troubles, thus giving credence to the claim. For an early discussion, see Charles S. Olcott, *William McKinley*, two volumes (Boston, 1916), Vol. 1, pp. 325–336. The offer to Sherman was made on 4 January 1897 and Sherman promptly accepted. Sherman was pleased with the appointment and, at the time, wanted to see Hanna appointed as his successor in the Senate. For a listing of the sources on this topic, see Clarence A. Stern, *Resurgent Republicanism: The Handiwork of Hanna* (Ann Arbor, 1966), pp. 74–75, n49.

7. Leech, pp. 100–101; Gould, p. 19; Morgan, pp. 191–193; and, for much detail, Everett Walters, *Joseph Benson Foraker* (Columbus, 1948), pp. 132–137. For a brief biography of Sherman, see ANB, 19:813–815; and for Foraker, ANB, 8: 198–199.

8. Leech, pp. 101–102; Morgan, pp. 194–195. Philip H. Burch has a detailed review of McKinley's Cabinet, this providing much information about the members' connections with the business world, in his *Elites in American History*, Vol. 2 (New York, 1981), pp. 136–144. Senator Sherman, for example, was a director of the Pittsburgh, Fort Wayne and Chicago Railroad from 1866 to 1898. His son-in-law, Colgate Hoyt, was a director of the Missouri, Kansas & Texas Railway from 1890 to 1898, and from "at least 1897" was a director of the Spanish-American Iron Company. No indication is given as to the significance, if any, of those ties.

9. Morgan, p. 195. Day's acceptance meant he "had sacrificed his inclinations and his practice, and whittled down his income to a salary of $4,500 a year." Leech, p. 152.

   One very knowledgeable person within the State Department was Alvee A. Adee, a carryover, a man with long experience. Morgan reports he "knew more details of foreign affairs than anyone else in Washington" and that McKinley found his service "indispensable" (p. 195).

10. Kohlsaat, p. 56, reports the acceptance and subsequent declination. See also, Leech, p. 104; Gould, pp. 14–15; Morgan, p. 196.

11. Morgan, loc. cit.

12. Richard E. Welch, Jr., *George Frisbie Hoar and the Half-Breed Republicans* (Cambridge, 1971), p. 201. Welch provides these comments about the relationship of businessmen and politicians: "Hoar, though strongly convinced of the national value of the business community, was no political puppet for any group or class . . . the term 'business community" is more an historian's convenience than an historical reality; there were many and differing groups of businessmen

with different and often conflicting aims" (p. 84). See also, Coolidge, *The Auto-biography of T. Jefferson Coolidge, 1831–1920* (Boston, 1923), p. 262. Coolidge had the backing of three prominent Massachusetts Republicans for this position, Charles H. Dalton, General Stephen M. Weld, and Governor P. C. Cheney. The three traveled to Canton "in the midst of winter" to argue his candidacy but clearly with no success.

Coolidge recommended a candidate to head the Boston Customs House and was "greatly irritated" when his recommendation was ignored. In July 1898, however, he was "seemingly mollified" when McKinley named Coolidge to serve on the Joint High Commission to settle the Alaskan boundary and fisheries questions. For this, see Ephraim K. Smith, "'A Question from Which We Could Not Escape': William McKinley and the Decision to Acquire the Philippine Islands," *Diplomatic History*, 9 (1985), p. 366. For more on Coolidge, see ANB, 5:425–427.

13. For a brief biography, ANB, 8:606–607; for more, see *Memoirs of Lyman J. Gage* (New York, 1937). Leech reports that Gage was a "gold Democrat" (p. 104) but in the *Memoirs* he states: "I have always been a Republican" (p. 90). Gould describes him as a "Republican with a difference"—he had supported Cleveland over Blaine in 1884 (p. 15).

    Gage served three terms as head of the American Banker's Association. Another biographical fact does not accord with the standard portrait of "bankers." He earned the respect of labor groups, among them, the Knights of Labor, for his extensive efforts on behalf of the men wrongly convicted of murder following the Haymarket Riot of 1886.

14. Kohlsaat, pp. 56–59; also, Gage, *Memoirs*, pp. 88–93. Those pages review the two men's discussions of the tariff and gold standard. They also report Gage's refusal of a $100,000 offer to compensate for "the sacrifice" he would be making.

15. Morgan, pp. 195–198, quotation from p. 197. Morgan suggests that it was Dawes who initiated the move and that McKinley himself had been considering Gage; p. 432, n33. In the original edition that note reports also that Kohlsaat's memoirs "are not always reliable." Morgan, 1963, p. 559.

    Two days after Gage's appointment, a young forty-dollars-a-week reporter, Frank A. Vanderlip, approached Kohlsaat and asked his opinion about going to Washington to serve as Gage's private secretary. Kohlsaat told him he was "too big a man" to be anyone's secretary but recognized that he would be useful to Gage in dealing with politicians and newspapermen. Vanderlip accepted the position. Three months later he was named as the Assistant Secretary of the Treasury, which provided "a salary of $4,500, more money than he ever received before in his life." In that position he came to the attention of James Stillman, the president of the National City Bank, a major New York City institution, who told Gage, "When you are through with that young man, I want him." Vanderlip was subsequently hired by Stillman and in 1909 he became president of the bank. From Kohlsaat, pp. 61–62.

16. Leech, p. 102; Gould, p. 16; Morgan, pp. 198–199. For a brief biography, see ANB, 1:288–289.

17. Leech, p. 103; Gould, pp. 16–17.

18. Leech, p. 104.

19. Gould, p. 17; Morgan, p. 198.

20. Graham A. Cosmas, *An Army for Empire: The United States Army in the Spanish-American War* (Columbia, MO, 1971), p. 58.

21. Leech, p. 106; Morgan, p. 199. Long was the only New Englander in the Cabinet. Burch notes that Long was related "through his mother and other family members to a number of Boston Brahmins and no doubt was thoroughly integrated into this close-knit group, as seen by the fact that he was appointed to the board of the United States Trust Co., of Boston in early 1901 (over a year before he resigned from federal office)," from his, *Elites*, pp. 138–139. Again there is no indication of significance, that is, whether the Brahmins or the Trust Company sought influence or, if so, whether Long complied.
22. Leech, pp. 136–137. For more details, see Morris, *Rise of Theodore Roosevelt*, pp. 555–561.
23. Leech, p. 137; Morgan, pp. 199–200. For more detail, see Lodge's letter to Roosevelt, 8 March 1897, in *Selections from the Correspondence of Theodore Roosevelt and Henry Cabot Lodge*, Vol. 1 (New York, 1925), pp. 252–254.
24. Leech, pp. 105–106; Morgan, p. 200. Leech and Morgan point also to regional representation as a factor in the appointment of Gary, Baltimore being counted as a gesture to "the South."

    These few sentences can provide only fragments of Payne's history. He was appointed postmaster of Milwaukee by President Grant and held that position for ten years. He left that job in 1885 with the accession of the Cleveland administration. Many years later, in 1900, after many important business and political efforts, he worked for Theodore Roosevelt's nomination to be McKinley's running mate. When Roosevelt became president, he "repaid his political debt" and chose Payne to be his postmaster general. See DAB, 14:326–327.
25. Kohlsaat, pp. 59–60; Morgan, pp. 200–201.
26. T. Bentley Mott, *Myron T. Herrick: Friend of France* (Garden City, NY, 1929), pp. 57–59.

    Burch also points to a big business connection, again suggesting influence: McKenna "had long been an intimate friend and loyal political supporter of railroad magnate Leland Stanford, and although this man had died several years earlier, it is unlikely that McKenna's basic economic views had shifted significantly in the interim." *Elites*, p. 139. A scholarly biography of the railroad magnate contains only a single sentence that mentions McKenna. He is listed there, along with six other men, as among Stanford's "closest friends" in Washington when Stanford served in the Senate. Norman E. Tutorow, *Leland Stanford: Man of Many Careers* (Menlo Park, CA, 1971), p. 283.

    McKenna served less than a year as attorney general. In December 1897, McKinley nominated him to be an associate justice of the Supreme Court. John W. Griggs, the governor of New Jersey, "a smart and sagacious lawyer who was close to Vice-President Hobart," was chosen as his replacement. Leech, p. 174.
27. Leech, p. 106; Gould, p. 14; Morgan, p. 201. The Morgan quotation is from the original edition, pp. 264–265.
28. Gould, p. 16; Morgan, p. 203. On Bliss, DAB, 2:369. McCook was a representative of American business interests in Cuba and also was connected with the Cuban Junta, supplying Assistant Secretary of State Day with materials provided by that organization. For this, see Philip S. Foner, *The Spanish-Cuban-American War and the Birth of American Imperialism 1895–1902*, Vol. 1 (New York, 1972), pp. 220–223.

    Mott misidentifies McCook, referring to him as Anson (*Herrick*, p. 58). Anson, a brother of John, was a prominent Episcopal clergyman based in Hartford, Connecticut. DAB, 11:603–604.

29. Hobart, Leech reports, was brought "into an integral relation with the administration." McKinley depended on his sound advice on many questions of government
policy," (p. 132).
30. Leech, p. 110; Gould, p. 19; Morgan, p. 204. Vice President Hobart died in November 1899, a position that remained vacant until March 1901, when filled by
Theodore Roosevelt.
31. These appointments also posed problems, ones requiring delicate negotiation.
Whitelaw Reid, another friend and sponsor, wanted the London position (to be
discussed below). New York's boss, Thomas Platt, had strongly opposed McKinley for the presidential nomination thus, under the ordinary rules, had reduced the
president-elect's obligation to the man. Platt, however, still made demands that
somehow had to be finessed. A dedicated enemy of Reid, Platt was adamantly
opposed to any concessions to the publisher's wishes. See Leech, pp. 108–110,
136–137 and Morgan, pp. 201–202. Morgan provides this summary observation:
"Diplomatic posts were often more open to politics than cabinet posts, for local
state leaders demanded such patronage in return for campaign funds and support"
(p. 268).
   The one-sentence descriptions of these men cannot begin to describe their careers
and achievements. In addition to founding Cornell, a remarkably advanced university, White had served as minister to Germany under Hayes and as minister to
Russia under Harrison. Tower, a lawyer and businessman, wrote a two-volume
biography of LaFayette (1895). He later served as minister to Russia and still later
was appointed, by Roosevelt, as ambassador to Germany (1902–1908). Hitchcock
followed Tower as minister to Russia. He later was named as Secretary of the Interior and continued in that office with Roosevelt. His great achievement there was
a prodigious "housekeeping" effort, that is, cleaning out corruption.
32. From John L. Offner, *An Unwanted War* (Chapel Hill, 1992), pp. 26, 22, and 40.
McKinley had great difficulty finding a candidate for the Spanish mission. He asked
John W. Foster, Henry White, Elihu Root, Jacob D. Cox, Seth Low, and Whitelaw
Reid, all of whom refused. New York's Senator Thomas C. Platt urged Woodford's
appointment. Offner, pp. 54–55. Woodford favored the Cuban insurgents. He was
listed, in 1897, as a member of the Cuban League and contributed to the insurgent
cause. He offered to withdraw when these facts became public but McKinley
declined. Woodford, it should be noted, performed very well in what was a very dif-
ficult mission. See also, DAB, 20:489–490 and ANB, 23:794.
33. Leech, p. 518. On the support for Rockhill, see Paul A. Varg, *Open Door Diplomat:
The Life of W. W. Rockhill* (Urbana, 1952), pp. 21–22. In May 1897, Varg reports,
McKinley appointed Rockhill, this eminent Far Eastern expert, as "Minister to
Greece, Rumania, and Servia, a diplomatic post of no vital interest to the United
States." Rockhill disliked the appointment but "had to accept for financial reasons."
   For a portrait of General Wilson, railroad entrepreneur, freelance writer, and
political operative, see Edward G. Longacre, *Grant's Cavalryman* (Mechanicsburg,
PA, 1996 [1972]), pp. 247–251. Wilson had traveled extensively in China, investigating rail line possibilities and had published a book on the subject. Longacre,
incidentally, gives a variant reading on the China appointment, indicating Wilson
as the disappointed candidate.
34. Varg, *Open Door Diplomacy*, pp. 42–44.
35. Samuel A. Schreiner, Jr., *Henry Clay Frick: The Gospel of Greed* (New York,
1995), p. 125.

36. George Harvey, *Henry Clay Frick: The Man* (New York, 1928), pp. 290–293. For the December 1896 efforts of Carnegie and Frick commending Knox to McKinley, see Joseph Frazier Wall, *Andrew Carnegie* (New York, 1970), pp. 644–645.

37. For a brief account, see ANB, 12:838–839. A note on a familiar cliché—"paying the piper." Frick had "supported Mr. Taft, as a 'regular,' from force of habit" giving through various channels some $50,000. When asked, late in the 1912 campaign, for additional support, he wrote back, refusing. He complained of the administration's unfair treatment of many of its warmest friends, mentioning specifically the suit against the United States Steel Corporation. For this, see Harvey, *Frick*, pp. 309–310.

38. Leech, pp. 567 and 13.

39. Leech, pp. 136–137; Morgan, pp. 201–202; and Duncan, *Reid*, pp. 167–173. In 1905, Theodore Roosevelt named him for a second tour as ambassador to Britain.

40. From Morris, *Rise of Theodore Roosevelt*, p. 559. For the deference to Foraker, see Leech, p. 138 and Walters, *Foraker*, p. 145.

41. Morgan, p. 200.

42. On this insurgency (and for the quotations), see Herbert Croly, *Marcus Alonzo Hanna* (Hamden, CT, 1965 [1912]), pp. 248–259. See also, Thomas Beer, *Hanna* (New York, 1929), pp. 183–188 and Walters, *Foraker*, pp. 136–140. For more, see Philip W. Warken, "The First Election of Marcus A. Hanna to the United States Senate" (Columbus, OH: unpublished M.A. thesis, The Ohio State University, 1960).

   There was another "pitched battle" between the Hanna and Foraker factions in June 1899. For a review of the later struggles in Ohio, see Walters, ch. 12. The attempt to displace Hanna in January 1898 was front-page news in Ohio newspapers, much use being made of the words "traitor" and "treason." For some more details, see ch. 6 below.

43. Croly, p. 252; Beer, p. 183; and Thomas F. Campbell and Edward M. Miggins, eds., *The Birth of Modern Cleveland, 1865–1930* (Cleveland, 1988), pp. 301–305.

44. Morgan, pp. 328–329. Another problem surfaced in this connection, one seen in connection with several other appointments: Root "risked an income in six figures for a government salary in four." For more on this appointment, see Philip C. Jessup, *Elihu Root*, Vol. 1 (New York, 1938), pp. 215–222. A remarkable array of participants became involved. New York Senator Thomas Platt, who disliked Root, had to be mollified. Cornelius Bliss and John Hay supported his appointment; Theodore Roosevelt was unenthusiastic, seeing the choice of a lawyer for the War Department as "simply foolish."

45. Burch, *Elites*, p. 142.

46. Michael Straight, Obituary, *New York Times*, 5 January 2004, A19.

47. Paul Sweezy, Obituary, *New York Times*, 2 March 2004, A25.

48. For this, and more, see David Rockefeller, *Memoirs* (New York, 2002), pp. 324–330. Nelson W. Aldrich, as seen, was a powerful United States Senator, the Republican boss of Rhode Island. Many years later, a great-grandson, then age sixteen, was attending St. Paul's, an elite preparatory school. His American history teacher suggested that he might want to "look into" the career of his illustrious ancestor and recommended Matthew Josephson's *Robber Barons* and Ferdinand Lundberg's *America's Sixty Families*. For "perspective," he also recommended *The Communist Manifesto*. His grandfather discovered these readings and attempted to make some correction. But the young man, now convinced that his ancestor was "an old crook,"

changed his planned history project and wrote instead on John Reed. The history teacher later became the principal of Exeter, another elite institution. For this, and more, see Nelson W. Aldrich, Jr., *Old Money: The Mythology of America's Upper Class* (New York, 1988), pp. 5–11. For a review of one famous instance of professorial influence, see Duane F. Alwin, Ronald L. Cohen, Theodore M. Newcomb, *Political Attitudes over the Life Span: The Bennington Women after Fifty Years* (Madison, WI, 1991). For the politics of professors (one, however, that does not measure influence), see Richard F. Hamilton and Lowell L. Hargens, "The Politics of the Professors: Self-Identifications, 1969–1984," *Social Forces*, 71 (1993):603–627.

For an account of one very rich and influential British-American family, several of whose members converted to socialism, see Christopher Sykes, *Nancy: The Life of Lady Astor* (London, 1971), pp. 451, 473, 478, 490–491, and 508 and Derek Wilson, *The Astors 1763–1992* (London, 1993), pp. 257–258, 332–336, 340–342, 356–359, 400–401.

4

The Decision for War

The Spanish-American War began with events in Cuba.[1] A war for independence had been fought there from 1868 to 1878, the Ten Years War, one that ended with a Spanish victory.[2] In 1895, the liberation struggle was renewed with many of the same leaders. General Maximo Gomez, who had lost the Ten Years War, now "employed a strategy of destroying the Cuban economy in order to persuade the Spanish to leave." The lesson drawn from his previous experience was that this rebellion "must be more savage if it was to succeed" and, accordingly, Gomez and his forces set out to turn the island into "an economic desert."[3]

Spain, at considerable cost, attempted to put down the rebellion, sending in large numbers of troops, ultimately the largest number ever sent to the new world. Given the elusive character of the struggle, with guerillas hiding among the civilian population, the military resorted to a standard practice, namely the resettlement of rural populations (here called *reconcentrado*). Reports of atrocities committed by the military followed, some of them accurate, some exaggerated, some fictional, all of this reported by the freedom-loving American press. The Cuban insurgents burned homes, plantation buildings, and crops and, of course, killed people. Both the insurgents and the Spanish used savage methods. The rebels "probably outdid their antagonists" in the commission of atrocities but this was not generally known since the press treatments of the war were remarkably one-sided.[4]

Most accounts of the Spanish-American War treat the Cuban insurgency as having an obvious cause—Spanish oppression—a fact requiring no further discussion or inquiry. But revolutions, on the whole, are rather complicated events. In other contexts, the sources, causes, or "preconditions" of such insurgencies have provided no end of material to challenge the thinking of subsequent commentators, academics, politicians, and revolutionaries. The antecedents in this case were reviewed in an important and much-cited source, Edwin Atkins' *Sixty Years in Cuba*. Atkins, a wealthy and politically influential Boston businessman, had a large sugar plantation in Cuba.

In the early 1880s, Atkins reports, Spain had a restrictive high tariff policy that gave preference to "Spanish goods in Spanish bottoms." The British evaded the policy through the use of British-owned "Spanish" ships and the transport of "Spanish" goods produced by British factories established in Spain. At that point, the United States sold little but coal and lumber to Cuba. That situation changed dramatically when the McKinley Tariff Law of 1890 put sugar on the free list and "included reciprocity provisions with Spain in regard to Cuba." Atkins claimed much of the credit for the reciprocity provisions, writing that they "were framed on almost the exact lines that I had outlined to [Secretary of State James] Blaine a few years before." The law provided a "tremendous stimulus" to sugar production and, obviously, to investment in that industry. But that stimulus disappeared in 1894 with the Wilson-Gorman Tariff that took sugar off the free list and abrogated the reciprocity arrangements.[5]

While that bill was pending, Atkins wrote to Senator Nelson Aldrich, among others, explaining the implications. The benefits of reciprocity, he reported, have "fully equaled the expectation of those interested in business between the United States and Cuba . . . a few years more of the present treaty [and] the United States will have the entire control of the markets of the Island, a condition which is more to be desired than annexation." Despite his efforts, however, the bill became law. Reciprocity ended and sugar was removed from the free list. Spain retaliated by returning to her old discrimination against United States imports to Cuba. Atkins summarized the impact on Cuba as follows: "[T]he cost of living . . . advanced and the price of sugar dropped, credit became impaired, the estates upon finishing their crop in 1895 discharged their hands, and the unrest flamed out into insurrection that ended in the Spanish-American War."[6]

The simplest of the formulas has it that Republicans favored high tariffs and Democrats favored low ones. Two important specifications should be noted. Republicans favored high tariffs *and* reciprocity, as was the case with the McKinley Tariff. A high tariff did protect American industry. The reciprocity clause provided an incentive for other protectionist nations to change their ways. If they opened their markets, the United States would do the same. The Cuban experience was exemplary.

The Democrats' tariff policy had an important correlate. The tariff produced a sizable part of federal government revenues, which meant that when tariff reductions were made other revenue sources had to be found to cover the shortfall. The Wilson-Gorman Tariff Act, accordingly, also provided for an income tax. Some conservatives, however, saw the income tax as a dangerous precedent. It was contested and quickly struck down by the Supreme Court. The tariff-tax connection would appear subsequently in Woodrow Wilson's administration. This time the problem was solved by a constitutional amendment that allowed the income tax.

The Wilson-Gorman Tariff Act provides a striking example of mismanaged legislation. Following the Democratic Party's program, the intent was to lower tariffs. The combination of ineffectual presidential leadership and lobbyists' zeal, however, produced a hodgepodge law with some 600 amendments. Cleveland was so dismayed at the product that he let it become law without his signature. This act of Congress proved to be helpful for the Cuban insurgency. The removal of sugar from the free list led directly to the discharge of farm laborers, many of whom, lacking other opportunities, found employment in the ranks of the insurgents. Joblessness "freed" the former farm laborers for the revolutionary tasks. Had matters continued as per Atkins's plan, the insurgents would have had difficulty finding willing recruits.[7]

One other consequence of the new tariff law should be noted. The removal of sugar from the free list clearly penalized American investors in Cuba. But that same provision meant roughly equivalent gains for sugar producers in the United States. It is not as if "capitalists" generally would have been faced with losses; some would have welcomed the change. Many others, those with investments in other areas, might well have been either indifferent or opposed to taking action, that is, unwilling to pay any "price" for regaining the Cuban opportunity. The exclusion of Cuban sugar, it should also be noted, would probably have meant some price increase, that is, a cost for American consumers.

From 1890 to 1894 American investors in Cuba had achieved a very satisfactory arrangement within the framework of Spanish sovereignty. Subsequently, with the developing difficulties, Atkins favored Cuban autonomy under continued Spanish sovereignty as opposed to annexation by the United States, a position stated repeatedly in his text. The first of several reads: "In the course of time I came to believe that autonomy was the only solution of the trouble, and while in the North, I worked in Washington toward this end and was able to continue my work for autonomy in Cuba [through] channels kept open to me." Writing from Cuba in mid-January 1898, he reported that he "found no opposition to autonomy anywhere." At the same time, however, he reported that, "a general sentiment now pervades the whole community for annexation. It is particularly strong among the Spaniards. All the better class Cubans fear independence." But as late as 11 April that year, Atkins still expected "a most liberal autonomy."[8]

Atkins estimated the American investment in Cuba at $30,000,000.[9] Early in 1898, one of the first steps in the movement toward war was the appropriation of $50,000,000 by the U.S. Congress. Later, of course, the costs, in money and men, went much higher. After the Teller Amendment, which prohibited an American takeover, Congress passed the Platt Amendment, which provided for an American "right" of intervention. The result, as of 1903, was an arrangement allowing "informal empire."[10] Had Congress rejected the problematic terms of the Wilson-Gorman Act in 1894, the existing investment pattern in Cuba would probably have continued and developed further. The 1898 war required payment of considerable costs for a result that was in place in Cuba in 1894, one that had been quickly and easily achieved.

The Cuban struggle began during President Grover Cleveland's second term of office. His popularity had suffered greatly due to the Panic of 1893 and his handling of the resulting problems. One consequence, as seen earlier, was the sizable Republican gain in the House of Representatives in the 1894 elections. Some public clamor developed over Cuba and Republican leaders made ample use of the opportunity. John L. Offner sums up as follows: "At the heart of the Cuban issue was partisan politics and the approaching election." Ohio's Senator John Sherman, a prominent Republican, one with presidential aspirations (and later McKinley's Secretary of State), was especially vociferous. The Spanish, he declared, were "barbarous robbers and imitators of the worst men who ever lived in the world." The American people, he announced, would soon intervene "to put an end to crimes . . . almost beyond description." His examples of "butchery and rape," however, were based on a *New York Journal* source, on an account soon proven false. Many Democrats, for other unrelated reasons, were disenchanted with Cleveland's leadership and some of them also joined in this enthusiasm for Cuban independence. President Cleveland and his Secretary of State, Richard Olney, conducted their foreign policy within this inauspicious context. Their policy, which proved remarkably consistent, favored nonintervention and continued Spanish rule. Olney told the Spanish minister, Dupuy de Lôme, that the United States opposed independence for Cuba. He did not view the insurgents as capable of self-rule and urged Spain to put a quick end to the uprising.[11]

In January 1896, Senator John Tyler Morgan, a Democrat from Alabama and an ardent expansionist, introduced a resolution calling for recognition of Cuban belligerency. Senator Don Cameron, Pennsylvania's Republican "boss," introduced a resolution calling for recognition of Cuban independence. The two motions were subsequently joined and debated for several months. The bipartisan resolution was passed in the House in April 1896. It called for recognition of Cuban belligerency, a move that would give equal status to both parties in the conflict, one that in effect recognized the revolutionary government. The proposal gained overwhelming support in both the Senate and House but, as a concurrent resolution had no practical importance. It was little more than an expression of opinion.[12]

Senator Morgan claimed wide popular support; the public wanted Congress to act. He introduced thirty-nine petitions "from all parts of country," adding that "the House had many more." Representative Robert Adams, Jr., chairman of the House Subcommittee on Cuba, said that his older colleagues could not recall "an issue that had aroused so much public support." Another member noted that "only the business community opposed congressional action." The subsequent Senate and House votes of approval, Offner notes, "contained a political message. The Republicans had succeeded in an election year in demonstrating greater commitment than the White House to Cuba . . ."[13]

After the 1896 election, during the rump session, the Senate Foreign Relations Committee passed another Cameron resolution, one that would "acknowledge" the independence of the Cuban Republic. It carried unanimously in the committee. The authors anticipated a Cleveland veto, a congressional override, and de facto recognition. But Olney quickly put an end to this, declaring that the resolution, even if passed over the president's veto, would have no force since under the Constitution the power to recognize a state rested "exclusively with the Executive." The event also provided some evidence of business sentiment. On clearing the committee, the resolution caused "a war scare, and stocks tumbled in New York and London."[14]

William McKinley was sworn in as president in March 1897. The House of Representatives and the Senate at that point were controlled by the Republicans, the latter by a very thin margin.[15] With the party of "big business" in power, supposedly, it would be easy—especially for distant observers—to conclude that the demand for war "reflected" their interests. But that conclusion would be mistaken. The Republicans, said to be the "party of big business," did push Cuban initiatives during the last years of Cleveland's presidency. But with McKinley in office, the pressures for intervention came largely from the Democrats.

Most Americans—it is said—favored Cuban independence. Most were opposed to continued Spanish rule, which was depicted as backward, authoritarian, and increasingly ruthless. The Monroe Doctrine was frequently invoked, the sense being that Spain, a tottering European power, should now, finally, give up its holdings in the Western hemisphere. That aim, sending the Spaniards home, could be achieved either by informal pressure, by negotiation or, ultimately, by war. There was, understandably, much division of sentiment over this issue. It was easy, in principle, to favor Cuban independence but the unforeseeable costs of military involvement could be considerable. Those estimates of public sentiment, it should be noted, were based on small and erratic "samples." With systematic public opinion polling still several decades away, politicians, newspapers, and magazines could easily claim sweeping support for their positions.

Many accounts portray that public clamor as large and insistent, a "force" that could not possibly be ignored. Ivan Musicant dates it from March 1895 when a Spanish gunboat fired on the *Alliança*, an American merchant vessel traveling six miles off the Cuban coast on route to New York City. "From every section of the country," he writes, "the press lavished rivers of headline ink on the incident, heralding a campaign of Spanish vilification that continued almost unabated for more than three years."[16]

The quantity and quality of messages coming to the president's attention give a markedly different picture of public sentiments. In the first three months of his presidency, McKinley's "Current Comment" scrapbook (newspaper clippings) contained only two Cuban references and only three letters on the subject. In that period, McKinley's

> . . . clippings and mail, like his thoughts, dealt with questions of patronage and jobs, both matters of greater political importance than revolution in Cuba.
> In the summer of 1897, McKinley finally turned his attention to Cuba, only to find that it commanded virtually no public interest. By then, even the few clippings and letters of the preceding months had disappeared from view, and there existed little if any public pressure upon the president to take steps to end the rebellion.[17]

McKinley exerted some pressure on Spain in the fall of 1897 to end the Cuban struggle. But even then, "he labored under little public pressure to intervene in Cuba. The public's interest in the island seemed at its ebb—a fact again apparent in the president's mailbags and scrapbooks . . ." From 2 June to 1 December 1897, Hilderbrand reports, McKinley again received only three letters from the public dealing with Cuba.[18]

The public clamor began with events in mid-January 1898. Even then, however, questions remain both as to the size and direction of those demands. In mid-April, McKinley's secretary, George M. Cortelyou, claimed that "at least 90 percent of the mail coming to the White House had supported the President's pacific course." His view was that: "The ranters in Congress, the blatherskites who do the talking upon the street-corners and at public meetings, and the scavengers of the sensational press misrepresent public opinion . . . when they assert that this country is for war except as a necessity and for the upholding of the national honor."[19]

The decisions for war and for territorial expansion are separate and distinct themes. Logically (and politically), the effort to liberate the Cubans could not end with the annexation of that island's population. This logic was emphatically supported when the Senate passed the Teller Amendment forbidding a takeover. On completion of the war, however, the question of "possessions" quickly surfaced. The war fought for Cuban independence ended with the acquisition of Puerto Rico and the Philippines. Simultaneously negotiations were begun to purchase the Virgin Islands from Denmark. The Hawaiian Islands, which had never been Spanish and were in not in any way involved in the struggle over Cuba struggle, became an American possession in a separate move just before the conflict ended.

The immediate policy options for the United States with respect to Cuba were:

First, non-involvement: The United States would not engage in Spanish and Cuban affairs. This, as seen, was the basic position of Cleveland and Olney.[20]

Second, Cuban autonomy (or home rule) with continued Spanish sovereignty, this to be achieved through negotiations and increased pressure on Spain. The advocates of this position cited the example of Canada, which since 1867 was an autonomous state within the British Empire. This position was emphatically rejected by the Cuban insurgents.

Third, Cuban independence, to be achieved through negotiations with and pressure on Spain. The Spanish government rejected this option and, as indicated, so did Cleveland and Olney.

Fourth, Cuban independence to be achieved through American intervention. This might involve official recognition of the insurgents and the granting of belligerency status (which would allow support, financial and military). It might, ultimately, mean direct U.S. military involvement. These choices were favored by some newspapers, by some politicians, and to some degree, it was said, by an aroused populace.

Fifth, support for Cuban "independence"—but with a hidden agenda, subsequent annexation by the United States.[21]

Most businessmen, as will be seen, favored the first of these options and some others preferred the second. Some persons who, early on, favored those options, later came to favor the third or fourth. One could favor "a war" without at the same time favoring expansion or imperialism, as for example was the case with William Jennings Bryan and Andrew Carnegie. Some people favored the fifth option, annexation. Some politicians and some Protestant clergy, for very different reasons, were of this persuasion. These are not the only possibilities. One could oppose the war but later see some advantages in the unexpected outcomes. Many businessmen, it is said, subsequently saw important gains in the Hawaii-Philippines-China linkage.

The causal processes involved in the two episodes, the origins and the outcomes, are markedly different. The events leading up to the war, effectively up to April of 1898, will be considered in this work. Those involving the outcome, the ending of hostilities, the signing of the Protocol on 12 August 1898, and the Paris peace conference where in December 1898 Spain ceded the Philippines to the United States, will be considered in a subsequent volume.

The American Revolution provided one part of the framework for interpretation of the Cuban struggle. Americans had been taught the lessons of freedom and independence in the schools, these reinforced in speeches at annual Fourth of July celebrations. When Cubans began their struggle against "Spanish tyranny," the effort was given sympathetic treatment in many newspapers and magazines. Given the dispositions, those evident earlier in Americans' support for Hungarian and Italian independence, the efforts in support of the Cuban insurgents, it is said, found a ready response. That assumption should, of course, be viewed as a hypothesis. And several related questions require consideration: How many, what portion of the citizenry responded to those appeals? Who responded—which persons or groups were so moved? Also, there is a prior question, that of agency: Which persons, groups, or media carried "the message" to the American populace?

The agitation for Cuban independence was the work of an unusual coalition of five diverse segments. These were: first, an organized pressure group; second, some important newspaper publishers; third, some Protestant denominations and clergy; fourth, a collection of politicians, most of them United States senators; and fifth, a small group of notables, most of them operating within the national government. These statements should be viewed as hypotheses. And, it should be noted, we have no precise measures of their influence, that is, how much impact each made in determining the outcome, the choice of war.

The pressure group, the Cuban Revolution Party, for short called the Junta, was an agency of the insurgent Cubans. In 1895 they established two centers, one in Washington the other in New York City, from which to conduct propaganda activities. The Junta also established a counterpart organization for American sympathizers, the Cuban League, with affiliated clubs operating throughout the United States. The League organized large meetings at which the Cuban position was advocated, with both Cuban and American supporters speaking for the cause. "Middle Western newspapers," it is reported, "gave unstintedly of their space and support to such assemblies at Chicago, Philadelphia, Cleveland, New York City, Cincinnati, Columbus, Detroit, and elsewhere. These gatherings were addressed usually by prominent local personages . . ." The organization, of course, also collected money for the cause.[22]

Reporters in New York and Washington "were encouraged to call each day" at the Junta's headquarters where "they received *gratis* the 'news' of the latest developments of the revolution." This included generous accounts of Spanish atrocities. With few reporters present in Cuba and no equivalent provision of "news" by Spanish authorities, the result was rather one-sided with editors cooperating in "depicting Spanish barbarities through editorial, cartoon, and verse."[23] The insurgents conducted filibustering expeditions, that is, deliveries of arms and ammunition to Cuba, those shipments originating from American soil. The Junta sought press support for these actions, the aim being opposition to the government's efforts to maintain its neutrality by blocking those expeditions. The Junta obtained the "de Lôme letter" and passed it on to

Hearst's *Journal*. The publication of that letter, on 9 February 1898, was one of several important antecedents to the war.[24]

The Cuban events were reported, in one way or another, by the nation's press. In New York City, the Cuban events gained special attention as a result of a newspaper war initiated by William Randolph Hearst. The publisher purchased the New York *Journal* in 1895 and, following the techniques he had used earlier in San Francisco, proceeded to gain circulation through sob stories, scandal, and sensationalism. His effort, for the most part, was directed against another popular, sensationalist newspaper, Joseph Pulitzer's *World*. When Hearst made use of the events in Cuba to further his aims, Pulitzer responded, as best he could, with a matching effort. Many accounts begin and end with the Hearst-Pulitzer press war. But their efforts had much wider ramifications. The New York *Sun* and the New York *Herald* also had "yellow" tendencies and they too sent reporters to Cuba. These four newspapers then sold their news and pictures to outlets elsewhere. The Chicago *Tribune* used the syndicated material of both the *Journal* and *World*. The Boston *Herald* and the Chicago *Times-Herald* used the New York *Herald* material. Hearst's material flowed as a matter of course to his San Francisco *Examiner*. The San Francisco *Chronicle* was supplied by the New York *Herald* and the *Sun*. The Associated Press transmitted material from all of these newspapers to outlets elsewhere. The AP also had its own reporters in Cuba. Many other newspapers had discovered that yellow journalism could help achieve financial success. The diverse contributions of "the press" will be reviewed in the following chapter.

The third segment of this coalition consisted of Protestant denominations and clergy. Spain did not allow Protestant missionaries within its possessions. The combination—Catholic Spain, tales of the Inquisition, the denial of access, plus the reports of atrocities—are said to have provided material for sermons. This subject, unfortunately, is very poorly researched. Pratt documents the positions of the various denominations as shown in their official publications. Evidence on sermons, however, is at best fugitive. Some sense of the impact, though, appears in a biography of Hanna. The man who beat Bryan, the biographer writes, "could not cope with women who were asking the pastor to write to Mr. McKinley about Cuba, and making children sign petitions to be sent to Congressmen." In January 1898, the president's brother wrote: "You have no idea of the pressure on William from religious people."[25]

The fourth segment of this interventionist coalition was a group of politicians, many of them members of the United States Senate. Among those active in 1897 and 1898 were Cushman K. Davis (Republican, Minnesota), Henry Cabot Lodge, (Republican, Massachusetts), William E. Chandler (Republican, New Hampshire), William P. Frye, (Republican, Maine), Joseph Foraker (Republican, Ohio), and John Tyler Morgan (Democrat, Alabama). Beginning in May 1897, Davis was the chairman of the Senate Foreign Relations Committee. Senators Foraker, Frye, Lodge, and Morgan were also members of that committee with Lodge heading its Cuba Subcommittee.[26] In addition, six "silver" Republican senators favored recognition of Cuban belligerency and independence. These were Henry Teller (Colorado), Richard Pettigrew (South Dakota), Lee Mantle (Montana), Frank Cannon (Utah), William Stewart (Nevada), and Frank Jones (Nevada). Most of these men, it should be noted, were interventionists who favored Cuban independence, not its annexation.

The fifth group, a loose coterie, convened for regular lunches at Washington's Metropolitan Club. Its unofficial leader was Theodore Roosevelt who as of April 1897 was the Assistant Secretary of the Navy in the McKinley administration. Several other members of the coterie worked in the executive branch and they also had some links with members of the senatorial group. Roosevelt's close friend, Henry Cabot Lodge, had ties with this coterie. It was largely through the senator's effort that Roosevelt had gained his position in the executive branch. Lodge had written the sentences in the 1896 Republican platform expressing sympathy for the "Cuban patriots" in their struggle against Spanish "cruelty and oppression." Senators Chandler and Frye were regulars along with Don Cameron, who, until March 1897, was a Republican senator from Pennsylvania. Also present were Commander Charles H. Davis, the chief of Naval Intelligence, and Clarence King, a member of the old John Hay-Henry Adams circle.

This group also had connections elsewhere. Representing the "Roosevelt point of view" in New York and London were, respectively, Charles A. Dana, editor of the *Sun*, and John Hay, then ambassador to the Court of St. James. Roosevelt was in active correspondence with Captain Alfred Mahan, whose extensive writings focused on issues of naval strategy. Mahan taught at the Navy War College and had influenced a generation of young officers. Whitelaw Reid, publisher of the New York *Tribune*, the Republican flagship newspaper, was a member of this group. He was later to be a member of the peace commission, the body that arranged the acquisition of the Philippines. Albert Shaw, the editor of the influential *Review of Reviews*, was a good friend of Roosevelt's. Commodore George Dewey was also involved with this circle. Later, through Roosevelt's adept intervention, Dewey was given command of the Far Eastern Squadron. The members of this coterie were proponents of the war effort within both the executive and legislative branches. Many of them, later, were active supporters of the subsequent annexations.[27]

Most of the individuals and groups concerned with the Cuban question, it should be noted, were arguing on humanitarian grounds. The problem was Spanish oppression and for these critics the solution was Cuban independence. Even Henry Cabot Lodge, who is often portrayed as a leading expansionist, took this position. The Republican Party platform statement, which he authored, called for the United States to "actively use its influence and good offices to restore peace and give independence to the Island." The previously discussed Cameron resolution demanded Cuban independence, not annexation. The "expansionists" among them had their eyes on different targets, those being strategic as opposed to economic. The Republican platform spelled out these aims, saying that the United States should control the Hawaiian Islands, should build, own, and operate the Nicaragua Canal, and should purchase the Danish Islands so as to "secure a much needed Naval station in the West Indies."[28]

The word coalition normally assumes contact, communication, and planning among the partners. But with one exception, this was not the case for these five groups. They were basically separate collectivities that early in 1898 favored the same general policy. Two of these groups were not on cordial terms. The Metropolitan Club group was Republican, many members with upper class backgrounds, many seeing themselves as defenders of culture and good taste. The two leading "yellow" newspapers, the *Journal* and *World*, were Democratic. Both publications made generous use of antiestablishment themes and both were of low intellectual quality.

The Cuban *Junta* was the obvious exception to this rule of "non-connectedness." The task of a pressure group, after all, is to "make connections." The organization supplied "news" to anyone willing to receive it, created support groups to disseminate their views and to collect funds, and was active in lobbying. One account details meetings of *Junta* members with Henry Adams and Lodge at the home of a neighbor, Senator Don Cameron. Those meetings led to the congressional resolution of January 1896 favoring American endorsement of Cuban independence and subsequently to Senator Cameron's provocative resolution in December of that year calling for U.S. intervention. The Cameron papers show that the Cubans addressed their letters to the senator's wife, Elizabeth Cameron, a procedure that would allow her husband and Lodge to deny direct contacts.[29]

The Hay-Adams circle broke up early in 1897 when Hay went to London as ambassador to the Court of St. James. Senator Cameron did not stand for reelection in 1896, having been deserted by the Pennsylvania Republicans (there was an alcohol problem). Henry Adams was an ardent interventionist in 1896. But in 1898, he and Hay, along with several others, were in Egypt on a Nile cruise from mid-January until the end of February when news of the *Maine* arrived. Unmoved, however, the group continued on to Athens. Hay then returned to London while Adams proceeded to Smyrna and later to Constantinople, to "study the antiquities of the Near East." He wrote his brother, Brooks Adams, that: "For two years, the Cuban business drove me wild. [Now] I've no more to do with it."[30]

The diverse pressures generated by this coalition converged on the president. McKinley was urged to recognize and support the Cuban insurgents or, the more ambitious demand, he should call on Congress for a declaration of war on Spain. McKinley, however, was opposed to American intervention and did all he could to avoid it.[31] McKinley's basic aim was to negotiate a settlement, one that would lead either immediately or in the short term to Spain's voluntary withdrawal. To achieve this aim, he undertook a range of initiatives, moves that in effect escalated the costs for Spain. It was a delicate operation. McKinley had to initiate these policies and plan responses to Spanish countermoves. And, at the same time, he had to restrain the demands of the Junta, of the "jingoes" in Congress, and of some important American newspapers.

Some congressional leaders saw the Cuban events providing opportunities for partisan advantage. That was the case with the Cameron resolution of December 1896, which had a clear political intent. The interventionists in the Senate Foreign Relations Committee sought to embarrass Cleveland. But that aim was thwarted by Olney's astute countermove and the resolution never went to the full Senate.[32]

A third attempt by members of Congress came in March of 1897. This effort was initiated by the Democrats, although it had significant Republican support. Alabama's Senator Morgan introduced a resolution recognizing Cuban belligerency, this in the same language as the April 1896 resolution. It was debated in April and May and ultimately carried in the Senate. The Democrats and Populists voted overwhelmingly for it. The Republicans were divided, eighteen in favor and twelve against, but with the majority abstaining. Some Republicans favored the motion but felt that such a test at this early point was unfair to the new president. In the House, Speaker Reed blocked its consideration and the resolution died.[33]

In his efforts over the coming months, McKinley had the support of many prominent Senate Republicans, most of them "stalwarts," the party's loyalists. This included the party's leaders, a group known as "The Four," Senators William Allison, Nelson Aldrich, Orville Platt, and John Spooner. In addition he could count on Hanna, Stephen Elkins, Thomas Platt, and several others. The Foreign Relations Committee, however, posed the most serious problem. Offner writes that the chairman, Cushman Davis, was "staunchly pro-Cuban, and all but one of his committee members shared that view." Up to thirteen of the forty-eight Republican senators, Offner reports, "were inclined to support the Junta's cause." In the House, the speaker, Thomas B. Reed, although not personally sympathetic to McKinley, provided the president with important backing. But McKinley and his supporters had limited control over the events in his first year of office or, put more precisely, they had limited control over the readings given to those events.[34]

Early in 1898 five events occurred that are said to have led to changes in both public and elite opinion. These were the riots in Havana led by colons and Spanish army personnel opposed to autonomy (January 12), the publication of the de Lôme letter (February 9), the explosion and sinking of the *Maine* in Havana Harbor (February 15), Senator Proctor's report on conditions in Cuba (March 17), and publication of the investigating committee's report on the loss of the *Maine* (March 28). The *Maine* catastrophe, understandably, was easily the most important of the five events.

In response to each of these events McKinley sought calm and delay hoping that the Spanish authorities would make the decisive concession. The Spanish government did concede much, instituting on 1 January 1898 a plan for Cuban autonomy, that is, for self-government in local affairs but with continued Spanish direction of foreign policy and trade. It also announced a willingness to end military operations—but only after a prior cessation by the insurgents. But the Spanish leaders did not concede on the key issue, that of independence, and the insurgents would accept nothing short of independence.[35]

McKinley's message to Congress was originally scheduled to be delivered on 5 April but, to allow the evacuation of Americans in Cuba and still hoping for concession, he postponed it until the 11th. The message, a long, complex statement, asked Congress for authority to intervene in Cuba, basically to bring peace to the island. The message did not call for war with Spain. Congress responded with the joint resolution on Cuba that was passed on 19 April. It "called for Cuban independence, immediate Spanish withdrawal from Cuba, and, if necessary, intervention by the armed forces of the United States. It disclaimed any American intention to absorb Cuba." The resolution, it should be noted, did not recognize the Cuban insurgents. The president signed the resolution on 21 April and Spain promptly broke off diplomatic relations. McKinley ordered a naval blockade of Cuba on 22 April. On the next day, Spain declared war. And on 25 April McKinley asked Congress for a declaration of war, a request that was speedily approved. The declaration was backdated to 21 April, the date henceforth taken as the beginning of hostilities.[36]

McKinley's message to Congress avoided recognition of the "so-called Cuban Republic."[37] An amendment put forth by Senators Turpie and Foraker sought to override the president on this point. It carried in the Senate but was defeated in the House. The struggle over the amendment allows insight into the underlying political motives. Senator David Turpie was a Democrat from Indiana. Senator Joseph Foraker was a prominent Republican and, like Hanna, McKinley, and Sherman, was from Ohio. But he was also a jingo, a presidential aspirant, and, as seen, an opponent of the McKinley-Hanna forces within the state. The measure was "designed in part to embarrass the President and in part to seize the initiative from him." It was seen as a Democratic measure—

twenty-nine of them voted for it, five against. It also had the support of eleven Populists and a handful of "silver" Republicans. Another resolution, one of considerable importance, the Teller Amendment, rejected annexation of Cuba by the United States. It carried easily in both chambers.[38]

Over the months, the pressures of press, pulpit, and public had moved some Republicans to the interventionist position. In the House of Representatives, the party had a solid majority that was under the direction of Speaker Reed— 204 seats, as against an opposition of 153 Democrats and Populists. The problem was in the Senate. The Republicans had forty-seven seats, the Democrats had thirty-four, and there were seven others (mainly Populists). That 47 to 41 edge, however, was tenuous given the presence of several Silver Republicans in their ranks and some others of doubtful loyalty. Garrett Hobart, the vice president (and presiding officer of the Senate) warned McKinley: "I can no longer hold back the Senate. They will act without you if you do not act at once." Many of those backing the president feared that inaction would be costly in the off-year elections coming in November that year. A committee representing some forty or fifty members of the Republican House caucus told the president that the party faced disastrous defeat unless he acquiesced to war. Lodge wrote the president, on 21 March, predicting that "if the war in Cuba drags on through the summer with nothing done we should go down to the greatest defeat ever known. . . ." It was those political considerations, the erosion of support within his own party and the fear of electoral losses that led McKinley finally to acquiesce to the demands for intervention. Offner summarized as follows: "In the final analysis, Republicans made war on Spain in order to keep control of Washington." And, in another statement: "But in the end, it was these [domestic political] pressures that brought about military intervention. Republican legislators made war on Spain not to obtain control of Cuba but to retain control of Washington."[39]

McKinley left virtually no written record of his thoughts or motives. But on two occasions, in private conversations, he reviewed his position. McKinley's friend and supporter, H. H. Kohlsaat, the Chicago newspaper publisher, provided an account of a meeting with the president in the spring of 1898. McKinley had requested the visit that took place in the White House. Kohlsaat describes the event as follows: "He was in much distress, and said: 'I have been through a trying period. Mrs. McKinley has been in poorer health than usual. It seems to me I have not slept over three hours a night for over two weeks. Congress is trying to drive us into war with Spain. The Spanish fleet is in Cuban waters, and we haven't enough ammunition on the Atlantic seacoast to fire a salute." At that point, Kohlsaat writes, "He broke down and cried like a boy of thirteen." By this account also, the impetus for war came from Congress with the president obviously showing considerable reluctance.[40]

A year later, McKinley reviewed these events in an extended discussion with another associate, Henry S. Pritchett, who had supplied maps for the president's war room. His account reports:

> The matter of which the President spoke with most feeling was his conviction that, if he had been left alone, he could have concluded an arrangement with the Spanish Government under which the Spanish troops would have withdrawn from Cuba without a war. Of this he spoke with great frankness, stating most explicitly his conviction that, but for the inflamed state of public opinion and the fact that Congress could no longer be held in check, a peaceful solution might have been had.

After reviewing the outcome of the war and the questions of annexations, McKinley returned to the war's origins, to the events of April. Pritchett summarizes as follows:

> The President spoke with more earnestness and with more definiteness as to his regret for the war itself than as to the complications which arose from it. There could be no question of his firm belief that, if left alone, he could have settled the matter without a war. The situation in Congress finally came to a point where, in his opinion, it was impossible for him to stop the war current. What the causes were which led up to this condition he did not indicate with great definiteness, otherwise than to mention incidentally the incessant newspaper agitation, the emotionalism of certain members of the House and of the Senate, and the stampeding of Congress under the impression that the country was demanding immediate hostilities. Whether this spirit could have been dealt with successfully by a man made of sterner stuff than President McKinley, it would be difficult at this time to say.[41]

The Kohlsaat and Pritchett accounts both justify Offner's summary conclusion—that the war was undertaken for a political purpose, to "keep control of Washington."

The nation's leading business leaders, it will be noted, were not involved with any of the five segments of the pro-intervention coalition. They do not appear to have made any contribution to the effort that led to the passage of the joint resolution. One should, accordingly, address this question: Where did "big business" stand on this issue? An answer to that question was provided, seventy years ago, by an eminent historian, Julius W. Pratt, a leading specialist on American expansionism. His answer was that business leaders opposed the venture. Here is his summary statement:

> That business sentiment, especially in the East, was strongly anti-war at the close of 1897 and in the opening months of 1898, is hardly open to doubt. Wall Street stocks turned downward whenever the day's news seemed to presage war and climbed again with information favorable to peace. . . . The "jingo" in Congress or the press, was an object of intense dislike to the editors of business and financial journals, who sought to counteract his influence by anti-war editorials in their

columns. Boards of trade and chambers of commerce added their pleas for the maintenance of peace to those of the business newspapers and magazines. So marked, indeed, was the anti-war solidarity of the financial interests and their spokesmen that the jingoes fell to charging Wall Street with want of patriotism.[42]

Pratt's review of business opinion begins with a comment on Mark Hanna: "No one was more unwilling than he to see the United States drift into war with Spain." Herbert Croly, Hanna's biographer, is quoted: "[T]he outbreak of war seemed to imperil the whole policy of domestic economic amelioration which he placed before every other object of political action." Hanna's opposition is reported also in Beer. One source reports a conversation with the senator, summarizing as follows: "His own aversion to a war was very plain. He said the economic condition of the country was just beginning to improve and that a war was undesirable from every point of view. . . . He was strongly in favor of getting the Cubans freed. But he said five or six times, 'I hate the thought of a war.' "[43]

In a supporting footnote, Pratt referred to biographies of four business leaders, steel manufacturer Andrew Carnegie, banker Jacob H. Schiff, and railroad magnates James J. Hill and E. H. Harriman, which he says attest to their antiwar sentiments. A fifth person, John Wanamaker, the department store proprietor, Pratt reported, was an exception, in that he "supported the war and raised a regiment." Pratt erred in his depiction of Carnegie's position, in his statement that to the surprise of many, Carnegie was not "strongly anti-war" but instead enthusiastically supported the military intervention. The problem stemmed from deficiencies in the two sources Pratt used.[44] More details on Carnegie's position will be provided below.

Pratt's statement about Wanamaker is misleading and misses some nuances. In mid-April 1898, Wanamaker telegraphed Alger, McKinley's Secretary of War, saying that he was "opposed to war, 'unless honorably unavoidable' . . ." When the war could no longer be avoided, he indicated his active support. His biographer writes that: "While opposed to war, if any peaceable means could be found to settle the Cuban question and deploring efforts of the 'yellow press' to force President McKinley's hand, Wanamaker let it be understood that he was ready to stand whole-heartedly behind the decision of Congress. He never made a secret of his hatred of war, and he abhorred jingoism. . . . [He] had always been interested in the movement for the emancipation of Cuba and had shown his sympathy with Cuban revolutionaries whenever the opportunity offered." Although opposed to war, it should be added, he "thought that military training was a splendid thing for young people."[45] The pages Pratt cited in the Schiff and Harriman biographies do not contain any information on their attitudes toward the coming of the war.[46]

Hill's position on the issue of the war and its antecedents deserves further attention. Early in 1898, Hill, whose home was in Minneapolis, wrote to a Minnesota congressman:

> From a national standpoint our blunder was first in bringing foreign matters, like Cuba and Venezuela, or the interests of any other outside people who have no interest or sympathy with us, national or otherwise, into our political contentions and making their conditions a part of our national platforms. Both parties have been guilty of the sin, and both parties ought to suffer the consequences. If we could learn to mind our own business it would save us a great deal of trouble.

That said, Hill then proceeded to the immediate lesson. After the destruction of the *Maine*, which he attributed to the duplicity of the Spanish government, he declared "there should be no halting or doubt as to the loyal support of the Government in whatever direction Congress and the President may find best. . . . We must now put on a bold front and bring the matter to a definite close." A later biography of Hill, by Albro Martin, contains nothing on the conflict. The index contains no references to Cuba, Spain, the Spanish-American War, the Philippines, or China. The pages covering the relevant years, 1895–1899, are devoted to reorganization plans for the Northern Pacific and the Great Northern Railroads. A still later biography, by Michael P. Malone, sums up his position in a single sentence: Hill "bristled at jingoism and nationalism and fit well the judgment of the school of historians who emphasize the fact that businessmen opposed war with Spain in 1898."[47]

If Lenin's claims about the imperatives of "monopoly capital" were accurate, businessmen and bankers should have been ardent proponents of the war and of the subsequent annexations. Given the urgent need for colonies, that issue ought to figure prominently in the biographical accounts. But Pratt reported an opposite finding: "Biographies of Morgan, Rockefeller, Frick, Robert Bacon do not discuss the attitude of those men to the war or imperialism." That conclusion, as will be seen immediately, holds also for many subsequent accounts. The imperialism issue appears to have been a very peripheral concern for these men.[48]

Three of the most important figures of American business at that point were John Pierpont Morgan, Andrew Carnegie, and John D. Rockefeller. The former, an investment banker, was the nation's leading "finance capitalist." As head of the House of Morgan he had reorganized railroads, sold American securities throughout Europe, and calmed investors in the Panic of 1893. Subsequently, he would organize some of the nation's leading firms—American Telephone and Telegraph, U.S. Steel, International Harvester, and General Electric. Carnegie was the proprietor of Carnegie Steel, by far the largest firm in the industry. And Rockefeller was head of Standard Oil, by far the nation's largest firm in that industry.

Two comprehensive histories describe the operations of the Morgan firm. The first, by Vincent P. Carosso, gives only a single page to the war: "Like many other Wall Street bankers, Morgan had hoped that the conflict might be avoided. He considered it pointless." Morgan and two other firms did however make separate offers to handle a $200 million war loan. But these were refused, a decision that tells something about the firm's power. The loan was "sold to the public, with small individual and institutional buyers taking most of it." The second account, by Ron Chernow, has only a brief paragraph on the Spanish-American War. The attitude toward the war is covered in a single sentence: "The Morgans had opposed the war, and Jack [the banker's son] . . . lamented the 'needless waste of life & property.'" The war, clearly, did not figure prominently in the affairs of the firm. That single sentence appears as an incidental comment in a brief paragraph that deals with a personal loss of property. At the outset of hostilities, the navy had conscripted Morgan's yacht, *Corsair II*, over the banker's "heated protest."[49]

A comprehensive biography of Morgan by Jean Strouse gives three pages to the war. The American business community "opposed the impending conflict as likely to disrupt international trade and jeopardize the recent economic recovery." Morgan was in Europe in the first months of 1898 spending some time in London then planning to winter in Rome. But the news from the United States, "the annoyance of war rumors," led him to return home. The biography contains no specific information indicating Morgan's attitude toward the war. A statement from Jack Morgan, the son and successor as head of the bank, is emphatically negative: "I do not like to see a civilized nation taking up the cause of the Cuban insurgents." The latter are described in very negative terms. The requisition of the *Corsair* is described—Morgan was paid $225,000 for the yacht and proceeded to the construction of a new one. Only a single episode of war planning is reported—early notification of the declaration allowed Morgan to lay in an ample supply of Cuban cigars. Three months later it was clear that war "did less damage to the economy than Wall Street had feared." The quick victory then brought up the question of possessions. Strouse thinks Morgan "probably sided with the Anti-Imperialists," but that is a conclusion based on a statement from the early eighties.[50]

The National City Bank was another major New York financial institution. Then under the direction of James Stillman, it later grew to be the "largest and strongest in the country." This bank had close ties with a wide range of business leaders, with William Rockefeller, H. H. Rogers, Harriman, Havemeyer, Pullman, Schiff, and many others. There was, as one might suspect, limited overlap between this group and those in Morgan's circle. The relevant chapter of the leading history of the bank covers the span from 1891 to 1908. It gives no indication of Stillman's position on the Cuban question or the war. The

Spanish-American War received only a few noncommittal sentences. The bond issue receives only a brief mention—the bank "agreed to underwrite any portion of the $200 million bond issue not taken up by the public."[51] A two-volume biography of Stillman contains three pages on the Spanish-American War. The bank "took an active part" in the financing of the war, with Stillman being "consulted at every step." Nothing is said there about the banker's position in the months leading up to the war.[52]

Andrew Carnegie was vacationing in Scotland in the months prior to the war. The response to the prospect of war fell to his second-in-command, Henry Clay Frick. Early in the year, Frick "was writing anxious letters to senators and congressmen, urging them to support McKinley's attempts to avoid war with Spain." When war came, late in April, "Frick and other conservative businessmen, who feared the effects of war on business conditions, blamed McKinley for yielding to the popular clamor for war." "A stronger man," Frick wrote to Carnegie, "would have held the Jingoes in check, and avoided war, at least until there was a good cause for one."[53]

Carnegie was a leading figure in the international peace movement and was well known for his pacifist sentiments. His support for the war, therefore, came as something of a surprise. But that support was based on his understanding of the war's purposes, on "McKinley's assurances that it was a war only to give Cuba its independence and to drive one more European nation completely out of the Western Hemisphere." It would, Carnegie thought, "cost America little in either men or material resources." It would also bring America and Britain closer together, one of his long-term aims. Laying aside "his pacifist sentiments for the duration," Carnegie offered diplomatic advice to the president and military advice to the American commander in Cuba.[54] Later, Carnegie would participate actively in the struggle over the annexation of the Philippines. He was probably the nation's most ardent opponent of that move.

The biographies of John D. Rockefeller published after Pratt's *Expansionists* contain no references to the war with Spain. This is most striking in Allan Nevin's extensive, detailed accounts, in his original two-volume study published in 1940 and in the revised account of 1953. Rockefeller had "various investments in iron mines" in Cuba, some 4,000 acres, plus a costly railroad and dock. He also owned a far more important property, the Mesabi iron ore field in Minnesota. The Cuban investment and/or market possibilities did not appear of sufficient importance to justify even a single sentence of comment from any Rockefeller biographers. A comprehensive history of the Standard Oil Company reports the presence of a refinery in Havana from 1881 and another in Puerto Rico begun in 1890. But it makes no mention of the Cuban revolution or of the Spanish-American War.[55]

Henry H. Flagler, an early Rockefeller partner, left the oil business in favor of Florida real estate, hotels, and railroads. He might be expected to have some interest in neighboring Cuba, but a recent biography reports "no evidence that he ever campaigned for American involvement in the Spanish-American War." After the war, he did invest in Cuba, in William Van Horne's Cuba Company, which owned the Cuba Railway (discussed briefly just below).[56]

A biography of Alfred I. du Pont contains several pages on the Spanish-American War. For well over a century the du Pont firm had been the nation's leading manufacturer of black powder, generally known as gunpowder. There is no suggestion, however, that the du Ponts were involved in the clamor for war or that they were actively seeking new markets either at home or abroad. The entire account focuses on the consequences of the war for the firm. They had to shift all of their production from black powder (a product used by hunters, miners, quarrymen, also in railroad and highway construction) to brown prismatic powder, a "smokeless" powder, an urgent wartime need. The firm met the heavy demand imposed by the Navy and War Departments. At the end of hostilities the Navy asked for an additional million pounds of brown powder but the firm tactfully refused, indicating their wish to return to their "useful, orderly business," to the manufacture of black powder, which had been neglected for some four months.[57]

Some of the complexities involved in "business" reactions may be seen in the positions and activities of another prominent businessman, Grenville Dodge. He had served in the Civil War, fought on many fronts, and was mustered out with the rank of major general. One of his wartime tasks was the reconstruction of rail lines destroyed by the retreating Confederates. After the war he made a fortune in railroad construction. His most important efforts involved the Union Pacific for which he was the chief surveyor, the Texas and Pacific Railroad (which linked up with the Southern Pacific at El Paso to become the second transcontinental line), and the Denver, Texas, and Fort Worth Railroad. Part of his fortune came through related real estate activity. He planned and surveyed cities along these railroads (three familiar ones: Cheyenne, Laramie, Dodge City, the latter named for him) and bought properties there. He was an "old and warm friend" of William McKinley who, after the 1896 election, offered him the position of Secretary of War. But Dodge turned down the offer and the position, as seen, went to another close friend, Russell Alger, the former governor of Michigan. Had Dodge accepted, he would have directed operations in the subsequent war.[58]

In the clamor over the events in Cuba, Dodge favored neutrality and made his views known to both McKinley and Alger. A week after the sinking of the *Maine*, he "begged McKinley to preserve peace." Senator Proctor's speech to the Senate, that dramatic firsthand report on conditions in Cuba, moved many political leaders at this crucial moment. Dodge challenged the senator's account, pointing to his short stay there, his ignorance of the language, and his dependence on interested sources. For Dodge, the accounts of Spanish atrocities "bordered on the ridiculous" since, as he well knew, the combatants in the Civil War had been far more ruthless than the Spanish were now. In a letter to Alger he spelled out some details of his own campaigns in Tennessee and Alabama—he had burned the Tennessee Valley "from one end to the other, driving its inhabitants out and concentrating them at our camps." Alger, however, disagreed with Dodge's arguments for neutrality. The Cuban problem, Alger wrote, was "a constant menace to the stability of our finances" and, at that point, war seemed an appropriate solution.

In another well-documented case, some businessmen from industrial Massachusetts attempted to influence their senator, Henry Cabot Lodge. One of these men was the previously discussed Edwin F. Atkins, described by Garraty as "a Bostonian with large sugar interests in Cuba" and also as "an active foe of American intervention." Atkins discussed the matter with Lodge in the spring of 1896 but there was misunderstanding on both sides, the "lesson" not adequately communicated or received. In December 1896, as noted previously, Senator Don Cameron had introduced the resolution calling for recognition of an independent Cuba, tantamount to a declaration of war, and Lodge had supported the measure. He was immediately "deluged with protests from Massachusetts businessmen." A Boston cotton broker, General S. M. Weld, complained that the lawmakers who were supposed "to help us . . . should get together and ruin us." Showing no sympathy for the Cuban insurgents, he declared they "are ruining our business." In a second letter, Weld remonstrated: "You were sent to Washington to represent one of the largest business states in the country" and those interests, he declared, require "peace and quiet," not war. Charles Francis Adams, Jr., formerly the president of the Union Pacific Railroad, objected to the resolution and to Lodge's support for it. The Cuban controversy was blocking the "return of business prosperity." Henry Lee Higginson, a leading banker, was a cousin and close friend of Lodge, also his personal financial adviser. He too joined in this opposition.[59]

Even in the agitation following the sinking of the *Maine* businessmen provided little support for intervention. One informant, John T. Morse, wrote Lodge that "I have not met a man . . . in the aristocratic upper crust in which you & I are imbedded, who considers that we have any justifiable cause of war. Below that crust . . . the wish for war is *almost* universal." Higginson wrote Lodge detailing his objections—"the economic dangers of fighting, the political damage to the G.O.P. if it precipitated an armed conflict, and the utter lack of evidence that the Spaniards had sunk the *Maine*." Lodge's friend, A. P. Gardner, traveled to Boston "to see what I could do about getting prominent businessmen to support the firm side," but he found that "business sentiment seems to have absolutely crystallized against war." Lodge made his own soundings in the state in mid-March. He claimed to have found views more to his liking, namely "an almost unanimous sentiment" favoring "settlement" of the Cuban crisis. Garraty thinks Lodge's own enthusiasm "colored his understanding," especially when he claimed, in a letter to McKinley, that "for business one shock & then an end was better than a succession of spasms," a conclusion that "conflicted with the tone of letters he was receiving from Boston." In the same letter he wrote that, "In a great, broad question like this, where right & wrong are involved, I believe profoundly in the popular instinct. . . . At such times the vast, utterly selfish money interests represented by a few men are perilous guides."[60]

As war approached, Lodge sought to achieve a united front within his own party. The business interests, however, were still "clamoring for peace." On another front, Bryan was "making political capital" through a series of speeches calling for Cuban independence. Lodge foresaw his party facing a Democratic campaign for "free Cuba and free silver" in 1900. He warned Higginson against this possibility, writing that his course "leads straight to free silver and Bryanism."[61]

Business attitudes changed only when war came. Higginson reported the dramatic fact—more than a tenth of the Knickerbocker Club enlisted. Writing to Lodge, the aging Civil War veteran stated that he too, "like an old fool . . . long to go into the service." The motivation at that time, it should be noted, was patriotism, not profits.[62]

The position of the Massachusetts business leaders, one they forcefully stated, was eminently clear: They opposed the prospect of war. Lodge's position was just as clear: Disregarding their demands, he favored the war. The business leaders made their views known but in this case "their" political agent acted with complete independence.

The business opposition to foreign entanglements and the independence of Lodge and other politicians had been demonstrated earlier in the Venezuela boundary dispute of 1895. President Cleveland took a very belligerent stand against Britain in this matter, his message producing "a wave of warlike enthusiasm in which Lodge wholeheartedly joined." According to Garraty, Higginson argued that, "America had enough trouble managing its own internal affairs without worrying about the rest of the world." In a letter to Lodge, the banker complained: "If England were to take Cuba tomorrow, it would not hurt us a bit. If she seized Mexico, we should be perfectly well off." Lodge replied: "The moment any question arises in which the honor of the country is involved and patriotism aroused, the opposition seems always to come from the bankers and capitalists." To his mother, Lodge wrote: "It was painful to read the telegrams & letters from frightened stockbrokers & bankers . . . asking me to eat my words . . . because stocks fell."[63]

An opposite claim, a suggestion of some important business support for military intervention, has been derived from one of Pratt's footnotes.[64] Pratt's source in this case is Thomas Beer's biography of Mark Hanna. Beer's father, William C. Beer, was a "political observer" who worked for the New York Life Insurance Company and for George Perkins, J. P. Morgan's "right hand man" from 1896 to 1904. Those chapters of Beer's work are based on his father's papers.

Early in March, a couple of weeks after the sinking of the *Maine*, Beer was hearing conflicting reports of Hanna's position, some saying he was trying to force a war on behalf of friends in steel and railroads and some others that he was "trying to prevent a war in the name of Wall Street." He heard in Washington that Wall Street was "solidly lined up against a war with Spain." But things were different in New York where

> men grabbed his arm as he entered his club, asking what this insane Hanna meant by trying to head off the war? He noted that the solidarity of Wall Street was imperfect. John Jacob Astor wore a buttonhole of red, white, and blue flowers. John Gates, Thomas Fortune Ryan, William Rockefeller, and Stuyvesant Fish all were sounded, before March 24th, and were found to be feeling militant. On March 28th it was announced by George Walbridge Perkins that John Pierpont Morgan was to put his yacht at the service of the government and that the financier saw nothing to be gained by more talk of arbitration. The news spread in the Lawyers' Club at noon, and men thought of their grown sons.[65]

Beer added some more details in a footnote placed after the words "feeling militant." His father, the "political observer," was in Washington collecting information about "a bank in South America," this on behalf of the "great life-insurance companies." He interviewed Colonel Astor and Mr. Ryan in the course of that inquiry. It was Beer's opinion "that the steady opponents of the war among financiers were simply the life insurance men and small bankers. A carbon copy of a letter to his friend Dudley Evans of Wells, Fargo and Company, dated March 26th, 1898, says: 'Nothing but war talk. Hill seems to be the only prominent railroad man who is fighting for peace. The Pennsylvania crowd say that nothing can be done to stop it since C. K. Davis and Alger are pushing the president. It can not be stopped from this end [New York] and I do not think Hanna can stop it in the Senate."

Pratt quoted the essence of this text (from the words "solidarity" to "militant"), one that indicates a change from the previous opposition by most businessmen. He also commented on this alternative seeing it, appropriately, as a response to the events of mid-March. On 17 March, Senator Proctor had reported to the Senate the findings of his recent visit to Cuba, an account of the terrible sufferings of the Cuban "reconcentrados." Pratt also quotes the *Wall Street Journal*, which reported that Proctor's speech had

> converted a great many people in Wall Street, who have heretofore taken the ground that the United States had no business to interfere in a revolution on Spanish soil. These men had been among the most prominent in deploring the whole Cuban matter, but there was no question about the accuracy of Senator Proctor's statements and as many of them expressed it, they made the blood boil."

Both Beer and Pratt, clearly, were reporting the angry sentiments of the moment, that is, a month after the sinking of the *Maine*. But both conclusions, it should be noted, are based on casual research procedures and both indicate a diversity of reactions.

Except for William Rockefeller, the persons mentioned by Beer were not top leaders in the business world, the other four being secondary or peripheral figures. This John Jacob Astor was a great-grandson of the founder of his family's fortune. He was thirty-four years old in 1898, at which point his major accomplishments appear to have been the management of the family estate and the building of "the Astoria section of the palatial Waldorf-Astoria Hotel." He was not, moreover, a late convert to the Cuban cause. In February 1897, he was a member of the executive committee of the Cuban League. In 1898, he loaned his yacht to the navy, volunteered for service, was present at San Juan Hill, and ended up as a lieutenant-colonel.[66]

John Gates, also known as "Bet-a-Million" Gates, was a troublesome promoter and speculator. One biographical statement reports that it was "chiefly as a marauder that he was known and feared on the Exchange." One account has it that J. P. Morgan intentionally ruined him financially. Still in his prime, Gates left New York and settled in Port Arthur, Texas, where, like "a Napoleon banished to St. Helena . . . he talked, gambled, invested, and promoted as though he were still in New York."[67]

Thomas Fortune Ryan was a financier, promoter, and Tammany man. In the 1890s, his fame rested on his efforts, as an ally of William C. Whitney, to gain control of streetcar lines in New York City. Stuyvesant Fish was a son of Hamilton Fish, Grant's Secretary of State. He began in banking but "Wall Street never appealed to him." He was then active in the Illinois Central Railroad and from 1887 to 1906 its president, extending the line's track mileage and increasing its receipts. Operating from the Great Lakes to the Gulf of Mexico, it was "almost the only north-and-south road of importance that prospered" in the years after the Civil War. In a subsequent clash, he was ousted by other Wall Street people, one of them being E. H. Harriman. William Rockefeller, a younger brother of John, was active in Standard Oil, in the National City Bank, and in several other joint efforts.[68]

During most of the months of agitation, business leaders were clearly opposed to any Cuban involvement. At a later point, in March and April, some business leaders, belatedly, joined with that "aroused public," at this point demonstrating their patriotism. Big businessmen clearly did not initiate the war policy. After the fact, they were reacting, adjusting, or "going along with" the decision generated by other elites.

Some commentators see these conclusions—passive or reactive business-men, big business losing in the contention over a major issue—as implausible and hence unacceptable. Accordingly, some effort has been given to putting "business" back at the center of things. One option has been to alter the "bal-ance" in Pratt's presentation, basically hedging his principal conclusion and putting Beer's statement about the late business enthusiasm "front and center" in the text. The five men listed by Beer are elevated in importance, the con-text—mid-March—is overlooked, and the suggestion is made that the opinions expressed are symptomatic of more general business preferences.

William Appleman Williams followed this strategy of elevation. Misrepre-senting Beer's sponsorship, he reports that a "special emissary sent by McKin-ley to sound out the New York area reported that such key figures as [Astor, Ryan, William Rockefeller, Fish] and spokesmen for the House of Morgan were 'feeling militant.' "[69] Walter LaFeber used a similar procedure. He describes Beer's casual survey as "a thorough survey of leading businessmen's opinion." The five men mentioned by Beer are introduced as "such giants as . . ." In every interpretative option, LaFeber portrays "business" as determining the course of events.[70] Foner follows the same procedure: "With the stock market moving from one level to another, there was an increasing cry from the business com-munity for an immediate solution. Such business giants as [Beer's five are listed] declared themselves for a more belligerent policy toward Spain."[71]

A similar misrepresentation appears in connection with an earlier effort by concerned businessmen. In May 1897, a memorial was signed by more than three hundred bankers, merchants, manufacturers, steamship owners, and agents and presented to Secretary of State Sherman. It called attention to the "serious losses" they had incurred as a result of the Cuban hostilities. To pre-vent further loss, to reestablish commerce, and to end the "unspeakable distress and suffering" of the Cuban population, they asked, in Pratt's words, that the government "take steps to bring about an honorable reconciliation between the parties to the conflict." A second memorial, signed by many of the same people, was presented to the president on 9 February 1898. It too stressed the economic losses that now, after three years of fighting, had reached a total of $300,000,000. This statement called for "prompt and efficient measures by our Government, with the sole object of restoring peace . . . and with it restor-ing to us a most valuable commercial field." Although the statements say "honorable reconciliation" and "restoring peace," one commentator reported differently, writing that "business interests accepted war as a necessary extension of the American Policy."[72]

The elevation-of-importance problem appears also in connection with this petition. The lead sentence of a New York *Daily Tribune* account refers to the presenters of the second petition as "a delegation of New-York business men representing a large number of well-known and influential firms in that city." LaFeber reports that passage without further identifying the members of the delegation. The four were W. M. Carson, of Morewood & Co., George Turnure, of Lawrence Turnure & Co., George R. Mosle of Mosle Brothers, and A. G. Smith, of James E. Ward & Co. None of those men are listed in the *Dictionary of American Biography* or in *Who Was Who in America*.[73]

Another frequently cited bit of evidence offered as proof that McKinley moved to war with the support of "big corporations" is the Reick telegram. On 25 March 1898, William C. Reick, the city editor of the New York *Herald*, sent a telegram to John Russell Young in Washington. Young, a former newspaperman, was then the librarian of Congress. The key sentences declared that: "Big corporations here now believe we will have war. Believe all would welcome it as a relief to suspense." Young gave the telegram to the Assistant Secretary of State, William R. Day, who presumably showed it to McKinley. The president's ultimatum to Spain was sent two days later, on 27 March 27. Reick did not name any of those big corporations. His next sentences point to another source, naming "Mr. B."—his employer, James Gordon Bennett, Jr.,—as one who "also agrees on these lines . . ." But Bennett, who resided "in Paris and on his yacht," would not have been well informed about such matters.

Reick would have been an unlikely spokesman for "the big corporations." If any corporate leaders wished to have an urgent message sent to the president, they certainly had better options, the route via Reick and the Library of Congress being circuitous and time consuming. The telegram appears to have been part of a flood of communications that flowed into the White House at this point. Lewis G. Gould, in a definitive assessment, compared two messages McKinley sent to Stewart Woodford, the American minister in Madrid, that reviewed his policies, one sent before, one sent after the Reick telegram. He found little difference between them, his conclusion being that the telegram did not alter the basic direction of McKinley's policy. Its effect on the 27 March message, he writes, "has not been demonstrated."[74]

Some authors assign an important role to the "sugar interests." But that theme, a recurrent one in discussions of the war, has long-since been rejected. The "sugar interests" would consist of American investors in Cuba, Atkins among them, and Henry O. Havemeyer's American Sugar Company, the "sugar trust" that controlled about four-fifths of the domestic market. As seen earlier, the two had sharply opposed positions with respect to the tariff. But both agreed on the need to avoid war. Pratt describes the efforts of Atkins as follows: He "was frequently in Washington, where he had influential friends, during both the Cleveland and McKinley administrations and *worked consistently against the adoption of any measures likely to provoke war*" (emphasis added). Garraty, as noted, described Atkins as "an active foe of American intervention."[75] Trask refers to an unpublished dissertation, from 1939, summarizing with this comment: "For well-documented arguments that American sugar interests did not play an important role in precipitating the war with Spain, see Richard D. Weigle . . ."[76]

One source of difficulty in discussions of positions and motives is the use of categorical formulations—the actors are either for or against expansion, for or against the war. Some sense of the complexities with respect to both Cuba and the possibility of war may be gained from a review of Henry Cabot Lodge's views, a man regularly described as a leading expansionist. At an early point, in January 1896, he stated his position with regard to Cuba in a letter to Henry Lee Higginson—"I think we ought to have Cuba for many reasons, although I recognize all the problems there." That expressed aim is followed by an equally clear statement of his justifications—". . . one reason for my desire for Cuba is that we should then raise all our sugar within the limits of the United States and another drain of gold would be stopped. We should no longer pay with drafts on London." The concern, clearly, was the balance of payments, not the well-being of American investors. The letter spells out several other measures needed to guarantee American prosperity—checking imports, increasing revenues, and stimulating domestic industry with a protective tariff. Lodge also wished for "discriminating duties" to favor American shipping and steamship lines. The letter says nothing about new foreign markets or investment opportunities.[77]

A year later, in a letter to Charles Francis Adams, Jr., Lodge provided another review of the Cuban problem. His position at that point is also clear and unambiguous: "I do not favor the annexation of the island." His preference was now for Cuban independence. The justification provided at that point was strategic: "I am strongly in favor of the removal of Spain from any possessions in this hemisphere. . . . The less of Europe we have in America the better in my opinion for the United States. It is the presence of a European power which makes trouble for us in any American state." The "true policy for the United States," he declared, "was to take vigorous measures to bring the war to an end." But Cleveland's administration, he added, "has decided otherwise" with the evident consequences of "constant agitation and disturbance of one sort and another . . ."[78]

Walter LaFeber draws on this same letter and provides a markedly different lesson, this in a paragraph dealing with "businessmen in Cuba [who] hoped that the annexation could be accomplished through peaceful means." Edwin F. Atkins is cited as one of those who thought "the best thing . . . would be the annexation of Cuba by the United States." Lodge's letter does declare, unambiguously, that Atkins was an annexationist but the senator had misinterpreted the businessman's point. LaFeber makes no reference to the rest of the letter thus omitting Lodge's clear anti-annexationist statement and his strategic concern. The innocent reader would sense that Lodge was responding to that presumed "business" sentiment where in fact, as he clearly states, he rejected the presumed recommendation. Atkins, Lodge wrote, seemed "to know but little of the question in its larger aspect and events have proved that he was very much mistaken as to some of the facts."[79]

Lodge's misinterpretation is of some interest in that it reveals his actual position. The senator had asked Atkins if he thought the Cubans could establish a stable government and the sugar planter "answered with an emphatic negative." Lodge indicated agreement, saying that "is exactly my opinion." Atkins deduced from this that Lodge opposed American intervention and instead favored some solution within the framework of continued Spanish rule, which was his solution, the autonomy option. He was surprised therefore when a few days later Lodge supported the resolution recognizing the belligerency of the insurgents. The senator's belief, expressed in a letter from March 1896, was that any Cuban regime "would be an immense advance over the government Spain would give them." Lodge also expressed another option, an assumed a right of intervention. Garraty summarized the position as follows: "If self-rule failed, America could step in." The Monroe Doctrine, Lodge wrote, "does not interfere in the least with anything we choose to do with regard to Cuba. There is nothing . . . preventing ourselves or any other American state from acquiring additional territory."[80]

The nation's leading businessmen, clearly, were opposed to the possibility of the United States going to war over Cuba, a fact that was well-known, very much in evidence in 1898. But later, some commentators neglected that evidence and argued—or insinuated—that "business" was somehow responsible for the outbreak of the war. Countering that development, Julius W. Pratt restated and documented the fact of business opposition in his *Expansionists of 1898* published in 1936.[81] That fact, it will be noted, provides a serious challenge for those many accounts declaring that "big business" was the dominant power in American society at least from the time of McKinley's 1896 election victory. Pratt inserted a late-conversion thesis in this chapter of the *Expansionists*—arguing that, "almost at the moment when the war began, a large section of American business had . . . been converted to the belief that a program of territorial expansion would serve its purposes."[82] That conversion occurred, Pratt argued, because of a threatened loss of the China market. But a late conversion, even if accurate, might influence the conduct of the war and its out-come. But a late conversion, an after-the-fact change of outlook, would have no relevance for explanation of the war's origins.

Overlooking Pratt's evidence on the attitudes of big business through to April 1898, William Appleman Williams, the leading figure in a later exposi-tion of the progressive tradition, provided this summary conclusion: "If there is any one key to understanding the coming of the war with Spain, it very proba-bly lies in the growing conviction among top economic and political leaders that American military intervention was necessary in order to clean up the Cuban mess so that domestic *and other foreign policy* issues could be dealt with efficiently and effectively."[83]

Walter LaFeber also implicates big business, assigning its leaders a central role in the decision for war. But the evidence provided in support of this argu-ment is thin, unreliable, and misleading. LaFeber's very tentative formulations signal the weaknesses of the claim: "It is possible to suggest . . . that by the mid-dle of March important businessmen and spokesmen for the business community were advocating war. It is also possible to suggest that . . . a shift seemed to be occurring in the general business community regarding its over-all views on the desirability of war. . . . A strong possibility exists that the antiwar commercial journals in New York spoke for the less important members of that financial community." In support of the latter possibility, LaFeber quotes Russell Sage, the financier and railroad magnate, who, shortly after the *Maine* explosion, claimed he spoke "not only my own views on this point, but those of other mon-eyed men with whom I have talked." If the battleship were blown up by an out-side force, "the time for action has come. There should be no wavering." If war did occur, he added, there "is no question as to where the rich men stand . . ."[84]

That report, however, is truncated, thus leaving a misleading impression. Sage was not arguing economic interest but, like many others at that point, was declaring a patriotic concern, one he stated unambiguously: "I am an American first and last, and purpose to stand by the flag. Party lines will be dropped. As for the stock market, that has got to take care of itself for the pre-sent. The ticker is now a secondary consideration. The honor of the Govern-ment comes first."[85]

Following his account of Sage's position, LaFeber reports Beer's observa-tions about the five business leaders who were "feeling militant." The busi-nessmen's petition to McKinley is reported, and that is followed by an account of the Reick telegram.[86] But Sage, as seen, was responding to the events, not initiating policy. He was not giving McKinley the "go-ahead." The three other bits of evidence were discussed earlier in this chapter. This evidence attesting to a change in "business" attitudes is perhaps best described as flimsy; it is certainly misleading.

A third review, this by Jules Benjamin, appears in a work that signals a debt to Williams and LaFeber. The Cuban insurgency, he states, threatened American trade and investment on the island. He writes of "the large U.S. trade with Cuba" and of the "growing North American investment there," suggesting these were significant concerns for some influential persons. President Cleveland's inaction "was becoming very unpopular at home, it was also becoming counterproductive." The 1896 election campaign pointed up some major domestic concerns. "[T]he silver issue," he writes, "symbolized a host of deep social tensions." President-elect McKinley faced a wide range of difficulties, the "tariff, the depression, the currency issue, the problems of overproduction and export expansion," all of which "pressed for attention." The "anarchy in Cuba" and a possible war with Spain would "interfere with conservative solutions to these pressing problems." But McKinley, Benjamin declares, "could not ignore the fact that Cuba was one of the largest U.S. export markets."[87]

The latter claim is accompanied by two footnote references, the first to "Langley, *Cuban Policy*, pp. 84–86."[88] Those pages contain a table showing United States' trade with Cuba, imports and exports, for the years from 1892 to 1898. Both fell off dramatically after 1894. Exports to Cuba peaked in 1893 at $24,157,698, fell somewhat in 1894, after which came the serious drop to $7.5 million in 1896. No comparisons appear there, none showing exports to other nations, which means those pages provide no support for Benjamin's claim that the Cuba market was "one of the largest."[89] Benjamin's second source, "Jenks, *Colony*, p. 21" is also a miscue. That page reviews the development of the sugar industry in Cuba in the years 1834 to 1867.[90]

A readily available source allows calculation of the importance of Cuban exports and gives some comparative figures: that $24 million in 1893 amounted to 2.8 percent of U.S. exports. The percentage fell to 1.6 in 1895.[91] Some recovery followed after the war but even in 1910, a relatively good year, the Cuban trade amounted to only three percent of total exports. The leading foreign outlets for American products in 1893 were (in millions of dollars): the United Kingdom, 421; Germany, 84; France, 47; and Canada, 47. For Europe, a large "Other" category accounted for $110 millions of American exports. Cuban exports, in short, constituted only a minuscule small part of American exports in this period.

Building on that infirm foundation, Benjamin turns next to the key political decision-makers: "As an ally (some would say representative) of big business, McKinley and his wing of the Republican Party were strongly committed to export expansion. . . . If conflict with Spain became the only alternative to the loss of the large U.S. stake on the island and the political initiative at home, McKinley was better oriented [than was Cleveland] to face the prospect of war." If that depiction were accurate, one would have to assume that McKinley and those big-business Republicans together were willing to pay enormous costs and take considerable risks for the sake of a very modest goal, maintaining or enhancing that minuscule share of American foreign trade. Total American exports at that point amounted to only six or seven percent of the gross national product. The game of hazard with respect to "the Cuban market" would presumably be played for a quantity amounting to roughly 0.2 percent of GNP. A simple question: Would such a gamble ever appear to be a reasonable course either for businessmen or for their political allies?

Three peculiar biases appear in Benjamin's account. First, there is a magnification bias—the commercial significance of Cuba is grossly exaggerated. Second, Benjamin goes out of his way to implicate "big business," suggesting that "they" somehow or other caused the war. The third bias involves that suggestion—"some would say"—that McKinley was the representative of big business. The "connective tissue," compelling evidence in support of these claims, is missing. The performance is all the more astonishing given the solid evidence against each of them. Both trade and investment in Cuba were very small; big business clearly opposed the war; and McKinley's choice was clearly a response to some other pressures, not those of "business." Those other pressures—the public clamor and party advantage—are given brief mention in the just-reviewed works. But there is no suggestion that one or the other, or both, were actually decisive.

The move to war required both the president's message and action by the Congress. In the Senate, as noted, two amendments to the original resolution were offered and debated. The first of these, the Turpie-Foraker amendment, called for "a free and independent" Cuba. It was defeated by a narrow margin. Senator Teller of Colorado offered the second, an amendment "disclaiming the intention of the United States to exercise sovereignty over Cuba, except for its pacification." The Teller Amendment was unanimously adopted by voice vote in the Senate and "cordially" accepted in the House. It was, perhaps, not a good test of imperialist strength since, as Margaret Leech put it, "only a small minority of extreme expansionists were ambitious for the acquisition of Cuba." There was the need for consistency: One could not support Cuban independence and then take it over. The amendment removed any reproach of "selfish ulterior aims."[92]

McKinley's decision-making efforts in the months from January to April 1898 have relevance to the first conclusion of the previous chapter, that attesting to his competence. For almost three-score years most scholarly and popular accounts portrayed McKinley as weak and vacillating, as a man with no clear policy. As "telling" proof, those claims were often embellished with Theodore Roosevelt's deprecating comment—"McKinley has no more backbone than a chocolate éclair!"[93]

In recent decades, a new view of McKinley has been presented and sustained. Several historians have shown that McKinley developed clear lines of policy and pursued them consistently and with considerable intelligence and capacity. From the start, he signaled a change from Cleveland's policy of noninvolvement. McKinley let it be known, quietly and indirectly, that he shared the view that "the Cuban cause should prevail." He also let Spain know that he was "more sympathetic to the Cuban cause" than Cleveland and "more responsive to Congress, and more willing to pressure Spain to end the Cuban war and the horrors of reconcentration."[94] These revisionists argue that McKinley's motives were humane, decent, and generous. He wished to end the bloodshed in Cuba. And he wished to avoid a larger conflict, one that would bring American involvement. Given the existing "clamor," it was a difficult strategy, one that could easily fail.

The revisionist reading—the argument that McKinley was a capable leader—was followed by another interpretation: that he was a Machiavellian, a man moved by sinister purposes. In his *New Empire*, Walter LaFeber agrees with the initial reading: "The President did not want war; he had been sincere and tireless in his efforts to maintain the peace." In a later work, however, LaFeber accepts the revised view of McKinley's competence and adds some very doubtful conclusions: "In the end, McKinley sought war and domination in the Caribbean and the southern Pacific . . . he needed war and an extended military commitment . . ."[95]

Notes

1. For accounts of the war see the following: Walter Millis, *The Martial Spirit: A Study of Our War with Spain* (New York, 1965 [1931]); Julius W. Pratt, *Expansionists of 1898: The Acquisition of Hawaii and the Spanish Islands* (Chicago, 1964 [1936]); Ernest R. May, *Imperial Democracy: The Emergence of America as a Great Power* (New York, 1961); Walter LaFeber, *The New Empire: An Interpretation of American Expansion, 1860–1898* (Ithaca, 1963); Walter LaFeber, *The American Search for Opportunity*, Vol. 2 of *The Cambridge History of American Foreign Relations* (Cambridge, 1993); Howard Wayne Morgan, *America's Road to Empire: The War with Spain and Overseas Expansion* (New York, 1965); John A. S. Grenville and George Berkeley Young, *Politics, Strategy, and American Diplomacy: Studies in Foreign Policy, 1873–1917* (New Haven, 1966); Hugh Thomas, *Cuba: The Pursuit of Freedom* (New York, 1971); Philip S. Foner, *The Spanish-Cuban-American War and the Birth of American Imperialism 1895–1902*, two volumes (New York, 1972); Gerald F. Linderman, *The Mirror of War: American Society and the Spanish-American War* (Ann Arbor, 1974); Charles S. Campbell, *The Transformation of American Foreign Relations, 1865–1900* (New York, 1976); David F. Trask, *The War with Spain in 1898* (New York, 1981); Louis A. Pérez, Jr., *Cuba between Empires 1878–1902* (Pittsburgh, 1982); Louis A. Pérez, Jr., *Cuba and the United States: Ties of Singular Intimacy* (Athens, GA, 1990);

John L. Offner, *An Unwanted War: The Diplomacy of the United States and Spain over Cuba, 1895–1898* (Chapel Hill, 1992); and Ivan Musicant, *Empire by Default: The Spanish-American War and the Dawn of the American Century* (New York, 1998). For a recent brief summary, see Offner, "McKinley and the Spanish-American War," *Presidential Studies Quarterly*, 34 (2004):50–61.

2. For more extended overviews, see Campbell, *Transformation*; Grenville and Young, *Politics, Strategy*; and Thomas, *Cuba*. Cuban's history was one of "chronic rebellion," something that troubled American leaders. From an early point, some American leaders favored annexation; some sharply opposed that option. In 1895, just prior to the Cuban revolution, the United States was involved in the Venezuela boundary dispute. The policies of President Cleveland and Secretary of State Olney brought the nation onto a collision course with Great Britain. It was a prelude to the subsequent drama, an episode that showed the demagogic possibilities of foreign affairs, one that aroused the "jingoes." See May, *Imperial Democracy*, p. 33 and Grenville and Young, *Politics, Strategy*, chs. 5 and 6.

3. Offner, *Unwanted War*, p. 5.

4. Campbell, *Transformation*, p. 242. In 1869, in the earlier liberation struggle, Carlos Céspedes, the nominal chief of the Cuban rebels, announced the plan to destroy the sugar plantations. His words: "Better . . . that Cuba should be free even if we have to burn every vestige of civilization" (Thomas, *Cuba*, p. 255). On events in 1895 and after, see his pp. 321–333.

5. Edwin F. Atkins, *Sixty Years in Cuba* (Cambridge, 1926), pp. 77.

6. Ibid., pp. 143–144. Atkins blamed the United States Congress for its shortsightedness; the new tariff halted and reversed the recent economic development and created the conditions that led to revolution and the subsequent war. Pérez's account, which makes extensive use of Spanish-language sources, contains a detailed review of the same legislative events. Cuban planters, especially the Creoles, he writes, blamed the Spanish government, faulting it for the punitive reaction. It was Madrid's "interference," he writes, that moved many of them to view independence with favor. Some others viewed annexation by the United States with favor. See Pérez, *Cuba between Empires*, pp. 31–35.

7. Tom E. Terrill, *The Tariff, Politics, and American Foreign Policy, 1874–1901* (Westport, CT, 1973), pp. 176, 185, 193–197; H. Wayne Morgan, *From Hayes to McKinley: National Party Politics, 1877–1896* (Syracuse, 1969), pp. 460–462, 473–476; Allan Nevins, *Grover Cleveland: A Study in Courage* (New York, 1933), pp. 563–588, 652, 667–668; May, *Imperial Democracy*, pp. 115–116; Pérez, *Cuba between Empires*, pp. 29–35; and Paul S. Holbo, "Economics, Emotion, and Expansion," pp. 204–207, in H. Wayne Morgan, ed. *The Gilded Age*, revised edition (Syracuse, 1970), ch. 10.

8. Atkins, *Sixty Years*, pp. 156–157, 236–237, 266, and 281.

9. Ibid., p. 209. The extent of the American involvement in Cuba has been variously estimated. Offner writes that the "exact amount of investment is unknown [but that] Secretary of State Richard Olney [estimated it] at $50 million." That figure, Offner adds, "was exaggerated" but, apparently, was widely accepted. *Unwanted War*, p. 15. Later, Offner reports that two House Republicans "estimated U.S. investment in Cuba at $20 to $30 million" (p. 20). Trask reports that "American investments [in Cuba] amounted to between $30 and $50 million and the annual export-import trade reached $100 million." *War with Spain*, p. 12. In 1963, LaFeber reported the U.S. investments in Cuba at "more than $33,000,000." *New Empire*, p. 334. In

1993, LaFeber referred to a State Department assessment that put "about $50 million in the island." *American Search*, p. 130. LaFeber cites Beisner (*Old Diplomacy*, p. 116) but no such figure appears there. On his p. 118, Beisner reports American investments in Cuba to be "worth about $40 million." LaFeber also cites May (*Imperial Democracy*, pp. 80–81) for support, but I do not find any relevant comment there. Lewis L. Gould reports that "the destruction affected the $50 million. . . . Americans had invested in Cuba," in his *Presidency of William McKinley* (Lawrence, KA, 1980), p. 63.

Those estimates say nothing about the overall importance of the Cuban investments, that sum as a percent of total U.S. overseas investment. One appropriate source gives the latter figure for 1897 as $700 million, U.S. Bureau of the Census, *Historical Statistics of the United States* (Washington, D.C., 1975), Part 2, p. 869. If Atkins' $30 million figure were correct, that would amount to 4.3 per cent of the total. If Olney's $50 million figure were correct, Cuba's share would be 7.1 percent. A question: Would other investors, the holders of the other 95 percent, be willing to risk their holdings for the sake of this 4–7 percent? A similar question may be asked with regard to the much larger domestic investment total: Would those investors be willing to take the risks and to pay the costs of a war?

10. On this, see Thomas, *Cuba*, pp. 453–456 and, for more detail, Louis A. Pérez, Jr., *Cuba Under the Platt Amendment, 1902–1934* (Pittsburgh, 1986).

11. Offner, *Unwanted War*, ch. 2 (quotations from pp. 17, 19); Trask, *War with Spain*, pp. 11–13; and Lewis L. Gould, *Presidency*, pp. 63–66. Some key chapters in the latter work have been published in a separate volume; see Gould, *The Spanish-American War and President McKinley* (Lawrence, KA, 1982). In the following, references to Gould are exclusively to his *Presidency*.

12. Foner, *Spanish-Cuban-American War*, Vol. 1, pp. 185–191; Offner, *Unwanted War*, pp. 18–22.

13. Foner, loc. cit. and Offner, *Unwanted War*, pp. 20–22. For more on Senators Morgan and Cameron and on the petitions, see below, ch. 6.

14. Offner, *Unwanted War*, pp. 32–33; Trask, *War with Spain*, pp. 11–12; and Nevins, *Cleveland*, pp. 716–722.

15. On McKinley and the events leading up to the war, see Margaret Leech, *In the Days of McKinley* (New York, 1959), chs. 6 and 7; Gould, *Presidency*, chs. 4 and 5; Trask, *The War with Spain*, chs. 1–4; and H. Wayne Morgan, *William McKinley and His America* (Kent, OH, 2003 [1963]), Chs. 15 and 16.

16. Musicant, *Empire by Default*, p. 81.

17. Robert C. Hilderbrand, *Power and the People: Executive Management of Public Opinion in Foreign Affairs, 1897–1921* (Chapel Hill, 1981), p. 13.

18. Ibid., pp. 14, and 208, n18.

19. Trask, *War with Spain*, p. 56.

20. Policies are rarely fixed or immovable. These statements provide only brief summaries of complex and changing circumstances and responses. While Cleveland's basic position was one of non-intervention, in his last message to Congress, that of December 1896, he did spell out another option, noting the conditions in which intervention was possible. See Grenville and Young, ch. 7, particularly, p. 197, and May, *Imperial Democracy*, chs. 5 and 6.

21. For strategic reasons, one might wish the acquisition of some bases in the area, to guard the approaches to the planned inter-ocean canal. The nation's foremost naval strategist, Captain Alfred Thayer Mahan, took this position but his aim was another

Spanish possession, Puerto Rico. See William E. Livezey, *Mahan on Sea Power* (Norman, OK, 1947), p. 139.

22. For a brief history of the Junta, see Foner, *Spanish, Cuban-American War*, Vol. I, ch. 9, especially pp. 163–168. See also, George W. Auxier, "The Propaganda Activities of the Cuban *Junta* in Precipitating the Spanish American War, 1895–1898," *Hispanic American Historical Review*, 19 (1939):286–305 (quotation from p. 295); Raymond A. Detter, "The Cuban Junta and Michigan: 1895–1898," *Michigan History*, 48 (1964):35–46; Ruby Weedell Waldeck, "Missouri and the Spanish American War," *Missouri Historical Review*, 30 (1936):365–400 (especially pp. 366–367); and Marshall MacDonald True, "Revolutionaries in Exile: The Cuban Revolutionary Party, 1891–1898," Charlottesville, VA: unpublished Ph.D. dissertation, University of Virginia, 1965, especially pp. 182–184 and 299–209. May reviews and explains Junta support "in unexpected places," including the Union League Club, various Civil War veterans organizations, and some trade unions, in *Imperial Democracy*, pp. 70–73. See also, Morton M. Rosenberg and Thomas P. Ruff, *Indiana and the Coming of the Spanish-American War* (Muncie, IN, 1976). They report Cuban League societies across the state with the largest unit in Elkhart (p. 7). An active League unit was reported in Oklahoma City, in David C. Boles, "Editorial Opinion in Oklahoma and Indian Territories on the Cuban Insurrection, 1895–1898," *The Chronicles of Oklahoma*, 47 (1969):258–267, see p. 266. For more on the League's activities, see chapter 6 below.

23. Auxier, "Propaganda Activities," p. 299.

24. A small detail: The family name of the Spanish minister was Dupuy de Lôme. Many American publications, then and later, made the abbreviation given here.

25. Pratt, *Expansionists*, ch. 8, "The Imperialism of Righteousness." The Hanna quotation is from Thomas Beer, *Hanna* (New York, 1929), p. 194. The words of the biographer and the brother, however, do not accord with Cortelyou's statement (quoted above at note 19), that written on 16 April 1898. Also, on the attitudes of "religious people," one researcher found that the Methodist press in the South did not favor a war to liberate Cuba but instead backed McKinley's effort to avoid a conflict with Spain; see Arnold M. Shankman, "Southern Methodist Newspapers and the Coming of the Spanish-American War: A Research Note," *Journal of Southern History*, 39 (1973):93–96.

26. The positions of these men, and several others, will be explored in chapter 7.

27. For information on this group and its network, see Warren Zimmermann, *First Great Triumph: How Five Americans Made Their Country a World Power* (New York, 2002); Edmund Morris, *The Rise of Theodore Roosevelt* (New York, 1979), especially ch. 22. For portraits of some of its members, see John A. Garraty, *Henry Cabot Lodge: A Biography* (New York, 1953), ch. 11; Bingham Duncan, *Whitelaw Reid: Journalist, Politician, Diplomat* (Athens, GA, 1975), ch. 13; Kenton J. Clymer, *John Hay: The Gentleman as Diplomat* (Ann Arbor, 1975), ch. 5; Lloyd J. Graybar, *Albert Shaw of the Review of Reviews: An Intellectual Biography* (Lexington, KY, 1974), pp. 123–124, also ANB, 19:734–736; and Philip Y. Nicholson, "George Dewey and the Expansionists of 1898," *Vermont History*, 42 (1974):214–227. For an account of the John Hay-Henry Adams circle, see Patricia O'Toole, *The Five of Hearts: An Intimate Portrait of Henry Adams and His Friends, 1880–1918* (New York, 1990).

28. Kirk H. Porter and Donald Bruce Johnson, *National Party Platforms, 1840–1968* (Urbana, 1970), p. 108.

29. O'Toole, *Five of Hearts*, p. 284; on Cameron, see ANB, 4:257–258.
30. O'Toole, *Five of Hearts*, pp. 283–286 and 295. See also, Clymer, *John Hay*, p. 114.
31. McKinley's opposition to the possibility of war is amply documented. In his inaugural address he declared that: "We want no wars of conquest; we must avoid the temptation of territorial aggression. Wars should never be entered upon until every agency of peace has failed; peace is preferable to war in almost every contingency." From Morgan, *William McKinley*, p. 247. See also Linderman, *Mirror of War*, pp. 29, 35. John D. Long, McKinley's Secretary of the Navy, believed that "if Congress had followed the suggestion of the President and left the matter in his hands the independence of Cuba would have been secured without a drop of bloodshed," (from Linderman, p. 189, n91). John W. Foster, a prominent diplomat and one-time Secretary of State, also saw McKinley as "strongly opposed to the war." Quoted in James Ford Rhodes, *The McKinley and Roosevelt Administrations 1897–1909* (New York, 1922), p. 64, n1. See also Hermann Hagedorn, *Leonard Wood: A Biography* (New York, 1931), Vol. 1, p. 141; and, Clymer, *John Hay*, p. 115. Leech writes of "McKinley's earnest will for peace," in *Days of McKinley*, p. 164.
32. On Cameron's December resolution, see Nevins, *Cleveland*, pp. 717–718. The congressional advocates portrayed themselves as representing constituent opinion. In support of this claim they pointed to the many petitions that, Foner reports, came "from all parts of the country [and] flooded both houses of Congress." Foner agrees with that claim, reporting the congressional moves as "reflecting widespread public opinion," in *Spanish-Cuban-American War*, Vol. 1, pp. 184–185, and 191. The petitions and their significance will be discussed further in the next chapter.
33. On the three resolutions, see Offner, *Unwanted War*, pp. 17–22, 32–33, and 43–45.
34. Offner, *Unwanted War*, p. 43; Leech, 184–185; Morgan, *William McKinley*, p. 257.
35. For reviews of these events, see: May, *Imperial Democracy*, ch. 12; Leech, ch. 7; Gould, *Presidency*, ch. 4; Morgan, *William McKinley*, ch. 16; Offner, *Unwanted War*, chs. 7–11; and Trask, *War with Spain*, ch. 2. McKinley described the de Lôme letter as a "comparatively unimportant matter," in Morgan, p. 272. For the significance of Proctor's speech, see Linderman, *Mirror of War*, ch. 2.
36. On the joint resolution and declaration of war, see Gould, *Presidency*, p. 88; Offner, *Unwanted War*, p. 190; and Trask, *War with Spain*, pp. 55–56 (the quotation is from p. 56).
37. May, *Imperial Democracy*, chs. 12 and 13.
38. On the Turpie-Foraker and Teller amendments, see Holbo, "Presidential Leadership"; Leech, pp. 187–189; Gould, *Presidency*, pp. 86–88; Offner, *Unwanted War*, pp. 188–189; and Trask, *War with Spain*, p. 55.
39. Offner, *Unwanted War*, pp. 88–89, the quotations are from pp. ix and 234. See also, Linderman, *Mirror of War*, p. 34; Jennie Hobart, *Memories* (Patterson, NJ, 1930), p. 60 (also, pp. 61–63); LaFeber, *New Empire*, p. 384 (for the Lodge letter); May, *Imperial Democracy*, pp. 146–147; Gould, *Presidency*, pp. 63–64; and Morgan, *McKinley*, pp. 279–80. See also Auxier's comments based on his review of Midwestern newspapers, cited in the following chapter.

In January 1898, Representative William Alden Smith told Speaker Reed that "his position with his constituents would be in danger unless some action were taken soon," as reported in Detter, "Cuban Junta," p. 42. Smith, a Michigan Republican and nominally loyal to McKinley, was working closely with the *Junta*. See also Waldeck, "Missouri," pp. 374–375.

40. H. H. Kohlsaat, *From McKinley to Harding: Personal Recollections of Our Presidents* (New York, 1923), p. 67. Gould reviews three descriptions of McKinley's appearance at this point. He does not mention Kohlsaat in this connection but does reject, without explanation, the notion of the president "in tears and despair," *Presidency*, p. 78. Leech reports Kohlsaat's account, provides a date, 30 March, and indicates no doubts as to its accuracy, *McKinley*, pp. 180–181.

41. Henry S. Pritchett, "Some Recollections of President McKinley and the Cuban Intervention," *North American Review*, 189 (1909):397–403, quotations from pp. 400–401.

42. Pratt, *Expansionists*, pp. 234–235. Business opposition to the war was widely recognized at the time, this indicated even after the *Maine* explosion. For evidence on this question, see: May, *Imperial Democracy*, pp. 139–140; Campbell, *Transformation*, p. 248; and William E. Leuchtenburg, "Progressivism and Imperialism: The Progressive Movement and American Foreign Policy, 1898–1916," *Mississippi Valley Historical Review*, 39 (1952):483–504, especially p. 497.

43. Pratt, *Expansionists*, p. 233; Herbert Croly, *Marcus Alonzo Hanna* (New York, 1912), p. 278; and Beer, *Hanna*, pp. 197–198.

44. Pratt, *Expansionists*, p. 234, n12. Pratt depended on Carnegie's autobiography and on the biography by Burton J. Hendrick. The former provides a brief description of the events leading up to the war, reporting it to be the result of a "wave of passion" that swept the nation. Apart from a faint sense of disdain and regret, it gives no clear indication of Carnegie's position. See *Autobiography of Andrew Carnegie* (Boston, 1920), pp. 349–350. Hendrick's work contains only a passing reference to the Spanish-American War, see *The Life of Andrew Carnegie*, two volumes (New York, 1921), Vol. 2, p. 176.

45. Herbert Adams Gibbons, *John Wanamaker*, Vol. 1 (New York, 1926), pp. 371–372.

46. See Cyrus Adler, *Jacob H. Schiff: His Life and Letters*, Vol. 1 (Garden City, 1928), pp. 307–309. The account contains only a faint suggestion of the banker's attitude prior to McKinley's message to Congress. On the day following delivery of that message he wrote to Adolph Ochs of the New York *Times* to say that: "Standing by the President has now become a patriotic duty, and in my opinion therein alone lies safety to the country and its best interest."

    Pratt cites George Kennan, *E. H. Harriman: A Biography* (Boston, 1922), Vol. 1, p. 170; Vol. 2, p. 1. Harriman's Union Pacific, Pratt reports, ultimately "profited from American operations in the Philippines." But Harriman did not appear to have foreseen this opportunity nor did he work toward annexation in 1898. He did not begin his Far East operations until 1905. A recent biography touches peripherally on the war but gives no indication of Harriman's position; see Maury Klein, *The Life and Legend of E. H. Harriman* (Chapel Hill, 2000), pp. 207, 283.

47. Joseph Gilpin Pyle, *The Life of James J. Hill*, Vol. 2 (Garden City, 1917), pp. 77–78; Albro Martin, *James J. Hill and the Opening of the Northwest* (New York, 1976); Michael P. Malone, *James J. Hill: Empire Builder of the Northwest* (Norman, OK, 1996), p. 194.

48. What is striking about the biographical accounts reviewed to this point, those cited by Pratt, is the paucity of comment on the 1898 events. The index to Kennan's biography of Harriman contains no entry under Cuba, Spain, Spanish-American, or McKinley. A chronology of the man's life contains the following entries under 1898: "Elected chairman of executive committee of Union Pacific in May. Made first trip of inspection over the road and called for an appropriation of $25,000,000

for betterments." Kennan, *Harriman*, Vol. 2, p. 402. Although not specifically cited, Pratt probably made use of George Harvey's *Henry Clay Frick: The Man* (New York, 1928). It contains nothing on the Spanish-American War, but, as will be seen immediately, Frick was very much opposed to the U.S. involvement. Harvey obviously did not judge this to be an important concern. A recent biography of the man also has nothing on the war, Samuel A. Schreiner, Jr., *Henry Clay Frick: The Gospel of Greed* (New York, 1995).

49. Vincent P. Carosso, *The Morgans: Private International Bankers 1854–1913* (Cambridge, 1987), p. 349; and Ron Chernow, *The House of Morgan: An American Banking Dynasty and the Rise of Modern Finance* (New York, 1990), p. 80. A different reading on Morgan and the yacht appears elsewhere, see note 65 below. The paucity of comment on the war in other relevant biographies is striking. The leading biography of George W. Perkins, Morgan's principal executive in this period, contains no index reference to Cuba, Spain, or the war; see John A. Garraty, *Right-Hand Man: The Life of George W. Perkins* (New York, 1960).

50. Jean Strouse, *Morgan: American Financier* (New York, 1999), pp. 369–371.

51. Harold van B. Cleveland and Thomas F. Huertas, *Citybank 1812–1970* (Cambridge, 1985), ch. 3 (quotation from p. 48). At a later point, after World War I, the National City Bank "plunged deeply into Cuba," this based on a boom in sugar prices. But those prices fell dramatically and "the bank's entire Cuban loan portfolio was frozen under a debt moratorium declared by the Cuban government." It was the "worst setback in National City's long history" and led Stillman to resign as president; see Cleveland and Huertas, pp. 104–110.

52. Anna Robeson Burr, *The Portrait of a Banker: James Stillman, 180–1918*, Vol. I (New York, 1928), pp. 138–140. Later the bank handled the transfer of the $20,000,000 indemnity to Spain as settlement for the Philippines. Apart from that, nothing is said about Stillman's position with respect to the outcome, that is, any possible concern with "expansion."

53. Joseph Frazier Wall, *Andrew Carnegie* (Pittsburgh, 1989 [1970]), p. 690.

54. *Ibid.*, p. 691. For another account of Carnegie's reactions, one that points up some significant contradictions in his position, see Robert L. Beisner, *Twelve against Empire: The Anti-Imperialists 1898–1900* (Chicago, 1992 [1968]), ch. 8. Carnegie "reconciled himself" to a possible annexation of Cuba. He favored, for strategic reasons, the taking of Puerto Rico and Hawaii (p. 176).

55. Allan Nevins, *John D. Rockefeller: The Heroic Age of American Enterprise*, two volumes (New York, 1940). For the Cuban iron mines see Vol. 1, pp. 359, 368, 377, 379, and 412. The other accounts reviewed are: Nevins, *John D. Rockefeller: A Study in Power*, two volumes (New York, 1953); Peter Collier and David Horowitz, *The Rockefellers: An American Dynasty* (New York, 1976); and John Ensor Harr and Peter J. Johnson, *The Rockefeller Century* (New York, 1988). The latter work contains a peripheral mention, a sentence reporting a "romantic trip to Cuba" in the spring of 1900 aboard the presidential yacht "to investigate conditions in the wake of the Spanish-American war" (p. 55). On board were John D. Rockefeller, Jr., plus Senators Aldrich, Teller, Allison, Spooner, and Beveridge. The trip was "romantic" in that Senator Aldrich was courting Abby, Rockefeller's daughter, at the time.

A recent biography of Rockefeller has nothing on the events leading up to the war, nothing on the magnate's position. Three fugitive mentions touch on some consequences, one dealing with malaria, one with yellow fever. See Ron Chernow, *Titan: The Life of John D. Rockefeller, Sr.* (New York, 1998), pp. 388, 487, 369. The comprehensive history of Standard Oil is by Ralph W. Hidy and Muriel E. Hidy, *Pioneering in Big Business, 1882–1911* (New York, 1955). The Havana and Puerto Rican refineries receive a single paragraph (p. 128) in this work of 800–plus pages. A footnote reports that exports of crude oil to Spain from 1894 to 1899 averaged 297,000 barrels per annum but the note makes no reference to the war (p. 747, n13). See also the work of Albert Z. Carr, discussed in note 71 below.

56. Edward N. Akin, *Flagler: Rockefeller Partner and Florida Baron* (Kent, OH, 1988), p. 169.

57. Joseph Frazier Wall, *Alfred I. du Pont: The Man and His Family* (New York, 1990), pp. 169–173.

58. The information in this and the following four paragraphs comes from Stanley P. Hirshson, *Grenville Dodge: Soldier, Politician, Railroad Pioneer* (Bloomington, 1967), ch. 16.

    None of the sources cited in chapter 3 mention McKinley's offer to Dodge. Hirshson writes that Dodge "withdrew" thus making way for Alger. He also provides documentation (pp. 227–228). Dodge would later head a presidential commission named to investigate the failings of the War Department under Alger's management; on this see Leech, pp. 315–319.

59. Garraty, *Lodge*, pp. 161, 180–184. The kinship tie is reported in Alden Hatch, *The Lodges of Massachusetts* (New York, 1973), p. 44.

    Henry Lee Higginson was indeed a leading banker but that statement, by itself, is seriously misleading. One biographical account states that he "never believed himself meant by nature to be a banker." His earliest interests were "reform movements and music." He gave up a clerkship, moved to Vienna, and intended to "make music his life work." Some "unexpected obstacles" prevented this and, after service in the Civil War, he joined the family's banking establishment. His most notable achievement, however, was not in banking. He was the founder and for many years the sole underwriter of the Boston Symphony Orchestra, at that time the "leading organization of its kind in America," from DAB, 9:12–13.

60. Garraty, *Lodge*, pp. 186–187.

61. Ibid., p. 189.

62. Ibid., p. 194.

63. Ibid., pp. 161–162. Lodge's position was disapproved by another elite figure, Harvard University's president, Charles W. Eliot. Writing in the New York *Evening Post* he referred to Lodge and Roosevelt as "degenerated sons of Harvard," from Garraty, p. 161, n4.

64. Pratt, *Expansionists*, pp. 246–247, n51.

65. Beer, *Hanna*, pp. 199–200. For public consumption apparently, Perkins reported Morgan's yacht being put "at the service" of the government. But as seen earlier, the yacht had been "conscripted" over the banker's objection. Beer, the "political observer," had picked up and given credence to the public relations statement. For more details on the conscription of the yacht, see the popular accounts by Andrew Sinclair, *Corsair: The Life of J. Pierpont Morgan* (Boston, 1981), pp. 108–109 and Edwin P. Hoyt, Jr., *The House of Morgan* (New York, 1966), pp. 268–269. The latter work reviews the problems posed by the confiscation of the yacht but says nothing about Morgan's position on the war.

66. These brief accounts are based, for the most part, on accounts in the *Dictionary of American Biography*. Astor's involvement in the Cuban League is reported in the

Review of Reviews, 15 (February, 1897), p. 137. Astor was definitely not a "giant" in the business world. The indexes to Carosso's *The Morgans* and to Chernow's *House of Morgan* contain no reference to the man. For a brief portrait, see Derek Wilson, *The Astors, 1763–1992: Landscape with Millionaires* (London, 1993), pp. 200–207.

67. Morgan had to deal with Gates in connection with United States Steel and again in another matter in 1902 but he "mistrusted and disliked [the man] and considered him an unfit custodian of other people's property." Carosso, p. 502. Chernow's *House of Morgan* portrays Gates as basically a nuisance. Gates is discussed at some length in connection with the 1902 issue in Garraty, *Right-Hand Man*, ch. 8.

68. One might expect that Stuyvesant Fish, whose Illinois Central railroad reached to New Orleans, would have more than average interest in Caribbean developments. But the index to a history of the line contains no reference to Cuba, to the Spanish-American War, or to McKinley. See Carlton J. Corliss, *Main Line of Mid-America: The Story of the Illinois Central* (New York, 1950). In 1898, the line, as the title suggests, had other concerns. It completed an extension to Peoria and began construction of the Fort Dodge & Omaha Railroad Company (p. 287).

William Rockefeller was allied with Jacob Schiff against Morgan in the struggle over the Chicago, Burlington and Quincy Railroad. There was some later involvement with Ryan in 1905 in connection with the Equitable Life Assurance Society.

69. In *The Tragedy or American Diplomacy*, revised edition (New York, 1962), pp. 36–37.

70. LaFeber, *New Empire*, p. 386.

71. Foner, *Spanish-Cuban-American War*, pp. 306–307. In a footnote (p. 307), Foner quotes Beer as saying that J. P. Morgan was "avidly for war." That phrase, however, does not appear in Beer's text (the entire passage is quoted here just above).

72. Nancy Lenore O'Connor, "The Spanish-American War: A Re-Evaluation of Its Causes," *Science and Society*, 22 (1958):129–143; the quotation is from p. 142. O'Connor declares: "We know that Edward [sic] Atkins during the latter part of 1897 urged President McKinley to take Cuba. Atkins held heavy sugar interests, it is true, but he was, in addition, a Morgan partner" (pp. 133–134). The only reference to Morgan in Atkins' *Sixty Years* is the following: "In 1889 I became a director of the Union Pacific . . . and was asked to be co-trustee with J. P. Morgan and F. L. Ames of the Omaha Bridge bonds" (p. 108). There is no index reference to Atkins in Carosso *The Morgans*, in Chernow *House of Morgan*, in Strouse *Morgan*, or in Garraty's *Right-Hand Man*. O'Connor was arguing against "the growing tendency among historians to lay the war at the door of the Populists" and for this purpose was reviewing "the weaknesses of Professor Pratt's thesis."

73. Pratt, *Expansionists*, pp. 248–250; LaFeber, *New Empire*, p. 387–88; and *New-York Daily Tribune*, 10 February 1898, p. 1.

To supplement Beer's findings, LaFeber added a paragraph describing the leadership of the Cuban League, this based on a brief account that appeared in the *Review of Reviews* (cited above in note 66), which, as noted earlier, was an expansionist journal. A self-selected group of supporters, however, cannot be taken as a representative sample of business leaders. LaFeber reports that several "militants" are listed, among them Theodore Roosevelt and Charles A. Dana. Five "conservative businessmen" are listed as vice presidents, the most prominent of these being Chauncey M. Depew, "railroad president and director of numerous railway and banking corporations" (p. 387). Depew's memoirs make no mention of the League; they say nothing about his attitude toward the Cuban events or toward the war; see Chauncey M. Depew, *My Memories of Eighty Years* (New York, 1922). Two members of the board of directors are named, one of them being Colonel John Jacob Astor. The leading biographies of Theodore Roosevelt do not report any Cuban League involvement.

74. For further details, see Lewis L. Gould, "The Reick Telegram and the Spanish-American War: A Reappraisal," *Diplomatic History*, 3 (1979):193–199. William Appleman Williams gives this report of the event: "[T]he President received by telegram the following intelligence from a New York correspondent . . ." *Tragedy*, p. 37.

   Walter LaFeber assigned considerable importance to this message: "Perhaps the most influential note received by the President was the telegram from Reick, a trusted political adviser in New York City . . ." *New Empire*, pp. 392–393. In a later work, LaFeber repeats the basic argument without any reference to Gould's critique, in *American Search* (p. 142). Foner views the telegram as somehow important; see *Spanish-Cuban-American War*, vol. 1, p. 307. The indexes in Leech, Gould, Morgan, Trask, and Offner contain no references to Reick.

75. Pratt, *Expansionists, 1898*, p. 250; Garraty, *Lodge*, p. 180.

76. Trask, *War with Spain*, p. 497, n23. The dissertation is by Richard D. Weigle, "The Sugar Interests and American Diplomacy in Hawaii and Cuba, 1897–1903" (New Haven, Yale University, 1939). See also Offner, *Unwanted War*, pp. 2, 25, 112. May also doubts the importance of the sugar trust; see *Imperial Democracy*, pp. 115–116.

   One account declares that McKinley "allowed the country to be pushed into war against Spain and sent American battleships and troops to Cuba, largely in the interest of the American sugar trust." But the author provides no evidence in support of that claim; see Albert Z. Carr, *John D. Rockefeller's Secret Weapon* (New York, 1962), pp. 110–111. Carr senses some advantage for Standard Oil: The war pushed its "sins" to the back pages of newspapers (p. 121).

77. Lodge to Henry Lee Higginson, 10 January 1896. For copies of this and the following letter, I wish to thank the Massachusetts Historical Society.

78. Lodge to Charles Francis Adams, Jr., 22 January 1897. Again, my appreciation to the Massachusetts Historical Society.

79. LaFeber, *New Empire*, p. 389. Two factual errors appear in LaFeber's account. He reports that, "as early as January, 1897, Atkins had written Lodge . . ." But in Lodge's letter of that date he reports an exchange of views "a year ago last November," and that in a personal discussion, not in a letter. As Lodge put it, "I talked with him for two or three hours . . ." Atkins was disappointed by the results of this conversation and thereafter, for several years, avoided contact with Lodge. See Atkins, *Sixty Years*, p. 212.

   In his later work, LaFeber again avoids the most obvious source for Atkins's views and again depending on this same letter writes in 1896 Atkins had favored autonomy but, "as the revolt spread and became more radical. . . . Atkins and his fellow planters began to consider outright U.S. annexation." At a later point, LeFeber reports that the "U.S. investors in Cuba, led by Atkins, wanted less dickering and quick annexation to the United States." *American Search*, pp. 130, 142.

80. For discussion of the misinterpretation, see Garraty, *Lodge*, p. 181. Lodge's statement of this right of intervention appears in a letter to Moreton Frewen dated

11 March 1896, that is, about two months subsequent to his letter to Higginson announcing that "we ought to have Cuba." Some additional complexities in Lodge's views will be reviewed below.

81. Pratt, *Expansionists*, ch. VII entitled "The Business Point of View." He cites only a single scholar, Professor Harold U. Faulkner, who argued the war was caused by "financial imperialism" (p. 232).

82. Pratt, *Expansionists*, pp. 233. The late-conversion thesis will be discussed further in the subsequent volume.

83. Williams, *Tragedy*, p. 29, his emphasis.

84. LaFeber, *New Empire*, pp. 385–386.

85. Russell Sage's statement appeared in the *New York Daily Tribune*, 27 February 1898, p. 5.

86. LaFeber, *New Empire*, pp. 385–393.

87. Jules R. Benjamin, *The United States and the Origins of the Cuban Revolution: An Empire of Liberty in an Age of National Liberation* (Princeton, 1990), p. 39.

88. Lester D. Langley, *The Cuban Policy of the United States: A Brief History* (New York, 1968).

89. The magnification of Cuba's significance appears also in Langley, who declares that: "At the end of the Ten Years' War [1878] the volume of trade between the United States and Cuba was greater than the total amount of United States trade with the remainder of Latin America." No source is given, but the *Historical Statistics* figures show that claim to be false. The combined exports to Mexico and Brazil were greater than those to Cuba at all points up to 1895. Total exports to "other" American nations (not including Canada) were significantly larger than "the Cuban market." U.S. Bureau of the Census, *Historical Statistics of the United States* (Washington, 1975), Part 2, pp. 904–905.

90. Leland Hamilton Jenks, *Our Cuban Colony: A Study in Sugar* (New York, 1928).

91. U.S. Bureau of the Census, *Historical Statistics*, loc. cit.

92. Leech, *McKinley*, pp. 188–189. Leech also reports a "general repugnance to the idea of admitting to the Union an alien and insubordinate people, Roman Catholic in faith, with a large admixture of Negro blood."

93. The statement appears, one example from among many, in Morris, *The Rise*, p. 610. As his source, he cites James Ford Rhodes, *The McKinley and Roosevelt Administrations, 1897–1909* (New York, 1922), p. 57. Rhodes, in turn, cites "Peck, 642," that is, Harry Thurston Peck, *Twenty Years of the Republic 1885–1905* (New York, 1907). The quotation appears there but no further information is given, nothing about the source, the date, or the context of Roosevelt's utterance. For a more extended review of this much-cited statement, see Richard F. Hamilton, "McKinley's Backbone," *Presidential Studies Quarterly*, forthcoming, 2006.

94. Offner, *Unwanted War*, pp. 41, 54; Gould, *Presidency*, pp. 6, 59, and 88–89. Gould credits Margaret Leech, H. Wayne Morgan, Paul S. Holbo, Grenville and Young, and Robert L. Beisner, among others, for the change in assessment of the man. For a brief summary of historians' views on McKinley, see Paul S. Holbo, "Presidential Leadership in Foreign Affairs: William McKinley and the Turpie-Foraker Amendment," *American Historical Review*, 72 (1967):1321–35, especially notes 1, 2, and 3. For more, H. Wayne Morgan, "William McKinley as a Political Leader," *Review of Politics*, 28 (1966):417–432; Joseph A. Fry, "William McKinley and the Coming of the Spanish-American War: A Study of the Besmirching and Redemption of an Historical Image," *Diplomatic History*, 3 (1979):77–97; Lewis L.

Gould, "Chocolate Eclair or Mandarin Manipulator? William McKinley, the Spanish-American War, and the Philippines: A Review Essay," *Ohio History*, 94 (1985):182–187; and John L. Offner, "McKinley and the Spanish-American War," *Presidential Studies Quarterly*, 34 (2004): 50–61.

Gould's essay reviews two books, one using the traditional approach, McKinley lacking backbone, the other in the newer tradition, McKinley as "imperialistic evil genius." They are, respectively, G.J.A. O'Toole, *The Spanish War: An American Epic—1898* (New York, 1984) and David Haward Bain, *Sitting in the Darkness: Americans in the Philippines* (Boston, 1984). That traditional approach, Gould wrote (in 1985), "extends an historiographical tradition that is more than six decades old."

95. LaFeber, *New Empire*, p. 400 and *American Search*, pp. 144, 135, 141, and 147.

5

Cuba and the American Press

Many accounts of the causes of the war assign prime importance to the demands put forth by an aroused and angry populace. William Allen White, the eminent Kansas publisher, a witness to those events, declared:

> That war revealed the blood hunger of a democracy. McKinley tried earnestly to prevent war. It is hard to realize, a generation after, how the waves of public wrath at the delay of the war with Spain beat in breakers about the White House. The tyranny of Spain in Cuba had excited the mob spirit in America. One wonders also if the deep lust for conquest was not in our heart in those days.[1]

Another such statement comes from Lyman J. Gage, McKinley's Secretary of the Treasury, a participant in the decision-making, a man who had "been there" and "seen it all." His account opens with a mention of the years of struggle on the island, a struggle in which "the sympathies of our people were wholly with Cuba." Then, "in the early months of 1898, the voice of our people, expressing itself through Congress, demanded intervention in Cuba's behalf and cried loudly for war." McKinley resisted, still seeking a peaceful resolution, but "the pressure from our people grew daily until it could no longer be resisted; it became plain that unless the President asked Congress to declare war, it would make such a declaration regardless of his protests or appeals." In Gage's reading, the causal chain had three links: the "voice of our people," the expression of Congress, and the decision of a reluctant executive. This conclusion was reached some time after the event, perhaps a "mature judgment" developed after some years of reflection.[2]

Judgments about mass opinion are easily produced. With a single declarative sentence, one having at least surface plausibility, the task is finished. Gaining accurate knowledge about such sentiments, however, is much more difficult, a task requiring extensive and complicated research. The basic problem with freely extemporized declarations may be seen by consideration of two earlier statements made by Gage. In the midst of the crisis, on 19 March 1898, he provided a much different reading of American public opinion. While on a visit to Cleveland he stated that the "people of the country are getting used to this war talk and they understand that it means little or nothing." Later the same day, speaking in Pittsburgh, his words were summarized as follows: "So far as the people were concerned, he was of the opinion that 90 per cent believed the explosion was an accident."[3]

Another declaration about the "state of the masses" was made by Pulitzer's business manager, Don C. Seitz. The second Cuban revolt, he stated, "had evoked wide sympathy in the United States long desirous of Cuba Libre." The sentiment in support of the insurgents, he declared, "was almost unanimous." In his account, the decisive event was the destruction of the *Maine*. "Popular opinion," he declared, "believed the ship had anchored over a harbor mine and that some Spaniard in the secret [sic] had touched this off." Although the affair "remains as much of a mystery as ever," it "did arouse opinion." Seitz says nothing about the Congress or the executive branch. Those "dynamics" were by-passed through his use of a passive voice construction—"the declaration of war, which came April 23 . . ."[4]

Decades later, a leading diplomatic historian, Thomas A. Bailey, provided an even stronger statement about the decisive role of the "war-mad" Americans. After the de Lôme letter and the sinking of the *Maine* "the American public was on fire for war." McKinley, Hanna, and Wall Street "did not want war. . . . But a frenzied public, lashed by the yellow press, clamored for war to free the abused Cubans. Overborne, the President finally yielded and gave the people what they wanted."[5]

Frank Mott, author of the leading history of American journalism, declared that the press, led by the *Journal* and the *World*, both published in New York City, created "an irresistible popular fervor for war."[6] An important unpublished 1970 dissertation by Mark Matthew Welter found similar statements in ten high-school histories and in fifteen university-level textbooks.[7]

A popular account, one written long after the events, reports as follows: "Despite the pacific intentions of McKinley, Hanna, and the established business world, the man in the street grew belligerent. Impelled by the heady winds of Manifest Destiny, stirred by manufactured Cuban atrocity stories, inflamed by the screaming headlines of Hearst and Pulitzer, the American public clamored for war even while forgetting its actuality."[8]

Claims about "public opinion," about orientations and intensity are easily stated. But the provision of confirming evidence, especially from times past, before the appearance of polls and surveys, is a much more difficult task. Intense mass reactions, moreover, must necessarily result from some other prior cause. From the beginning in this case, it was alleged that those forceful public demands stemmed from sensational press coverage, from demagogic portrayals of Spain's repression of the Cuban insurgency.

Accounts of that press coverage begin, typically, with reviews of the competition between Joseph Pulitzer's *World* and William Randolph Hearst's *Journal*, two mass-circulation New York City newspapers. The content of those newspapers was reviewed and documented in a comprehensive study by Joseph E. Wisan published in 1934. Another key study, by Marcus M. Wilkerson, published two years earlier, reviewed the content of newspapers in other large cities, those of Philadelphia, Chicago, St. Louis, and San Francisco. Both works argued that the "sensational" depictions of the Cuban events began with New York's "yellow press." Both claimed that "the press" elsewhere imitated that performance. And that imitation, in turn, generated the national public clamor.[9]

The Pulitzer- and Hearst-centered depictions of the 1898 events radically simplify a much more complicated reality. New York City had twenty-seven daily papers in 1897 with widely varying orientations and circulations. An early content analysis by Delos Wilcox classified them as follows: eleven "yellow," ten "conservative," and six uncertain.[10] Most accounts do focus on the *World* and the *Journal*, but two other New York papers, the *Sun* and the *Herald*, although not quite so vociferous, also provided strong support for the Cuban insurgents.

The *Herald* and the *Sun* were New York's largest circulation newspapers in the 1870s and early 1880s. Both were popular; both provided "sensational" content. In the 1890s, the *World* and later the *Journal* far surpassed them in circulation and also were of much lower quality. One fact regularly overlooked in those many depictions of the "clamoring masses" is that all four of those large-circulation newspapers usually favored the Democrats. Charles Anderson Dana (1819–1897), the long-time publisher of the *Sun*, had a personal dislike for Grover Cleveland and in 1884 changed to support the Greenback-Labor candidate for the presidency. One consequence was that the *Sun* experienced a serious loss of circulation as many readers shifted to a new entry in the city, to Pulitzer's *World*. In 1896, three of the four newspapers distanced themselves from Bryan's candidacy, the exception, as seen, being the Hearst newspaper.[11] It is easy to think that profit making was a principal concern for these "sensational" newspapers. One source however, quotes Arthur Brisbane, a "Hearst stalwart," who declared that their reporting of the war had been "ruinous financially."[12]

Wilcox reported that in 1897 the United States had 250 dailies with a circulation of 7,500 or more. Over half of these were based in five states: New York, forty-eight; Pennsylvania, twenty-nine; Ohio, twenty-three; Illinois and Massachusetts, twenty-one each. Sixteen states had no daily with that minimum circulation.[13] Wilcox declared further that the "*New York World* and the *New York Journal* have an incalculable influence in the United States. During the late war they claimed a daily circulation of more than a million copies each, and they were hawked upon the streets of distant cities." But in one important respect his evidence shows their influence to have been very limited. Wilcox tabulated "exchanges" (reprinted stories) found in his sample of 147 dailies. From a total of 1,601, the *New York Sun* led the list with seventy-five exchanges while "only 15 and 14 were taken from the *World* and the *Journal*, respectively."[14] At the outset, it would seem unlikely that the Republican press would make use of material provided by such competitors. The neglect of partisanship allows a considerable magnification of the presumed Pulitzer-Hearst influence.

Wisan's 1934 review of the key causal sequence provides an exemplary instance of this kind of neglect, his summary paragraph making no mention of the partisan factor. His account begins as follows: "The Spanish-American War, so momentous in its consequences, was a popular crusade. Neither the business interests of the nation nor the Government executives desired it. The public, aroused by the press, demanded it." Wisan's compendious account reviewed the content of New York's daily newspapers, focusing primarily on the *World* and *Journal*. His final conclusions, presented without any appropriate evidence, contain the following declarations:

> The *Journal's* sensational innovations won immediate national attention and some imitation. When New York's powerful newspapers emphasized Cuban news, it was natural that others should do the same.
>
> From March, 1895, until April, 1898, there were fewer than a score of days in which Cuba did not appear in the day's news. The newspaper reading public was subject to a constantly increasing bombardment, the heaviest guns booming for "Cuba Libre." The effect was cumulative. . . .
>
> Little wonder that the "average reader," indoctrinated with these opinions, called on his Government for War.[15]

Marcus Wilkerson mentions "partisan newspapers" in his 1932 study but moves on without signaling the possible, the likely difficulty. His summary paragraph reads:

> The sensational press had finally triumphed. Led by the *World* and *Journal*, partisan newspapers, after carefully arranging the stage for the final act in the drama of war propaganda, "played up" the Maine explosion without restraint and left the American public reeling from a bombardment of half-truths, misstatement of facts, rumors, and faked dispatches. Sensing the popular tide, a hesitant administration, egged on by a "jingo" Congress, proposed war with a nation already on the verge of collapse from internal strife and rebellion.[16]

Several years later, in 1940, George W. Auxier provided an important criticism of this long-established wisdom:

> American historians have long emphasized the important part played by American newspaper propaganda in precipitating the Spanish-American War. This emphasis has resulted primarily from the assumption—arrived at *post hoc propter hoc*—that the sensational methods employed by William Randolph Hearst and Joseph Pulitzer, in their ruthless exploitation of the Cuban crisis for purposes of increased circulation of their respective papers in New York City, were universally imitated by the newspapers throughout the "entire" United States and that sensational journalism was accordingly the paramount factor which culminated in war with Spain over the Cuban question.

Auxier raised an important question: Was that assumption—universal imitation—justified?[17]

Still later, Harold J. Sylwester published another important critique. He began with a similar statement: "Writers of American history continue to mention the press as one of the causes for the Spanish-American War in 1898." In support of that claim, he quoted two prominent diplomatic historians, Thomas A. Bailey, cited just above, and Samuel Flagg Bemis, who wrote that: "Irresponsible and self-interested journalism must bear its large burden of responsibility for the Spanish-American War . . ." Sylwester cites a dozen other leading historians who made similar claims.[18] Both Auxier and Sylwester, as will be seen, provided evidence casting doubt about the sweep of those claims.

A basic problem that appears in many of those discussions of "the press" and its presumed influence is that of sampling. The accounts focus on a very limited sample of metropolitan newspapers. But only a small minority of the nation's population lived in the nation's largest cities at that time. As seen in chapter 2, in 1890 only eleven cities had a population of 250,000 or more and they contained only 11.0 percent of the nation's population. More than three-fifths of the American population lived in unincorporated rural territory.[19]

Most people in the nation would probably have never seen a single issue of any "scandalous" New York City newspaper. For those living in the towns, villages, and countryside, almost everything known about distant events, those occurring in Washington, New York, Havana, or Madrid, would have been transmitted through the local press. Some information, perhaps, would have come from local citizens or groups speaking on behalf of the Cuban cause. It is important therefore to have some sense of how people in other regions and those in smaller cities, in the towns and villages saw things. What did the people living there know of those distant events? And how did they react? What demands, if any, did they make? And how were they expressed?

A small, scattered, and largely neglected literature gives some sense of what the vast majority of Americans living outside the handful of large cities would have been told. With one exception, this literature will be reported in sequence, taking the items according to the dates of their appearance.

An early study by Ruby Weedell Waldeck reviewed events as reported in Missouri newspapers. The article provided information on mass meetings, petitions, Junta activities, and press content. In the three years before the war, petitions were sent to Congress urging recognition of belligerency or independence. These came from St. Louis, Kansas City, and several smaller communities, Jefferson City, Sedalia, Windsor, and Bonne Terre. Meetings were held to collect money and supplies for the suffering Cubans. A society to aid the Cuban cause was formed in St. Louis in 1895 and branches were established in some smaller communities. The St. Louis unit was in close touch with the Junta in New York. The efforts of Senator George Vest and several of the state's Democratic congressmen placed "Missouri definitely among the leading states active in the interest of Cuba and for intervention." The majority of Missouri newspapers were Democratic and they, Waldeck reports, were "heartily in favor of war with Spain." When war came, the declaration brought "an outburst of enthusiasm all over the State. In St. Louis bells rang, guns boomed, and flags waved."[20]

Waldeck's article gives wide coverage to the developments in Missouri. There is little reason to doubt the statements about the positions of the state's press and politicians. This brief article, however, could not provide much detail about the content of the state's newspapers and is limited to a report on editorial positions. A more serious problem appears there in that gratuitous judgments about press influence are made throughout the article, for example: "[T]he political views of party leaders and newspapers profoundly influenced the attitude of the general public." But no evidence on the attitudes of that "general public" is reported. Some citizens probably did not read any newspaper, some would have been opposed to intervention, and some would have had no opinion.

An article by J. Stanley Lemons reviewed the performance of forty-two Missouri weekly newspapers from "county seat towns" (the population range, 500 to 5,600 persons), none of them having a daily paper. One principal finding: "In the Missouri country press the Cuban question failed to be a campaign issue at any time between 1895 and the coming of the war." Yellow journalism to that point was "scarcely a factor." After the sinking of the *Maine* the state's largely Democratic press was "heartily in favor of war with Spain." Within that rank, there was a division along the gold-silver line. The gold papers "counseled moderation." The "silver press" led with "the most bitter, denunciatory statements [and] righteous fury." One denounced President Cleveland as "The Second Judas" while another saw McKinley as "the creature of evil men."

Patriotism was equated with the "crusade for silver." The war was "a holy war" against "Wall Street, Great Britain, Jewish Bankers—the whole 'international gold conspiracy.' "[21]

The previously mentioned study by George Auxier gives a wide-ranging comprehensive review of editorials in more than forty Midwestern newspapers, these from large and middle-sized cities ranging from Chicago to Omaha. That article also, necessarily, is summary in character, little detail being possible in eleven pages. These newspapers, he states, focused on four themes. There was, first, "the basic interest of the United States in the Caribbean . . . stated in terms of economic imperialism, military stratagem, political idealism, and a large measure of humanitarianism." The second theme, a repeated complaint, was that Spain had "violated" those interests. Third, he reports the newspapers "served as a vehicle for the propaganda of the Cuban *Junta*." The fourth theme was the evident partisan use made of the insurgency. Those factors are suggested as the "real causes" that led to the war with Spain. Auxier rejects the view that the demand for intervention stemmed from sensational content with the aim of increased circulation. In this connection, Auxier refers to the "objective manner" in which the editors suspended judgment with respect to the de Lôme letter and the sinking of the *Maine*. These newspapers showed a "decided provincial antipathy to the 'yellow sheets' of the East . . . throughout the course of the Cuban revolt."[22]

Since so often overlooked, Auxier's comments on partisanship deserve special emphasis. The editorial columns of these Midwestern newspapers, he wrote, indicated that attitudes on the Cuban question were "influenced to a large extent by political considerations. . . ."

> In seeking to discredit Cleveland's policy of neutrality the Republicans introduced the Cuban issue into American politics. . . . The partisanship of the Republican press toward Cleveland's policy of neutrality was apparent as early as midsummer, 1895, and became increasingly evident with the approach of the presidential canvas of 1896. . . . Immediately after the election in November, Republican editors reversed themselves and advised a Cuban policy equally as cautious as that which the Democrats had pursued under Cleveland. . . . [The Republicans] received much retributive denunciation from Democratic editors, who pointed out the inconsistencies of their political foes and sought to embarrass them precisely as they had been embarrassed by the Republicans during Cleveland's regime.[23]

A dissertation by Richard Anthony Matré reviewed the editorial positions of seven leading Chicago daily newspapers in the years from 1889 to 1902.[24] An unexpected linkage appeared here in that the *Tribune*, an ardently Republican publication, subscribed to both the New York *World* and *Journal* Cuban news services from an early point. From an early point, the *Tribune* was aggressive, bellicose, and jingoist in its foreign policy recommendations. With one exception, these newspapers were either Republican or independent. McKinley's supporter, Herman H. Kohlsaat, the owner of the *Inter-Ocean*, bought the Democratic *Times-Herald* in 1895 and turned it into a Republican paper running a challenge to the *Tribune*. A new Democratic paper, the *Chronicle*, was founded in the same year.

The attention paid to Cuban events by these seven newspapers over some four years fluctuated in much the same pattern as seen elsewhere. Here too, as elsewhere, there was partisan differentiation. This was clearly the case with respect to the December 1896 Cameron resolution. The Republican papers supported it, subjecting Cleveland and Olney to heavy criticism. Four newspapers—two independents, the Democratic *Chronicle*, and, unexpectedly, Kohlsaat's *Times-Herald*—did not join in the attacks. The Chicago experience differs from that found elsewhere in that the partisan reversal did not appear after McKinley took office. The same division appeared in the first months of 1898 as with the Cameron resolution. The three Republican papers "ardently" favored intervention. The two independents, plus the *Chronicle* and the *Times-Herald*, did not favor such action.[25]

A study by William J. Schellings of eight leading Florida newspapers in the period 1895–1898 brought some additional unexpected findings. Florida, he reports, "presented the unique picture of being the only state in which all important newspapers were united in opposition to war. The journals continued to oppose it right up to the day on which President McKinley signed the joint resolution of Congress . . ."[26] One ground for this opposition was concern about the possibility of attacks by the Spanish fleet, a fear, Schellings says, that was shared by every city and state on the Gulf and Atlantic coasts. That opposition also "undoubtedly" reflected "the opinion and attitude of a large and influential group in the state, the business interests." The editors and business people saw war as "an interruption of business" that would halt the expansion and growth of the state's industry, tourism, and agriculture. Another fear was that victory in the imminent war would bring the annexation of Cuba. And that would put Cuba within the tariff wall thus providing competition that "could not be met."

Some 8,000 Cubans lived in the state, most of them in Tampa and Key West, most employed in the manufacture of cigars. As noted previously, they provided generous support for the Cuban Junta. Floridians generally, it is said, showed sympathy for the Cubans in their struggle with Spain. These complications led the newspapers to follow a "middle course." Opposing war but giving no suggestion of favor to Spain, they "expressed their sympathy, contributed to funds for Cuban relief, and wished the rebels good luck in their endeavors." They gave "little heed" to the Hearst-Pulitzer demands for intervention, some occasionally faulting the New York journals for "their jingoist tendencies."

Following that middle course, the Florida press gave "a rather surprising" amount of attention to "the Spanish side of the story." In February 1898, it played down the implications of the de Lôme letter, depicting it as "a regrettable, somewhat stupid error, but one that should cause no difficulty." In regard to the *Maine* explosion, most editors "gave the story full coverage, but cautioned . . . that no judgment should be passed until the Navy had made its investigation." The Tampa *Tribune* suggested the explosion had been an accident. If not an accident, the editor suspected the rebels, seeing them as the most likely beneficiaries. With the approach of war, the press opposition softened. The newspapers' conversion, their full acceptance of the war, came with the passing of the Teller Amendment that ended the threat of Cuba's annexation.[27]

A review of North Carolina press commentary by George H. Gibson reports "no lack of sympathy" for the rebels. In response to General Valeriano Weyler's ruthless tactics, the "United States" became "more vocal in its protests" and it was "widely urged" that the insurgents be granted belligerent rights. One response, as seen earlier, was the passing of the Morgan-Cameron resolution by Congress in April 1896. Gibson reports that North Carolina's senators, one Republican and one Populist, voted for it. The vote in the House is reported as follows: "Five North Carolina Representatives (one Democrat, two Populists, and two Republicans) voted for the action, one (a Democrat) voted no, and three (all Democrats) were recorded as not voting." The distribution suggests partisanship rather than a response to clamorous public demands.[28]

One paragraph reports representations from the state's citizens directed to the United States Congress. The first, dated 13 January 1896 and of unstated origin, asked for recognition of the insurgent Cubans as belligerents. The second, dated 16 January 1896, was from "G. H. Brown, Jr., and 19 other Citizens of Washington, N. C." The third, dated 28 June 1897, was the "Petition of T. H. Hathcock, mayor of Norwood, N.C.," and "579 citizens of Norwood and vicinity" favoring belligerent rights for "suffering Cuba." Those are the only indications in the article attesting to direct communication between North Carolina's "public" and their representatives in the Congress.

As evidence of popular concern, however, these reports are incomplete, telling next to nothing of their origins or about any subsequent impacts. The *Congressional Record* gives little more detail. The report of the first of those submissions tells that Mr. Lockhart (the representative from Wadesboro) introduced two petitions, one submitted by the heirs of a deceased constituent in reference to an unresolved war claim. The complete report of the second, the Cuba petition, reads: "Also, petition for recognition of the insurgent belligerents in their struggle for freedom—to the Committee on Foreign Affairs." No indication is given as to origins of this petition, nothing said as to how many signed or how many communities were represented. And nothing is indicated about its impact on the Congress. Apart from the members of the Foreign Affairs Committee it is possible that few other congressmen even saw it.[29]

The second petition, also from January 1896, reported the sentiments of some twenty persons in a small community, one with 4,842 inhabitants in 1900. This was one of many resolutions received by the Congress at this time, several calling for immigration restrictions, several protesting Turkish atrocities in Armenia. Most of these entries are brief, basically three-line reports similar to the one just cited.[30]

The third petition, that with 579 signatures, was submitted by Mayor Hathcock of Norwood, North Carolina, a village approximately thirty miles east of Charlotte. The village had a population of 663; the township had 2,315 persons. Hathcock must have been an unusually charismatic figure to generate such support from that small community. That petition was also consigned to the Committee on Foreign Affairs. The Cuba question, it will be remembered, was an unexpected theme for the first session of the 55th Congress, its main purpose being to produce the Dingley Tariff. Most of the petitions received at that time, not surprisingly, dealt with duties on cigar wrappers, goatskins, dressed bristles, onions, sheep dip, hops, and many other products.[31]

These observations point up an important methodological consideration. Many accounts of those Cuba petitions contained in the relevant literature may, because selective, give a false sense of the extent of public concern. And similarly, selective reporting would also give a false sense of the pressures from constituents felt by the members of Congress.

Gibson's narrative covers the principal subsequent developments, providing also an assortment of press comments on each. His conclusion about public opinion in the state reads as follows:

> If public attitudes can be accurately gauged by newspaper editorials, editorials, public pronouncements of political figures, and petitions of ordinary citizens, North Carolina had only a slight war fever. Public opinion was not inflamed by the de Lome letter; North Carolinians adopted a wait-and-see attitude after the sinking of the "Maine"; and editors decried the yellow sheets of metropolitan cities which were spreading war germs.[32]

The study by Harold J. Sylwester, as noted, provides a comprehensive analysis of the Kansas press including that of the smaller towns and also of the weeklies.[33] His principal conclusion is that with two exceptions, those newspapers did not lead "the masses to clamor for war." Instead, they "tended to follow a cautious course and generally came to endorse war only after McKinley had declared its necessity." A second conclusion is that "while some Kansas papers were 'jingoistic,' more were not. A few even violently attacked the 'yellow press.'"

Sylwester indicated the political uses of the Cuban conflict by the major parties. He also commented on the Populist papers that "sympathized with the Cubans and wanted action in their behalf" but opposed war because "it would only benefit the rich at the expense of the poor." The Populist editors, it will be noted, were out of touch, unaware of the actual preferences of their big business opponents. Sylwester's summary conclusion is that "the Kansas press alerted its readers to Cuba's needs but it hardly led them to demand war."

Mark Welter's dissertation reviewed a sample of eight Minnesota newspapers.[34] This included newspapers from large cities, St. Paul, Minneapolis, and Duluth, and some from smaller towns, Crookston and Fergus Falls. The eight were selected from all regions of the state and also, although most of the state's newspapers were Republican, some Democratic and independent journals were also represented. Welter compared New York and Minnesota press accounts of the initial Cuban rebellion, filibustering, atrocities, belligerency, official U.S. policies, the Havana riots, the de Lôme letter, and the *Maine* disaster. He found "conspicuous" dissimilarity in the reports provided by New York's "yellow press" and the Minnesota press.

At the end of 1895, the first phase of the conflict, Welter concludes that, "Minnesota reporting did not—in contrast to its eastern counterpart—significantly alter its course in the direction of the spectacular. Far from having 'scarcely a day pass' without its mention, Cuba was referred to infrequently; often weeks, even months, went by between references. When it was printed, coverage was brief, usually objective and at times filled with penetrating insight into the character of the struggle. . . ." News of Cuba "virtually disappeared" from the pages of the Minnesota press in the second half of 1896 when "every publication" was "saturated with stories on the evils of free silver and the blessings of 'sound' money." From "the beginning of the rebellion to the conclusion of its third year," Welter reports, the Minnesota accounts "differed distinctly from the New York style." Anti-administration criticism "was significant" in the East, but in the West it was "slight." Minnesota evaluations, he wrote, fell between "the poles of respectful dissent and complimentary agreement."[35]

The Havana riots on January 1898 "created no great stir" in Minnesota's press. Most in fact "ignored the outbreak altogether." The reactions to the de Lôme letter were quiet and subdued. It was an "indiscretion," a problem that was quickly resolved, in short, "no cause for alarm." None of the eight newspapers demanded an immediate overt response to the sinking of the *Maine*. The responses again were calm with much attention given to the possibility of an internal explosion. The basic recommendation was to suspend judgment, to await the results of the inquiry. Senator Cushman K. Davis, the state's senior senator and chairman of the Senate Foreign Relations Committee, urged caution. In another summary, one that covered reports through to mid-April, Welter stated that, "In lieu of the 'Demand for War,' witnessed in the East, the Gopher State press offered its readers a 'demand for peace.'" When Pulitzer and Hearst material was reprinted, which was not often, it was typically accompanied by another story that challenged the "sensational" claims. Some carried pointed critiques as, for example, an editorial entitled "Free Speech vs. Free Lying." The Duluth *Herald* was an "incomplete exception" to the dominant pattern. Its editorials matched those of "the East," but its news pages were little different from the seven other papers reviewed.[36]

A 1970 dissertation by Edward M. McNulty reviewed the performance of New Jersey newspapers with respect to the Cuban crisis. His compendious study focused on the editorials and news columns devoted to the Cuban crisis that appeared in some thirty newspapers—from larger city dailies to small rural weeklies. It also placed the Cuban news "in the context of other news, local, state, national, and foreign." McNulty summarized his findings as follows:

> (1) New Jersey news columns gave little prominence or sustained attention to the Cuban question until after the sinking of the *Maine*; the editorials seldom echoed jingoism, although they occasionally evidenced anti-Spanish bias; (2) there was no significant pattern, political, regional, or geographic, in news and editorial emphasis with regard to the Cuban struggle; (3) the state' editors revealed sympathy for the insurgents as the underdog in a struggle against colonialism, but they remained most reluctant to suggest American military involvement; (4) there were manifestations of nationalistic truculence with regard to American rights, insults to the flag, etc., and of latent Anglophobia, but almost universal anti-jingoism with regard to Cuba until after the news of the *Maine*; (5) not only did Garden State editors avoid "yellow journalism," "news fabrication," and "sensationalism," but many of them expressly condemned the "New Journalism" in New York City; and (6) New Jersey editors were apparently innocent of the growing concept of "manifest destiny" and did not visualize an American empire until after Dewey's Manila Bay victory.

That fifth conclusion deserves special attention. If the New Journalism was as powerful as is often alleged, one should find the Pulitzer-Hearst influence extending across the Hudson River. But that, clearly, was not the case. McNulty provided an alternative conclusion as to the principal cause of the war—again it was the partisan factor. His study indicated "the significance of Congressional agitation over Cuba and the impact of Senate bellicosity . . ."[37]

A dissertation by William J. Donahue, also from 1970, reviewed more than 260 newspapers across the nation to ascertain their reactions to the sinking of the *Maine*. He found that in 1897 the majority of the leading journals "refused to copy the methods employed" by the New York yellow journals. Even after the destruction of the *Maine*, he found "over one hundred" papers that condemned the practices of the sensational journals. Donahue concludes that the "overwhelming pressure . . . began to mount" only after McKinley's message to Congress following the Court of Inquiry report. Although he was reviewing newspaper content, Donahue concludes that the pressure for intervention was coming from "the public and Congress."[38]

Daniel Simundson reviewed the editorials in twelve of the thirteen newspapers in South Dakota from March 1897 to the outbreak of the war in April the following year.[39] These papers, he indicates, exerted pressure on the president for a more aggressive policy. The anti-administration editors "continually scolded [him] for what they considered to be his lack of initiative." The Republican editors "tried to defend [him] but when his peaceful policy became unpopular with the electorate, they withdrew their support." That declaration of cause and effect, it should be noted, is an unsupported inference.

Simundson also reported the frequency of editorial comment on Cuba in 1897 but did not discuss the implications. McKinley's Cuban policy was discussed in "at least forty instances" in the four months from March to June. Attention declined significantly in the following six months with a total of "less than twenty" editorials. In the first period that would mean those South Dakota papers did not average even one editorial per month. In the second period, it would mean, on average, fewer than two editorials per paper for the entire period from July to December. For them, Cuba was clearly not a pressing issue, hardly the source of a public "clamor."

Simundson also indicated a "distinct difference" in the approach of the New York press and that of South Dakota: "While the Hearst and Pulitzer papers were struggling for circulation, most South Dakota papers were struggling to survive. They had neither the editorial staff, the inclination, nor the ability to dwell on Cuban sensationalism, especially when state-wide issues often seemed to be more important." Some instances did appear but "such writing was comparatively rare." The sinking of the *Maine*, for example, did not bring immediate accusations against Spain. Only one paper immediately blamed Spain while "at least five" considered the possibility of an accident. One paper faulted the *New York Journal*'s performance, describing it as a "vulgar bit of self seeking enterprise . . ." One headline read: "Let Us Suspend Judgment." But eventually, in the following weeks, the press generally, including the Republican papers, shifted and called for war.[40]

A brief monograph by Morton M. Rosenberg and Thomas P. Ruff reviews the developments as reported in the Indiana press.[41] One important difference here was that Claude Matthews, Indiana's governor, was a Democrat. He was also an ardent supporter of the Cuban insurgents, which put him in direct opposition to the policies of President Cleveland. Support groups were formed throughout the state with "Cuba Libre" clubs and "Cuban League" societies said to be "numerous." The press, here as elsewhere, was divided along party lines but here there was the additional split within the Democratic ranks. Initially the press offered a wide array of comment on Spain and Cuba but over time, the authors report, some newspapers began to emulate the New York "yellow journals." One reason for this was that "virtually all news items available on the subject originated from New York." In January 1896, for example, four Indiana newspapers published a Cuban Junta report from New York, one excoriating Weyler. The local support groups at that point "flooded" Congress with petitions demanding belligerent rights.[42]

Cuban affairs gained some attention early in 1896 when both house of the Congress approved belligerency resolutions that Cleveland and Olney subsequently ignored. The Cuba issue then disappeared for some months, basically for the period of the 1896 presidential election, during which time, as one newspaper put it, the Cuban issue was "virtually nonexistent." The pressures resumed during the first session of the 55th Congress, which was called to revise the tariff. Governor Matthews urged the General Assembly to petition Congress on behalf of the Cubans. Democrats in the Assembly introduced three motions in support of belligerent rights but all of them were defeated by the Republican majority. In Washington, the newly elected Republican senator, Charles W. Fairbanks, "reflected his party's position of moderation" and opposed all interventionist efforts. Indiana's other senator, David Turpie, a Democrat, was an ardent supporter of those same efforts. In the last half of 1897, the Hoosier press was anything but warlike—"President McKinley's approach to the Cuban question received approval from most of the Hoosier press. His caution, patience, and temperate attitude as he sought to resolve the highly charged problem were applauded."[43]

The press responses to the sinking of the *Maine* were also striking in their moderation: "[E]ditors generally assumed a posture of caution and restraint. Even the Democratic papers opted for a nonwar approach to the crisis." Several are quoted as calling for suspension of judgment, at least pending the result of the investigation. Several directed anger against "the eastern journals," faulting them for their inflammatory reporting.[44]

Following the declaration on 25 April, the authors state that: "Hoosiers welcomed the war with Spain despite the fact that they had earlier been cautious in their behavior and reaction, antiexpansionist and antijingoist in their outlook." That conclusion, however, is not justified. The monograph reports an assortment of newspaper comment. But it provides no serious evidence on public sentiments within the state.[45]

These accounts of newspaper content in the period leading up to the war, understandably, used different approaches and had different emphases. This "sample" moreover is clearly not cross-sectional. It gives us some information about Missouri, the Midwest, Florida, Kansas, South Dakota, Minnesota, New Jersey, and Maine but obviously tells us nothing about the remaining states and regions. Those studies, however, provide the best available information we have on press performance across the nation in those years. That scatter of evidence, accordingly, provides a better basis for analysis than those many ad hoc declarations about "the press" and its presumed impact on "mass sentiments."

The accounts of public opinion reviewed in the first pages of this chapter claim a strong, single-minded tendency among the American citizenry. "The public" was making imperious demands for intervention in Cuba; those demands, in turn, resulted from an equally single-minded tendency found in "the yellow press." The studies of press content reviewed here provide no serious support for the latter reading.

In contrast to those declarations of single-mindedness, these studies show differentiation, that being perhaps the most important of the findings. Missouri dailies were "heartily in favor of war." But for that state's weeklies war was not even an issue. Florida's newspapers showed sympathy for the Cubans but were opposed to war, to American intervention. As for the impact of New York's "yellow" press, disdain or hostility toward those sources was a frequent finding. As opposed to the notion of insistent attention to Cuban affairs, one study found infrequent mention. As opposed to the notion of persistent demagogic agitation, there were frequent calls for calm consideration even after the sinking of the *Maine*.

Finally, these studies report differentiation by party with the Democratic press, following McKinley's inauguration, generally favoring intervention and the Republican papers favoring caution and avoidance of war. This finding, partisan division, is reported in eight of the thirteen studies reviewed here. Florida was an exception, a special case, two studies finding opposition to intervention by all newspapers. Partisan division deserves emphasis given the persistent preference in much of the relevant literature for undifferentiated portraits of both "the press" and "the masses."

The clamor for war begins, supposedly, with those "sensational" New York newspapers. But, as indicated, the fact that those were Democratic journals is rarely noted. Another line of differentiation should be noted. Among the Democratic journals, those of the Bryan, silver, or Populist persuasion generally favored intervention; the conservative or "gold" papers generally took an opposite stance. In addition to the role of the parties and the party-related press, several of the studies reviewed here reported another effort of agitation, the contributions by individuals or groups having ties with the Cuban Junta or its local Cuban League affiliates. But little direct evidence was provided in these accounts attesting to the state of public opinion, evidence about "grassroots" sentiment in those states and communities. Direct evidence on this subject, local reactions and initiatives, is sparse both in the press reports and in subsequent monographic studies.

One other consideration should be noted: The news from Cuba had a seasonal character—fighting there normally abated in the hot summer months. The history, in short, was not continuous. Americans were not provided with a steady diet of stories about Cuba. The history was not cumulative, as Wisan claimed, each account adding to a widespread sense of outrage.

Those Cuba-centered—or Cuba-obsessed—narratives give little or no attention to other competing news events in the years from 1895 to 1898. Some of those events to be sure were far from American shores—the Sino-Japanese War ended with China's defeat; Armenians were massacred in Turkey; an Italian army was defeated by Abyssinians; the Jameson raid in South Africa was followed by Kaiser Wilhelm's telegram to Kruger; Greece and Turkey went to war over Crete; Germany took Kiao-chow from China; Russia took Port Arthur; Lord Kitchener, fighting in the Sudan, reached Fashoda; a revolt broke out in the Philippines; the Dreyfus affair, including the trial of Emile Zola, continued in France; and gold was discovered in the Klondike. Closer to home, two major events pushed Cuba off the front pages for months: President Cleveland and Secretary of State Olney challenged Great Britain, threatening war in the Venezuela boundary dispute, and for many months the 1896 presidential campaign dominated all else. The struggle in Cuba, in short, was only one of many subjects reviewed in the pages of American newspapers.

A sizable disparity appears in much of the literature dealing with the origins of the 1898 war. Bold assertions are presented telling of the "powerful forces" said to be "driving" events. But all too often, the evidence offered in support of those claims proves very thin. In some cases no evidence at all is presented, as if the declaration itself were sufficient. Such is the case with the flamboyant statements of William Allen White, the Kansas-based editor, those quoted at the beginning of this chapter. His declarations stand in sharp contrast to Harold Sylwester's findings reported here, those based on a review of the Kansas press. That press, he reports, "alerted its readers to Cuba's needs but it hardly led them to demand war." White's report of "blood hunger," "public wrath," and "mob spirit" is difficult to reconcile with Sylwester's evidence, that showing the Kansas press recommending a "cautious course."[46]

The leading current American history textbooks show little recognition of the findings contained in the studies reviewed here. Divine et al. declare that "a wave of sympathy for the insurgents" was stimulated by "the newspapers," a statement that again neglects the partisan division within the press. That is followed by an unambiguous statement that the "so-called yellow journalism did not cause the war." The conflict "stemmed from larger disputes in policies and perceptions . . ." The review of causes ends with the statement that "in the end, the conflicting national interests of the two countries brought them to war."[47]

Norton et al. review the Cuban insurgency, telling of United States investments going "up in smoke" and a trade that was dwindling. One is then told of the "reports of atrocity and destruction [that] became headline news in the American yellow press [and that] Americans sympathized increasingly with the insurrectionists."[48]

Nash et al. review those same events reporting that "Americans were outraged" and that "An outpouring of sympathy swept the nation." "Sensationalist newspapers . . . competing for readers, stirred up sentiment with pages of bloody stories of atrocities." The New York *World* is cited in this connection. "The Cuban struggle," this account continues, "appealed to a country convinced of its role as protector of the weak and defender of the right of self-determination." The American populace became enraged as Hearst's New York *Journal* called De Lôme's letter "the worst insult to the United States in its history." The partisan division of the press and the public goes unmentioned.[49]

Henretta et al. report the Cuban insurrection and emphasize the role of the exiles, of the *junta* who set up shop in New York City. They came on the scene at a "critical juncture," that is, at the same time as Hearst purchased the nearly moribund *Journal*. He and Pulitzer then engaged in "a furious circulation war," both papers elevating Cuba's "agony into flaming front-page headlines." The next sentence declares that, "Across the country powerful sentiments stirred . . ." And, "Congress began calling for Cuban independence." Two full pages follow, these devoted to "William Randolph Hearst: Jingo."[50]

None of these textbooks report the principal findings in the literature reviewed in this chapter. The differentiated performance of "the nation's press" is not reported. And, most importantly, the party linkage, the partisan usage of the Cuban struggle, is not mentioned.

The assertion-evidence disparity may be seen in one recent compendious history of the 1898 conflict. Ivan Musicant reports that in the weeks following the destruction of the *Maine*: "The American public, already aroused by the Dupuy de Lôme scandal, was driven to new heights of hysteria. . . . Public disgust with Spain's conduct in Cuba intensified." For support, he provides first a statement from Secretary Long's journal—"Public sentiment is very intense"—then adding this information: "Three mass meetings in Buffalo alone demanded a declaration of war. The Naval Veterans' Association of Brooklyn offered its services in any fight with Spain. In Lehigh, Pennsylvania, college students drilled under a banner stating, 'To Hell with Spain.' The tide of intervention swept across the national consciousness . . ." It is a modest array of evidence to support such an important conclusion.[51]

Notes

1. William Allen White, *Masks in a Pageant* (New York: Macmillan, 1928), p. 176. For a brief account of the man, his work, and his importance, see ANB, 23:251–253.
2. Lyman J Gage, *Memoirs* (New York, 1937), pp. 125–126.
3. The *Evening Dispatch* (Columbus, Ohio), 19 March 1898, p. 1. The statements by White and Gage differ from most other accounts in that they do not explicitly mention newspaper reports as sources of that popular arousal.
4. Don C. Seitz, *Joseph Pulitzer: His Life and Letters* (New York, 1924), pp. 238–239. A small detail, the declaration of war was passed by the Congress on 25 April.
5. Thomas A. Bailey, *The American Pageant*, second edition (Boston, 1961), pp. 617–618.
6. Frank L. Mott, *American Journalism: A History: 1690–1960*, third edition (New York, 1962), p. 527.
7. Mark Matthew Welter, "Minnesota Newspapers and the Cuban Crisis, 1895–1898: Minnesota as a Test Case for the 'Yellow Journalism' Theory" (unpublished dissertation, University of Minnesota, 1970), pp. 3–4. This work will be discussed further below.
8. Francis Russell, *The President Makers: From Mark Hanna to Joseph P. Kennedy* (Boston, 1976), p. 30.
9. Joseph E. Wisan, *The Cuban Crisis as Reflected in the New York Press, 1895–1898* (New York, 1934) and Marcus M. Wilkerson, *Public Opinion and the Spanish-American War* (New York, 1967 [1932]).
10. Delos F. Wilcox, "The American Newspaper—A Study in Social Psychology," *Annals of the American Academy of Political and Social Science*, 16 (1900): 56–92.
11. For brief biographies of Dana, see DAB, 5:49–52 and ANB, 6:55–58. For more detail, see Janet E. Steele, *The Sun Shines for All: Journalism and Ideology in the Life of Charles A. Dana* (Syracuse, 1993), chs. 8 and 9. Steele gives the daily circulation of the *Sun* in 1897 as 120,000, well ahead of the *Herald*, *Times*, and *Tribune* but far behind the *World*, p. 143.

    An important source of information on newspapers (all kinds) is *N.W. Ayer & Son's Newspaper Annual: 1898* (Philadelphia, 1898). For information of their procedures, which included sworn statements, see p. 16. The *World* and *Journal* did not provide Ayer with circulation figures in 1898, 1899, and 1900. Their self-reported circulation figures, clearly, should not be trusted.
12. See Sidney I. Pomerantz, "The Press of a Greater New York, 1898–1900," *New York History*, 39 (1958):50–66, quotation p. 54.
13. Wilcox, "American Newspaper," pp. 77, 58–59.
14. Ibid., pp. 81–82.
15. Wisan, *Cuban Crisis*, pp. 455, 460.
16. Wilkerson, *Public Opinion*, p. 132. The meaning, moreover, is not clear—it might refer to partisanship on behalf of Cuba.

17. George W. Auxier, "Middle Western Newspapers and the Spanish-American War, 1895–1898," *Mississippi Valley Historical Review*, 26 (1940):523–534, the quotation, p. 523.
18. Harold J. Sylwester, "The Kansas Press and the Coming of the Spanish-American War," *The Historian*, 31 (1969):251–267.
19. U.S. Bureau of the Census, *Historical Statistics of the United States* (Washington, D.C., 1975), Part I, p. 14. Most contemporary American history textbooks have chapters dealing with the "growth of the cities." Few of them suggest the actual distributions indicated here. Large cities were growing: In 1900 there were fifteen with 250,000 or more population. The number of persons living in the large cities increased by just over 4 million between 1890 and 1900. But in the same decade, the number of persons living in places of 5,000 or less (again including rural territory) also increased—by more than 5.6 million.
20. Ruby Weedell Waldeck, "Missouri in the Spanish American War," *Missouri Historical Review*, 30 (1936):365–400.
21. J. Stanley Lemons, "The Cuban Crisis of 1895–1898: Newspapers and Nativism," *Missouri Historical Review*, 60 (1965):63–74.
22. Auxier, "Middle Western Newspapers," see especially, for discussion of Junta activities, pp. 525–528.
23. Ibid., pp. 528–530. For much more detail, see Auxier's dissertation, "The Cuban Question as Reflected in the Editorial Content of Middle Western Newspapers, 1895–1898" (Columbus: Ohio State University, 1938), pp. 148–160, 205, and 214.
24. Richard Anthony Matré, "The Chicago Press and Imperialism, 1889–1902" (Evanston, Ill., unpublished Ph.D. dissertation, Northwestern University, 1961).
25. Ibid., pp. 103–106, 119–124.
26. William J. Schellings, "Florida and the Cuban Revolution, 1895–1898," *Florida Historical Quarterly*, 39 (1960–1961):175–186. Another article by Schellings reviews events in the first months of the war, "The Advent of the Spanish-American War in Florida, 1898," *Florida Historical Quarterly*, 39 (1960):311–329.
27. A review of six Southern Methodist newspapers found that they also "did not favor a war to liberate Cuba." While not indifferent to Cuban suffering and encouraging charitable assistance, these newspapers "did little to encourage a martial settlement" and instead supported McKinley's efforts to avoid war. Only after the war began did they favor the expulsion of Spain from the island; see Arnold M. Shankman, "Southern Methodist Newspapers and the Coming of the Spanish-American War: A Research Note," *Journal of Southern History*, 39 (1973):93–96.
28. George H. Gibson, "Attitudes in North Carolina Regarding the Independence of Cuba, 1868–1898," *North Carolina Historical Review*, 43 (1966):43–65, pp. 56–57.
29. *Congressional Record*, 54th Congress, 1st Session, 1896, Vol. XXVIII, pp. 642.
30. Ibid., p. 757.
31. Ibid., 55th Congress, 1st Session, 1897, Vol. XXX, p. 2085. Population figures from *12th Census of the United States* (1900), Vol. I.
32. Gibson, p. 64.
33. Cited in note 18 above.
34. Cited in note 7 above.
35. Welter, "Minnesota Newspapers," pp. 36, 56, and 141.
36. Ibid., pp. 154, 160, 191, and 210.

37. Edward M. McNulty, "The Cuban Crisis as Reflected in the New Jersey Press, 1895–1898" (unpublished Ph.D. dissertation, Rutgers University, New Brunswick, New Jersey, 1970), pp. iii–iv.

38. William J. Donahue, "The United States Newspaper Press Reaction to the Maine Incident—1898" (unpublished dissertation, University of Colorado, Boulder, Colorado, 1970), pp. 230, 232, and 238.

39. Daniel Simundson, "The Yellow Press on the Prairie: South Dakota Daily Newspaper Editorials Prior to the Spanish-American War," *South Dakota History*, 2 (1972):211–229.

40. For details on the choices facing the state's editors, politicians, and parties, see pp. 226, 228. Another of the gratuitous declarations about mass opinion and its effects appears there: "Publishers on the prairie, like those elsewhere, were reflecting the national mood of manifest destiny."

41. *Indiana and the Coming of the Spanish-American War* (Muncie, IN, 1976).

42. Ibid., pp. 7, 16. The authors tell of "the huge flow of petitions" from Indiana on behalf of the Cubans, but the information contained in their source, the *Congressional Record*, shows that report to be selective (paralleling the practice reported in notes 26–28 above). Petitions came in on a wide range of topics, all of these directed to the appropriate committees. Almost as many expressed concern about outrages in Armenia as for those in Cuba.

43. Ibid., pp. 20–23.

44. Ibid., pp. 25–27.

45. Ibid., p. 30. At one point they report "vehement" press responses to Spain's actions, those it is said "reflected the critical reaction of the public" (p. 6).

46. A later account by White gives a markedly different reading of "the causes." There he emphasized the "many hundreds of millions of American dollars" invested in Cuba, most of it in sugar and rum. American sympathy for the oppressed, he declared, "was following the American invested dollar and beckoning the American flag." The local congressman, Charley Curtis, "made some speeches, as did most of our Congressmen . . . about the oppression of the Cubans." But he was "after votes to hold his job, and 'free Cuba' was a vote-getter." White wrote editorials on the subject but did not remember "which side I took." Like "Our Charley," he "knew nothing about the deeper currents of imperialism that were sweeping the world . . ." One would not sense any "waves of public wrath" from this whimsical account. See *The Autobiography of William Allen White* (New York, 1946), pp. 305–307. A scholarly biography of the man makes only two very peripheral references to the war, Sally Foreman Griffith, *Home Town News: William Allen White and the Emporia Gazette* (New York, 1989), pp. 52, 150.

47. Divine, et al., pp. 654, 656.

48. Norton et al., p. 643.

49. Nash et al., pp. 641–642.

50. Henretta et al., pp. 680–684.

51. Ivan Musicant, *Empire by Default: The Spanish-American War and the Dawn of the American Century* (New York, 1998), p. 152. The secretary's words are from Margaret Long, ed., *The Journal of John D. Long* (Rindge, N.H., 1956), p. 216. No source is given for the events in Buffalo, Brooklyn, and Lehigh.

    Wisan might have been the source for the first of those events. He reports, "Three mass meetings in Buffalo requested President McKinley to declare war against Spain," in *Cuban Crisis*, p. 403. He gives his source as the New York *World*, 18 February [1898]. I did not find any mention of mass meetings in Buffalo in the issue indicated. Mass meetings at that point would seem unlikely given that the *Maine* explosion occurred on 15 February, only two days earlier. My inquiry addressed to the Research Library of the Buffalo and Erie County Historical Society brought this report: A check of their newspaper index revealed no articles about mass meetings in Buffalo in 1898. And a check of a few newspapers around the indicated date yielded the same result. I wish to thank Laura Schiefer for this assistance.

6

A Mobilization of the Masses?

To obtain a better appreciation of public reactions to the events in Cuba, this chapter will examine the experience of one middle-sized city, Columbus, the capital of Ohio. The purpose of this inquiry is to obtain some sense of the impacts of press, pulpit, and Cuban support groups on the attitudes and behavior of local citizens. The contents of the city's three daily newspapers will be reviewed. The specific aims are, first, to see how they reported the pertinent national and international events in the early months of 1898, and second, to look for accounts of local reactions to those events. The prime concern is to discover evidence of public reactions, of any "inputs" that might have "compelled" belligerent responses by political leaders, local, state, or national. Although obviously limited in scope, this review will allow somewhat better informed conclusions about that elusive subject, public opinion.

Columbus, the capital of Ohio, was the state's third largest city, after Cleveland and Cincinnati. Like most other cities, it too showed rapid growth, increasing from 88,150 in 1890 to 125,560 in 1900.[1] Many readers of the city's three daily newspapers would have lived in the surrounding towns, villages, and countryside of Franklin County. The detailed reports on matters outside the county suggest that all three had even wider outreach with some readers living in the towns and villages of surrounding counties.

The *Ohio State Journal* reported a daily circulation of 13,163 and a Sunday circulation of 17,471.[2] A morning paper, it was clearly aligned with the Republicans, offering strong support for McKinley and, in state affairs, for Mark Hanna and his faction. The daily editions contained some ten or twelve pages of news, international, national, state, and local. The Sunday editions ran to roughly twenty pages. Most of the information provided on Cuba, understandably, focused on distant events with very little said about the local reactions. Most of the accounts gave the Associated Press as the source, most items indicated as originating in the various capital cities.

The *Evening Dispatch* reported a circulation of 18,500 (but no Sunday edition). Although described in Ayer's as "independent," it clearly favored the

Republicans in 1896. It's pre-election editorial put some "pertinent questions," such as: "Do you want to vote for a candidate for president who stands on a platform whose principles would precipitate on the country a calamity equal to that of the civil war, and destroy all that has been accomplished in the last 30 years? . . . If you do, then vote for Bryan and the Chicago platform." Another editorial offered "A Final Word to Workingmen." The advice: "Cast your ballots for business prosperity, financial honor, law and order, and a 100-cent dollar. Your work and your wages, your homes and your happiness, are now at stake" (*Dispatch*, 2 Nov 1896:4). The *Dispatch* put out four editions per day. All citation here is from the final edition. Much of its national news came from the New York *Herald* via the Associated Press. On occasion it published articles from Pulitzer's *World* but these were temperate accounts, not at all of the sensational variety.

The *Evening Press* announced the "Largest Circulation in Central Ohio." No circulation figure was given in Ayer's *Annual* but an unsworn statement contained there gives it as 32,000. The paper appeared Monday through Saturday followed by a Sunday edition called the *Morning Press*. The firm, the Press-Post Printing Company, also put out a weekly edition, called the *Press*, that appeared on Thursdays. In 1898, on 1 March, the name was changed from *Evening Press* to the *Press-Post*.[3]

This paper was clearly Democratic. Just before the 1896 election, one front-page cartoon showed the leaders of the "U.S. Gold Syndicate." Two of its members, both fat and ugly men, were identified as J. P. Morgan and Mark Hanna. Attached to Hanna by a chain was a tiny knee-high creature identified as McKinley (1 Nov 1896:1). The main front-page headline the day before the election declared that: "The Cause of the Plain People Will Triumph!!" (2 Nov 1896:1). That was followed by pictures of Bryan and of John Jacob Lentz, the local congressman, both identified with the "Success of Silver." The paper catered to a large local ethnic group, putting the principal lessons, in script, in German—"Für Präsident William Jennings Bryan" and "Des Volkes Stimme muß triumphieren!"

On the day following the election, the main front-page headline announced— "Triumphant Victory!" The subheads provided further specification: "William J. Bryan Next President of the United States. . . ." The story itself gave a more "mixed" picture while the editorial in the same issue, entitled "The Next President," reported "all indications pointing to the election of Mr. McKinley as president . . ." (4 Nov 1896):1, 4). A comment on the following day blamed the Associated Press for the erroneous declaration (5 Nov 1896:4).

The *Evening Press* also provided enthusiastic support for *Cuba Libre*. Unlike Florida, Minnesota, and New Jersey, Columbus had an important press organ that, like the New York *World* and *Journal*, did its best to generate public support for American involvement in Cuba.

Another agency needs to be considered. The Cuban League, as seen in the previous chapter, was an important pressure group in this period. The local unit, the Columbus Cuban League, was organized, on New Year's Day 1897, in the home of James Kilbourne, who was chosen as its president. One of the city's most prominent citizens, he was the president and general manager of Kilbourne and Jacobs, the city's largest employer, a manufacturer of hardware. As might be expected, he was very well connected, sitting on the boards of numerous fiduciary organizations. Kilbourne was a Democrat, a leading and active member of the party.[4]

Three members of the League's executive committee were partners in leading law firms. One of them, Thomas E. Powell, had a national reputation as a lawyer. He represented some major corporations, several of his most important cases being tried in New York. He was a leader of the state's Democratic party, a candidate for several offices including at one point that of governor (he lost to the incumbent, Joseph Foraker).[5] Daniel Joseph Ryan was a lawyer, the president of a company, "an enthusiastic Republican," and the author of several historical monographs.[6] Henry Judson Booth was another "prominent attorney and man of affairs" in the city. He was a partner in a leading law firm, a founder of several public service organizations, and served as a trustee on several boards.[7] The League had important newspaper support: Dewitt C. Jones, the editor of the *Evening Press*, was also a member of the executive committee. And last, but not least, Charles B. Galbraeth, the state librarian, a Republican, was a member. One biographical account states that it was Galbraeth who, under the direction of Colonel Ethan Allen of New York, organized the Columbus branch of the Cuban League. The Columbus unit was reported to have had 2,000 members, which, if accurate, would be a large number at any time for a community organization. It seems likely that the membership was drawn, disproportionately, from the city's well-off and influential citizens.[8]

The most important activity of the Columbus Cuban League in the first months of 1898 was charitable in character, managing the collection of funds for Cuban relief. President McKinley had appointed a central national committee to manage Cuban relief efforts. That committee called on the governor, Asa Bushnell, to help in this effort and he, in turn, placed the matter in the hands of the Cuban League (CED, 21 Jan:8; and CEP, 21 Jan:10). It was clearly not a grassroots initiative.

The content of the three Columbus newspapers will be reviewed in the following pages. The aims are twofold, to indicate what the three reported about Cuban events and to seek evidence of public responses in the period from

January to April of 1898. To simplify somewhat, each of the many events will be covered in the following sequence: *State Journal, Dispatch*, then *Evening Press* (later, *Press-Post*).

The New Year's Day issue of the *Ohio State Journal* in 1898 carried a page-one note from Havana reporting a meeting of the new Cuban cabinet, the group that would work out the autonomy arrangement scheduled to begin that day. On Monday, 3 January, a note reported the appeals of McKinley and Secretary of State Sherman asking for contributions for Cuban relief. A long account that day reviewed events in Cuba—the insurgents were doing very well; the Spanish authorities were disheartened; the general population was doing poorly, many dying of smallpox and the fevers.

All three newspapers gave several columns to church news in their Saturday issues, listing sermon topics, musical offerings, and other items of interest. Most of the sermons, understandably, dealt with religious, not political, subjects. Church news appeared also in the Monday issues with summaries of several sermons, evening lectures, and comments on their musical presentations. On this Monday the *State Journal* gave two columns for a lecture, "Retrospect and Prospect: The Old Year and the New," by an influential local clergyman, the Reverend Washington Gladden, a man with a national reputation.[9] Gladden reviewed several disappointments beginning with the failure of a plan for arbitration of international conflicts. He faulted the European powers for not coming to the aid of insurgents in Crete, for their failure to end the "detestable and degrading rule of the Turk." He discussed Cuba: The insurgents there were unwilling to accept autonomy; he thought the Cubans incapable of self-rule but offered no solution. On another topic, Gladden recommended "the extension of civilization and good government," of American rule, to Hawaii. The next paragraph dealt with Germany's recent move in China and the prospect of further efforts of partition by the major powers.

The principal news topic in the first week of January was the attempt by Governor Bushnell and others to displace Mark Hanna, to remove him from the Senate. These events filled the news columns from Tuesday to Saturday and continued into the following week. The *State Journal* strongly favored Hanna. The Saturday edition contained a brief note with some details on Cuban relief (8 Jan:6). On page eight, a meeting of McKinley's cabinet was reported. Their most important concern was Germany's role in China.

On Monday, 10 January, the Senate was considering the annexation of Hawaii, a topic that appeared regularly in the following weeks. President Dole, the islands' leader, visited the United States in this period seeking support for that move. From Havana there was a report about Cuban appreciation for the first distribution of American supplies. The lead editorial, drawn from a Cuban newspaper, asked "in the name of humanity" that the insurgents lay down their arms and make peace. The next day's issue reported at length on the activities of Frederick Funston, an American who had fought with the Cubans.

In the first days of January, the lead news stories in the *Evening Dispatch* also, understandably, concentrated on the struggle over Hanna's seat. The treatment of this contest was more restrained than that of the *State Journal* but here, too, the paper favored Hanna, as is seen in two editorials, "Bushnell's Attitude Indefensible" and, after the outcome, "A Victory for the People" (CED, 3 Jan:4; and 11 Jan:4). Little attention was given Cuban events in this period. A front-page story (taken from the New York *Herald*) reported that General Gomez, the leader of the insurgent forces, rejected autonomy (CED, 6 Jan). In another report, Gomez called on Blanco to end the war and again declared independence as the only way (CED, 12 Jan:2).

The contest to replace Hanna also dominated in the headlines of the *Evening Press*. It clearly supported the effort, sounding a note of jubilation in many headlines: "Death Knell of Hannaism," "Mark's Throne Tottering," "The End Is Very Near," and "Mark Hanna is Caught." The latter introduced a related theme: "Bribery Is Imputed to the Cleveland Boss." Hanna's narrow victory was reported the following week under this headline: "$ HANNA'S $ ONE $ VOTE $" (12 Jan:1). Cuban affairs also received much attention, more than in the other Columbus papers. This insurgency was also viewed with favor in stories with these headlines: "Cubans to Win Independence," "Patriots Victorious," and "1500 Spaniards Join Cuban Insurgents." Secretary Sherman's appeal for Cuban relief was also reported.

The Havana riots, the demonstrations by colons and Spanish military personnel opposed to autonomy, occurred on Wednesday, 11 January. Although signaled as an important event in later American history textbooks, the event that would bring the *Maine* to Havana, the first mention in the *State Journal* appeared two days later and then only in a brief note reporting that quiet had been restored (OSJ 14Jan:2). The Saturday edition reported actions in the House of Representatives the previous day. Because of the "excited condition of affairs in Havana and the wildly exaggerated reports afloat," the House had decided to avoid the possibility of opening up a Cuban debate by turning to other, more pedestrian matters.

A first-page headline in the *State Journal* Sunday edition announced "The Crisis Reached"—but that was an account of a murder case in Wilmington, Ohio (16 Jan). A story on page two reported "Disquietude in France," it dealing with the Dreyfus Affair. The latest report from Cuba, on page three, was headed "All Quiet in Havana." Another account, an editorial, "Poor Cuba," appeared in the same edition. It told of the widespread suffering there, commented on the impact of the anti-autonomist rioting, and ended with this statement: "The end of the Cuban rebellion is close at hand." A front-page story in the Monday edition spelled out the likely topics for that day's House discussion of foreign relations including the Cuban situation, the annexation of Hawaii, and the "designs of the European powers toward China." The house managers, it was reported, "do not want an extended debate on Cuba . . . but the minority is determined to press the question . . ." The Hawaiian annexation treaty would occupy the Senate at this time. A story on page two described Havana's streets as "perfectly tranquil." The rioting in the previous week was now described as "merely a flurry" that spent itself in a few hours (OSJ, 17 Jan:2).

The Havana riots were reported on the front page of the *Evening Dispatch* in an account headed "Hot Time in Havana" (13 Jan:1). The subheads reported much concern: "May Result in Intervention by Uncle Sam," "Get Ready to Sail," and "Situation Serious." A linked story told of the *reconcentrados*, this under the heading "Thousands Are Starving." A regular feature, "Special to the Dispatch," reported editorial opinion in the New York newspapers. Those reports on the following days indicated that the tempest had passed—"All Calm in Havana" (14 Jan:1), "Quiet Restored in Havana" (15 Jan:1). Another story, from the New York *Herald*, described the "Work of the Insurgents." It told of their contribution to the misery through the destruction of crops.

The *Evening Press* reported the Cuban disorder beginning with "Mob Rule in Havana" (13 Jan). Their reports differed from the two other papers in that violence was said to have continued for several days: "Big Panic in Havana, Terror Reigns," and "The Reign of Terror Continues." Three days later a front-page story reported "Critical Situation Still Prevailing in Havana." Well down in this account was a message from Counsel Lee in Havana that declared "Everything tranquil" (16 Jan:1).

Also in the 16 January issue, an editorial commended a motion put forward in the state legislature, one calling for the recognition of Cuban independence and demanding an end to hostilities. The "people of Ohio," it declared, are "thoroughly united" on this question and if put to a "vote of the people the resolution would carry without opposition." A front-page story the following day, from Havana, told of the conditions on the island: "Dying of Starvation," "Horrible Situation in Cuba," "Frightful Loss of Life Among the Concentra-dos," "The Most Terrible Ravages of Famine All Over the Island." *Evening Press* stories typically indicated a place of origin, Havana for example, but rarely indicated the agency, whether a press association or another newspaper.

On Wednesday, 19 January, the *State Journal* published a brief page-one report on a question then under consideration—"A Warship for Havana." It was followed by a note from Havana, one declaring "All's Quiet." A page-three story reviewed events in the House of Representatives the previous day. A Missouri Democrat attempted to attach a rider to the diplomatic and consular appropriation bill that would have recognized the insurgents as belligerents.

The struggle was intense but the motion was ultimately defeated. This Associated Press report was very detailed and neutral in tone but a note of evaluation—"The Ruse Fails"—appeared in a headline. The House debate, also reported in the *Dispatch*, told of the defeat of the "Agitators" (19 Jan:1). The *Evening Press* headline read: "Czar Reed Squelches the Cuban Resolutions in the House" (19 Jan:1).

Several stories involving Cuba appeared in the *State Journal* issue of 21 January. The administration in Washington was said to feel that more time should be allowed for working through the autonomy plan. Another indicated that no uprising threatening American interests in Cuba was anticipated, but if one did occur United States naval vessels would be in Havana harbor within six hours. De Lôme had some misgivings about the movements of the American vessels. A small band of insurgents surrendered in Cuba. A headline—"Sensational Episode"—introduced a two-column report of another tumultuous session in which the Democratic partisans of Cuba in the House of Representatives confronted Speaker Reed and his Republican allies.

The House session was the subject of an editorial in the *Evening Press* entitled, "Do the People Rule?" (21 January:4). There is no doubt, the editorialist declared, "that 90 per cent of the people of the United States are in favor of recognizing either the belligerency or independence of Cuba." The problem lay with the Republican leaders—"Mark Hanna is almost the only opponent that brave people have in the senate, and Chairman Hitt and Speaker Reed are their chief if not only enemies in the house." Congress has "not been able to give voice" to this popular sentiment because "Speaker Reed will not permit it." The "people of the country" must "be aroused to the dangers," otherwise they might lose political power entirely. On the same page, another editorial, "Bryan the Peerless Leader," warned against the efforts of conservative Democrats, the Van Wyck-Whitney-Hill-Belmont crowd in New York, to block Bryan's candidacy in 1900.

The *State Journal* Saturday edition contained a page-two account of the fighting in Cuba under the heading "Insurgents Defeated." A page-four story, headlined "Cuban Relief," reported a meeting of the executive committee of the local Cuban League. With the support of Governor Bushnell, they were planning arrangements to publicize their campaign throughout the state. This report appeared also in the *Dispatch* (21 Jan:8).

To this point, the *State Journal*'s readers would have read nothing that would provide grounds for concern. Very little was reported that would indicate local sentiment with regard to Cuba. The accounts of the relief efforts, understandably, emphasized the suffering there, but this newspaper's accounts were not partisan with respect to the causes. The insurgents fired on a train, killing several animals in one of the cars; another group of insurgents entered "the cultivated zone" of a town near Havana and destroyed "all of the huts and the crops that had been planted." An Associated Press account from Havana told of "widespread revolutionary incendiarism" with the insurgents "burning the canefields on the central plantation, Teresa, at Celba Hueca" and the fire spreading to neighboring plantations. The next sentence reported the 16,403 deaths in the province in 1897 and told of the extensive relief efforts (OSJ, 24 Jan:1, 2).

The movement of the *Maine* to Havana was first-page news in the *Dispatch* on 24 January. The essentials were summarized in the headlines: "Ordered to Havana, . . . on a Mission of Peace and Friendship; Will Mark the Resumption of Friendly Intercourse by the American Navy." Several senators were quoted expressing their approval. Senator Teller wanted to see "the harbor of Havana filled with American ships." A long inside-page story reported the Columbus League's "earnest appeal" for Cuban relief. It condemned Spain's policies in Cuba, detailed the resulting suffering, and called on citizens to contribute food, clothing, and medicine. The *Evening Press* also carried the notice, "An Appeal for Cuba." The League's statement was reported as having been prepared by Mr. DeWitt Jones, the publisher of the *Press* (24 Jan:7).

On 25 January, the front page of the *State Journal* contained three Cuba-related stories, the most important of them headed "Maine to Go to Havana." Assistant Secretary of State Day was quoted at length saying that the move was not at all unusual but "simply the resumption of friendly naval relations with Spain." Another account reported former President Cleveland's reiterated opposition to involvement in Hawaii and Cuba. A Cuba Resolution was passed in the state legislature calling on the Congress to grant belligerent rights. The measure was sponsored by Senator John Pugh, a Democrat from Franklin County (which contained Columbus). The inside pages contained an editorial defending McKinley's policies with respect to Cuba.

The following day, 26 January, a page-one headline in the *State Journal* announced: "Maine Arrives at Havana." The customary gun salutes were exchanged. Consul General Lee reported that the ship "had been received with every courtesy" and that the commanders of the German and Spanish ships of war in the harbor had called on Captain Sigsbee and that he had returned their calls. Lee added that "everything was tranquil in Havana." The next day it was announced that a Spanish warship, the *Vizcaya*, would visit American ports. Secretary Sherman indicated he would be glad about the exchange and Secretary Long said he would be "delighted" by such a visit. Much of the same content appeared in the *Dispatch*. It reported that other nations, France and Germany, had sent ships to Havana, that the *Maine* was "Quietly at Anchor" in Havana, and also that the Ohio legislature had debated and adopted Senator Pugh's measure on granting belligerent rights (26 Jan:1; 27 Jan:1, 10).

The *Evening Press* continued its front-page accounts of war and turmoil in Cuba—"Terrible Fighting," "Riots in Matanzas," "Military Train Blown Up by Cubans," and "Bribery in Cuba." One front-page story reported "Czar Reed Lauded by Madrid Paper" (24–27 Jan). The most "startling" revelation was contained in a brief account telling that: "Havana Harbor Mined and Drawn Off Into Squares of Subterranean Dynamite. With the Pressing of a Button the Battleship Maine Could Be Blown Out of Existence in an Instant." The account carried a Washington dateline but provided no further information as to its source (27 Jan:1).

The Sunday *Morning Press* contained a long front-page report by an American, Samuel Morrell, a resident in Havana (30 Jan:1). Dated 19 January, it told of the uncertainty and fears felt especially by Americans after the earlier riots. "Why does not Congress act?" he asked, "Why does the President hold back?" But if action were taken "every Spanish officer would issue forth, armed with a machete, to wreak vengenance [sic] upon every American he met . . ." "There is a crisis in the air. . . . The famine is coming too."

Shortly thereafter, the *Dispatch* carried a brief report by an Ohio man who had recently returned from Cuba. It was headed: "Is Not in Sympathy." He reported that "the Cubans are a bloodthirsty lot" and that the native Spaniards "penned in the cities" were the ones suffering while the insurgents roamed the interior where "tropical products grow in abundance." His portrait of the insurgents was very negative: They destroyed 6,000 acres of growing sugar on one plantation whose owner had refused a $30,000 demand to carry on the war. They later returned and "mutilated everything possible in the planter's house" (5 Feb:2).

The *State Journal* published an editorial entitled "Cuba: Why Our Government Does Not Interfere" (6 Feb). It expressed great sympathy for the insurgents and detailed the Spanish horrors. It reviewed two similar cases where Spain had viciously repressed independence movements, Chile in 1810 and Mexico 1815 to 1823, and where American presidents had not intervened. It recommended continued confidence in McKinley's leadership. In the following days the *State Journal* published reports on the fighting in Cuba, the sufferings of the Cubans, and the inadequate relief measures. Three measures were introduced in the Senate to recognize Cuban belligerency, this reported in account headed: "Jingoes at It Again."

The *Dispatch* reported the Senate debate under the heading: "Gala Day for Cuba." The texts of the resolutions, all strongly condemning Spain's efforts, were reproduced. All of them, the headline stated, had the "Same End in View, Freedom of Cuba" (8 Feb:1; and CEP: 8 Feb:9). More on this subject was reported the following day—"A Cuban Field Day Again Indulged in by Members of the Senate."

The de Lôme letter was published in the New York newspapers on 9 February. The *Dispatch* that day carried a brief note reporting the event. The account, with a Washington dateline, said nothing about the circumstances of its first publication and, showing some caution, indicated some doubt as to its authenticity (9 Feb:1). The newspaper's later reports were calm but insistent beginning with a headline "De Lome Must Leave" (10 Feb:1). A temporary "last word" on the subject was indicated several days later: "End of the Episode Expected at Any Moment by the Washington Authorities" (15 Feb:1).

The *Evening Press* carried an extensive account on the ninth under the headings "Climax Coming" and "Spain Has Recalled De Lome." A subhead announced, prematurely, that it "Costs a Man His Place and May Give to Cuba Its Independence." The paper vouched for the authenticity of the letter, reporting the frank statement of Horatio Rubens, the Junta lawyer, that it was stolen, adding, "All is fair in love and war." The headlines in the next days announced "De Lome Out" and "Uncle Sam Very Hot." "Let Him Go Home" was an editorial recommendation. Five days later, readers were informed that the Spanish government had disavowed the letter and that the episode was "All Settled . . . the Row Closed Up" (15 Feb:1).

At the same time, the *Evening Press* continued its steady flow of partisan comment—"Cuban Army Growing" and "Enthusiasm Everywhere in Cuba for the Patriots." Tampering with the United States mail sent to the *Maine* was reported—"Spanish Authorities Caught in a Sneaking Act." In that connection, readers were told: "McKinley's Administration Likely to Compromise With Spain on Easy Terms So as Not to Wound the Sensitive Feelings of the Haughty Dons" (14 Feb:1).

The de Lôme letter was first reported in the *State Journal* on the tenth with news and commentary over the following week. Most of these stories were from the Washington office of the Associated Press. They describe the "sensation in official Washington" and reported many of the outraged reactions. The reports in the *State Journal* in the following days however were calm and factual, not expressing any of the outrage found in the sensational journals.

The two moderate Columbus newspapers were generally evenhanded in their reports on Cuba up to this point. Apart from an evident sympathy for the suffering Cubans and approval of humanitarian aid, there were few indications of demands for more serious American involvement. The change in orientation came with the sinking of the *Maine* on the evening of 15 February.

The *State Journal* reported the event on 16 February—"U.S.S. MAINE BLOWN UP." The regular edition was followed by an extra that carried the same heading but in larger type. One subhead declared "CAUSE OF THE EXPLOSION a Mystery." That was followed by another, a hypothetical statement—"SPANISH TREACHERY/On Board or Spanish Torpedoes in the

Harbor May Have Done It." The account, by the Associated Press from Havana, reiterates the first of these statements—"As yet the cause of the explosion is not apparent." A follow-up report that same evening offered a "first theory"—that there had been a preliminary explosion "with powder or dynamite below the water." Spanish officials and navy vessels were helping the *Maine*'s crew "in every way possible."

A note on terminology: Stationary underwater explosive devices were first developed at the time of the American Revolution. Then and for more than a century thereafter, those devices were called torpedoes. When Admiral Farragut said "Damn the torpedoes," he was referring to what later generations would call mines. Self-propelled underwater explosive devices, those later called torpedoes, were invented in 1870. Some limited use of these occurred during the Spanish-American War. Frequent use, however, did not come until the Russo-Japanese War, 1904–1905. As of 1898, military professionals would have adopted the modern usages. But the nineteenth-century usages continued among non-professionals, including many journalists. One result, as may be seen in the previous paragraph, is that the meanings are often not easily discerned.

A dispatch from Washington told of Secretary Long's reaction. He described the catastrophe as "an accident" with two possibilities suggested, "a fire in the bunkers, heating the bulkhead near a magazine" or an accident while inspecting high explosives.[10] The extra edition carried a dispatch from Captain Sigsbee, released by the Navy Department. It asked that public opinion "be suspended till further report." The headline stated that "many Spanish officers, including representatives of General Blanco, now with me and express sympathy." Another story from Havana reported that: "The wildest consternation prevails in Havana. The wharves are crowded with thousands of people. It is believed the explosion occurred in a small powder magazine."

The *State Journal*'s Thursday edition, 17 February, contained several pages on the catastrophe, leading with a large-type heading: "Two Hundred and Fifty Brave Men Die for Their Country." A large subhead declared: "Cause of the Terrible Explosion Still a Mystery." The lead story reviewed possible causes. Divers would be able to establish whether the hull plates bulge out, signaling an internal explosion, or whether driven in "as would result from the attack of a torpedo or the explosion of a mine beneath the ship." That investigation, it was indicated, would take some time. The story continued with a report that the "large majority of naval officers are inclined to the belief that the explosion resulted from spontaneous combustion of a coal bunker; the overheating of the iron partitions between the boilers and the magazine or from the explosion of a boiler, though the last theory finds little support."[11]

Also on the *State Journal*'s front page was a boxed item with an equally large head: "Blown Up by a Spanish Torpedo." This report, out of Key West, reads: "The correspondent of the Associated Press has been assured in a reliable quarter that Captain Sigsbee is under the impression that the warship Maine was blown up by a floating torpedo, and that he has communicated his impressions to Washington, asking at the same time that the navy department should send naval engineers and mechanics to investigate the explosion." The Key West dispatch with the floating torpedo allegation was shown to a Navy Department spokesman who emphatically rejected the claim. No second dispatch from Sigsbee had been received; the spokesman did not think the torpedo theory tenable and did not believe Captain Sigsbee had "expressed such a theory." A small item at the bottom of the page reported the view of Rear Admiral George Belknap, retired (from the Associated Press out of Boston)—"he was inclined to think that the Maine was blown up by a torpedo."

This welter of material in the *State Journal*'s first report of the catastrophe may be summarized as follows: some people, Sigsbee and Long among them, called for investigation and for reservation of judgment pending the result. Two causal hypotheses were offered: the internal versus external cause, those summarized as an "accident" versus a torpedo, a mine, or some other external source. A peculiarity of the placement, and emphasis, should be noted: Reading down the page, the lead headings signal the fact, the 250 men dying, then the cause "still a mystery," then the boxed item, "Blown Up by a Spanish Torpedo," and finally, "Sigsbee Says Investigation Is Necessary."

The *State Journal* provided a balanced statement in an editorial entitled "The Loss of the Maine" (17 Feb:4). It signaled the just-noted tendency, the press for judgment, and also reported a problem with the accident thesis:

> The destruction of the Maine, according to the best advices, was caused by an explosion, the nature of which is not known even to Captain Sigsbee. It is still a mystery with many very peculiar circumstances surrounding it. When the news first reached this country there was a strong disposition to charge the catastrophe to Spanish hands, but this is so far only a suspicion. It is possible it was simply one of those accidents liable to happen on any warship, with thousands of pounds of powder and guncotton aboard. But this explanation will not satisfy the American public unless it is supported and borne out by the fullest investigation. . . . It is a possible explanation, but it involves such a reflection upon the American navy that the public will hesitate to believe it. Naval circles discredit it . . .

The contention of claims appeared also in the headlines of the Friday edition, 18 February. The main head reads: "How Are the Plates of the Maine Bent?" And several subheads follow: "Till That Question is Answered a Nation Waits, but Mourns Her Untimely Dead," and "The Treacherous Plot of the Spaniards," and further down, "The Navy Department Will Investigate," "Officers and Men All Differ in the Theories of the Cause . . ." The same issues were reviewed in an editorial entitled "May Be a Casus Belli." It began with a bit of speculation: "In the absence of certainties, conjectures of every kind are made. It is well known that the harbor of Havana was planted with torpedoes, as New York harbor is today. These terrific engines of destruction were so plentiful that it was necessary for the Spanish naval authorities to make the way of the Maine when she reached Havana . . ." The principal conclusion, still hanging on a conditional, reads: "If it is shown that the Spanish are responsible for the horrible affairs, a declaration of war against Spain is inevitable and it should come at once."

Friday's *State Journal* contained a boxed item with a large headline: "General Booth on Cuban Situation." This was General William Booth of the Salvation Army, who was then touring the United States. He declared that the "Cuban butchery should stop. It should stop, if need be, by the intervention of the United States." This recommendation, a news report it will be noted, was the first such demand to appear in this newspaper in its 1898 issues.

The Saturday edition, 19 February, contained some cautionary words from Secretary Long: "As yet there is no indication of design. Therefore my impression has been all along, and I rather think the general opinion preponderates in the same direction, that it must have been accidental." He went on to describe the claim that Captain Sigsbee had warned the department about submarine mines or torpedoes, declaring those claims as "utterly without foundation." In the adjacent column, under "Plot Unearthed," the reader was told about a plan to blow up Consul General Lee and the American Consulate in Havana. Across the page, under "A Hot Debate Precipitated," was an extensive report on the Senate debate about the sinking. Senator Mason of Illinois had made an "Attack Upon the Navy Department" and was "Sharply Answered." The people, Mason asserted, are demanding a congressional investigation. He did not wish "to reflect on the motives or honor of anybody, but he suggested that the officials of the navy would be trying their own case, and would naturally endeavor to cover up any blame that might attach to them." The senator disparaged the policy of autonomy and put forth a resolution for intervention.

The lead item in four columns of church news that Saturday was the announcement of a memorial service organized by the First Baptist Church and scheduled for the following evening (OSJ, 19 Feb:4). This was to take place in the Great Southern Theatre. Invitations had been sent to the governor, the state legislature, members of the state supreme court and other state and local potentates. The program was listed, complete with the speakers and the musical offerings. The church service would then be "merged" into a mass meeting of Columbus citizens and appropriate resolutions would be presented.

The usual extensive listing of church services and sermon topics followed. With only a couple of exceptions, those continued to focus on religious themes.

One church announced a program of "a patriotic order" with the pastor giving a "brief patriotic address" to be followed by a flag salute. The other exceptions, those touching on patriotic themes, centered on presidents' birthdays rather than on the recent catastrophe. One sermon dealt with "Washington and Lincoln," another was entitled "George Washington, the Joshua of America."

On 20 February, the *State Journal* published a front-page account that originated with Pulitzer's reporter Sylvester Scovel in Havana and was transmitted by the Associated Press. "The consensus of opinion of those who have studied the wreck closest," Scovel reported, "is now that the explosion was caused by a submarine mine." The "fearful damage" was too great for "any but an extremely large torpedo." "All the American officers," the report continued, "are internally boiling. There is not one of them, from Captain Sigsbee down, who is not fairly convinced a government submarine did it." An additional note: "The Spanish dailies are loudly clamoring 'Accident, accident . . .'" Also, it was agreed that Spain would conduct its own investigation but that it would be independent of the ongoing American effort.

On Monday, 21 February, the newspaper carried a similar account, one with a similar lesson. The lead headline announced "A 'Spanish Outrage'." The following headlines reported that the court of inquiry was sailing for Havana and would begin its work "today." This account, however, begins with some conclusions: "Sailors of the battleship Maine, suffering from wounds in the Key West hospital, are smarting over the delay of the government in punishing what they term a 'Spanish outrage.' In their minds there is no doubt as to the cause of the explosion . . ." A boxed note there carries a large-type headline: "Commander Barnett Gives Facts." He was quoted as follows: "You want the facts. I can tell you there are ninety-five chances out of a hundred that the investigation will show that the forward magazine of the Maine did not blow up first, if it exploded at all." He told an Associated Press correspondent, in Washington, that, "The condition of the wreck when first studied and a later careful scrutiny make this an almost absolute certainty."

Another *State Journal* account, also on the front-page that Monday, reported in detail on the Sunday evening memorial meeting. It was attended by "fully 2000 people" with many standees and many others turned away.[12] The Reverend Herman H. Barbour delivered the principal address, opening with an "eloquent tribute" to George Washington and his compatriots, then turning to the "awful disaster" and the loss of lives. He reviewed the situation in Cuba, "now ravaged by fire and sword [and] ground beneath the heel of a relentless despotism." Barbour then took up a new theme:

> Oh, if it shall be found that the blood was shed by design, and not by accident, that those men went to their death through the instrumentality of Spanish intrigue and

deviltry, then! Then, if the spirit of '76 still lives, if the descendants of Washington are not poltroons and cowards, that explosion in Havana harbor shall yet be spoke of, like the first gun fired at Lexington, a sound heard round the world, and for every murdered American tar a hundred haughty dons shall bite the dust, and for one ruined American battleship a score of Spanish vessels shall go down beneath the waves!

That was followed by "Prolonged applause and cheers." Reverend Barbour reminded his listeners that he was a minister of the "Gospel of Peace." But that Gospel preached that "they who take the sword shall perish by the sword." He also referred to the Good Samaritan and reminded his hearers of their charitable obligations—"binding up the wounds of those who have fallen among thieves." Dr. Barbour then turned the meeting over to Governor Bushnell who was the presiding officer.

The governor also gave a stirring patriotic address that, among other things, urged reservation of judgment until the investigation of causes was completed. Bushnell then recognized Mr. Thomas E. Powell, who noted that the origins of "this deadly work" had "not yet been accurately ascertained." In the next sentence, however, he declared that "we are justified in the belief that the machinery which worked out this dire disaster would never have been set in motion except for Spanish duplicity and Spanish treachery." Powell then introduced two motions, the first asking for the support of the wounded sailors and for families of the dead, and the second declaring that "the patriots of Cuba should not only be accorded belligerent rights, but should be given the pronounced and active support of our people in their struggle for liberty." Several seconding speeches followed. Governor Bushnell then put the question and asked for a show of hands. The resolutions "were declared adopted unanimously." The meeting ended with the singing of "America."

The same issue of the *State Journal* contained a long interview with Dr. Charles N. Thomas, who had recently returned from a two-month stay in Cuba. His message, contained in headlines and text, was that "Cubans Will Never Submit Again to Spanish Rule, Neither Will They Accept Spain's Offer of Home Rule." His lectures on this topic were "attracting considerable attention."

The bellicose tendency evident in the opening pages of this issue of the *State Journal* were then countered by a page-four editorial commending McKinley's quite course: "While the air is filled with the cries of jingoes and demagogues, who have no responsibility, the president goes serenely on, enforcing a policy, that, according to the opinion of the Cuban junta themselves, will bring independence to the island within the present year without any declaration of war against Spain or disturbance of the commercial and industrial interests of this country." McKinley's "wisdom, firmness and self-command will eventually solve the present difficulties in a manner that will satisfy all reasonable and justice-loving Americans . . ."

This memorial meeting for the dead sailors was the first local event reported in 1898 that might be taken as evidence of a public clamor for a stronger American response. But even that gathering can hardly be read as an expression of "mass" demands. It was conducted, clearly, by persons who were highly placed in state and local affairs. It seems likely that much of the audience would also have been of high status. The *State Journal* provided little information on the sponsorship of this meeting, noting only that the First Baptist Church was making the arrangements. Although not indicated, two of the speakers, Thomas E. Powell, who introduced the resolutions, and Henry J. Booth, were members of the Cuban League executive committee.

Prior to the sinking of the *Maine*, the *State Journal* had reported events in a balanced manner. The direction commended was to support President McKinley's pacific course. Those earlier reports had emphasized the suffering the Cuban population and readers were urged to support efforts for their relief. The demands for a more "forceful" response reported by that newspaper were made by local notables or by political leaders elsewhere, members of the state legislature or, with much greater frequency, members of United States Senate. Following the *Maine* catastrophe, however, tendentious presentations alleging Spanish involvement were "the rule." These accounts, typically based on flimsy sources, were judged as deserving front-page treatment. The words of caution, those asking readers to await the results of the investigation, now appeared as notes on the inside pages.

A later front-page story told of a steamer arriving in New York from Havana (OSJ, 22 Feb). Its passengers were "generally of the opinion that the Maine was destroyed by design." The ship had arrived in Havana the day after the explosion. Among other things, passengers cited "the fact" that the Spanish man-of-war, Alfonso XII, "which was anchored near the Maine CHANGED HER MOORINGS just previous to the disaster." One passenger, who presumably boarded in Havana, had seen "a boat go near the Maine a short time previous to the explosion." The attitudes of Spaniards in the city were reported as either indifferent or offensive.

On the 24th, a front-page account revealed more suspicious findings: "Maine's Plates Blown Upward" and "Explosion from Without." A "Masterful Debate" in the Senate was reported, the issue being the question of belligerent rights for the Cubans. A headline, also on the front page, quoted Senator Foraker: "The Time is Coming When We'll Become Involved in a War With Spain." The same issue contained a brief statement, on page two, from Senator Hanna. His conclusion: "I honestly and frankly do not see any reason for the excitement that is being created. There will be no war."

On the 26th, the *State Journal* published a denial by the Cuban chargé d'affaires in Washington. On page three, boxed and with a bold type heading, it reads: "This Is What He Says"—"no mine exists inside or outside of Havana harbor; nor is there any submarine defense of any kind." Reports to that effect, he stated, were "absolutely false and ridiculous . . ." They were produced by "persons anxious to incite the evil passions of both nations for their own miserable ends."

A long front-page account on 28 February written by a special correspondent of the *Ohio State Journal* reported the "Pathetic Stories of Starving Cubans." It contained an extensive and very positive account of the reactions of Cubans to the Americans for their losses. Well down in the story is a statement that "In all probability it was an accident." At the worse, "the horrible crime was committed by some irresponsible lunatic, like Guiteau, or Booth . . ."

On the same page, another story carried this headline: "How Maine Was Blown Up." The explanation was contained "in a letter forwarded by a secret Cuban club in Havana to J. M. Govin, a Cuban insurance agent there." It was written in English and signed "Maquinista." In an old warehouse, some 200 yards from where the *Maine* was moored, "some diving apparatus had been hidden." From there "two divers had worked by night and filled the torpedo holes of the Maine with dynamite cartridges" and connected them with wire to the battery on the land . . ." The last sentence of this Associated Press account read: "An officer of the Maine, whose attention was called to the story today, asserted positively to this correspondent that the torpedo holes of the Maine had not been open during her stay in the harbor." The account of the nefarious plot was given almost all the attention; the rejection of the claim received only a brief last-line notice.

Some of the circumstances involved in this report should be noted. An Associated Press reporter picked up (or was given) this questionable account. The reporter checked it out, heard the disconfirming statement, but nevertheless wrote it up and sent it on to Key West. At some point, an AP wire editor judged it as newsworthy and sent it on to member newspapers. Editors at the *State Journal* also judged it newsworthy and thought it deserved a place on the front page. The likely impact would hardly be countered by a page-four editorial that day, one commending President McKinley's attitude—"patiently waiting for the facts concerning the Maine disaster." That policy "is warmly praised by thinking men on every side . . . with the exception of a few Jack Falstaffs who are fairly bubbling over with the spirit of war, and are ready to wipe Spain off the map . . ."

The 28 February issue contained three accounts that give some limited sense of the then current opinion. A *State Journal* reporter interviewed a group of men with Ohio's Seventeenth Regiment. After a hesitant beginning the reporter asked, "Don't you think the dons deserve a first-class thrashing?" One man's "growled" reply was, "They do that." Another "snarled" that he "would like to get at them." And a third "chimed in" with: "Who'd want anything easier than a lot of garlic-eating greasers." One man declared that "it looks now as if they were going to prove" Spanish culpability. On the prospect of war, that respondent thought the United States army "will be glad of it as a mere diversion."

One regular feature in the *State Journal* was a review of "College News." This gave brief summaries of the happenings in Ohio's universities. At Miami University, in Oxford Ohio, it was reported that the "war spirit is running high." The previous Monday, despite inclement weather, a procession "formed at the gymnasium, headed by the 'varsity band, [and] marched to the public square, where De Lome and Blanco, together with the Spanish flag, were burned in effigy. At least 1000 of the village folks were out. . . . The entire night was spent in building bonfires and holding war meetings." This was the only event of its kind reported from the colleges to this point.

The church news in the 28 February edition of the *State Journal* contained a strikingly pacific message. Three of the five columns were given to Dr. J. W. Barnett's sermon on "The Church's Attitude in the Present Crisis." He argued against "the loud voice of the agitator" whose "first impulse in such cases is for revenge." He also against the current "fanaticism," citing the example of Senator Mason, something found also in the press, and, "to their shame . . . in some pulpits." But, in an important qualification, he declared these to be the position of minorities—"we ought to thank God that the number of newspapers which are doing so is comparatively small." The first task, he argued, was calm, patient investigation, even if it took six months. If that investigation established "treachery" then, his second point was an emphatic commendation of arbitration. "War belongs to barbarism," he declared, "Jesus nowhere sanctions it." Scripture was cited to support this position: Jesus, the Prince of Peace, told Peter "to put up his sword into its place."

The *Dispatch* reports on the *Maine* catastrophe and its aftereffects cover much the same ground and show similar policy emphases. The initial report was headed: "BLOWN TO PIECES!" From the start, the same scatter of guesses appeared along with assorted words of caution. The initial report, for example, carried these headlines: "Spanish Torpedo Theory Not Credited by Officials . . . Speculation Offers Many Theories as to Cause, but All Is Yet a Mystery." Also on the front page were these headlines: "THEY ALL HESITATE To Say What Wrecked the Battleship, But the Mystery Will Be Probed to the Very Bottom." Below this story was a small entry under the heading "Spontaneous Combustion." The Navy Department had been "greatly troubled" by such complaints in recent years, citing relevant instances. The lead editorial that day reviewed the catastrophe. It noted the "strong Anti-Spanish sentiment which has raged in

Washington for some days" but argued "there is still the greatest necessity for a careful investigation," signaling the possibility of danger from the ship's own explosives (16 Feb:1, 4).

A page-one headline the next day reported a diver's discovery of an eight-inch hole below the *Maine*'s waterline, one "Charged to a Torpedo." But the next headline reported that the "Idea is Ridiculed in Washington by Naval Authorities." Two fragmentary accounts by Sylvester Scovel of the New York *World* appeared on the same page. The editorial that day recommended "Fact Before Action" (17 Feb:1 and 4).

The *Dispatch* reported the memorial meeting at the Great Southern Theatre in detail (CED, 21 Feb:5). The content was similar to that contained in the *State Journal* that morning. The next day, some indications of public reactions were reported. The cash register company in Dayton was holding a convention of its agents from all over the world; some workingmen pulled down Spanish flags and tore them to shreds. The president of the company, however, ordered them replaced (22 Feb:1). About nine-tenths of Governor Bushnell's mail and that of Adjutant General Axline were "devoted to war matters." The next sentence reported that "Almost every letter" contained reference to the "strained relations" between the United States and Spain and, furthermore, that "the universal sentiment" was that the writers' names should be "considered as on file and ready for duty at a moment's call." The "tone of these letters clearly demonstrated that the feeling of patriotism is growing and that in the event of war with Spain thousands of men in the state would be ready to spring to arms in defense of the nation's honor" (22 Feb:7). No source is given for this report nor is the number of letters indicated.

The thrust of that message was countered in the *Dispatch* the next day with a page-one story headed: "THERE'LL BE NO WAR Is the Way Hanna Puts Sensational Rumors to Rest. No Excuse for It." A long editorial that day, entitled "Sensation Mongers," faulted the presentations appearing in the New York *Herald*, pointing out the disparities between its assertions and its own evidence. Two days later, in a front-page story, the *Dispatch* published a statement ("to the Herald from Havana") reporting there "is no longer any reason to doubt" that the explosion was external and that the magazines "had nothing to do with the initial explosion." A story in an adjacent column, with the heading "An Outside Agency," offered the same conclusion, this based on information received from "the highest authority."

An indirect report about the views of the nation's "highest authority," President McKinley, appeared under a small heading on the same page. The Chicago publisher, Henry H. Kohlsaat, who was "very close" to the president, stated that "neither the president nor Secretary Long is in possession of a single fact or report in regard to the Maine disaster that they have not made public."

"Every official connected with the investigation," he added, "is under an oath of secrecy" and the wreck itself "is sacredly guarded from unofficial approach." The targets of Kohlsaat's remarks were "the daily sensations from Havana and the stock jobbing forebodings of war from New York and Washington."

An editorial the following day, "More Sensationalism," took to task the *Commercial Tribune* of Cincinnati. Among other things, it claimed that Spain would not fight alone, that Austria was "to have the advantage of striking the first blow." But, pointing to that state's internal discord, the editorialist thought it unlikely that Hungarians could be induced to take up arms for this purpose. The last sentence read: "They will forget Kossuth first" (26 Feb:4). Under the heading "Vicious Journalism," another editorial quoted the proprietor of a "sensational New York newspaper" who was said to have telegraphed these words to his Washington correspondent: "Damn the truth, give us something that will sell the paper" (28 Feb:4).

The *Evening Press* account of the catastrophe was highly inflammatory. It provided immediate, unambiguous judgment with respect to the cause of the catastrophe. The main heading read: "American Blood at Door of Spain." A subhead declared "Without Possibility of Interior Causes." McKinley and Long asked "Suspension of Public Opinion Pending Investigation" while another subhead announced "The Country Demands Action by the President—American Honor at Stake." A boxed and framed notice at center-page carried these headlines: "The Disaster Predicted, Startling Confirmation of Evening Press Dispatches of January 27." On that day, as indicated above, they had printed a report about Havana harbor being mined, drawn off into squares, with each square connected with a "particular button" such as could blow the *Maine* "out of existence" (CEP, 16 Feb:1).

That same day, an editorial began with a statement that it is "not certain" the vessel's destruction was "by treacherous Spaniards, yet the indications strongly point in that direction." It ended with this thought: "The day has come now to put an end to the most barbarous war of the century, and the American people will scarcely be further suppressed by the pro-Spanish policy of the president, in whose breast every sentiment of Americanism seems to have perished." Another editorial that day reported that McKinley's Spanish policy "has been a deep disappointment to a large majority of his own party, and the butt of ridicule to the people of every other party in the land."

Much more material of the same sort appeared in the following days: "Torpedo Beneath Maine. . . . Torpedo Responsibility Affirmed From Four Sources of International Origin" (17 Feb:1). A "Black Boat" had circled the *Maine* several times before the explosion; "The New York World and Journal Both Reiterate That Explosion Took Place Outside of Hull" (19 Feb:1). And also,

"A Great Hole Blown in Bottom of Maine, Inward from the Port Side is the Startling News" (21 Feb:1).

Also on the 21st, the *Evening Press* reported some public reactions to the *Maine* catastrophe under this headline: "Uprising in Chicago and Other Cities." The subhead reported "Chicago Stirred Up" but the uprising there proved less than citywide—"From the flag draped pulpit of Centenary Methodist church, the Rev. A. C. Hirst Sunday night said that the Spanish nation should be obliterated from the face of the earth. No sooner had the high pitched utterance died out than the vast congregation joined in an outburst of applause. Such expressions as 'good,' 'That's right' 'That's the way to talk!' came from men and women in all parts of the auditorium." The disjunction between headlines and stories, the former with sweeping declarations of magnitude, appeared regularly in this newspaper's subsequent reports.

Governor Bushnell and Mayor Black, it was reported, had received telegrams from the publisher of the New York *Journal* (identified as W. E. Hearst) asking them to serve on a national committee to erect a monument for those lost on the *Maine* (CEP, 21 Feb:2). Both signaled their agreement. An editorial, entitled "A Spanish Organ Among Us," condemned the performance of the *Ohio State Journal*—". . . not content to express its sympathy with Spain, and its admiration and delight at the present do-nothing policy of Mr. McKinley, it proceeds to insult those whose sympathy with Cuba has led them to express impatience at the trifling and inefficient policy of the administration, now condemned by nine-tenths of the people regardless of politics or religion."

Last, but not least, that issue of the *Evening Press* carried a detailed four-column account of the Great Southern Theatre memorial meeting on the previous evening. It was an overflow audience, with all seats taken, the lobby packed, and "hundreds" not able to gain admittance. The event could "hardly have called out more of [the city's] prominent citizens." Many of them, those on the stage or in the boxes, were named. Also many members of the legislature and state officials were "scattered about the audience." Dr. Barbour's stirring words were reported at length (CEP, 21 Feb:4).

The following day, the *Press* quoted Ohio's Senator Foraker—"Spain Is Responsible." That was the case, he held, even if the explosion proved to be the work of a fanatic—"Spanish Government Cannot Shirk the Blame." And a brief account reported a public reaction—"The War Spirit"—from Ybor City, Florida, where "A crowd of cigar makers and others dragged the red and yellow flag of Spain in the dirt Monday night and ended by tearing it into pieces. All kinds of threats were made in case the government failed to take prompt steps in the Maine affair. The war spirit is growing" (22 Feb:1). The demonstration by Miami University students was reported. In their account it consisted of two hundred students who marched through the town; the band played and citizens cheered. An editorial that day explained "Why Cuban War Is Not Stopped." The explanation was that bankers, among them, J. Pierpont Morgan, would suffer major losses if Spain's bonds worth $400 million were repudiated.

The accounts in the following days told more of the "Spanish Plot," of McKinley's efforts of avoidance, and now, with increasing frequency, of American military preparations. As evidence of "An Outside Torpedo," *Press* readers were offered the following: "Washington, Feb. 26.—The navy department has a letter written by Astrologer Paine, of New York, two days after the Maine disaster, in which he says the Maine was destroyed by an outside torpedo . . . The man who did it is well-built, middle stature, broadface, complexion dark and swarthy . . . he is an officer of the Spanish navy."

As for public reactions, readers were told that a man in Shelbyville, Indiana was arrested and required to leave town because of his "Hurrah for Spain." And, closer to home, from Delaware, Ohio, the readers learned that "about 100 students at Wesleyan university [were] willing to fight for their country. . . . The feeling is intense in Delaware, and every word from the seat of war is caught up and heralded to all parts of the town." The last sentence added that the *Evening Press* "leads all 'city' papers in circulation coming into Delaware" (26 Feb:9).

Another indication of public outrage came from Sherman, Texas. Under "Texas True as Steel," it was reported that: "A big anti-Spanish demonstration was held on the public square at night. Cries of 'Cuba Libre,' and 'Down with Spain,' were heard, but further than this no demonstration was made." Another story announced that the bureau of navigation was being "submerged" with "an ocean of letters. . . . A million men would answer the first call for volunteers" (27 Feb:17).

An unexpected report came from Ohio's Adjutant General Axline, who had been in Washington for several days working with the officers of other states to increase appropriations for the national guard. He said "there was no war excitement in Washington" (28 Feb:6).

That same day in Columbus, Mayor Black named a committee of leading citizens to the Maine monument committee. Although the connection was not indicated, five of the men named were members of the Cuban League executive committee. The two others named were the Reverend Herman H. Barbour, the principal speaker at the memorial meeting, and John J. Chester, a prominent local attorney and a speaker at the Great Southern memorial meeting. The next day, to make the committee more representative, the mayor added some others, one man from each of the daily papers plus several from smaller journals (*Press-Post* 1 Mar:8).

A major front-page article that day reported the words of a New York tobacco merchant who had recently arrived from Cuba. He had "certain" information that the Spanish knew in advance of the Maine explosion. Another report, from Havana, told of "Spanish Joy over Disaster to the Maine." A minor entry revealed the source of the dynamite used in the effort—"An agent of Weyler came to St. Louis, where he purchased six tons . . ." And another public reaction was reported—an "immense meeting of ladies" in Port Clinton, Ohio appointed a committee to solicit aid for the suffering Cubans. Also, resolutions "condemning the lenient policy of the administration on the Cuban question as a sample of weak-kneed poltroonery were adopted with rousing cheers by the patriotic ladies."

The *Press-Post* continued its sensational revelations. From the New York *Journal*, they had a report that "remnants of a submarine mine" along with "wire attachments" had been recovered in Havana and brought to Key West. Also on the front page was an account by a widow in St. Antonio telling about elaborate underground passages, beginning at the Morro Castle and reaching for miles under the harbor (CPP, 2 Mar:1). Pennsylvania's Senator Quay was quoted saying the loss of the Maine was not a cause for war, the matter could probably be settled with an indemnity; that was in a brief seven-line note (2 Mar:1). The next day, Senator Foraker's words were given a half column: "There'll Be War" and "There is No Doubt in the World But that Spanish Treachery Blew Up the Maine" (3 Mar:10).

The next day a *Press-Post* report declared "War Is Near at Hand." It was accompanied by an account telling that the "Latest Discoveries of the Divers Settle the Fact." Another story, taken from a Cuban paper in Key West, told that "Diver Barquin Did It. He Put Mine under the Maine. He Went Home and Told the Whole Story to His Wife." Another front-page story reported that the Chicago *Times-Herald*, H. H. Kohlsaat's newspaper, described as "McKinley's personal organ," had urged immediate intervention in Cuba. Elsewhere in this issue, McKinley's supporters were referred to as "Spanish Republicans." It was indicated further that "Czar Reed's Castilian Gang Earns Its Dividends" (CPP, 4 Mar:1,10).

In the first days of March the *State Journal* continued to publish speculative accounts of the ongoing investigation plus news of the difficulties such as divers contending with mud. The speculations about the explosion, the claims and counterclaims, continued, although in most of the accounts, as before, an external source is insistently suggested as the most likely conclusion. Senator Proctor, now in Cuba, called on Blanco. The *Viscaya* left New York and arrived in Havana. Another story about a "floating mine" was front-paged. Many tons of relief supplies provided by Americans arrived in Cuba. Several stories told of preparations for war by both Spain and the United States.

A long, three-column account by a *State Journal* correspondent provided "Pathetic Pictures of Life in Cuba" (6 Mar:1). Spain requested the American government to withdraw General Lee as consul general in Cuba. McKinley, in a "Prompt and Decisive Action," refused the request. This front-page news was accompanied by a large-type boxed entry declaring that the *State Journal* was the only Columbus paper that had reported "this exceedingly important news" the previous day. The 8 March issue reported at length on the introduction of "a resolution carrying $50,000,000 for the public defense." Also on page one was an account of the preparations then under way: "Grim Visaged War Now Whets His Sword," and "Though the Officials at Washington Do Not Expect War, They are Discreetly Preparing for Such an Emergency."

The Cannon resolution asking for the $50 million was approved unanimously in the House (OSJ, 9 Mar: 9). Fifty-nine "rousing" speeches were delivered. The galleries were "jammed with enthusiastic spectators [who applauded] the sterling patriotism of the words of eloquence uttered by the members on the floor." The following day, a front-page story announced that the measure had passed unanimously in the Senate. The work was done with "enthusiasm, fervor and promptness almost unparalleled in the senate in time of peace. . . . Seventy-six short, sharp and emphatic speeches were delivered in favor of the bill."

The *Dispatch* carried similar accounts in its early March issues, much of it also unfounded speculation about the *Maine* and the likely conclusions of the inquiry. Much of this speculation also suggested Spanish involvement. Some stories reported preparations for the possible conflict. Two *Dispatch* stories however anticipated a peaceful resolution, the first, indicating the judgment of some United States officials: "No War Is Expected" (5 Mar:1). The second, entitled "Effect of War," reported the judgments of local businessmen. John G. Deshler, a prominent banker, declared "there isn't going to be any war!" When pressed about the possibility and likely impacts, he stated that: "A war scare has the same effect on business as a rainy day, but there will not be any war outside the 'yellow newspapers.' They are doing more than anything else to injure business and their editors ought to be hung for printing such ridiculous stuff . . ." (5 Mar:5). All of those interviewed, it was said, were of the opinion that "war would cause a great depreciation in values and investments." Six of the seven men interviewed made that prediction, but one, General John Beatty, anticipated only a short break in stock prices to be followed by a quick recovery. "Practically," he said, "it would not have any effect on values." His comments appeared in the final paragraph of the report.

William Jackson Armstrong lectured on "Castelar and Spain" at the First Congregational church with Dr. Gladden presiding (OSJ, 9 Mar:7). Armstrong, a very forceful speaker, was a participant at the Great Southern meeting. He commended Castelar, a Spanish statesman and a consistent champion of republicanism whose efforts had failed. Armstrong then sharply condemned American policies:

> Had we dealt justly or humanly by the Cuban patriots the Maine catastrophe would never have come to pass. It is our blood atonement for treason to American traditions . . . it is time to say that the arm of this republic shall put an end to Spanish butchery there. That is today the demand of the American heart and conscience from sea to sea. Liberty and humanity are dearer to Americans than peace with Spain. Let swift liberty to the struggling patriots be the indemnity for the Maine disaster! Let free and independent Cuba be the monument of our fallen heroes!

The "enthusiastic audience" listened attentively and applauded from time to time.

The *Dispatch* reported the quick passage of the fifty million dollar appropriation (along with reports of falling stock prices). A page-one account carried this headline: "Every One in Havana Now Knows That the Battleship Maine Was Blown Up." This conclusion was based on a remark to a Key West reporter made by Colonel M. M. Parker who accompanied Senator Proctor on his Cuban journey. Parker's revelation came via Pulitzer's *Evening World* (CED, 10 March:1).

The same issue of the *Dispatch* contained another front-page story—"Italy to Supply Spain"—this too was from the *World*. Its correspondent had learned "on authority" that "large orders for ammunitions of war have been received from Spain." Both of the "moderate" Columbus papers, it will be noted, were playing a hypocritical game: While emphatically opposing "yellow press" excesses, they nevertheless reported and gave credence to "sensational" accounts.

The *Press-Post* of 9 March reported the Senate's unanimous passage of the $50 million appropriation—"Quick on the Trigger"—along with reports of "Cuban Victories," of "Miles' Orders," and another report on Spanish involvement in the *Maine* explosion. A brief note from South Bethlehem, Pennsylvania, also on the front page, told of "Students' Patriotism"—"The war spirit has attacked the students of Lehigh university and daily drills and parades are held on the campus. At noon about 300 of the students headed by a drum corps, paraded through town cheering for Uncle Sam and jeering Spain. A banner had the inscription: 'To Hell With Spain.'" Another report, "Ohio Aroused," told that applications to organize new companies of the Ohio National Guard had been received from more than nine communities. In Chicago, a Spanish actor who was playing the role of "a Spanish villain in a lurid naval melodrama" was "assaulted by a crowd of young men as he was leaving the theatre."

The same issue of the *Press-Post* reported a local expression of opinion— "Students' Mass Meeting" (9 Mar:9). But this clamor had nothing to do with the impending war—"The students at the [Ohio State University] demonstrated Tuesday evening that they intend to clear up the athletic horizon at that institution in short order. The mass meeting was presided over by Professor Thomas, who . . . has always been a strong supporter of O.S.U. athletics." Four other professors spoke, "advancing ways and means of making up the deficiency." This mass meeting was "the largest held for some years and shows that the students are tired of affairs as they have been going on in the past."

The following day another expression of sentiment in the university was reported, this headline reading: "Dancing Don't Go." The students had presented a petition to the trustees "requesting the use of the gymnasium for dancing" and the trustees had passed the question to the faculty for resolution. The professors "decided that the university buildings could not be used for such purposes" (10 Mar:9).

The principal lesson with respect to mass sentiment in Columbus to this point may be summarized as follows: No serious evidence of a "grassroots" demand for war had been reported. All local interventions in favor of Cuba originated with highly placed persons in the community, much of it generated by the Cuban League. The evidence attesting to a "war spirit" was of a fugitive character, a scatter of instances from distant locations.

Another instance of this sort appeared that day on the front page of the *Press-Post*—"Cowboys For War" (10 March). It reported, from Washington, that Judge Jay L. Torey, of Wyoming, had been presented to McKinley by Senator Warren. The judge asked the president for authority to organize "twelve troops of cowboys" for service in the event of war. The president made no promises but assured his visitors that "in any case of necessity the cowboys should be remembered."

From central Ohio, also a front-page story, came a brief report from a village just north of Columbus. Under the heading "Westerville Awake," it was announced that the "most energetic and wide awake citizens" had met in the mayor's office. A spokesman declared it was "the universal agreement of all present" that of the things the city needed "street improvements is paramount." Also, in the same story, a debate between two local colleges, Denison and Otterbein was reported. The subject: "Resolved, That the punishment of criminals by the state should be reformatory rather than punitive."

That evening, Thursday, 10 March, the day those commonplace local events were reported, a mass meeting was held to raise funds for the Hearst-inspired memorial for the dead seamen of the *Maine*. This was the largest local Cuba-related gathering in the months that led up to the war. Like the Great Southern Theatre meeting, it was organized by highly placed local citizens; it too was a "top-down" effort. The new Columbus Auditorium was "well filled" with "representative citizens of the city and their wives and daughters" (OSJ, 11 March).

Samuel L. Black, the mayor, chaired the meeting. Because of the haste involved, several invited speakers, Governor Bushnell, Daniel J. Ryan, and H. J. Booth, were unable to attend. The governor was addressing a meeting "of like character" in his home city of Springfield. Bushnell and Ryan sent letters that were read. Although not identified as such in any of the three local dailies, Ryan and Booth were members of the Cuban League executive committee.

Lieutenant Governor Jones, the principal speaker, said that the explosion may have been an accident; he hoped that was the case. However, if war should come he hoped it would not close "until the Cubans are freed from oppression. If we must have war it must not stop till we have driven the Spaniards from out of this quarter of the globe." The next speaker, Ohio's Adjutant General, Henry A. Axline, asserted that "when honorable peace was no longer possible, he was for honorable war and for it in earnest."

Judge D. F. Pugh was then introduced and "Everybody prepared to hear something stirring . . ." He declared that: "We are here to assist in doing honor to the first American martyrs to Spanish treachery. The time for hearing evidence . . . has passed; the time for judgment, for verdict, has arrived." He spoke of those "crushed to death by the cunning and force of an invisible and cowardly enemy." "I will tell you what killed them," he continued, "It was the cowardly spite of some Spaniard or Spaniards; it was the fingers of assassins which dabble in the bloody knife at the throats of old men on sick pillows, and of women and children in their peaceful homes—called by some war—that killed these soldiers and sailors of the Maine." His comments were reported at length.

This meeting was also reported by the *Dispatch* (11 Mar:5). Their account was in substantial agreement with that of the *State Journal* except for the indications of the audience size. The *Dispatch* account spoke of the "hundreds of earnest patriots" in attendance but indicated also that the occasion "ought to have brought out a larger audience . . ." Roughly the same content appeared in the *Post-Press* (11 Mar:11).

The potpourri of news items continued in the following week with fact and flotsam sharing the front pages. The *State Journal* and the *Dispatch* continued to favor caution and restraint; the *Press-Post* became even more vociferous in its demands for war.

A front-page headline in the *State Journal* reported that: "Divers Say 'Twas a Mine" (11 Mar). This was based on a letter, dated 3 March, sent by a sailor from Key West to his parents in Williamsport, Pennsylvania. The Associated Press had picked it up and passed on the main lesson: "The Maine was blown up by a mine—that is what both divers say." A similar hearsay account appeared in the *Dispatch*, also on the front page, this headed "A Significant Fact." A survivor from the *Maine*, John R. Lead, on shore leave, was living with his brother-in-law, Louis Heineke, in Jersey City. Police Captain

Archibald McKaig reported that Lead, although guarded in his statements to reporters, had told his friends that "the launch of the Maine, which was at a little distance from the ship, blew up before the Maine did." This information was reprinted from the New York *Herald* (CED, 12 Mar).

A front-page headline in the *Dispatch* that same day announced that "Germany Is With Us." This was followed by a story with an opposite lesson: At a family dinner party in the royal palace, Kaiser Wilhelm is supposed to have declared that as long as he is emperor of Germany, "the Yankees shall not take possession of Cuba." This hearsay report appeared in the *Madrid Correspondencia* that was quoting an unidentified person who had it from "a sure source." This account was picked up by the *New York World* and then by the *Dispatch*.

The rumors, speculation, and demands continued in the following days. The *Press-Post* reported: "Congress Up in Arms and McKinley's Knuckling to Spain. Administration Wants Peace at Any Terms Obtainable." One subhead provided words of explanation: "Wall Street and Business Interests Wish No Fighting." Another pointed up an implication: "And Uncle Sam Will Likely Squat Down Before the Haughty Dons With Meek Demands" (15 Mar:1).

Many accounts reported American preparations for war. Spain objected to those efforts saying, among other things, that they encouraged the insurgents (OSJ, 17 Mar:2). Declarations about the causes of the explosion continued to appear along with speculation about the timing of the official report. Spain's ambassador met with President McKinley to "avert calamity."

The *Evening Dispatch* gave front-page attention to an item taken from the *New York World* (17 Mar). Michigan Senator Julius C. Burrows, in a signed statement, announced that: "In a very few days the government will receive the report of the court of inquiry." Burrows stated that the finding "will be" that "the Maine was destroyed by the explosion of a Spanish mine or a torpedo." His expectation was that war would follow. Burrows admitted some uncertainty as to the perpetrator but, nevertheless, faulted Spain. His words: "I care not whether the explosion was through the connivance or a Spaniard or Cuban, Spain's responsibility for the deed is not lessened thereby." This report, it will be noted, began in Washington, was then transmitted by a New York newspaper, then passed on by a local paper to its readers.

On 18 March, the front page of the *State Journal* was filled with Cuba-related accounts beginning with: "Two Nations' Hearts Beat More Quickly." This announced the imminent reports of the American and Spanish investigations. It contained an account (from the New York *Journal*, via the Associated Press) under these headlines: "Weyler's Work Come to Light, Tell-Tale Letter Which Discloses His Scheme to Blow Up American Ships in Havana Harbor." The letter was reproduced under a subhead—"The Alleged Letter," signaling a need for caution. Senator Proctor's speech, given the previous day, was presented as "The Story That Will Give Freedom to Cuba." The entire speech appeared there under a subheading—"An Accurate Picture . . ." In the same issue, a two-column box at center-page contained a statement from the Cuban Junta: "Independence or Death." Fearing the possibility of further concessions by Spain, this was intended, presumably, to block consideration of any options short of independence. The statement appeared on the same day in the *Dispatch*.[13]

Saturday's church announcements indicated most sermons still on religious themes. The Reverend Gladden's Sunday morning "discourse" was entitled "We Are Saved by Help." That evening his subject would be "Predestination, Foreordination, Election, Reprobation: What Does It All Mean?" (CED, 19 Mar:16). Reverend Barbour's topic, however, was "Christ and the War." The college news column reported events at eight institutions, but nothing there suggested the imminence of war. The *Dispatch* gave more attention to the Columbus city council election than to the possibility of war.

On Sunday the Y.M.C.A. auditorium was filled to hear Dr. Charles N. Thomas talk on "Cuban Conditions" and also to hear the singing of the Columbus Republican Glee club (OSJ, 21 Mar:5). The speaker told of the suffering he had seen in Cuba. He also commented on the concerns of Spain's leaders and on the military situation. The meeting ended with a request that the mayor be asked to call a mass meeting to secure supplies and clothing for the suffering Cubans. The *Press-Post* issues published anti-McKinley and anti-Hanna cartoons, also an article on "Starvation in Cuba," and one telling that Congress was "Becoming Restless." In all three papers, speculation continued about the timing, content, and implications of the Board of Inquiry report.

The *Dispatch* published a letter from Fidel G. Pierra of the Cuban Junta— "Cuban Indemnity. Junta Says Island Cannot Pay Spain" (21 Mar:5). This rejected one possibility that had been discussed, that of buying Cuba's independence. The letter, a well-reasoned statement, indicated that the devastated island could not possibly pay the $300 million debt that Spain had incurred in connection with Cuba. Charles B. Galbreath, the state librarian, was the initial recipient of this letter. The report did not indicate that Galbreath was a member of the executive committee of the Columbus Cuban League.[14] This account appeared also in the *Press-Post* (21 Mar:2).

The bold-faced heading on the front page of Tuesday's *State Journal* read: "Two Days More and Then—" (Mar 22). It announced that the *Maine* report would reach Washington on Thursday. On the following day, the front page of the *State Journal* was filled with reports of an entirely different problem, a local catastrophe—"Waters of the Scioto Overflow Its Banks." An extra edition declared it the "Most Destructive in the History of the City." These accounts continued in the following days—"Ohio Valley Devastated by Floods." The flood news filled the pages of all three newspapers. The threat of war was moved to the inside pages.

Later in the week, the *State Journal* reported that the president had conferred with congressional leaders; Long and Alger were actively preparing for the likely war (a brief mention of Theodore Roosevelt appeared here); and there was more on the "Horrors and Cruelties" (24 Mar:9). On Friday, the war threat was again on the front page, "Spanish Fleet Sails, U.S. Prepares for War." A brief account updated the flood news, "Scioto Receding."

The *Dispatch* that week carried an account, a "Special to The Dispatch," under this heading: "Voice From the Dead." The voice "Tells of a Mine Discovered Under the Ill-Fated Maine." Lieutenant Jenkins, who died in the explosion, had written to his mother in Pittsburgh a few days before the explosion. The letter stated "that he had discovered a mine under the Maine." Much more of "a startling nature" was contained there but the relatives "refuse to make it public." The letter was sent to Mrs. William H. Jones, a cousin living in Lima, Ohio. It was through her that the abbreviated account came to the attention of the *Dispatch* (24 Mar:1).

The *Press-Post* signaled the results of the forthcoming inquiry—it was not an accident, but "Some Form of Torpedo. By Persons Unknown" (22 March:1). That day they published an editorial on "Bryan and the War." The next day, another editorial, "Hoaxing the People," commented on McKinley's policies.

A *State Journal* story from London reported that the crisis had "prompted financiers to make efforts to avert war. A movement to this end is on foot in Lombard street and American bankers, who are leading it, are supposed to have the sympathy and perhaps the co-operation of the Rothschilds" (25 Mar:2). The *Press-Post* reprinted a story from the New York *Sun* on the same subject, this with a much more vehement tone: "'Business Interests' Rapped by the New York Sun." "The Commercial Men Betraying Cuban Liberty," it was said, "And Truckling to the Very Basest Instincts of Greed. They Are Still at Work Silently and Secretly" (25 Mar:1).

The *State Journal* Saturday edition reported the Board of Inquiry findings under a bold-type heading: "Spain Is Responsible for the Destruction of the Maine" (26 March). The subheadings announced that the American court of inquiry found the explosion was external while the Spanish inquiry had demonstrated the explosion was internal. Most of the rest of the front page detailed the resulting concerns and preparations. An editorial, entitled "The Hour Strikes," began with reference to the Proctor and Thurston reports and proceeded with a declaration that "the wisdom and disposition of the people is in hearty accord with their sentiments." And that it "is now full time for this country to interfere in Cuba to put an end to the present sacrifice of life on the island." Without any inquiry as to "the state of the masses," the writer declared the "American people are united as one man upon that proposition, and the president, backed by a loyal congress, without regard to party bias, should at once declare that the slaughter shall no longer continue . . ." The previously moderate newspaper had converted, now giving full support for intervention.

The *State Journal* lead headline—"Spain Is Responsible"—was not accurate. That assertion does not appear anywhere in the account, an AP report out of Washington. The court of inquiry concluded that the explosion was due to an external cause, "a mine was exploded under the ship on the port side." But the court also declared that it "cannot find evidence to fix responsibility." This was revealed in a "Complete Abstract" of the report presented on the front page of the Monday edition (28 March). Most of the subsequent accounts bypassed that open question. The basic message, reiterated by many commentators, was simple: Spain was responsible.

The *Press-Post* published its report of the inquiry that Monday, along with another first-page account denouncing McKinley's "Judas Iscariat Policy" (28 Mar:1). Another account that day reported the reactions in Congress under these headlines: "Hades Is Stirred Up. President McKinley's Spanish Policy Denounced. Congress to Take the Matter Out of the Hands of Executive." Then, moving from Congress to the public, the next subhead declared: "Whole Nation Aroused at Uncle Sam's Subserviency" (28 Mar:1, 7). This story predicted that: "There will be an outbreak in both senate and house should not the president's message contain more ginger . . ." It added that: "If the president does not march at the head of the American people, they will lead him, is the way a number of staunch Republican members of the house put it." Congressman Butler, of Pennsylvania, said the president "has a chance to lead the American people now. He'd better look out, or he'll have to take a back place in the procession. The time for action has come. Spain must leave Cuba." Congressman Gibson, of Tennessee, said: "We're going to get that [Spanish] flag off the island peacefully, if possible; with bullets and powder if need be."

The key message was reiterated in *Press-Post* headlines the next day, these beginning with: "SIGNS POINT TO WAR." The subheadings read: "The Nation Stands By the Star Spangled Banner. McKinley's Peace Policy Apparently Unable to Control the Congress. Resolution Declaring Immediate War Against Spain Introduced in the Senate. Followed by Another Recognizing the Independence of the Republic of Cuba. Foraker, Frye, Allen and Rawlins Lead With the Most Radical Legislation. Inspiring Scenes in the Senate Chamber—Great Crowds Surround the Capitol. Senator Mason Scores the President and Declares Himself Tired of Delay." And finally: "No Telling What Will Be the Next Step in the March of Events—Administration Influence at a Low Ebb—the Voice of the Country Heard Through the People's Representatives—No One Knows What a Day May Bring Forth" (CPP, 29 Mar:1).

With one exception, those statements provide a reasonably accurate summary of the day's activity in the Congress. The exception is the causal claim about the "Voice of the Country" and its impact since at that time there was no serious way to measure mass opinion. That declared truth was reiterated later in the article where *Press-Post* readers were told that: "The Great Heart Of the People Beats for Freedom and Not a Flunk." An inside page story reiterated the same themes, making the same points in even stronger language: "Crawfished" was the lead, that referring to "M'Kinley's Pacific Attitude, Uncle Sam's Base Surrender to the Spaniards." The correlate, stated in a subhead, was: "Congress to Take the Matter Into Its Own Hands." Another story that day told of further delay: "M'Kinley Rattled. President Uncertain Whether He Has a Backbone or Not . . . a Most Pusillanimous Policy." One-sentence statements from more than a score of congressmen were reported, all favoring some tougher action. That issue did report one public reaction. The headline read: "President M'Kinley Burned in Effigy by the Infuriated Colorado People." The story reported an event in Durango, Colorado.

The clamor in Congress was reported, more temperately, in the *State Journal*—"House Restless. Murmurs of Dissatisfaction That Will Be Hard to Control—Want Immediate Action" (29 Mar:1). The following day *State Journal* readers were told: "Indications Congress Will Declare War; Four Resolutions on the Cuban Question Offered in the Senate Yesterday Which May Hasten the Irrepressible Conflict; Senator Foraker Moves for Independence; Senator Mason Vigorously Declares for War." Mason's comments brought a "storm of applause" from the galleries; Vice President Hobart had difficulty suppressing the demonstration (30 Mar:1). The next day saw more of the same: "Most Dramatic Scene in the House; Members and Spectators Wrought Up to High Pitch of Excitement" (31 Mar:2). Speaker Reed blocked action, but two Republicans defected and "about a dozen" did not vote. A majority of the Republican House members met later that evening to work for their main demand, "complete independence of Cuba." They agreed to give the president additional time for negotiations; they also formed a "Committee of Eleven" to acquaint the president with their sentiments.

The *Press-Post* continued its insistent advocacy. It announced, among other things, that the "Ohio People Want War—If Sentiments of [state] Legislators Are Any Indication." Based on many interviews, the report concluded that "it is safe to say that the majority of the people of Ohio are for war." An editorial reviewed once again the "submarine mine" thesis. Hanna was denounced at a mass meeting in El Paso, Texas. Meanwhile, in the Congress, "Czar Reed and His Spanish Allies Hold Down the House." On an entirely different theme, the forthcoming visit to Columbus by the "most illustrious living American,"

William Jennings Bryan, was announced. He would speak on "Bimetallism" (30 Mar:3, 4, 5).

The Washington-based clamor continued in the following days. The *State Journal* headlines reported McKinley's work on his message to Congress, congressional demands for "Vigorous Action," and various military preparations. But there were few signs of clamor in central Ohio. An instance of public outrage was reported in Bucyrus, 70 miles north of Columbus, where 500 locals burned a Spanish flag. The church news was introduced with this headline: "Celebration of Holy Week in City Churches." Six columns of detail were reported, these overwhelmingly on religious themes. Lazarus, the city's leading department store, published a full-page advertisement for a sale of spring overcoats. It was embellished with American flags with a vague tie-in to the current crisis (2 Apr:12).

The *State-Journal* headline in the Sunday issue, 3 April, read: "Peace or War: Which Shall It Be?" There was also a long account: "Senators Want War." On Monday, the lead headline was: "The Crisis at Hand." Numerous conferences between leaders in Washington were reported. Congress "Will Wait for the President's Message," but "Great Difficulty May Be Experienced in Holding the Radical Republicans in Line After Monday."

Comments by local citizens were still infrequent. In his Sunday sermon, the Reverend Gladden asked for caution and restraint; the headline read: "If War Must Come Let It Be the Holiest War that Was Ever Waged."[15] On the same day President Bashford of Ohio Wesleyan University (in Delaware, 25 miles north of Columbus) spoke briefly on the Cuban question in Grey chapel. Cuban independence, he said, "ought to be recognized at once by the United States" and, if Spain refuses "our requests" or should hinder our efforts for the starving Cubans, "we should begin war at once." While the impending war gained most attention in the front pages, other news dominated the remaining pages, much space being given to the Columbus city council elections (4 April) and to catastrophic floods in Illinois (5 April).

The *Press-Post* covered the same events with its insistent tendency and greater fervor. An editorial faulted McKinley for ignoring "the wishes of 95 per cent. of his countrymen." A news story reported that the president was preparing his message to Congress. It appeared under these headlines: "No Backbone. A Milk and Water President. McKinley Halting and Wavering in His Course" (3 Apr:4, 7). The next issue carried accounts of Wall Street opposition to war— "Working for Peace." On the local scene, Fred Lazarus, the proprietor of the local department store, together with some other local businessmen, sent a wire to Congressman Lentz urging Congress to give McKinley more time. Another headline declared: "Congress Clamorous" (4 April: 3, 7, and 9).[16]

McKinley's policy was the subject of a heated debate in the Ohio legislature. The *State Journal* tagged the effort as "Democratic Buncombe" and declared that the "Republicans Have All the Best of the Argument" (6 Apr:1). Several speeches in the U.S. Senate called for "Vigorous and Instant" action. Under "Situation in a Nutshell," the reason for McKinley's delay, it was explained, was to allow all Americans to leave Cuba (7 Apr:1). In Columbus, a play, described as a "Great Scenic Production," opened for a week of performances. Entitled "Cuba's Vow!," it was "A Story of Spain's Cruel Oppression of Cuba's Loyal Patriots."

In Urbana, Ohio, 40 miles west of Columbus, an "enthusiastic meeting" at the Opera House proposed the creation of a volunteer military company. Resolutions were adopted, one to "avenge" those murdered on the *Maine*, the other a demand to "move upon the enemy at once." A front-page story told of Bryan's visit to Columbus and his "Bimetallism" lecture. The hall was reported to have been only half full (OSJ 7 Apr:1).

The *Press-Post* shifted its focus in early April, giving much attention to Bryan's visit, announcing it several times and encouraging attendance. His arrival and reception in the city was reported at length and the speech itself was described as a "Masterly Address." In striking contrast to the *State Journal* report, the audience was said, by a conservative estimate, to be 3,500 but their report thought 4,000 probable (7 Apr:6). The news from Washington was still given prominence as in this headline: "Not Today. President Postpones Again."

The *State Journal* digressed from the main themes of the week to reprove the local congressman, John J. Lentz, a Bryan Democrat, who had stated that McKinley's delay in sending his message to Congress was "directly traceable" to the influence of Wall Street. The heading renamed the offender, calling him "Jawn Jingo Lentz, Demagogue." He was "taking his cue from the New York Journal, the most notorious and unreliable of the numerous yellow journals of the country." Lentz was described as a "conscienceless agitator" who was "out of place in the American congress" (9 Apr:4). The next day, another editorial dealt with "The Yellow Journals and the President." The main lesson was that the "thinking people of this country are heart and soul with President McKinley." A later issue had several columns of comment from newspapers elsewhere in the state condemning Lentz's performance. The *Press-Post* reported the same events, but with opposite assessments. An editorial that day was headed: "When Will the Shame End?" (8 Apr:3, 4).

The clamor, the tumult, the "loud voices," as seen, were found in the nation's capital, most of them in the legislative branch. The congressional pressures on McKinley, reported in the previous chapter, were amply confirmed in the local press. The front page of the *Dispatch*, for example, on 30 March carried these headlines: "Thomas Reed Is Still Ruler of the House, The Democrats Attempt to Overthrow Him, But Time for Cuban Action Was Not Ripe." A smaller story carried this headline: "Even the Senate Cannot Be Much Longer Held in Restraint." One important local action was reported two days later under the headline "They Want War." But this again was a report of elite preferences as opposed to some voices from "the masses." The opening sentence read: "The Ohio legislature is on record in favor of recognition of Cuban independence, and war, if necessary" (1 Apr:6).

McKinley's message was read to Congress on 11 April. A *Dispatch* headline that day gave this summary: "War Must Stop And Give Way to Stable Government." The following day a front-page *Dispatch* headline announced that: "The Warlike Spirit, Is Hard to Keep Down Among the Members of Congress." The president's message was discussed in the Congress, this summarized as follows: "Get Out of Cuba/Is the Order Given to Spain by Uncle Sam/ . . . And the President Is Directed to Use All the Force/Of Both the Army and Navy" (13 Apr:1).

The headlines in the following days detailed the events leading up to the war. No useful purpose is served by a step-by-step summary. Both houses of Congress struggled with the wording of the Cuban resolution, finally adopting a version that did not recognize the Cuban republic or the Junta. The headlines in these days provided both fact and celebration—"One of the Most Memorable Days in the History of the American Congress Ends Triumphantly for Cuba" and "President McKinley, Commander-in-Chief, Will Hurl Thousands of America's Bravest Men Against Spain's Rotten Rule in the War-Swept Queen of the Antilles." The effort was described as the "Holy Crusade Against Spanish Cruelty and Spanish Tyranny to Drive Them from Western World" (OSJ, 19 Apr:1).

The *Press-Post* summarized events under these headlines: "On the Rampage Are the Sneaking Spaniards. Vote in the Senate Has Set the Heathen in a Rage, And They Howl in Madrid Like the Mad Hyenas" (18 Apr:10). One modest sign of local sentiments appeared at this time. The citizens of one south-side neighborhood paid their "respects to Weyler" by hanging him in effigy (OSJ, 16 Apr:8; CED, 16 Apr:6; CPP, 16 Apr:6). It was a rare indication of local sentiments. Nothing was said about the size of the crowd.

A few days later, the local press reported the first and only instance of "mass" participation. On 18 April, the Seventeenth Regiment marched through the city to the depot from which they would be transported to Tampa. The *Press-Post* headlines read: "Forward! March! The Gallant Seventeenth Leaves for the Front, Grand Patriotic Demonstrations All Along the Line of March." Also: "Business Suspended Altogether and the Sidewalks Lined With Cheering Men, Women and Children. Columbus Takes Part in a Patriotic Demonstration of Which Coming Generations Will be Proud" (19 Apr:1). The *State Journal* report was headed: "Outpouring of People: Magnificent Demonstration by the Citizens of Columbus in Honor of Seventeenth Regiment: Triumphal March." "No demonstration in the history of Columbus," it was reported, "equals that of Tuesday, when the people of Columbus turned out en masse to wave a last farewell to the brave boys in blue who go to fight their country's battles. . . . Nearly everybody in Columbus saw the parade. . . . The streets were never so crowded before. Never before were people so enthusiastic" (20 Apr:1). The *Dispatch* also reported this send-off, referring to what was "perhaps the wildest and most patriotic demonstration ever recorded here . . . the crowd numbered thousands." (CED, 20 Apr:5).

Everything had been done to ensure a large turnout for the sendoff. The event had been announced in the previous days; streetcars were removed from the route; schools, shops, and factories let out; factory whistles and church bells announced the beginning of the march. At this late point, the "masses" finally came "on stage." Their role, however, was approbation, the giving of approval to an action taken by others, by the members of Congress. This ratification was obviously not causal. It was clearly "after the fact," after the decision had been made in Washington.

Few signs of local public reactions appeared in the days that followed. Professor George Welles Knight gave a lecture on Cuban-American relations during the chapel hour at Ohio State University. The lower floor was packed with "enthusiastic students" who greeted the professor with a "triple cheer after a resounding college yell" (CED, 22 Apr:7). The professor reviewed Cuban events from 1868 and indicated the reasons for the American intervention. "Technically," he added, "we are, as I understand international law, aggressors . . . [but] Morally, we are entirely and unqualifiedly right. Of our motives there is no question" (CPP, 22 Apr:7).

Some activity was reported at other universities. Weyler effigies were hanged and burned at Yale, Dartmouth, and Connecticut Wesleyan. A thousand students paraded at Princeton (the "greatest student demonstration since the civil war"). Ex-President Cleveland addressed them, welcoming the evidence of their patriotism (CED, 22 Apr:7, 12). The *State Journal* reported some public activities in surrounding communities. The citizens of Westerville were arranging "A Great Parade" and Lancaster was showing "War Fever."[17] Something was happening in Fremont and elsewhere. In the Columbus churches, it was announced, "War Will Be the Theme of Many Ministers" (OSJ, 23 Apr:8, 9). Another report there indicated that "Nearly Five Hundred" area citizens had enlisted in a regiment of Ohio volunteer infantry. These signs of arousal, like the great send-off, also appeared after the fact, after the decision for war had been taken.

The United States' government took the final legal step a few days later. The *Press-Post* headline read: "Declaration of War Made." Several enthusiastic subheads followed: "Uncle Sam Flings the Star Spangled Banner to the Breeze and Says the Fight is On, Everything Now Goes and the Americans Will Quickly Sock It to the Haughty Dons." A late report from Washington indicated that: "In Two Minutes the House Unanimously Votes War to Lick Spain" (25 Apr:1).

* * *

The principal lesson to be drawn, a negative one, may be stated as follows: No significant mass demand "for war" was evident in Columbus or in central Ohio in the months prior to the declaration. Any argument for the public-clamor thesis based on the Columbus daily newspapers must depend on a handful of episodes in small communities elsewhere in Ohio, in Oxford, Port Clinton, and Bucyrus, or at a greater distance, on the scatter of events in El Paso, Durango, and New Haven. That negative conclusion—no mass demand for intervention from Ohio—is reinforced by another striking fact, the absence of reports of clamor in Ohio's largest cities, no reports from Cleveland or Cincinnati, nothing from Toledo, Youngstown, or Akron. From Dayton, there is only that brief Spanish-flag episode.

The most vociferous clamor reported in the Columbus newspapers, the demands that would have carried weight in the McKinley's decision for war, were those located in the nation's capital, just down the street from the White House in the United States Senate and House of Representatives.

At home, on the streets of Columbus and in the neighborhoods, there was little to report. Apart from the flood, things were generally quiet; life went on as usual. Apart from a single episode, Weyler burned in effigy, the few local actions favoring support for Cuba and its citizens were initiated by high-status citizens. The most important of these was the Southern Theatre meeting sponsored by a downtown Baptist Church, with significant involvement by state and local political leaders and the Columbus Cuban League. The resolutions passed called for belligerency rights and, somewhat vaguely, the "active support of our people" in Cuba's struggle for freedom. The greatest indication of mass support, the 19 April send-off for the troops came after the decision to intervene. That late demonstration by "the masses," in short, was a gesture of approval, a ratification of an action taken by the president and the Congress.[18]

The positive lesson should also be indicated. If the citizens of central Ohio were not clamoring for war, what were they doing? That, too, is indicated in the daily newspapers: The answer is that everyday life appears to have continued with little change. April 8 was Good Friday. The Saturday edition of the *State Journal* reported the sermon themes for Easter Sunday. As usual, they dealt with religious subjects, these embellished with a wide array of musical offerings. A week later, just after the send-off of troops, the headline announcing the church offerings indicated that some ministers "Will Discuss the War Situation," one topic being "Our National Crisis." But the overwhelming majority, judging from the titles, still focused on religious subjects. The local clubs and lodges continued to meet. Local "society" events were reported with no sign of change, all three Columbus papers giving many columns to reports of travels, of visits, and parties. On Sunday, 17 April, the day after the Senate passed the Foraker-Turpie resolution, a *State Journal* headline announced: "Baseball Season Opens."

This search for evidence of mass sentiments in the first months of 1898 reports a very limited "sample" of experience: a single city, Columbus, or at best a single region, central Ohio. This "case study," however, is of more than ordinary interest because of its distinctive circumstances. The city's largest circulation newspaper was an ardent advocate of the Cuban cause; it had close ties to the local Cuban League; and it made generous use of "sensational" methods. There was, in short, a lot "going for" the mobilization effort. Yet, as far as one can tell, the Columbus "masses" remained largely unmoved. Put more precisely, there were few visible signs from "the grassroots" that would have forced action by reluctant members of Congress to go to war. The local congressman, John J. Lentz, clearly favored "forceful action," but for that he needed no instruction or direction from "the masses."

This account says little about the experience elsewhere in the nation. Other communities, Chicago, Cleveland, Cincinnati, and Canton, might have shown more zeal for the Cuban cause. If so, it was not reported in any Columbus newspaper. If Pittsburgh, Detroit, or San Francisco were "up in arms," why would it not be reported in the *Press-Post*? Why, instead, did they report the reaction in Durango, Colorado? If the citizens of Cleveland were outraged, why not report that? Why, instead, tell of the ladies in Port Clinton, Ohio?[19]

The experience of Columbus (or of central Ohio) indicates that the "aroused masses" assertion—that the "tide" of opinion was the decisive cause for American entry in the war—must be counted as not supported or, put more strongly, as unlikely. Pending the presentation of compelling evidence demonstrating the existence of a "mass demand" for war, that claim should be recognized as, at best, an untested hypothesis.[20] Assessment of public opinion is difficult at all times. Even with the polls and surveys developed in later decades, given the complexities of sampling, question wording, response rates, and weighting of possible causes, such judgment is difficult. But, as of 1898, none of that research apparatus was available. Nevertheless, many commentators, then and later, showing no caution whatsoever, boldly declared what "the masses" were thinking and doing.

If mass sentiment is rejected as "the cause," one must look for some other cause (or causes) to explain the decision for war. The most likely alternative indicated both in the previous chapters and in the newspaper experience reviewed here, is that the clamor was a joint effort stimulated by a political opposition (parties and their supportive press) and by an advocacy group, the Cuban League. The clamor for war was based in Washington, not in the nation's cities, towns, villages, and farms. More precisely, that clamor came from within the ranks of the Congress, from the Junta's advocates, and from groups of high-status individuals, many of them with ties to the Cuban League. Most of the advocates at this point were aligned with the Democratic Party.

Notes

1. The State of Ohio, Anthony J. Celebrezze, Jr., ed., *Number of Inhabitants Urban and Rural Population (Twentieth Federal Census)* (n.p., 1980), p. 154.
2. These figures, based on the publisher's sworn statements, are from *N.W. Ayer & Son's Newspaper Annual: 1898* (Philadelphia, 1898).
3. The weekly edition was listed as Independent in Ayer's, 1898, p. 636. The following year, the *State Journal* reported a circulation of 13,511 (sworn); the *Dispatch* reported 20,000 (unsworn); and the *Press-Post* reported a circulation of 23,500, (sworn), from *Ayer's*, 1899, pp. 641–642. There is a significant disparity between the *Press-Post* figures for 1898 and 1899. For some background on the city's newspapers, see Alfred E. Lee, *The History of the City of Columbus*, two volumes (New York, 1892), Vol. 1, chs. 27 and 28. See also note 20 below.
4. Kilbourne was the grandson of another James Kilbourne, one of Ohio's founders. See Historical Publishing Company, *Franklin County at the Beginning of the Twentieth Century* (Columbus, 1901), pp. 47–48 and Osman Castle Hooper, *History of the City of Columbus Ohio* (Columbus, 1920), pp. 291–293.
5. Charles B. Galbreath, *History of Ohio*, five volumes (Chicago, 1925), Vol. 4, pp. 6–7; Opha Moore, *History of Franklin County Ohio*, three volumes (Topeka, 1930), Vol. 2, pp. 833–835.
6. Charles B. Galbreath, *In Memoriam: Daniel Joseph Ryan, 1855–1923* (Columbus, 1924).
7. Hooper, *History . . .* , p. 295.
8. Historical Publishing, *Franklin County*, pp. 309–310. Galbreath was also an author, as seen in the previous notes. His *History of Ohio* contains a brief paragraph on the Cuban League; see Vol. 1, p. 624. See also Kilbourne's letter in the *Columbus Press-Post*, 22 April 1898:3. Congressman Lentz commended the work of the Cuban League in his address favoring the $50 million defense appropriation. *Press-Post*, 31 March:4. I did not find any information on T. C. Clark, the seventh member of the executive committee.
   From this point the following abbreviations will be used for citations in the text: *Ohio State Journal*, OSJ; *Columbus Evening Dispatch*, CED; *Columbus Evening Press*, CEP; and *Columbus Post-Press*, CPP.
9. See Washington Gladden, *Recollections* (Boston, 1909) and Jacob Henry Dorn, *Washington Gladden: Prophet of the Social Gospel* (Columbus, 1967).
10. Long's diary entry Wednesday evening, 16 February, reads: "My own judgment is, so far as any information has been received, that it was the result of an accident, such as every ship of war; with the tremendously high and powerful explo-

sives which we now have, on board; is liable to suffer," from Margaret Long, ed., *The Journal of John Davis Long* (Rindge, NH, 1956), p. 215 (punctuation as given). Some small differences appear in this version as compared to an earlier publication of Long's journal. In that version another sentence follows those just given— "The best way, however, seems to be to suspend judgment until more information shall be had." From Lawrence Shaw Mayo, *America of Yesterday* (Boston, 1923), p. 164.

11. Admiral Hyman J. Rickover's review of the *Maine* catastrophe concluded that spontaneous combustion was the cause. Coalbunkers were located adjacent to magazines to "give additional protection from enemy projectiles," but that brought the risk that "spontaneous combustion of the bituminous coal would overheat the magazines." He lists more than a dozen such bunker fires since 1895, several "almost" causing the magazines to explode, in his *How the Battleship Maine was Destroyed* (Annapolis, 1995 [1976]), p. 20.

12. After being closed for many years, the Great Southern Theatre is again in active use. In 2003, it had a total of 933 seats.

13. It appeared also on the same day in the *Detroit Free Press*; see Raymond A. Detter, "The Cuban Junta and Michigan: 1895–1898," *Michigan History*, 48 (1964), p. 43. The Cuban Junta again is shown to be a very adept pressure group.

14. Sometime before, the Columbus Cuban League brought Pierra to Columbus where he addressed "a large meeting." He "made a most favorable impression in Columbus, where he was entertained by Colonel Kilbourne and other prominent citizens." From Galbreath, *History of Ohio*, Vol. I, p. 624.

15. Gladden has been described as a pacifist, but some exceptions, clearly, had to be considered. See Donald G. Baughman, "Washington Gladden's Attitude on War," (unpublished M.A. thesis, Ohio State University, 1960). On Sunday, 17 April, Gladden spoke on "Our Nation and Her Neighbors." "That good will come out of this war," he said, "is certain" (CED, 18 Apr:5).

16. The difficulties involved in assessment of opinions may be seen in a couple of fragmentary reports out of New Haven. One *Press-Post* notice announced "Yale Students on the Warpath" (2 Apr:1). A few days later, another report appeared under a deprecating headline: "Yale College Faculty Stick Their Noses in for Peace." President Timothy Dwight had conferred with the members of the several faculties and on that basis sent a telegram to President McKinley expressing "cordial satisfaction" for his efforts to settle the difficulties without resort to war, this "on terms just and honorable to both nations." As that message was sent, "a crowd of men in the eastern part of [New Haven] were burning President McKinley in effigy on a telegraph pole" (5 Apr:1).

17. Westerville, just to the north of Columbus, had a population (1900) of 1,462. The same news item reported also a local college event, that the Otterbein baseball team would go to Gambier where they would "contend with their old rival, Kenyon."

18. A peripheral finding: Later biographies, monographs, and textbooks give prominence to the ever-active Theodore Roosevelt. But the local newspaper accounts dealing with naval affairs center almost exclusively on Secretary Long. In those accounts, Roosevelt, the assistant secretary, is practically invisible. Given the secrecy involved, it is understandable that the *State Journal* reported nothing of the momentous orders to Admiral Dewey sent out on 25 February. The first report of the Pacific squadron's movements appeared in the *State Journal* on 4 March, a brief page-two AP dispatch from Madrid. Under the heading "Preparing For War,"

readers learned that the Spanish public was "much exercised" over the reported presence of American warships at Hong Kong where "it is presumed the vessels intend to threaten Manila, the capital of the Philippine islands, in the event of war between the United States and Spain."

19. The leading newspapers of Cleveland and Cincinnati were reviewed. The findings for those cities were similar to the Columbus result: The demands for intervention came from highly placed persons, many of them with links to the Cuban League. No serious indications of demands from "the masses" were discovered.

20. Another lesson should be noted. A standard assumption of the mass society theory is that sensationalism (or demagoguery) is a profitable tactic, that it pays off. But in Columbus, the *Press-Post* circulation was stagnant, never reported as more than 25,000 in later years. By 1908, the positions were reversed. The *State Journal* was then the largest paper, with 45,000 subscribers, followed by the *Evening Dispatch*, with 31,331. The last issue of the *Press-Post* was published on 11 July 1909.

7

Public Pressures and the Congress

The dominant, long-standing explanation for the United States' intervention in 1898 has it that "Americans," outraged by the Spanish depredations in Cuba, clamored for war. And, responding to their constituents' "imperative" demands, members of Congress, both senators and representatives, initiated measures to support the Cuban insurgents. McKinley and his loyal supporters did what they could to fend off those pressures but ultimately they, too, were forced to go along.

The popular clamor was stimulated, presumably, by "sensational" press reports, many accounts, as seen, beginning with the efforts of Pulitzer and Hearst, with their mass-circulation "yellow" newspapers, the *World* and the *Journal*, both based in New York City. The "news" they produced in the metropolis was sent out by the wire services and was reproduced in newspapers across the land. The evidence reviewed in the two previous chapters showed that those claims of a "sweeping" press influence are open to serious question.

A second test of that generally accepted causal argument is possible. If the public-clamor argument were accurate, the members of Congress should have been overwhelmed with demands from their constituents. The volume of letters, petitions, and personal contacts calling for American intervention would have been enormous, like nothing seen in previous memory. If that were the case, evidence attesting to the "clamor" should be found, writ large, in the memoirs and biographies of the leading members of the Congress.

Given the differentiated press performance seen in the previous chapter, one should also expect to find corresponding differentiated reactions on the part of the nation's senators and representatives. Given the virulence of the New York City press, New York's two senators, Republican Thomas C. Platt and Democrat Edward Murphy, Jr., should have been moved by the Pulitzer-Hearst press agitation. Yet neither man appears on the lists of the clamorous senators; they gain only fleeting mention in discussions of events leading up to the war. The same holds for all but one of the state's representatives. The chapter of Platt's autobiography that reviews 1897–1898 contains only two fugitive mentions of the Spanish-American War. Nothing is said there about any pressures, from press or constituents. That chapter focuses on the dynamics of state politics.[1]

A neighboring state, New Hampshire, not known for its sensationalist press, produced two ardent interventionist senators, William E. Chandler and Jacob H. Gallinger. Missouri, as seen in chapter 5, had a vociferous press and one of the state's senators, George Vest, did prove to be an especially active interventionist. The Florida press, as seen, was strongly opposed to American intervention in Cuba. But one Florida senator, Wilkerson Call, ignored those press "demands" and was an active proponent of Cuban initiatives. Ohio's two senators represented the same constituents but, as seen, they made opposite choices, Foraker ardently favoring some Cuba action and Hanna ardently opposed to such interventions.

Another possibility needs consideration: Correlation does not establish causation. Was Senator Vest responding to the demands of Missouri's press? Or was he proceeding independently, moved by other causes? Another example is relevant: Senator William Vincent Allen of Nebraska had been a foremost advocate of the Cuban case for seventeen years. From 1878, in every session of Congress, he had introduced a resolution of sympathy for the Cuban people, all of this long before Pulitzer and Hearst appeared on the scene, long before the 1895 Cuban uprising.

The received hypotheses assume a combined influence of "the press" and concerned citizens, both making forceful demands on the nation's elected officials. The question to be addressed in this chapter is: Was that actually the case?

Evidence relevant to that question should appear in the memoirs and biographies of those elected representatives. Those sources should give some indication of the pressures exerted by the press and the public as well as some account of the representatives' reactions to those "imperative" demands. This procedure, to be sure, presents some problems. One could easily select, say, a one-in-five random sample from among the ninety senators and 357 representatives in the 55th Congress. But the probability of finding relevant information on the members of that sample would be very small. Such works are available for the most prominent members of the Senate and House but sparse for most of the others. Two examples follow:

Robert Adams (1846–1906) was a capable man, one with wide-ranging experience, much of it involving Latin America. He was elected to Congress in 1893, representing "an important business district" of Philadelphia. In April 1898, he was the acting chairman of the House Committee on Foreign Affairs. When President McKinley sought the authority to end hostilities in Cuba, it was Adams who saw the measure through the House and headed the conference committee to resolve the differences with the Senate version. On 25 April, in the space of one hour, he drafted, introduced, and "forced through the House" the declaration of war against Spain. The *Dictionary of American Biography* contains a brief biography of Adams. No full-length biography had been written at that time, 1928, and none has appeared subsequently.[2]

Robert R. Hitt (1834–1909) was another congressman who had demonstrated much ability. He worked first as a journalist, reporting on important events at home and abroad. He was appointed as secretary of the legation in Paris where he worked for seven years. Later, for a brief period, he served as the Assistant Secretary of State under James Blaine. Elected to Congress from an Illinois district in 1882, he served continuously until his death. He was a member of the Committee on Foreign Affairs and, when the Republicans were in the majority, served as its chairman, the longest stretch being from the 54th to the 58th Congress. Brief biographies appear in the DAB and NAB but, like Adams, there was no full-length biography.[3]

In some instances, biographical information is almost entirely absent: John McDonald, a Republican, was elected to the 55th Congress from a rural Maryland district and served only the single term. His descendants have searched for information on the man but their efforts have been largely without success.

The available accounts, biographies and other materials, moreover, are organized on diverse principles, each author making different judgments with respect to importance and coverage. They differ also in the extent and quality of the use made of source materials. One should note also a likely source of bias. Authors of memoirs are not likely to confess that they were "blind" or helpless followers of opinion, either that of the press or the public. Nor would they be likely to give full and accurate accounts of questionable behavior such as the advocacy of war for the sake of party advantage. Another source of bias is likely with respect to the biographies. Few authors would find either the interest or the time to research and record the actions of unthinking or deferential conformists.

The people to be discussed here were all prominent persons with known positions, both pro and con, on all of the major issues. Advocates would probably have been selective in their "targeting," avoiding their known opponents and favoring the sympathizers. They might also, with good reason, have paid greater attention to the "undecideds" and the "don't knows." These would probably have been less prominent persons, people who, like John McDonald, left no extensive records, documentary or biographical. Researching the suggested option, following through with a random sample, would be an impossible task.

The following pages report instead on an odd-lot sample of congressmen. Some prominent advocates of the Cuban insurgents will be considered first.

Some accounts of their opponents, the McKinley backers, will follow. One biographer had provided short lists of the contending "sides."

> The war party . . . was led by Morgan, Democrat from Alabama, and he was supported not only by such independent Republicans as Chandler and Teller but by many so-called administration Senators, Lodge, Cullom, Foraker, and Frye. Opposed to them were the "Big Six"—Aldrich, Allison, Hanna, Hoar, [Orville] Platt, and Spooner; they rallied around the President as he endeavored to avert a war.[4]

The memoirs and biographical accounts of these individuals will be reviewed in the sequence indicated. First however some words of caution may be useful. Lists of those "for" and "against" are easily produced and may seem plausible. But such categorical statements hide much complexity and may even be erroneous. As will be seen, one of the senators listed is clearly misplaced and another hard to place.

Another author provides more extensive lists of both the proponents and opponents of intervention. The former does not include Senators Morgan, Cullom, and Frye but adds several others. The second list does not include Senator Hoar among the opponents. Another author refers to the "Big Four" Republican leaders, a "fraternity" that in 1897 had been a "full sixteen years in the making." This leaves out Hanna, a recent arrival in the Senate, and an older Republican potentate, Senator George Frisbie Hoar of Massachusetts.[5]

Senator John Tyler Morgan of Alabama (1824–1907) is described by a biographer as "one of the principal firebrands in the coming of the war. Few, if any, public figures had been more vocal and harsh in condemning Spain and (until early 1898) in calling for the recognition of Cuban belligerency and independence."[6] His larger agenda included many items traditionally favored by southern Democrats—"state banks to make credit more readily available, lower tariffs to decrease the cost of manufactured goods, and an income tax to raise the relative tax burden of the more prosperous North." He also favored free coinage of silver. When faced with a threat from the Populists, he "emphasized race" and worked for the disenfranchisement of the black population.[7]

Morgan served on the Senate Foreign Relations Committee from 1878 until his death in 1907. For much of that time he was the ranking Democrat on the Committee. In the 53d Congress, from 1893–1895, he served as its chairman. His aims there were to increase the South's exports of cotton, coal, iron, and timber and to generate indigenous sources of capital "to free Dixie from the control of northern and British merchants and investors." He also hoped to add new territories to the nation so as to allow the formation of new states sympathetic to the Democratic South. He "championed a canal through Nicaragua," seeing Mobile as a key port for international trade and Mount Vernon, Alabama as a shipbuilding center. Morgan worked "tirelessly" for "expanded trade with Latin America, Asia, and the Congo, endorsed the construction of a modern U.S. Navy and merchant marine, welcomed the annexation of Hawaii, Puerto Rico, and the Philippines." Morgan thought that the new states created in the annexed territories might become "havens for colonized American blacks."[8]

Morgan, in short, had a clear and consistent agenda, one he pursued long before Pulitzer and Hearst began their agitation. His position was distinctive, one not shared by most southern congressmen and, given his distinct regional concerns, one rarely shared by leading Republican expansionists. Morgan sharply opposed President Cleveland in 1893–1894 because of his failure to annex Hawaii. This brought criticism from the Democratic press and commendation from Republican papers. Fry describes him as "an aggressive expansionist and a political maverick on foreign policy issues."[9]

In the first years of the Cuban struggle, Morgan "consistently supported the Cuban insurgents, harshly criticized the Cleveland administration's pro-Spanish neutrality, and helped stimulate the heightened United States emotionalism regarding Cuba." In those efforts, Morgan drew on consular reports, on committee hearings he and Cushman K. Davis conducted, and on American newspapers. He also used "materials provided by the Cuban junta (with whom he was in close communication)." Morgan proved to be more favorably disposed to McKinley than he had been to Cleveland, a fact recognized by both the New York *Journal* and the Montgomery *Advertiser*, both judging him "far too cozy with the GOP on Cuban policy." Throughout the summer of 1897, Morgan "forwarded letters from Cuban leaders and proinsurgent newspaper clippings" to the new president, "always in a friendly manner." This restrained quiet backing of McKinley continued even after the de Lôme letter and the sinking of the *Maine*. That support for McKinley is explained by Morgan's sense that "the new president shared [his] expansionist agenda." Accordingly, he objected to measures "designed solely to embarrass the president."[10]

Morgan's biographer, Fry, has a paragraph telling of the "emotional demands for war" that "burst from all sections of the country" following the *Maine* catastrophe. Without any mention of the nation's press, it centers on the partisan reactions—"numerous Populists, agrarian Democrats, and even Cleveland Democrats began to push for war" and William Jennings Bryan "joined the chorus." In response, he writes, GOP stalwarts "frantically urged the president to act." Those sentences report events happening elsewhere, things impinging on other decision-makers. Fry portrays Morgan's politics as largely self-determined. The senator generated and reached out for supporting materials, including aid from Junta sources. Nothing contained in Fry's pages, however, suggests a response to sensational newspaper content.[11] Nothing is reported there about a clamor, about pressures from the "grassroots."

William E. Chandler (1835–1917), a Republican senator from New Hampshire, is often counted, along with Morgan, as one of the leaders of the interventionist forces. His biographer reviews the question in a chapter entitled "An Apostle of War."[12] There one is told that McKinley's course concerning Cuba was "not essentially dissimilar to that of Cleveland. . . . The business interests, which had elected him and to which he owed his first allegiance, were utterly opposed to war, and [McKinley] put forth his best efforts to avert it." Although a Republican, Chandler was "entirely hostile" to the president's course. From the first, he "took the extreme view that the United States should intervene actively to secure the freedom of the island, even if war should result."[13]

The "sympathy of the United States," Richardson reports, "had ever been extended to countries contending for self-rule, as instanced by former enthusiasms for the Greeks, the Hungarians, and the rebelling peoples of South America . . . but the Cubans were at our very door." Although sympathetic, probably not "one in ten" Americans in the early months of 1898 would have chosen "actual warlike interference . . ." But that all changed with the sinking of the *Maine*. The "outpourings of the yellow press" are mentioned, these described as "positively disgusting" in their misrepresentations. But the author thinks "the course of events probably would have been much the same" without those efforts. By mid-April, McKinley had "yielded completely to the forces of aroused public opinion and political pressure."[14]

The quotations in the previous paragraph report the author's inferences about public opinion and its effects. The next pages of the chapter report Chandler's activities and the actions taken in the Senate in the months from February to April including discussion of the various resolutions offered, the votes taken, the actions of Reed in the House, and the subsequent compromises. Those pages report nothing about "grassroots" pressures or sentiments that might have touched and moved Chandler.[15]

Henry Moore Teller (1830–1914), a senator from Colorado, was the state's "most popular and foremost politician." Originally a Democrat, he joined the Republicans at the time of the Civil War. Later, in the 1890s, he became a Silver Republican, the leader of those who demonstratively exited the party's convention in 1896 following the adoption of the gold standard. Teller supported Bryan and later, in 1901, rejoined the Democrats.[16]

Teller was the author of the Teller Amendment, the measure rejecting a possible annexation of Cuba. It may come then as a surprise that his biographer should report that in 1898 Teller "was an expansionist" and that he favored "an absolute incorporation" of Hawaii. In the Senate, he declared that: "I am in favor of the annexation of Cuba; I am in favor of the annexation of the great country lying to the north of us. I expect in a few years to see the American flag floating from the extreme north to the line of our sister Republics on the south.

I expect to see it floating over the isles of the sea . . . ." But, at the same time, he also indicated a limiting condition, that of consent—"If the Canadians do not choose to come to us we shall never get them. . . . I do not believe that by conquest we should take anything."[17]

The discussion of Cuba again provides "the basics" telling of the insurrection, of Spain's "cruel methods," the press role, plus a statement that it "was natural for the public to sympathize with any people struggling for independence." Teller favored recognition of the belligerency of the rebels but denied that it would "give Spain any cause for complaint, much less for war." He was "not favorable toward a war against Spain" and his voice was usually raised "for moderation and for calm decision." Even after the sinking of the *Maine*, he "cautioned against hasty action or judgment."[18]

The various measures discussed in the Congress are then reviewed, much attention being given Teller's proposal. Again the partisan division is evident, the measure being adopted by "the combined votes of Democrats, Populists, Silver Republicans, and a small group of regular Republicans who had been favorable to the Cuban cause." The measure, the author reports, "was unquestionably distasteful to the convinced imperialists, because it pledged the United States to make Cuba independent." The measure, the author claimed, "represented the wishes of the public at large at this time." The latter, he adds, "was sympathetic toward the cause of Cuban independence, and was not motivated as yet by too obvious desires for territorial expansion." Nothing is reported as to the sources of that knowledge. One additional comment should be noted: "Many, probably including Teller, felt that an independent Cuba would eventually ask for annexation." Apart from those unsupported judgments, those pages report nothing about demands "from below," demands that might have influenced Teller's judgments.[19]

The relevant chapter in Garraty's biography of Henry Cabot Lodge opens with a comment about public opinion. It announces the "natural sympathy of Americans for an underdog people seeking freedom from the rule of a foreign monarch," a disposition that guaranteed "the revolutionaries a favorable press and powerful economic assistance."[20] Lodge's involvement began early in 1896 when Senator John Sherman, the chairman of the Foreign Relations Committee, named him to a subcommittee on Cuban affairs along with himself and Senator Morgan. The assignment put him "in close contact with the whole problem." Lodge then began "to see a good deal of the unofficial representatives of the revolutionaries in Washington, 'interesting young fellows' who thanked him for his efforts in behalf of Cuba's freedom . . ." Cleveland's policy of strict neutrality "exasperated Lodge."[21]

Lodge supported the Cameron resolution in December 1896, which Garraty describes as "a virtual declaration of war on Spain." But the senator, as seen earlier, was then "deluged with protests" from Massachusetts businessmen. Garraty gives an entire page to the business reactions, but Lodge made no concession, arguing instead the merits of the "strong stand." Then, as seen, Secretary of State Olney effectively tabled the measure. The pro-Cuba agitation subsided in the months following McKinley's inauguration.[22]

Garraty then reviewed the events following the sinking of the *Maine*. American opinion, he wrote, "skillfully stimulated by the newspapers, demanded revenge" and at once the nation "was on the verge of war with Spain." But Lodge "did not share in this hasty reaction." His position was that: "We must keep silent until the facts are known." He continued to see "the Cuban question" as problematic, as something to be "settled quickly." His view, in late February, was that if the government stood "perfectly firm," a settlement could be accomplished peacefully. To support that "firm" course, he "continued to believe in preparing for war."[23]

The comments of three Boston business leaders (those reviewed in chapter 4) appear here, one announcing that not one member of the "aristocratic upper crust" considered war to be justified while elsewhere, below that segment, the "wish for war is *almost* universal." In mid-March, Lodge returned to Massachusetts "to attend the Nahant town meeting and sound out public opinion." The senator also reported talks with business and professional people in Boston and with workingmen, tradesmen, and mechanics in Lynn. "He professed to find," Garraty reports, "an almost unanimous sentiment in favor of demanding reparations for the sinking of the *Maine*, and the 'settlement' of the Cuban crisis." Garraty suggests this was a distorted reading, one that conflicted with "the tone" of letters he was receiving from Boston. It was a reading that favored Lodge's own policy recommendation.[24]

In mid-March, Lodge assured the president that he "still saw no need for war, arguing only for reparations and the recognition of Cuban independence." That recognition, in itself, would not be a cause for war, but if "Spain makes it so, the country is united as one man & public opinion the world over will be with us." Throughout those days, he "was determined to avoid any rash action." In the Senate, he urged "silence and patience" until the board of inquiry reported. As a member of the Foreign Relations Committee, Lodge met "almost daily" with the president and "honestly co-operated with his efforts to avoid a fight." In early April, he wrote that he had "done all in my small way that I could to help [McKinley] to keep Congress from breaking away & acting without him." That work had "not been easy & the pleasure has not been enhanced by frantic telegrams from frightened brokers & bankers calling for me to stand by the president just as if I was fighting him." Garraty emphasizes the point, declaring that Lodge's "desire to keep Congress from acting on its own hook amounted almost to a fixation."[25]

Lodge was moved by two prime concerns, the first being patriotism. He wrote a friend that, "I want my country in a conflict with another country to present a united front." The second concern was partisan: He feared a "political disaster" if the president and the Republican-dominated Congress were to divide. Business interests were clamoring for peace; Bryan was "making political capital" with speeches calling for an independent Cuba. The problem he foresaw was a Democratic campaign for "free Cuba and free silver" in 1900. Early in April, he warned "peace-minded" Henry Lee Higginson that his course would lead "straight to free silver and Bryanism."[26]

Up to this point, Garraty has made no mention of demands from "the masses" directed to the senator. In early April, Lodge wrote a trusted friend and requested assistance: "Tell me what you think of public opinion and whether the masses of the party want us to back down . . ." Only after McKinley's message to Congress did Lodge speak openly in favor of American involvement. Only then is reference made to pressures "from below." At that point, "the vast bulk" of Lodge's mail "was now favorable to his stand."[27]

Lodge's position appears to have been largely self-determined. There is nothing in Garraty's text to suggest he was responding to the demands of "clamoring" masses. One indirect report appears there, that from the businessman who sensed a "universal" wish for war. But that claim is countered by Garraty's statement about the "tone" of letters Lodge was receiving and also by the senator's sensed need for that sounding of opinion.

This portrait of Henry Cabot Lodge as a strong backer of McKinley is unexpected given the earlier statements that depict him as a leading interventionist. He did favor a "larger" policy; he was, unquestionably, an expansionist. In 1897 he wrote of his desire to "get Europe out of America . . . I believe entirely that Canada ought to become part of the United States . . ." But in the first months of 1898, he evidently felt that support of the president was the best course of action, the best means for achieving those "larger" goals.[28]

Shelby M. Cullom (1829–1914) was a Republican senator from Illinois. Although listed by Fowler as a leader of the pro-interventionist forces, two sources give a markedly different picture of his position. Cullom's memoirs, published in 1911, offer a very favorable picture of McKinley and give positive assessments of his cabinet appointments. Most striking, perhaps, is his portrait of Mark Hanna described as "probably the most caricatured man in public life . . . usually pictured as being covered with money-bags and dollars." But, Cullom reports, as of 1900 "he really became one of the popular figures in American politics."[29]

Cullom's review of the war's origins is very brief, limited to two long paragraphs. His discussion of the causes begins with a vague passive voice statement—". . . conditions were leading up inevitably" to the war. The next sentence reports the "enthusiasm" of two senators, Senator Proctor of Vermont and his own colleague, Senator Mason of Illinois, these two being "so intense" as to bring on the war "before the country was really prepared for it." McKinley, knowing the horrors of war, "held back," wishing to avoid "hostilities with any other country." But for the destruction of the *Maine*, Cullom felt, war could have been averted. After that catastrophe, he writes, "The country forced us into it . . ." His account does not indicate that he was an interventionist. The account, moreover, contains nothing about newspaper agitation. Apart from that all-embracing reference to "The country," he does not report any grassroots pressures. He and Senator Mason might have faced similar pressures from within the state but here too, as in Ohio, the senators made opposite policy choices.[30]

A later biography of Cullom also gives only brief attention to the events leading up to the war. "Americans became alarmed almost at once," this author declares, "To some extent they were impressed by the sensational newspaper journalism of the period . . ." Some loose speculation about the likely sources of the public reactions is provided beginning with the partisan linkage, that "it was the rural Democrats and Populists who most agitated in Congress for American intervention in Cuba." But ultimately "Republicans, too, began to climb onto the band wagon." Cullom made a single contribution to this effort when, in December 1896, he introduced and defended a resolution calling for an end to Spanish rule in Cuba. This contribution amounted to an attack on Cleveland's policies.[31]

Apart from one passing comment, Cullom "took no further notice of the Cuban situation until mid-April, 1898." The passing comment was a wish, expressed in the Senate, for the body to "dispose of a resolution calling for the island's freedom so they could consider an appropriation bill." It was two months after the de Lôme letter and the *Maine* catastrophe that Cullom next "came forward to voice his support of the administration's course." The biography says nothing about constituent pressures on the senator. Clearly, Fowler erred in listing Cullom as a leading pro-interventionist.[32]

Ohio's Joseph Benson Foraker produced a large, two-volume autobiography.[33] Therein he reports his "maiden" speech in the Senate in May of 1897 shortly after joining that body. The speech was in support of Alabama Senator Morgan's resolution that would give belligerent rights to the Cuban insurgents. He spoke later "two or three times" on the same general subject. Those pages spell out briefly the logic of his position.[34]

Foraker portrays the sinking of the *Maine* as the decisive event. The six weeks of activity following the "great tragedy" is summarized in a single paragraph, indicating that "sooner or later we would have had war anyhow." When "this great tragedy occurred, and investigation confirmed the belief that our ship . . . had been foully dealt with, public sentiment was so aroused that it was impossible longer to delay positive action to put an end to the trouble." Over two pages he reports the introduction of his resolutions that, after amendment and a deletion, were "finally adopted by both Houses." And "thus it was," he concludes, "that our intervention in Cuba and the Spanish-American War that followed were based on the resolutions I offered." His view that "the Republic of Cuba was entitled to recognition" was "in harmony . . . with the majority of my colleagues, and an overwhelming majority of the American people . . ." Foraker rejected another reading, that the recognition was "a proposition brought forward in a spirit of jingoism, as charged by the representatives of the anti-war spirit in the Senate and in the press of the country." It was rather "a sound and valid conclusion that had the approval of so conservative an official as Senator Sherman [it being] based on official information and documents, which no one could successfully contradict or challenge."[35] His account contains nothing on the quantity or quality of communications received from his constituents.

Foraker's account is confirmed in all essentials in a subsequent biography. He first joined the Senate 1897 and was named to the Senate Foreign Relations Committee where he "studied at length" the voluminous official literature on the Cuba question. This extensive research convinced him that the United States should recognize the state of belligerency in Cuba and recognize the Republic of Cuba. Mention is made of Hearst's activity and a sentence declares that the "press was stirring up nation-wide excitement." But nothing is said about grassroots pressures on Foraker, nothing about the possible impacts of Cincinnati newspapers. The biographer reports simply that "he knew what the people wanted . . ."[36]

There is no book-length biography of Maine's Senator William Pierce Frye (1831–1911), who was a conservative Republican, a leader of the party's "Old Guard." He was a popular figure, a conciliator popular with both parties. McKinley later named him to the Paris peace commission. Frye advocated taking the Philippines, specifically taking "everything in sight," this "for the good of the people who inhabit them, and for the immense advantage, commercially, they promise us."[37]

Fowler, as seen, listed the following senators as the leading McKinley backers and as opponents of intervention: Aldrich, Allison, Hanna, Hoar, Platt, and Spooner.

Nelson W. Aldrich (1841–1915), a senator from Rhode Island, was a conservative Republican and a businessman with wide-ranging interests. He was one of the acknowledged leaders of the Senate Republicans and, not surprisingly, was a strong supporter of McKinley. There is only a single biography of the man. Published in 1930, it has been described as "florid and unremittingly celebratory."[38] The relevant chapter, entitled "Enter Imperialism," opens with one of the most flamboyant depictions of public reactions in the entire literature on the war.

> A bolt fell out of the blue!
> Or, it might be truer to say that all of a sudden the earth trembled, and vapors arose before the sun, and the face of the world was changed. The political forces, the powers and principalities that had seemed of late years to possess America, that had been threatening it with revolution, were covered over as in the twinkle of an eye by thick darkness. Other things took their places. A whole nation became dizzy. . . . America went wild over Cuba in the spring of this fateful year.[39]

Stephenson gives three possible causes for this spectacular public response. The first involved big business—"It was whispered that American money invested in Cuba wanted to get rid of the rule of Spain." Then there was the "Cuban revolutionary junto" in New York that "chanted hysterically the woes of the distracted isle." And thirdly, the "most passionate propagandists for Cuba" were the New York *World* and *Journal*. Those factors, however, did not explain what happened. At that point, with "a powder magazine of raw emotion in America" the blowing up of the *Maine* "was only the lighted match."[40]

A fourth factor is indicated, activities in Congress that are described as follows: "When the Cuban fury, after repeated failures to infect Congress, suddenly turned a corner and captivated the imagination of Congress, [Aldrich's] opposition was instantaneous." The other members of "the Four" took similar views. With his "ardent legalism," it is said, Senator Spooner "was not to be duped by the furious special pleading of the yellow press." The following pages of the text review the events in greater detail, the emphasis being given to developments in the Senate—"Party ranks in the Senate were broken. Mr. Chandler and a few others . . . deserted to the opposite camp. . . . Mr. Chandler and the sentimental radicals, Mr. Teller and the silvermen, the rank and file of the Democrats eager to force the President into a quandary, all fell in line for extreme measures." Against "this violent coalition," the four Republican leaders, Aldrich, Allison, Platt, and Spooner, "stood firm."[41]

This biography also reports an unexpected linkage—"Several senators were induced by the New York *Journal*" to investigate conditions in Cuba. The Spanish government could hardly refuse access and, shortly after their return, their speeches in the Senate reported things that would "shock the hardest heart." A Nebraska Republican, Senator John Thurston's impassioned and "brilliantly delivered" speech was especially effective given that his wife, who had accompanied him, died while en route.[42]

More information on this contribution to the war effort appears in Swanberg's biography of Hearst. The relevant paragraph reads:

> Hearst had rounded up a carefully-selected group of jingoistic legislators who were not averse to a free trip to Cuba. Senators Hernando Money of Mississippi, John W. Thurston of Nebraska and J. H. Gallinger of New Hampshire, and Representatives William Alden Smith of Michigan and Amos Cummings of New York, embarked from Fort Monroe on the Hearst yacht *Anita* as "*Journal* Commissioners" to make a survey of conditions on the island and to write reports for the *Journal*, their expenses being paid by Hearst. Representatives Smith and Cummings were members of the House Foreign Affairs and Naval Affairs committees respectively. The *Journal* meanwhile appealed to its readers to write their Congressmen, and said it had so far relayed 15,000 such letters demanding war.[43]

Stephenson's biography of Aldrich continues with a review of the struggles in the Senate, this now complicated by William Jenning Bryan's intervention on the side of the insurgents—"the Democrats had seen a chance to play politics." In opposition, "the Four" made strenuous but futile efforts to deflect those moves. Stephenson's account contains nothing about grassroots impacts, nothing about any "imperious demands" put to Senator Aldrich by Rhode Island's citizens.

Senator William Boyd Allison (1829–1908) was the most powerful of Iowa's political leaders. For more than a third of a century he was the state's Republican "boss." He preferred the term "regency," a more "benign appellation" for a group that included several leading railroad executives, among them, Grenville Dodge of the Union Pacific. Allison's biography gives one and a half pages for a review the Spanish-American War from onset to victory. The account opens as follows:

> The tariff issue, so important in 1897, was pushed into the background in 1898 by outside events. For years America had been watching the growing seriousness of the plight of the Cubans under Spain's harsh rule. The sinking of the *Maine* on February 15, 1898, awoke the indifferent and the casual lookers on and converted many of them, temporarily at least, into firebrands, while others retained their equanimity and opposed intervention as unnecessary and unjustified. Allison and most of his friends were definitely ranked on the side of the antiexpansionists, the isolationists of the day.[44]

Among those friends were: his colleague, Senator John H. Gear, Richard P. Clarkson of the Des Moines *Register*, General Dodge, and "most notably and positively," Allison's great friend, Congressman David B. Henderson. The latter, a colonel and friend from Civil War days, had received letters on the subject from his constituents. Henderson's response was a "brief but pointed speech" in Congress on March 8, 1898:

> I have had letters from my people wanting us to take Cuba, to punish Spain. I simply write back that no international law makes the United States the regulator of the wrongs of the earth. God has written no motto on the banner of our country that demands of us the regulating of the wrongs of other countries to their people. We all sympathize with the liberty-loving and fighting Cubans, but they are citizens of another Government. So long as that question is before us, I follow the advice of Washington, recommending that we mind strictly our own business.

Joseph Medill, publisher of the Chicago *Tribune*, "took sharp issue" with that statement. Congressman Henderson then sent a clipping of Medill's editorial to his close friend, Clarkson, "with instructions as to its use in the *Register*."

But despite the opposition of leading senators and representatives, "the fateful step" to war was taken. A rather obscure summary sentence reports that "it is pretty well agreed that certain special groups and individuals, inflamed with 'the martial spirit,' led the country into an unnecessary conflict." Once engaged, Allison and Henderson "had to take a real interest in the conflict and help to support it." The biography reports nothing about the relationship of Allison and his constituents on this issue.

The two biographies of Mark Hanna contain very little on the events leading up to the war. Croly has a brief discussion of the special session intended for tariff revision that some used also for a resolution to recognize Cuban belligerency. Croly describes the effort as partisan, reporting nothing about demands from the public—"Almost all the Democrats and a minority of the Republicans wanted to bring about war." Hanna "voted uniformly with the minority" but the measure was carried with a sizable majority. The Dingley Bill is then discussed in some detail.[45]

In the first session of the 55th Congress the Republican leaders planned to "transact only necessary business" and then to adjourn, they hoped, by 1 May. This would aid the return of prosperity and leave "the administration free to deal with the Cuban situation without interference from Congress." But those plans were frustrated by "the increasing fury of the demand for intervention in Cuba." Those demands culminated following the sinking of the *Maine*. Several statements review the causal dynamics—"Congress wanted war and had the power to declare it. The people were willing. . . . Public opinion had come to believe that the independence of Cuba was the only satisfactory cure for the maladies of Cuba; and it was willing, if necessary, to fight for that conviction." Nothing in those pages tells of demands made by Hanna's constituents. There are no indications of what he heard from them or of how he reacted.[46]

Beer's biography of Hanna appeared some years later, this based on the extensive materials left by the author's father.[47] It contains a brief one-page review of the events leading up to 1898. Hanna's reactions are discussed, those centering on his expectation of some European involvement, judgments however that are indicated as having a flimsy basis. The efforts of "the Protestant sects" and their pressures are reviewed in a long paragraph, this being the strongest "input" statement found in any of the biographies reviewed here. But it is an odd assortment, including letters "from English Methodists" reaching the White House in late January and, at the same time, a report that Hanna "was denounced in a Baptist church of San Francisco for holding Mr. McKinley back." But most of the account deals with a "candid war party" in the capital, one with allies in the cabinet. A conversation at a social gathering is reported with Hanna, Orville Platt, Cushman Davis, Theodore Roosevelt, and others in attendance. Hanna's aversion to war was plain; he was also "strongly in favor of getting the Cubans freed." The reactions in Wall Street, those discussed in chapter 4, cover more than two pages. The Pope made an intervention, this bringing a response by "dozens" of Protestant pastors who "at once saw a profound danger to American independence." In early April a "vacuous note" was received from the ambassadors of six European nations hoping for further negotiations to restore order and maintain peace.[48]

Beer described the final steps as follows: McKinley "was an American" and the "will of majorities had a special meaning for him."

> War cries banged in his ears. Roosevelt had said across a dinner-table to Mark Hanna, "We are *going* to have this war!" Cushman Davis, Alger, Frye, a mob of Congressmen and officials, his own brother, and his friend Herman Kohlsaat were telling [McKinley] to go ahead. He delayed. He would not send his message to the Capitol unless he heard that all Americans were out of Cuba. Then, on April 11th, he sent what it wanted to Congress. . .

The passage begins with the reference to "majorities," but the "cries" reported were from a collection of notables, most of them based in Washington. Hanna, clearly, was disappointed: "If Congress had started this," he said, "I'd break my neck to stop it." But, Beer added, "his own President had let Congress have the lead."[49]

George Frisbie Hoar (1826–1904), a conservative Republican, was Massachusetts' senior senator. From the outbreak of the Cuban revolution, Hoar indicated his sympathy with those oppressed by Spanish rule but consistently opposed the "clamor" for American intervention. Relations with the Cuban insurgents, he held, should be "based on facts and not rumor," American policy should not be determined by the "excitements of the moment."[50]

In December 1897, Hoar urged a Boston businessman to "see his fellow financiers" and tell them of the president's wish for contributions to the Cuban relief fund. Those monies would serve "diplomatic as well as charitable" purposes, the former described as "keeping this country out of war." The events of February through April 1898 "eroded" Hoar's hopes and eventually he "was prepared to support military intervention if the President was convinced that there was no other way to achieve Cuban peace and liberty." It was a reluctant conversion given his recognition that war "would unsettle business." It would also, he sensed, "excite the cupidity of those who wished for America a colonial empire" and would probably bring a "wave of corruption and scandal" such as followed the Civil War.[51]

Hoar's biographer made no mention of a press-inspired clamor or of insistent demands from "the masses." The only mention of constituent pressures, a single sentence in a footnote, reports insistent opposite demands: "As late as mid-April 1898 Hoar was the recipient of scores of letters from Boston merchants and bankers, as well as Unitarian ministers and women's rights leaders, opposing a war with Spain and urging the 'wide and courageous course of negotiation.' "[52]

Orville Hitchcock Platt (1827–1905) was a Senate Republican leader and a supporter of McKinley. His biographer reviews the Cuban events beginning with Marti's landing in February 1895 and the early successes of the insurgents. American sympathy was "aroused by constantly increasing newspaper exploitation of the gallant struggle for liberty," this as the 1895–1896 session of Congress approached. "There was," the biographer declared, "an insistent demand that the sentiment of the American people should find voice at Washington."[53]

Cleveland and Olney were "opposed to any action" and "the attention of the Cuban sympathizers was turned to Congress." Many resolutions were introduced, with options ranging from intervention to neutrality. Platt felt that Congress, "for the time at least should keep hands off," recognition of belligerency being a matter for the executive branch. This position, it is reported, was "far from popular" since the "trend of sentiment everywhere was unmistakably toward the recognition of the insurgents." The yellow journals were "inflaming the public mind," with Connecticut being "no less Cuban-mad than other States." But Platt, who was facing reelection, "did not care what effect his attitude might have on his personal fortunes." He indicated this in a Senate speech in mid-January 1896 that backed Cleveland's restraint. Platt continued on that course throughout the year.[54]

This biography differs from those reviewed previously in that it provides long excerpts from the Senator's speeches and excerpts from his letters to various notables encouraging their efforts to counter the demands for involvement.

The twin sources of the problem were stated in a letter to a correspondent at the New York *Tribune*. These were: "The newspaper rot about what is going on there, though published one day and contradicted the next . . . and the Cuban junta or legation, or whatever it is called, is active and pestiferous in circulating its views of the situation."[55]

With the destruction of the *Maine*, the "smoldering embers of war broke into flame" but even then, Platt "maintained his poise." His "counsel was sought constantly" by President McKinley. And in several lengthy letters to constituents, he argued his case, that the relations between Spain and the United States "are quite susceptible of amicable adjustment . . ." The principal problem reported in his letters was with anxious members of the Congress. Writing to Governor Cooke, he indicated his belief that "the sober second thought of the American people will keep us out of war." But members of Congress, he wrote, are "so frightened . . . lest they should be defeated in case absolute independence is not secured either by negotiation or by hostilities." He counseled against putting Connecticut's National Guard "in a state of efficiency," saying it "would, of course, add at once to the general alarm." He recommended that the governor should "come down and talk it over with the President and Secretary of War." At about the same time, in a press statement, he said: "I think there is altogether too much war talk. . . . I do not think the sober second thought of the American people is for war, and I believe that our relations with Spain are susceptible of an amicable adjustment."[56]

In a letter dated 6 April, Platt summed up as follows:

> A good many of us believe the recognition of independence is entirely unnecessary and would like something in the way of a resolution which will give Spain an opportunity to back down before actual hostilities are begun on our part.
> The war party is evidently in the majority and will push its views thinking that no one dare stand up against it.

Again bellicose members of the Congress are declared to be the prime source of the difficulty. Platt hoped the president's views would prevail at a meeting of the Foreign Relations Committee on the following day but, he added, "Foraker has seemed to dominate the Committee and any change will have to be over his head."[57]

Foraker and three Democratic members of the Committee introduced the amendment that would recognize the republic of Cuba. A "spirited debate" followed "wherein bitter attacks were made upon the motives of the administration." Finally, a "little band of ten Republicans, headed by Chandler and Foraker, stood out with the Democrats and Populists for the minority amendment," which was adopted by a vote of 51 to 37.[58]

The active agents in this account were those "yellow journals" that inflamed "the public mind" and the diverse coalition of senators. Nothing is said about direct pressures "from below." There was a public "clamor" but it apparently did not touch or influence Platt.

John Coit Spooner (1843–1919), a Wisconsin senator, is declared by his biographer to be a "Defender of Presidents." The brief review of the war begins with the 1895 insurgency led by "some Cubans" desiring complete independence, a reference to the "revolutionary junta" organized in New York City. The revolutionists and Spanish armies "embarked on a campaign that threatened to devastate the whole island." General Weyler's atrocities "made headlines for the yellow press," the "American public became very emotional over the plight of the unhappy Cubans," and "Congressmen excitedly took up the issue."[59] The pages that follow provide a brief review of executive and legislative actions. A single sentence summarizes the events of early April declaring that, "the yellow press and the jingoists in and out of Congress shouted for war." Against them, "President McKinley and a small group of Senators bent every effort to bring about a peaceful settlement . . ." Those efforts are reviewed over several pages. Again, the striking fact about the narrative is the absence of any report on "voices from below" pressing the senator for support of intervention.[60]

The leader of the Democrats in the House of Representatives, Joseph Weldon Bailey (1863–1929), is another person who deserves attention. Usually referred to as Joe Bailey, he was from the Fifth District of Texas, from Cooke County, located to the north of Fort Worth and Dallas. Bailey was very capable, a fact indicated by his party's choice of a thirty-five-year-old to lead the struggles against the much older and more experienced Thomas R. Reed, the powerful and adept Republican "boss" in the House of Representatives. Bailey's biographer, Sam Acheson, describes him as "one of the authors of the Spanish-American War."[61]

Acheson's depiction of the Cuban issue is phrased, for the most part, in terms of partisan (or factional) struggle. President Cleveland had indicated his opposition to any involvement there. The Republicans, in the closing months of his administration, "had developed a tendency to harass the President" with their demand for belligerent rights. Some Democrats shared the same tendency. At the national convention in Chicago in the summer of 1896, delegates saw an opportunity to "voice disapproval of the outgoing President" and went "on record as sympathetic with the Cuban patriots." In the same paragraph, Acheson points to the "great moral and religious sentiment" then "mobilizing in behalf of freedom for the patriots," this being generated by the "geniuses of inflammatory journalism."[62]

Early in 1897, a special session of Congress met to revise the tariff. Sensitive to the Cuban issue, Republicans introduced a measure for the relief of American citizens living there. Bailey used the occasion to ask unanimous consent for recognition of belligerent rights. The request was, of course, peremptorily refused. "From that instant," Acheson reports, "the Democrats were on the offensive, driving their opponents unsparingly with the spur of popular sentiment pressing deeper and deeper into the flanks of the cautious leaders of the majority."[63]

The Congress reassembled in December 1897. In the intervening months "sympathy" had been awakened for Cuba and "many a Republican lawmaker" now returned with a "more tolerant view." The House Democrats met in caucus to define the party's policy. Bailey spoke again in favor of Cuban belligerency. The caucus, it was reported, accepted the proposition without any dissent.

The sinking of the *Maine* is described as a disaster, one that "threw the American people into a state of great excitement; in Texas the war spirit now flared into a frenzy." The Dallas *News* reported that, "The President has received telegrams from every quarter of the disposition of the people to rush into war if he will but say the word." But while the administration "sat tight on the lid at Washington," Acheson continues, "the Democratic policy of 'action' was fast becoming the policy of the people back home."[64] That sentence indicates a causal sequence: The Democratic policy was being adopted by the "people back home." The political fact, the choice of policy, came first; then came the supportive sentiment from the citizenry.

Mass meetings, Acheson states, were "now the order of the day." The only explicit report of local "grassroots" sentiment from Bailey's home area tells of a meeting in Dallas. On Sunday, 27 February, "over 700 citizens choked the city-hall auditorium in celebration of the third anniversary of the outbreak of the Cuban revolt." The mayor presided and twelve "leaders" addressed the gathering, eleven of them speaking in favor of war with Spain.[65]

At no point does Acheson portray Bailey as responding to popular sentiment. Bailey's attitude, he declares, was "nine-tenths feeling," one based on his experience as "a child of the Reconstruction in the South," now moved by the picture of a "subject people ground under the heel of a military government."[66] Another, a more immediate cause, is indicated—Bailey "fraternized with the Cuban representatives in Washington; he took them into his home and broke bread with them . . ."[67]

* * *

If "irresistible demands" from "the masses" were the decisive cause that led to (or forced) the choice of war in 1898, clear and abundant evidence of those pressures should appear in the biographies reviewed here. If the public clamor argument were accurate, evidence indicating the quantity and insistence of those demands should have been present in all fifteen accounts. But instead, what one finds is a peculiar disjunction. The "aroused masses" are "off-stage," the clamor occurs elsewhere, in different, usually unspecified contexts. Typically, some depiction of the clamor is made but nothing follows to indicate how those demands affected the subject. The disjunction is most striking in Stephenson's biography of Nelson Aldrich, easily the most flamboyant of all the accounts.

Two biographies do report direct constituent pressures, but that influence was not from "the masses" but rather from local notables. Senators Hoar and Lodge, both from Massachusetts, were under considerable pressure from local businessmen who demanded that they do everything possible to avoid a war. Another direct influence reported was that of the Cuban Junta. Several congressional advocates, it was seen, had direct ties with this advocacy group. The Junta provided them with information and they "served its interests."

The claims of mass demands as the key factor accounting for American intervention in the Cuban struggle, those many assertions, are clearly unwarranted. Put differently, that major causal statement is not supported by the evidence reviewed here, all of which has been readily available now for several decades.

As opposed to the vaguely sketched accounts of "the masses" and their presumed influence, these accounts point to three other influences. The first and most prominent of these is political: the expectation of partisan advantage. Republicans and dissenting Democrats, as late as December 1896, pushed the Cuba issue to embarrass President Cleveland. Then, a few months thereafter, Democrats (and a few others) used the same issue to press President McKinley. The point is stated with eminent clarity in one of the biographies: "Both parties played rather disgraceful roles . . . with regard to the Cuban agitation. The Republican line politicians used it to embarrass Cleveland in 1896, the Democrats to embarrass McKinley in 1897." That frank declaration is relegated to a footnote.[68]

On the same point, partisan advantage, Garraty points to "one rather sordid aspect" of the Cameron resolution. If war broke out before inauguration day 1897, Cleveland would "bear the responsibility." "By pushing matters to a head quickly," Garraty writes, "the Republicans could escape the onus of starting the trouble and claim the credit for carrying the fight to a successful conclusion." McKinley had told Lodge in Canton the previous November that he wanted the crisis settled "one way or the other" before he took office and the Cameron resolution "seemed designed to accomplish this objective." Sturgis Bigelow, a good friend of Lodge, wrote him, saying that "Cameron ought to be clubbed." "A war," he continued, "is a damned sight too big a chip to play party poker with." Lodge wrote back indicating that, as Garraty put it, the Democrats "would certainly make a party issue of Cuba after McKinley's inauguration."[69]

A complete review of "the case" for the public-clamor argument, it was noted, would require information on all senators and representatives. A next-best procedure would be to review information on a representative sample from among those bodies. But both procedures, as noted earlier, would be problematic given the likely shortage or complete absence of the needed information. The procedure adopted here, use of a clearly non-representative sample, is perhaps the best feasible alternative.

Again, one should remember the difficulties. The thirteen senators discussed were all prominent persons whose positions, both those for and against, were well known. And their choices, moreover, were not likely to change. For Cuba's advocates, pressures exerted on the president's dedicated supporters might seem pointless. And pressures exerted on dedicated supporters of Cuban independence would seem unnecessary. The pressure groups, the press, and concerned citizens might have targeted less-known figures, recent arrivals in the Congress or perhaps those with a less secure base. To research the experience of vulnerable legislators would also be a formidable task, one especially likely to be complicated by absence of information. One might focus on a key group, the Republican defectors. But that, too, would be a complicated task, one where needed information would probably be in short supply.

Two such defections appeared in a study of the Missouri experience where again the partisan linkage is clearly evident. One of Missouri's senators, George Vest, a Democrat, was a leading advocate of the Cuban cause. All twelve of Missouri's Democratic congressmen ultimately supported the Cubans. And two of the state's three Republicans ultimately defected, abandoning McKinley and joining in the clamor. All three of these Republicans represented districts "in and about St. Louis," a city in which the three "great metropolitan dailies" ultimately favored intervention. From the start, the two Democratic papers, the *Republic* and the *Post-Dispatch*, "took a bellicose attitude toward the Cuban situation." The Republican *Globe-Democrat*, "after an uncertain beginning, departed from the path President McKinley was following and by the end of February was calling for war." The three, one author reports, "must have exerted an enormous influence in shaping public opinion in favor of war."[70]

Richard Bartholdt, one of the defecting Republican congressmen, upheld McKinley in the spring of 1898 but came under heavy pressure to change his position. In contrast to the other accounts reviewed in this chapter, Bartholdt's autobiography reports that "messages by the score poured in on me peremptorily demanding that I either vote for war or resign." Even here, it should be noted, the pressure did not come from "the masses." Most of those messages, he reports, "were signed by responsible party leaders and personal friends."

There was "but a single letter to the contrary." Bartholdt writes that he voted to "represent their views rather than in accordance with my own conviction." In his autobiography, published more than three decades later, he wrote: "I regret that vote to this day."[71]

The conditions leading to Bartholdt's defection were, first, strong (ultimately complete) local press support for intervention in Cuba, and second, a concerted effort by local advocates, by people close to the congressman, in support of that policy.

This "case study" indicates the need for partitive formulations. Uniform press recommendations would probably have been infrequent in any city. And advocates, individuals and groups, would probably have been selective in their efforts. The most cost-effective procedure for the advocates would be to concentrate attention on those who were wavering and/or those who were vulnerable. The lesson: One does not need to invoke the "clamorous masses" to explain the move to war. The need is for explanation of the choices made by the small number of Republican defectors.

Bartholdt gives strong emphasis to the partisan factor, to the political causes of the war. The small "band" of Republican insurgents, he writes:

> . . . was vigorously backed by the Democratic minority, whose leader boldly threatened the Republicans in open session with the words: "We will take you by the scruff of your necks and drag you into it!" Unfortunately, Republican insurgents and Democrats combined formed a clear majority of the House, and it was this majority which, in fact, was responsible for the war.[72]

Notes

1. *The Autobiography of Thomas Collier Platt*, compiled and edited by Louis J. Lang (New York, 1910), pp. 354, 364. For a brief account, see ANB, 17:587–588.

   The one exception was New York City Congressman Amos Cummings. He was an advocate of Cuban involvement and, as will be seen, had some involvement with the Hearst organization. On this connection, see note 43 below.

   References to the press and/or to the war in another account are best described as fugitive, this in Harold F. Gosnell, *Boss Platt and His New York Machine* (Chicago, 1924). Another account of possible relevance would be the work of De Alva Stanwood Alexander, *Four Famous New Yorkers: The Political Careers of Cleveland, Platt, Hill, and Roosevelt* (New York, 1923). The index contains no reference to Hearst or Pulitzer. There are thirteen index references to McKinley but none to the Spanish-American War.

2. DAB, 1:94–95. No biography of Adams appears in the ANB.

3. DAB, 9:80–81; ANB, 10:879. Some additional information on these two men appears in John L. Offner, *An Unwanted War* (Chapel Hill, 1992), pp. 20–21, 97–98, 151–152, and 187–188 and in Philip S. Foner, *The Spanish-Cuba-American War and the Birth of American Imperialism, 1895–1902*, Vol. 1 (New York, 1972),

p. 188. Adams was the chairman of the Foreign Affairs Committee's subcommittee on Cuba.

4. Dorothy Ganfield Fowler, *John Coit Spooner* (New York, 1961), p. 224. Fowler cites five biographies as providing the basis for these two lists.

5. Everett Walters, *Joseph Benson Foraker: An Uncompromising Republican* (Columbus, 1948), p. 148. The "big four" are described in Nathaniel Wright Stephenson, *Nelson W. Aldrich* (New York, 1930), ch. 9. The omission of Hoar from the Republican leadership group is easily explained, his "tendency to independence" making him a difficult co-worker. For a brief portrait, see Robert L. Beisner, *Twelve Against Empire: The Anti-Imperialists 1898–1900* (Chicago, 1992 [1968]), ch. 7; also, ANB, 10:888–889.

   Fowler's lists contain the names of key senators who might be described as "regulars" among the major parties. Paul S. Holbo lists two additional groups of Cuba supporters, four Populists and six Silver Republicans. McKinley, he writes, could usually count on forty-three loyal Republicans plus one "cooperative independent," James Kyle of South Dakota, and a "few helpful Democrats," among them George Gray of Delaware. See Holbo, "The Convergence of Moods and the Cuban-Bond 'Conspiracy' of 1898," *Journal of American History*, 55 (1968):54–72, specifically, pp. 58 and 56, n8.

6. Joseph A. Fry, *John Tyler Morgan and the Search for Southern Autonomy* (Knoxville, TN, 1992), p. 164.

7. For a brief summary of his issue positions, see Fry, "Morgan," ANB 15:841–843; for more detail, see Fry, *Morgan*, ch. 4.

8. Fry, *Morgan*, chs. 3 and 5. The quotation, p. 154.

9. Ibid., pp. 80–88 155.

10. Ibid., pp. 159–160. Morgan was one of the few Democrats who voted against the Turpie-Foraker proposal. In the contention over the final intervention measure, Morgan supported the majority proposal, one that followed McKinley's wishes. Senator Chandler, a "Republican jingo," contended that the "radicals" would have prevailed "were it not for the defection of Morgan" (p. 163).

11. Newspaper reports are noted throughout Fry's biography. The Mobile *Register* objected to Morgan's condemnation of "timid businessmen" and it "bristled" over the senator's "contempt for our business interests." Again, the senator was showing independence. Fry, p. 157.

12. Leon Burr Richardson, *William E. Chandler, Republican* (New York, 1940), ch. 25. For a brief account, see ANB, 4:667–668.

13. Richardson, *Chandler*, pp. 570–571.

14. Ibid., pp. 571–575.

15. Ibid., pp. 575–581.

16. ANB, 21:432–433 and Elmer Ellis, *Henry Moore Teller* (Caldwell, Idaho, 1941), ch. 20.

17. Ibid, pp. 307–308.

18. Ibid, pp. 308–309.

19. Ibid, pp. 310–312.

20. John H. Garraty, *Henry Cabot Lodge* (New York, 1953), p. 180.

21. Ibid., p. 181.

22. Ibid., pp. 182–183.

23. Ibid., p. 185.

24. Ibid., pp. 186–187.

25. Ibid., p. 188.
26. Ibid., pp. 188–189. On Higginson, see ch. 4, note 59.
27. Ibid., p. 190.
28. Ibid., pp. 184–185.
29. Shelby M. Cullom, *Fifty Years of Public Service* (Chicago, 1911), pp. 276–282. The judgments contained in this work are generally very positive. Cullom sought the Republican presidential nomination in 1896 but, as seen in chapter 2, was thwarted by the McKinley forces. At that time, his view of McKinley was quite different. In a letter to the *New York Times* (9 March 1896), he declared that, "McKinley is less qualified for the office than any other conspicuous candidate. He has less courage, less knowledge of national and international affairs than any one of the others." Cullom was "bitterly disappointed" about his defeat, this from James W. Neilson, *Shelby M. Cullom: Prairie State Republican* (Urbana, 1962), pp. 166–170.
30. Cullom, *Fifty Years*, pp. 283–284. For information on William E. Mason (1850–1921), see DAB, 12:397.
31. Neilson, *Cullom*, pp. 171–172.
32. Ibid., pp. 170–173.
33. *Notes of a Busy Life*, two volumes (Cincinnati, 1916). The Spanish-American War is discussed in Vol. 2, ch. 31. See also, ANB, 8:198–199.
34. Foraker, *Notes*, pp. 17–18.
35. Ibid., pp. 19–23.
36. Walters, *Foraker* (cited in note 5 above), ch. 10, specifically pp. 144, 147, and 150.
37. Lewis L. Gould, "Frye," ANB 8:531–532.
38. Stephenson, *Aldrich* (cited in note 3 above). The description is from the ANB, 1:246–249.
39. Stephenson, p. 151. The florid comment continues also on the next page.
40. Ibid., p. 151. Lodge's business constituents communicated directly and insistently, leaving an ample documentary record. The equivalent groups in Rhode Island, presumably, left only reports of "whispered" communications. In a note it is reported that McKinley's efforts to maintain peace were supported by Harvard's President Eliot and eighty-five faculty members, by Bishop Walden of the Methodist Church, and by John F. Dryden, the president of the Prudential Insurance Company (p. 447, n4).
41. Ibid., pp. 152–154.
42. Ibid., p. 154. Stephenson mistakenly included Vermont's Senator Proctor among those sponsored by Hearst.
43. W.A. Swanberg, *Citizen Hearst* (New York, 1961), pp. 139–141. Each of the five "brave congressmen" wrote articles for the *Journal* "describing the suffering they saw." While in the harbor of Matanzas, Mrs. Thurston "suffered a heart attack and died aboard the Hearst yacht—a misfortune the *Journal* blamed on the destitution she had seen" (p. 140).

This linkage of Hearst and members of Congress does not appear in many standard sources. There are no index entries for four of the five congressmen in two later Hearst biographies, those of Ben Procter, *William Randolph Hearst* (New York, 1998) and David Nasaw, *The Chief* (Boston, 2000). A passing reference to Cummings appears in Nasaw in a different context, p. 160. For more on Cummings see DAB 4:593–594.

Margaret Leech reports that Thurston "shook the Senate with a tearful tribute to his wife, who had died on their trip to Cuba with a plea for the suffering population on her lips"—but says nothing of Hearst's sponsorship. From *In the Days of McKinley* (New York, 1959), pp. 173–174. Another source reports that Thurston ended his tribute in "wretched taste . . . by calling for war because it 'would increase the business and earnings of every American railroad [and] it would increase the output of every American factory." Walters, *Foraker*, p. 148.

44. Leland L. Sage, *William Boyd Allison* (Iowa City, 1936). The war is reviewed on pp. 271–273. For a brief portrait of Allison, see ANB, 1:365–367.
45. Herbert Croly, *Marcus Alonzo Hanna* (Hamden, CT, 1965 [1912]), pp. 274–275.
46. Ibid., pp. 277–278.
47. Thomas Beer, *Hanna* (New York, 1929).
48. Ibid., pp. 191–201.
49. Ibid., p. 202.
50. Richard E. Welch., Jr., *George Frisbie Hoar and the Half-Breed Republicans* (Cambridge, 1971), p. 212. Hoar produced a large two-volume memoir, *Autobiography of Seventy Years* (New York, 1903). Volume II, chapters 21–30, review events in his life from 1896 to 1898. They contain no discussion of the events leading up to the war and nothing on the conduct of the war. Welch describes the work as "an essential source and a difficult one . . . in some ways most interesting for its omissions." Its organization, he reports, "is chaotic, reflecting the fact that much of it first appeared as separate articles in *Scribner's Magazine*" (p. 346).
51. Welch, *Hoar*, pp. 212–213.
52. Ibid., p. 213, n25.
53. Louis A. Coolidge, *An Old-Fashioned Senator: Orville H. Platt of Connecticut* (New York, 1910), p. 260. See ANB, 17:586–587. The author, Samuel T. McSeveney, refers to Platt as one of the "Big Five" of the Senate, adding Eugene Hale of Maine.
54. Ibid., p. 261.
55. Ibid., pp. 261–266. Platt noted also an element of hypocrisy, pointing to an event in Texas where some 7,000 "yelling people" were "not fluttered" when "a negro was covered with kerosene oil and burned to death on a public platform." But now people were "shedding tears over the sad fate of Maceo" (p. 266).
56. Ibid., pp. 269–275.
57. Ibid., pp. 277–278.
58. Ibid., p. 280.
59. Fowler, *Spooner*, pp. 223–224 (cited above in note 4).
60. One other episode in Spooner's career should be noted. In the late 1880s, Wisconsin's Republican governor sought to require English in public and parochial schools. This episode of nativism brought a reaction in that German Lutherans abandoned the party, thus giving the Democrats a victory in the 1890 election. One further consequence was Spooner's removal from the Senate, the victors giving that position to one of their own. But following the 1893 depression, in 1894 the Republicans regained power and in 1897 Spooner was again named to the Senate. On this, see Fowler, pp. 144–153, 177–79, and 197–198. For a brief account, see ANB, 20:491–493.
61. Sam Hanna Acheson, *Joe Bailey: The Last Democrat* (New York, 1932), p. x.
62. Ibid., p. 84.
63. Ibid., pp. 84–85.

64. Ibid., pp. 91–93.
65. Ibid., p. 93. Although not stated, this meeting of notables was probably stimulated by Hearst's effort to collect funds for a monument for the *Maine* victims. As seen in the previous chapter, a similar meeting took place in Columbus on the same day.
66. Ibid., p. 95. Acheson offers a brief explanation for the mass sentiment, for the "mobilization of the American spirit in 1898." Making no reference to the role of the press, he declares that "in the beginning, at least, [it was] the natural child of America's emotionalism, born in the loosely sentimental pocket of the mass mind out of which from time to time issue crusades against the Saracens, attacks on wind-mills, and wars to end war; in short, the altruistic idealism of civilized beings" (pp. 94–95).
67. Ibid., p. 95.
68. Stephenson, *Aldrich*, p. 447, n1.
69. Garraty, *Lodge*, p. 183. There was a further round in this "sharp exchange" before the two let the matter rest.
70. James W. Neilson, "Congressional Opinion in Missouri on the Spanish-American War," *Missouri Historical Review*, 51 (1957):245–256. The Cuban Junta was "most active" in St. Louis, its first support organization appearing there in 1895. For this see Ruby Weedell Waldeck, "Missouri in the Spanish American War," *Missouri Historical Review*, 30 (1936):366–368.
71. Richard Bartholdt, *From Steerage to Congress: Reminiscences and Reflections* (Philadelphia, 1930), pp. 160–161. Neilson describes the two other Republican congressmen, Charles F. Joy and Charles Edward Pearce, as "ready for war" but only one of them appears to have voted for it. Pearce was "an enthusiastic expansionist, well acquainted with the work of Alfred Thayer Mahan . . ." The state's Democrats opposed the annexation of the Philippines. The three Republican congressmen "loyally upheld their party leader." None of the three congressmen, incidentally, is listed in the *Dictionary of American Biography* or in *American National Biography*.
72. Ibid., pp. 159–160.

8

On the Various Readings

Four tasks were announced in the opening chapter. Three of these were to review and assess accounts of key events in American history in the years 1896 to 1898. The first of those events was the 1896 presidential election campaign, the struggle between Bryan and McKinley, the latter's win often described as a victory for "big business" and a defeat for "the people." The second task was to review McKinley's staffing decisions, his choice of cabinet members and diplomats. The third of the announced tasks was to review the events that led to the Spanish-American War. The fourth of the announced tasks was to review and assess the theoretical frameworks that have been used to summarize and make sense of those three topics.

Many accounts of the 1896 election tell of a transcendent struggle, of "big business" versus "the people," a struggle in which Mark Hanna, fronting for "Wall Street," took control of "the government." As seen chapter 2, those accounts are mistaken and very much in need of revision. One man who knew both men reported that McKinley "was the master and Hanna the faithful lieutenant." That was a judgment shared by John Hay, who said, "[T]here are idiots who think Mark Hanna will run him!"

The review of McKinley's staffing decisions, his choice of cabinet members and ambassadors, also attested to his independence, his distance from those "big business" sponsors, as shown in chapter 3. McKinley was moved, primarily, by political considerations, by the wants (or demands) of party leaders, their interests taking precedence over those of business elites. Mark Hanna refused a cabinet position, choosing instead to serve in the Senate, a choice that removed him from the immediate "center of power." Again, the need for revision is evident.

The third event, the decision for war, was much more complicated. The major antecedent event was the Cuban insurgency that began in 1895. Many commentators have treated "the press," "the public," and "the Congress" as the key agencies that linked those distant Cuban events with the decisions taken subsequently by the president and the Congress. This argument, in its extreme formulation, holds that two competing New York City press lords generated and published the "sensational" accounts that were picked up and republished by other newspapers across the nation. An enormous public uproar resulted, a clamor that politicians could not afford to ignore. Following the destruction of the *Maine*, the reluctant president yielded and asked Congress for the authority to intervene on behalf of the Cuban insurgents. The Congress granted that authority and the war began.

Two persistent methodological problems appear in those discussions of the presumed causal linkages. The first is the problem of categorical usage. Apart from the president, each of the above agencies (those put in quotation marks) may be differentiated, with the subgroups having diverse views and reactions. The "public," for example, could divide on any issue—some for, some against, some unsure, some indifferent, and some completely unaware of the issue, the familiar "don't knows." The categorical reading—that "the masses," some ninety-plus percent of them, were "for war"—would be a very unlikely hypothesis.

The second problem is to estimate, or better, to research and determine the quantities: What percent of the citizens were for, against, indifferent, etc.? And, a more difficult quantitative question: How much "weight" or importance did a given factor have in determining the outcome? In addition, it should be noted that attitudes and weights are not constant; the recognition of change is always appropriate.

Alfred North Whitehead, the noted philosopher, provided a useful reminder with respect to this second concern. The world, he reminds us, ". . . is infected with quantity. To talk sense, is to talk in quantities. It is no use saying that the nation is large,—How large? It is no use saying that radium is scarce,—How scarce? You cannot evade quantity."[1] Many people, however, do attempt to evade quantity and, regrettably, many others accept and go along with those evasions. Many commentators, as seen, have solved these problems "by declaration," providing statements about the "powerful" factors, "decisive" concerns, and "forceful" public opinion alleged to have determined some end result.

A third methodological concern should be kept in mind: the need to consider alternative hypotheses. Categorical treatments exclude consideration of alternatives. A declared solution, for example, that the war was a response to "a public clamor," excludes all other options. But there are other possibilities, such as: the efforts of expansionist ideologues, of military leaders moved by strategic considerations, of some interested business leaders, or of interested politicians seeking partisan advantage. Or, still another possibility, that the war resulted from the efforts of Cuban insurgents and their interest groups. There is still another option, that the war resulted from some combination of those factors.[2]

In 1898, the principal agency for the transmission of information about world affairs (among these, about events in Cuba) and about national, state, and local affairs would have been "the press," principally newspapers (and, to a much smaller extent, magazines). At that time, the United States had approximately 2,200 daily newspapers, 13,000 weeklies, and 600 semiweeklies. These publications, as seen, varied enormously in both the quantity and quality of their coverage. They also varied enormously in circulation.[3]

The analysis of that press content was possible from the moment of publication in 1897 or 1898. As seen in chapter 5, that content has been reviewed in many publications in the intervening years. Much of that information, however, appeared in unpublished theses and dissertations and much in specialized state and local histories. Diverse performance is a recurrent finding in those studies. More precisely, "the press" was sharply differentiated along partisan lines. One partisan pattern was found in the last years of Cleveland's presidency with Republican congressmen demanding United States aid for the insurgent Cubans. A strikingly opposite pattern appeared in the early months of McKinley's presidency. Democratic newspapers (plus some of the Populist and "silver" Republican persuasions) then became the advocates of American intervention. And the Republican newspapers, backing McKinley, then chose the moderate course.

That insistent fact, partisanship, was so clear and obvious it could not be missed. But from an early point, the "obvious fact" was neglected and another reading was substituted and given credence. The party affiliation of the two leading "sensational" newspapers went unmentioned. And it was assumed that, in one way or another, the rest of the nation's press picked up and transmitted that "scandalous" content.

Categorical statements about the "powerful" (or compelling, or irresistible) effects of press content in the formation of public opinion abound in "the literature." Here is an example from a recent textbook, a "forceful" statement of the press role that makes no mention of the partisan factor. The Hearst and Pulitzer newspapers

> . . . competed to see which could stir up more public support for the Cuban rebels . . . politicians ignored the public outcry at their peril. . . . Americans were outraged. An outpouring of sympathy swept the nation. . . . The Cuban struggle appealed to a country convinced of its role as protector of the weak and defender of the right of self-determination.[4]

More than a century after the event, another account offers this depoliticized explanation for the coming of war: Thanks to Hearst's New York *Journal* and Pulitzer's New York *World*, "the country erupted in righteous anger and patriotic fervor. On April 25, 1898, Congress declared war on Spain."[5]

Although newspapers are a useful and readily accessible source, as indicated, some important information about them and about their impacts is unavailable. We may have circulation figures (some of dubious merit) but beyond that we know next to nothing about the characteristics of their readers. And, a much more important problem, we have no systematic evidence at all about their readers' reactions to the newspapers' stories or to their editorial recommendations. Whether a given audience read, believed, and was moved by a newspaper's reports on Cuba is effectively unknown. We have, as seen, several studies of press content. But these tell us next to nothing about audience characteristics. And they offer nothing, no serious empirical studies, of readers' reactions. Wayne Morgan stated the lesson succinctly and accurately: "Just how potent the press actually was in fomenting the war with Spain was unanswerable."[6]

Some authors report public views as "reflecting" newspaper content, as if a mirror image, but that metaphoric usage is also speculation, unsupported hypothesis. If argued, however, an important implication follows. Since newspapers' positions on "the Cuba question" were linked to partisan preferences, any sweeping declarations about "Americans," "the public mind," or a "national mood" should, from the outset, be rejected as inappropriate. If one accepted the "reflection" hypothesis, it would be necessary to report the party linkage and to suggest at least two strikingly different "moods" within "the public."

Again, other hypotheses are possible and should be considered, such as— readers gave little or no attention to the Cuba stories; or they read the stories, but did not believe them; or they assessed them differently (for example, seeing the insurgents as causing the suffering); or they read the stories but had more urgent immediate priorities (low earnings, paying bills, illness, etc.).

Of all the "forces" considered here, "the public" (also referred to as "the masses") is clearly the most difficult to study. In 1898, that collectivity consisted of some 75 million persons.[7] Just over half were twenty years old or over. Those younger than twenty were not likely to have exerted much political influence. Just under half of those older persons were women, not yet with voting rights and also not likely to have exerted much influence. Some of the adult males would have been foreign born, many of them not yet citizens. And the adult black males, most of them, were denied the exercise of the vote. Enfranchised adult males, numbering perhaps fifteen million, would probably have been the most active participants in public affairs. But we know nothing further about the quantities. The key questions: How many were very active or even moderately active? How many wrote letters? How many signed petitions? Or participated in demonstrations? And, how many were apathetic or indifferent?

Those Americans lived in cities, towns, villages, and countryside, settings that would have differed widely in access to (or knowledge of) the major events of the age. The quality of newspapers in those locations would have differed significantly. The best of the newspapers would ordinarily have been found in the large cities, although with circulations much smaller than those of the scandal sheets. The quality of the press generally fell off in the smaller cities, the towns and villages. Several other possibilities should be kept in mind: Some people did not read anything and some had only limited contact with those news sources, either for lack or interest or by reason of illiteracy or limited literacy.

Some basic "facts of life" should be kept in mind. Persons in the labor force around 1900 worked long hours, the prevailing standard being sixty hours—ten hours per day, six days a week. For most people that work would have been physically exhausting. One must consider in addition the time (and effort) required for travel to and from the workplace. For housewives, life in those "good old days" would also have meant long hours of exhausting, never-ending tasks—washing, drying, ironing, and mending clothes, cleaning house, shopping, preparing meals, child care, etc. Children too, from an early age, would have been assigned housekeeping tasks, those once-familiar chores. Many of them, at an early age, would be taken out of school and sent into the labor force.

Those "facts of life" should be kept in mind when assessing the plausibility of the many sweeping claims provided by later commentators. Richard Hofstadter, for example, reports the existence of an "observable crisis of the national consciousness" in the 1890s: "The general depression . . . the widespread anxieties and discontents of the era, clearly had important bearings on questions of war and empire, and must be seen as major instrumentalities of history."[8] Some questions need to be raised and addressed: How would one "observe" such a crisis of consciousness? How would one do that several decades after the fact? And, how would one establish importance, whether the anxieties were a major, middling, or minor instrumentality?

The just-reviewed facts of everyday life suggest another, a more plausible hypothesis—that few Americans would have had the time, energy, or interest to participate in any "clamor" for the relief of suffering in Cuba. Some basic questions ought to be addressed: After returning from work, washing up, and having supper, would those exhausted factory workers have gone out in the evening to participate in protest meetings? And what of the farmers who lived miles away from the next town? Would they hitch up the horses and drive off to attend protest meetings or to collect signatures on a petition? And what of the wives of those workers and farmers, after washing the dishes and putting the children to bed, would they go off to participate at protest meetings for the relief of Cuba?

One should consider this alternative hypothesis about "the masses"—for most people, for the overwhelming majority, the provision of sustenance and caring for the well-being of the family required so much time, attention, and effort as to prevent any serious interest or concern for distant events, either those in Washington or Havana. Even if interested, the exhausted farmer, factory worker, or housewife would have had little time, energy, or opportunity for such matters. This speculation suggests that "public opinion," a general "clamor" by "the masses," should be recognized as an unlikely, as an implausible hypothesis. Put differently, perhaps only seven, five, or three percent of "Americans" were "clamoring" for war. And, if that were the case, the appropriate tasks would be to research and discover first, who they were, and second, the sources of their exceptional behavior.[9]

Two important implications follow: First, if the quantities are unknown, the most appropriate conclusion for any serious commentator should be a statement to that effect, one indicating that *we do not know*. And the second, rather than an exclusive focus on that single hypothesis, a near-total popular mobilization, other possibilities ought to be considered. A very limited public mobilization might suffice to gain American involvement.

After "the press" and "the people," the third of the agencies considered here is the Congress. We have much better information about congressmen than about the American masses. Congress at that point consisted of ninety senators and 360 members of the House of Representatives. Both bodies were divided by party, the largest in both houses being the Republicans, followed by the Democrats and a scatter of others. Although not a perfect measure of congressional opinion, we have the evidence of their voting records. And, although not as accessible and much less systematic, we have many expressions, public and private, of opinions expressed by many members of the Congress. Congressional opinion, as seen, was sharply divided with respect to Cuba. From early 1897, Democrats and a few others made Cuba an issue and pressed the president and his party for intervention. McKinley's problem was the clamor coming from the capitol building, a few blocks away on Pennsylvania Avenue, not one coming from distant towns and villages. McKinley also had to deal with losses in his own congressional following as some Republicans converted, shifting to support intervention in Cuba.

The well-documented linkage of political party and position on Cuba has an important implication, again that partitive statements are appropriate. And those statements should also be accompanied by words of explanation telling why Democrats, Populists, and some silver Republicans favored intervention while the Republican stalwarts, generally, opposed any such move. The latter observation, that the "party of business enterprise" opposed the war, should be clearly stated along with the obvious implication—that the party and its "powerful" sponsors lost in this important contest.

Another possibility follows from this discussion, that of a disjunction between party leaders and their constituents. The just-reviewed argument is that most voters, including the Bryan Democrats and Populists, were quiescent.

Except for some small minorities, most citizens would have been occupied by those omnipresent and pressing concerns, those of family sustenance and welfare. The argument, in short, is that "the action" began with the choices made by leadership groups within the Congress, choices aided and abetted by a supportive partisan press and, of course, by the Cuban support groups.

Elected officials in democratic regimes regularly depict their decisions as responses to underlying popular sentiments—they are obeying the "will of the people." But those statements might be of doubtful validity. Such claims provide legitimation for what might easily be seen as questionable behavior, the advocacy of war for the sake of partisan advantage. Those statements, accordingly, should also be viewed as hypotheses, as declarations needing independent confirmation.

Two other agencies worked to bring about American intervention. The Cuban Junta, as noted, campaigned within the United States. Its offices in New York City and Washington were both active and effective in gaining support from willing newspapers and parties. To gain additional influence, the Junta established local support groups, the units of the Cuban League. These were headed by local citizens, most of them persons of some eminence, in larger American communities. These agencies exerted influence through sympathetic local newspapers that in turn gave space and support to the League initiatives. The League units would have had direct contact with local citizens, with those small minorities, the seven, five, or three percent hypothesized earlier. Most of those reached would have been upper or upper-middle class citizens, persons with more time and money than most, and also, persons who typically were not engaged in physically exhausting labor.

Membership and involvement in associations is at all times more frequent among better-off segments of the population.[10] Outside of the South, the upper- and upper-middle classes in 1898 would have been overwhelmingly Republican. Cuban League membership, accordingly, would probably have been recruited disproportionately from among the Democratic minority, from among the "outsiders" within the privileged ranks. The suggestion, still hypothesis, is that a serious appearance-reality gap exists in the many reports from 1898 and in many subsequent accounts. It is the difference between "aroused Americans" as the relevant category and perhaps one American in twenty who was so moved.

Another "agency" that needs to be considered in this review of the influences contributing to the decision for war is "big business." Big businessmen did, as far as we can tell, have a common position with respect to the possibility of war—they were opposed to it. A war would be a "disturbing factor," diverting efforts and resources in problematic directions. The financial costs would mean increased taxes and, simultaneously, decreased purchasing power. A war, moreover, with all its uncertainties, could easily upset the recovery from the recent depression. An appropriate conclusion would be that "big business" lost in the contention over Cuban policy. Put differently, Wall Street was defeated in the struggle, its "forces" overwhelmed by the pro-intervention agencies.

That conclusion, however, is rarely expressed in the sizable literature on this war. Instead, one finds a recurrent insinuation, a frequent claim that somehow or other "big business" was responsible for the war. In 1898, the fact of business opposition was clear and unambiguous. But in the Beards' influential work, *The Rise of American Civilization*, business involvement and support was argued or, more precisely, was declared.

In 1936, in an important work, Julius Pratt found it necessary to restate the original conclusion, business opposition, this with provision of evidence contained in later biographies. But even Pratt, as noted, provided a "role" for big business with his declaration of a late conversion in those ranks. The logic, however, is problematic. Businessmen are routinely portrayed as men dedicated to maximizing their profits. Would such men be willing to pay the heavy (and uncertain) costs of a war? Would they do that in order to "save" someone else's market, most especially one as small at that of Cuba?

The principal conclusion of this work is that the clamor for American intervention in Cuba was generated by a coalition of advocates consisting of the Cuban Junta, its Cuban League affiliates, and some supportive newspapers. The Junta had Republican support through to the early months of 1897. After McKinley's inauguration the partisan support for Cuba now came, most of it, from the Democrats. The Cuban insurgents, in short, had developed a brilliant strategy, one that gained them the support of two key elite segments, Democratic newspaper publishers and Democratic congressmen. And the resulting mobilization was sufficient to give at least the appearance of a broad-based mass movement. Some Republican newspapers and congressmen also, somewhat belatedly, joined the movement, their conversion ultimately leading McKinley to change his position. It would be a mistake to see all of those advocates, the publishers and party leaders, as driven exclusively by self-interest. Some of them, undoubtedly, were moved by humanitarian concerns, by a desire to end the death, suffering, and destruction on the island.

Our knowledge of the agencies discussed in these pages varies considerably. As indicated, we have no serious studies of public concerns, attitudes, media attention, or, of attempts to exert influence from this period. We have much better information on the content of newspapers from the period, much of that content still available, still part of the "public record." We have some information on the Cuban Junta and the Cuban League, but little of this could be called detailed or systematic. Our best information is on the United States Congress. We have a complete listing of the members and records indicating the partisan divisions on issues brought before them. And we have a wide scatter of statements, speeches, and later, for some of those involved, memoirs and biographies. It was their voices and their votes that provided the greatest problems, the most direct concerns for McKinley and his closest advisors. Study of "the clamor" that moved the president should therefore concentrate on that agency, on the increasingly aggressive demands made by some members of the House and Senate.

While certainly of interest, it is not necessary that we know the precise configuration of attitudes and demands found among "the masses." The most appropriate conclusion with respect to this collectivity, as indicated, is "I don't know." Authors who assert otherwise are purporting to know things that could not possibly be known—how "the American public," the citizens of Cambridge, Canton, Chicago, Coon Rapids, Cheyenne and elsewhere—"saw" and reacted to the Cuban events.

In his 1970 dissertation, Mark Welter expressed astonishment that the "yellow press" explanation for the war's origins "has been essentially unchallenged and unaltered" for so many decades.[11] What is even more astonishing is that the twin "truths," the arguments of press-influence and outraged-masses, should have survived in many accounts for still another three decades. Welter argued the need for an alternative hypothesis, specifying the political option, the struggle for party advantage.

The causal process in 1898, it should be noted, was exceptional, perhaps unique in all of world history. A minority within the Congress, later to become a majority, was threatening use of its war-making powers, essentially forcing the issue on a reluctant executive. The evidence reviewed in chapter 7 suggests that congressional leaders were acting without serious evidence of their constituents' opinions. Some of them, clearly, were acting independently, or even in defiance, of the opinions of their constituents.

* * *

The fourth of the announced tasks is to consider the theoretical implications. The basic question: Which theory or theories would be most useful for analysis of the events reviewed here?

The accounts of American history in the late nineteenth century have been "framed" in an unusual manner. The leading history texts tell of urbanization, industrialization, and the growth of "big business." Those processes reach a culmination point, presumably in the 1896 election, which is portrayed as a monumental contest between "farmers and workers" on the one hand and "big business" on the other. On the one side were the forces of progress, led by William Jennings Bryan, now in control of the Democratic Party. Pitted against them were the Republicans, the forces of reaction led by William McKinley but actually "managed" by Mark Hanna who was "serving the interests of" big business. The result, as depicted in this oft-recited tale, was that Hanna's machinations brought victory for "the interests" and defeat for the "the people." It is a theory of class dominance, one that "works" equally well in both the progressive and the Marxist readings.

Less than two years later, however, those same masses are said to have been "aroused" by some other "forces," ones that achieved another remarkable "success." Led by "the press," those other agents forced McKinley and his associates—including the manifestly unenthusiastic big businessmen—to make war on Spain. For this purpose another theoretical framework is invoked. The class-dominance position is dropped and, in its place, those same commentators provide an analysis based on the mass society theory.

The explanation for the choice of war centers on the two "press lords" who were engaged in a "sensational," or perhaps better, a demagogic campaign, intended to enhance circulation. Other newspapers disseminated that "scandalous" material, passing it on to readers throughout the country. The choice of war in 1898 is portrayed as a tale of clamoring masses compelling a response from the Congress and forcing a decision for intervention from the reluctant president.

That theoretical disjuncture, the sudden "paradigm shift," needs some justification. But that is rarely the case. Instead, one narrative follows the other without any comment or justification. Robert L. Beisner, for example, opens a discussion of public opinion with an appropriate statement of uncertainty—"Although hard to measure . . ." But the sentence then continues with a declaration of complete certainty—"public opinion was a factor of fundamental domestic importance." In the period from 1865 to 1900, he writes: "Popular sentiment unquestionably played roles . . . pushing the United States and Spain to the precipice of war in the 1870s, and toppling them over the brink in 1898." Another declaration touches on the question of causation: "Then, as now, officials could create 'public opinion' from scratch or massage it into desired shape."[12]

But if that were actually the case, why did McKinley not undertake the task? Or, perhaps appropriately, why did Hanna, all-powerful Warwick, not intervene to halt the "clamor" that became such a problem in 1898? Mark Hanna makes only a fugitive appearance in the accounts of 1898 events. His opposition to a war is sometimes indicated. But nothing is said about his sudden insignificance and evident helplessness.

* * *

The prevailing mode of analysis present in the received literature to explain the 1896 election outcome is best described as a class-dominance theory. The election outcome was a victory for "big business," for the leading capitalists, the proprietors of the major industries, railroads, and banks. Those men are said to share basic interests. They are also portrayed as acting together with high intelligence and efficiency to achieve their purposes.

The alternative argued here borrows from and modifies two other theoretical positions, elitism and pluralism. The elitist position holds that modern societies have developed specialized organizations, called bureaucracies, to perform the tasks necessary or desired for survival and well-being. Among these would be the tasks of governance, those of the economy, of education, of religion, of policing and defense, and, in recent times, the provision of information and entertainment. Those tasks are usually undertaken by bureaucratic organizations created and led by trained and experienced specialists. Those specialized leadership groups are referred to as elites.[13]

Most discussions of bureaucracies and their leaders focus on an "end-state," on what Max Weber referred to as the "fully-developed" form. But that suggestion of a static end-state is misleading since at all times we are dealing with continuous, ongoing processes. One giant business firm, the United States Steel Company, was created by J. P. Morgan on 1 April 1901, an amalgamation of all major producers, the most important being Carnegie Steel. But then, as opposed to the assumption of continued linear development, ever bigger, ever more powerful, within a decade the firm faced serious competition with the opening of Bethlehem Steel, which specialized in sheet steel, a product required for an important new market, automobiles. Another problem for the class-dominance argument needs explanation. Two Republican presidents, Roosevelt and Taft, instituted antitrust suits against giant capitalist enterprises, among others Rockefeller's Standard Oil and two J. P. Morgan creations, United States Steel and an important railroad trust, Northern Securities.

Governments, national, state, and local, were slowly and reluctantly bureaucratizing. Civil service reforms, the requirements of training, examination, and guarantees of tenure, came haltingly, much of this in the face of opposition from the political parties. In this respect, the United States was laggard in the development of its civil service, coming decades after similar achievements in France, Germany, and even Britain.

McKinley did seek capable appointees (with some notable exceptions) but his assessment of their abilities depended on casual acquaintance and impressions rather than on years of professional training and subsequent examinations. In making those choices, McKinley's primary concern, as seen, was political, the needs and obligations of party, not those of big business. One consequence, at this early stage of bureaucratization, was frequent instances of amateurism as with those diplomats lacking diplomatic experience and having no knowledge of the necessary languages. One further consequence was movement from one bureaucracy to another, for example, from business to government (and back again), this being relatively easy and frequent. That does not necessarily mean those businessmen were "serving capitalist interests" while in the government. Again, research is necessary to establish any such claims.

The key feature of the elitist theory is the notion of multiple, diverse leadership groups, each with some degree of autonomy. Those specialized elites would have separate and distinctive training and careers. And the everyday routines of each would also, ordinarily, be separate and very different from those of other leadership groups. Business elites spend long hours attending to the affairs of a given firm. Government elites spend long hours with the affairs of a foreign ministry, or a finance ministry, or a welfare agency. Military leaders, both army and navy, would also have separate training, separate careers, and very different everyday tasks. Members of legislatures would deal with still other tasks, with the writing of new (or corrected) legislation. Many of them would have received their early training in law schools and subsequently would have worked in law offices.

One implication of this division of tasks and specialized training is that the various elites would have some degree of independence, some basis for autonomy in the conduct of their affairs. And the needs of a given agency would ordinarily be given precedence over the needs of other elites. The leaders of army, navy, and coast guard might each wish more money for men and equipment; business leaders might wish lower taxes; the president (and his cabinet) would have to judge the priorities and undertake some initiatives; the Congress, particularly the House (and more specifically, its Ways and Means Committee), would have to adjudicate the demands and then make a first authorization of the expenditures.

Degrees of independence or autonomy would pose a challenge to the principal assumption of the class-dominance position, to that assumption of hierarchy with "business" having "the power" in any contention. As opposed to a near-automatic assumption of collusion, for instance "business pulling strings," one should, at the outset, recognize the possibility of independence or autonomy and also, the possibility that other elites might be powerful and in some struggles might even win.[14]

Another possibility should be noted. As opposed to the "dialectical" imagery, that of opposing "forces" each aiming for a decisive "win," the possibility of compromise adjustments should be considered. Polarized conflicts are costly and can have long-lasting detrimental effects. Recognizing those facts, elites might be disposed to accept compromise solutions. It is not "in the cards" that one set of leaders will direct or control the activities of the others. A mutual agreement, an elite settlement, is both possible and likely.

Ruling elites are usually portrayed as very knowledgeable, as highly rational decision-makers. But that assumption, too, should be viewed as hypothesis rather than as established fact. Executives who spend long hours managing the affairs of a Wall Street bank would not ordinarily know the needs of a Pittsburgh-based steel company, or the internal "dynamics" of the United States Senate, or anything at all about the "opportunities" provided in Latin American markets. As opposed to an initial assumption of "perfect knowledge," the assumption of imperfect (or bounded) knowledge—or even ignorance—would be more appropriate. If ignorant, of course, they have the "resources" needed to allow them to remedy any obvious deficiencies. But that assumption, too, is problematic: Could they, without fail, find the appropriate experts? Which of seven contending experts "really" knows the subject in question?

Formulations of the elitist theory typically have little to say about "the masses." The underlying assumption is that the thoughts and actions of those millions count for little or nothing in the determination of public affairs. The masses, presumably, have no independence, no autonomy. One way or another, their attitudes are determined by cunning demagogues, either by those arising "out of the ranks" as with Bryan, or those from among the privileged, as with Pulitzer and Hearst. But here, too, the exclusive, all-or-nothing formulations seem inappropriate.

The pluralist theory contains some insights that, with appropriate modification, prove useful for analysis of the United States' choice of war in support of Cuban initiatives. Early in the development of the American democracy, Alexis de Tocqueville recognized and wrote of the importance of associations.[15] Individuals, he wrote, would ordinarily be powerless, unable to influence government decisions in any way. But individuals sharing a common concern could come together and form associations that would be able to exert influence and affect policy. Tocqueville and his many successors focused on sentiments issuing from the "grassroots," from the American citizenry. But the experience reviewed here signals the need for a modification: Open democratic societies also allow others, persons from outside the nation, to participate in the "struggle for power." The Fenians, Kossuth, and Garibaldi, as seen, campaigned in the United States in support of, respectively, Irish, Hungarian, and Italian liberation movements.

The Cuban Junta was more successful than its predecessors, in part due to geographic proximity, the homeland being only ninety miles from Key West. Previous experience was another factor—the Cubans had done it before. The Cuban insurgents had sought American support during the Ten Years War, 1868–1878. Profiting from that experience, having learned many useful lessons, they could now proceed to the task with even greater skill.

Tocqueville pointed also to the role of newspapers in the "aggregation" process. They perform an important mediating function. Newspapers in the late 1890s told readers of the Cubans' grievances and also of the associations present in the local communities working for solutions. Unfortunately, the evidence on Junta activities is thin, much of it anecdotal. We have no detailed study of its operations. Most importantly, we have little information on how they managed with such success to secure the support of local elites in so many American cities. Archival records in many of those communities would allow research on this topic, even at this late date.

* * *

Three subject matters have been reviewed here, the 1896 election, the subsequent staffing of the executive branch, and the 1898 choice of war. Some of the received explanations have been reviewed and criticized and some better alternatives suggested. In all three instances, we have been exploring the causal connections, looking for the factor or factors that brought about the indicated results.

A causal statement is a sentence asserting influence or impact, one linking some factor (or factors) to a subsequent effect. By themselves such statements are no more than declarations. If nothing else is provided, such declarations should be recognized as hypotheses. More precisely, they should be recognized as unsupported hypotheses. Unfortunately, many authors treat such statements as if they were fully and convincingly supported.

The problem, one seen repeatedly in these pages, might be termed Truth by Declaration. Declared truths are expressed, typically, in florid prose as seen in the writing of the Beards and William Allen White.[16] One recent publication making use of this procedure provides many more such sweeping categorical formulations, colorful metaphors, and vaguely specified causes, including "ominous forces," a "national mood," and a "climate of fear." There are also unquestioned judgments of weight or importance—"provided a powerful impulse" and "a principal impetus . . ."[17]

The obvious alternative to the declared truth would be the researched truth. That would also begin with a declaration, an hypothesis, but would recognize its tentative character and the requirement for a follow-up procedure, for investigation to discover whether the claim is valid. That research, normally, would also inquire about alternative hypotheses, about other factors that might bring about or contribute to the result in question. That research might also investigate questions of weight or impact, a given factor possibly having no influence, a minor, middling, or significant impact in determination of the result.

As noted in the Prologue, wars have three very diverse components or episodes: origins, conduct, and outcomes. Political elites typically dominate in the first and last episodes. Military elites, understandably, dominate in the conduct. Other elites may "play some role" in all three activities, but their efforts typically would be of less importance, more likely to be advisory. The class-dominance framework reviewed here figures prominently again in accounts of the outcome of the Spanish-American War. In that process, the United States gained a "new empire," a settlement said to "reflect" the wishes of "big business." That topic will be the subject of the subsequent volume.[18]

Notes

1. Alfred North Whitehead, *The Aims of Education* (New York, 1957), p. 11.
2. See T. C. Chamberlin's article on multiple working hypotheses, cited in ch. 1, note 78.
3. Alfred McClung Lee, *The Daily Newspaper in America: The Evolution of a Social Instrument* (New York, 1937), ch. 4 and pp. 715–717.
4. Nash et al., pp. 640–641. For more examples and comment, see Louis A. Pérez, Jr., *The War of 1898* (Chapel Hill, 1998), pp. 64–80.
5. Chalmers Johnson, *The Sorrows of Empire: Militarism, Secrecy, and the End of the Republic* (New York, 2004), p. 40. Another easy declaration appears on the previous page—". . . the press was manipulated to whip up a popular war fever . . ."
6. H. Wayne Morgan, *William McKinley and His America*, revised edition (Kent, OH, 2003), p. 252.
7. Department of the Interior, United States Census Office, *Twelfth Census of the United States, 1900* (Washington, D.C. 1902), Volume II, Population, Part II, pp. xvii–xix, xxxvi–xxxviii, l–li.
8. Richard Hofstadter, *The Paranoid Style in American Politics* (Chicago, 1979 [1965]), p. 146. This is from a chapter entitled "Cuba, the Philippines, and Manifest Destiny."
9. The problems involved in ascertaining attitudes in 1898 may be better appreciated when compared with the attempts made in later decades when surveys, many of them, had become available. For a modest contribution, see Richard F. Hamilton, "A Research Note on the Mass Support for 'Tough" Military Initiatives," *American Sociological Review*, 33 (1968):439–445. For a compendious study, see John E. Mueller, *Wars, Presidents, and Public Opinion* (New York, 1973). And for a compendious analysis of a later struggle, see Stanley A. Renshon, ed., *The Political Psychology of the Gulf War* (Pittsburgh, 1993). For a general empirically based exploration of public concerns, see Richard F. Hamilton and James D. Wright, *The State of the Masses* (New York, 1986). On the central importance of marriage and family, see ch. 3.
10. For discussion and evidence, see Richard F. Hamilton, *Mass Society, Pluralism, and Bureaucracy* (Westport, CT, 2001), pp. 77–80.
11. Mark Matthew Welter, "Minnesota Newspapers and the Cuban Crisis, 1895–1898: Minnesota as a Test Case for the 'Yellow Journalism' Theory" (unpublished Ph.D. thesis, University of Minnesota, 1970), p. 231.

12. Robert L. Beisner, *From the Old Diplomacy to the New, 1865–1900*, second edition (Arlington Heights, IL, 1986), p. 5. Beisner reviews several other factors in the pages that follow, one of these being party politics—"one party always stood ready to harass and embarrass the other over foreign policy issues" (p. 6).

13. For an introduction, see G. Lowell Field and John Higley, *Elitism* (London, 1980). This theory assumes bureaucracy to be the dominant organizational form in modern societies. For an important and influential early statement, see Max Weber, "Bureaucracy," ch. 8 of H. H. Gerth and C. Wright Mills, eds., *From Max Weber: Essays in Sociology* (London, 1948). For criticism and relevant evidence, see also, Hamilton, *Mass Society, Pluralism, and Bureaucracy*, ch. 3.

14. Business leaders in Austria-Hungary, Germany, and Great Britain opposed the choice of war in July and August of 1914. In all three cases, their views were disregarded by the more powerful political elites. On this, see Richard F. Hamilton and Holger H. Herwig, eds., *The Origins of World War I* (New York, 2003), pp. 483–501. Those cases, it will be noted, are a precise match to the American experience in 1898.

15. Alexis de Tocqueville, *Democracy in America* (New York, 1963 [Reeve translation, 1840]), Vol. 2, Second Book, ch. 5, entitled "Of the Use Which the Americans Make of Public Associations in Civil Life." Tocqueville's chapter 6 discusses the role of newspapers in aiding the formation of those associations.

   Most discussions of pluralism and the role of associations begin with Tocqueville. Pressure group activity in Great Britain some years earlier brought two major legislative achievements, first, the ending of the slave trade, then the ending of slavery itself within the British Empire. In both instances well-organized humanitarian groups defeated some of Britain's most "powerful" economic elites. For this, see Adam Hochschild, *Bury the Chains: Prophets and Rebels in the Fight to Free an Empire's Slaves* (Boston, 2005).

16. Beards, quoted in the first pages of chapter 1; White, in the first pages of chapter 5.

17. Thomas R. Hietala, *Manifest Design: American Exceptionalism and Empire*, revised edition (Ithaca, 2003), pp. 7, 9, 10, 51, 54, and 55.

18. Richard F. Hamilton, *President McKinley and America's "New Empire"*, forthcoming.

Index

Adams, Charles Francis, Jr., 125, 131
Adams, Henry, 115
Adams, Robert, Jr., 108–109, 214–215
Aldrich, Nelson, 15, 57, 106, 116, 223–225
Alger, Russell A., 87–88, 96, 97, 120, 124, 127
Allen, William Vincent, 214
Allison, William B., 84, 90, 92, 116, 225–226
Ambassadors (or Ministers), 91–92
Anti-Semitism, 14
Armour, Philip, 53
Astor, John Jacob, 9–10
Astor, John Jacob IV, 127–128
Atkins, Edwin F., 105–107, 125, 130–132

Bailey, Joseph Weldon, 230–231
Bartholdt, Richard, 233–234
Beard, Charles A., and Mary R., 1–4, 61, 246, 252
Beer, William C., 127–128, 129, 133, 227
Belmont, August, 14, 61
Benjamin, Jules, 134
Bennett, James Gordon, Jr., 130
Big business, problematic usage, 12, 97–98. *See also*, Elites, business
Bliss, Cornelius, 62, 90, 96
Boer War, 6
Bourgeoisie. *See* Elites, business
Brisbane, Arthur, 151
Bryan, William J., 2, 59–62, 64–65, 69–70, 111, 126, 200, 202–203, 204, 225
Burch, Philip H., Jr., 12–13, 97

Burrows, Julius Caesar, 87, 198
Bushnell, Asa, 85, 94–95, 173, 175, 177
    opposition to Hanna, 85
    Business leaders. *See* Elites, business

Cabinet, 19–20, 84–98
    Agriculture, 90
    Interior, 89
    Postmaster General, 89
    Navy, 88–89
    State, 84–86
    Treasury, 86
    War, 87–88
    See also McKinley
Call, Wilkerson, 214
Cameron, Don, 108, 114, 115, 232–233
Cameron, Elizabeth, 115
Cameron resolution, December 1896, 116, 125, 156, 219
Canada, 218–219, 221
Carnegie, Andrew, 11, 63, 67, 111, 120, 121, 123
Categorical usages, 240
Chandler, William E., 89, 113, 114, 214, 218
China, 91–92
China market, the, 26
Civil service, 18
"Clamor," re Cuba. *See* Public pressures
Class dominance theory, 67, 247–248
Cleveland (city), 95, 96
Cleveland, Grover, xii, 16, 17, 51, 107, 108, 116
Clichés, 4–5, 14, 29, 52–53, 94, 96, 97–98, 109–110, 163, 242, 250
Cline, John, 90
Collum, Shelby, 86, 221–222

255

Columbus, ch. 6, *passim*
  colleges, universities, 188, 192,
    195–196, 203, 206
  Columbus Auditorium meeting,
    196–197
  Cuban League, 173, 178, 196, 199,
    207
  Great Southern Theatre meeting,
    183, 184–185, 189, 191, 192
  History, population, 171
  Maine monument committee, 192
  newspapers, 171–172; for contents,
    entire chapter
  sendoff parade, Seventeenth
    Regiment, 187–188, 205
  sermons, 183–184, 188, 194–195,
    199, 203, 207–208
Conger, Edwin H., 92, 96
Congress, xiii, 116, 207, 244–245, and
    ch. 7, *passim*
  petitions re Cuba, 157–158, 163,
    202
  See also Senate
Conkling, Roscoe, 15–16, 24
Coolidge, Thomas Jefferson, 86
Corporations, large, 12–13
Cortelyou, George M., 110
Crimean War, 6
Cuba, 68–69, 105–136, 164
  autonomy plan, 117
  insurgency, 105, 179
  policy options, 111
  U.S. exports to, 134–135
  See also Spanish-American War
Cuban Junta (Cuban Revolution Party),
    112, 115, 154, 156, 199, 217,
    219, 224, 231, 245, 251
Cuban League, 112, 128, 154,
    161–162, 173, 177, 245
Cummings, Amos, 225

Dana, Charles A., 114, 151. *See also*
    New York *Sun*
Davis, Charles H., 114
Davis, Cushman K., 113, 116, 127,
    160, 217
Dawes, Charles G., 48, 63, 68, 86–87,
Day, William R., 46, 53, 85–86, 130
Decision-making, xi–xii

Declared truths, 252
DeLome. *See* Dupuy de Lôme
Democratic Party, 21–23, 68–69
Deshler, John G., 194
Dewey, George, 114
Dick, Charles, 48
Dingley, Nelson, Jr., 86
Dodge, Grenville, 124–125, 225
Du Pont, Alfred, 124
Dupuy de Lôme, 108, 117, 180

Edison, Thomas, 12
Elections: 1876–1896, 23–24; 1884,
    24; 1894, 108; 1896, 7, 24,
    60–68
Elites, diverse roles, 9–21
  business, xiii, 4, 7–8, 12–14, 96
  opposition to war, 119–135, 192,
    200, 220, 228, 245–246
  political, 14–20, 96, 227
Elitism (theory), 27, 29, 67, 96,
    249–251
Elkins, Stephen, 116
Experts, expertise. *See* Technocratic
    assumption

Fairbanks, Charles W., 162
Fenians, 6
First National Bank of New York, 13
Fish, Stuyvesant, 127, 128
Fisk, Jim, 10, 12, 14
Flagler, Henry M., 11, 123
Foraker, Joseph B., 51, 55, 87, 94, 94,
    113–114, 117, 135, 191, 214,
    222–223, 229
Franco-Prussian War, 6
Frick, Henry Clay, 11, 53, 92, 123
Frye, William P., 113–114, 223

Gage, Lyman J., 86–87, 96, 149–150
Galbraeth, Charles B., 173
Gallinger, Jacob H., 214, 225
Gardner, A. P., 125
Garibaldi, Giuseppe, 6
Gary, James A., 89, 94
Gates, John, 127, 128
Genêt, Edmund Charles, 6
Gladden, Washington, 174, 199, 203
Godkin, Edwin L., 17

Gold, issue, 59
Gomez, Maximo, 105
Gompers, Samuel, 66
Gould, Jay, 10, 12
Grant, Ulysses S., 15, 16, 20
Greece, 5
Greeley, Horace, 16

Hale, Eugene, 92
Hanna, Marcus A., 1–2, 8, 15, 20, 24,
        27, 46–47, 50–51, 53, 54, 56–57,
        58, 68, 86, 88, 89, 94–95, 113,
        120, 127, 175, 214, 226–227, 239
    contest for Senate, 94–95
    and election, 1896, 62–64
    meeting with J. P. Morgan, 57
    relationship with McKinley. *See*
        McKinley
Harriman, Edward H., 10, 12, 13, 14,
        120, 122, 128
Havana riots, 117, 175, 176
Havemeyer, Henry O., 122, 130
Hawaii, 68, 110, 115
Hay, John, 18, 49, 53, 83, 88, 91, 115,
        239
Hearst, William Randolph, 14, 18, 113,
        152, 165, 213. *See also* New
        York *Journal*
Henderson, David B., 57, 225–226
Heraclitus, 30
Herrick, Myron, 47–48, 53, 54, 68, 88,
        89–90
    meeting with J. P. Morgan, 56–57
Hicks, John D., 3
Higginson, Henry Lee, 125, 126, 131,
        221
Hill, James J., 10, 14, 62, 63, 67, 120,
        121
Hitchcock, Ethan Allen, 91, 96
Hitt, Robert R., 215
Hoar, George Frisbie, 86, 227–228, 232
Hobart, Garret A., 58, 118
Hofstadter, Richard, 1, 243
Huntington, Collis P., 10

Income, politicians' sacrifice of, 46, 86
Inflation, 60–61
Influence, failed attempts, 89, 92–94
Intellectuals, 6, 29

Johnson, Tom L. 95
Jones, DeWitt, 178
Jones, James K., 64

Kennedy, Joseph, 14
Kilbourne, James, 173
King, Clarence, 114
Knox, Philander, 53, 92–93
Kohlsaat, Herman Henry, 49, 53, 83,
        86, 96, 118, 156, 189–190
Kossuth, Louis, 6, 190

LaFeber, Walter, 129, 131–133, 136
LaFollette, Robert, 89
Lee, Fitzhugh, 91, 178, 194
Leninism, 26
Lentz, John J., 203, 204, 208
Lodge, Henry Cabot, 15, 86, 88, 92,
        113–114, 118, 125–127, 131,
        132, 219–221, 232
Long, John Davis, 86, 88–89, 178
Longworth, Nicholas, 10, 50

Mahan, Alfred, 114
Maine, battleship, 117, 178, 180–184,
        186–187, 188–189, 190–191,
        193, 194, 200, 201, 218,
        222–223, 226, 229
Manley, Joseph H., 57
Marx, Karl, 4
Marxism, 26, 67
Masses, the. *See* Public
Mass society theory, 26–27, 248–249
Mayer, Louis B., 14
McCook, John J., 90
McKenna, Joseph, 89
McKinley, Abner, 48
McKinley, William, xii, xiv, 2–3, 8,
        43–81, 95–96, 124, 130, 162,
        187, 201, 221
    "bosses," and, 57
    Cabinet selection, 83–98
    colleagues (coterie), 46–50
    Cuba, and, 110, 116, 119
    éclair image, and later critiques,
        135, 203
    election, 1896, 58–67
    message to Congress, 11 April
        1898, 117, 205

McKinley, William (*continued*)
  political career, 44–46
  relationship with Hanna, 52–53,
    67–68, 83, 172, 239
  Walker episode, 53–54
  youth and early career, 43–44
  See also Spanish-American War
McKissen, Robert E., 95
Medill, Joseph, 85, 226
Metropolitan Club group, 114–115
Mines, naval, 181, 193, 197–198, 200, 202
Ministers (or Ambassadors), 91–92
Missouri, 233–234
Money, Hernando, 225
Monroe Doctrine, 68, 132
Morgan, John Pierpont, 12, 14, 56–57, 59, 61, 67, 121–122, 127, 128
J. P. Morgan & Co., 13, 14, 122
Morgan, John Tyler, 108, 113–114, 116, 216–217
Morison, Samuel Eliot, 3
Morse, John T., 125
Murphy, Edward, Jr., 213

Nation, The, 17
National City Bank of New York, 13, 122–123, 128
New York Herald, 18, 113, 151
New York Journal, 18, 108, 113, 115, 150, 151–152, 165, 241
  sends senators to Cuba, 224–225
New York Sun, 18, 87, 113, 114, 151
New York Tribune, 16, 17, 49, 130, 229
New York World, 18, 113, 115, 150, 151–152, 165, 241
Newspapers
  audiences of, 242
  and Cuba, 18, 69, 112–113
  "exchanges," 152
  Maine and, 160–161
  number of dailies, circulation, 151–152, 241, 247, 252
  role of, xii, 153, 242
Newspapers: cities
  Chicago, 155–156
  Columbus, ch. 6, *passim*
  Florida, 156–157
  Kansas, 158–159

  Indiana, 161–162
  Minnesota, 159–160
  Missouri, 233–234
  New Jersey, 160
  North Carolina, 157–157
  South Dakota, 161
Nicaragua, 68, 115
Northern Securities Company, 93

Olney, Richard, 108, 116
Osborne, Will, 48, 85
Otis, Harrison Gray, 89

Panic, 1893, 108
Parties, political, 21–22. *See also*
  Democratic Party; Elections;
  Political issues; Populists;
  Realignment, of parties;
  Republican Party; and "Silver Republicans"
Partisanship. *See* Spanish-American War
Payne, Henry B., 18, 56, 89, 94
Payne, Oliver H., 56
Penrose, Boies, 91
Perkins, George Walbridge, 127
Philippines, 110, 223
Platt, Orville, 116, 228–229
Platt, Thomas, 15, 57, 87, 88–89, 116, 213–214
Pluralism, 28–29, 251–252
Political leaders. *See* Elites, political
Political issues, 22, 59–62
Populists (People's Party), 59–60, 69
Porter, Addison, 48–49
Porter, Horace, 91
Power. *See* Who rules?
Pratt, Julius W.
  thesis of, 119–133, 246
  late conversion claim, 132–133
Press, the. *See* Newspapers
Pritchett, Henry S., 119
Proctor, Redfield, 117, 124, 127–128, 198–199
"Progressive" tradition, 1–4
Public, the, xii–xiii, 5–6, 8, 150–151, 207
Public pressures, re Cuba, 109–110, 149–166, 209, 213, 230, 231–234
  implausibility of argument, 242–244

Puerto Rico, 110
Pulitzer, Joseph, 18, 113, 152, 213. *See also* New York *World*
Pullman, George, 53, 122

Quantification, need for, 240
Quay, Matthew, 15, 50, 57, 87

Railroads, 10–11
Real estate, 9–10, 11
Realignment, of parties, 1894–1896, 24–26, 66–67
Reed, Thomas B., 56, 58, 89, 116, 204–205
Reick, William C., 130
Reid, Whitelaw, 17, 59, 83, 93, 114
Religious groups, influences, 113, 174, 191, 227
Republican Party, 21–23, 58, 68–69, 115
Rockefeller, John D., 11, 14, 54–56, 67, 121, 123
Rockefeller, William, 62, 122, 127, 128
Rockhill, William W., 91–92
Rogers, H. H., 122
Roosevelt, Theodore, 17, 86, 93, 114
Root, Elihu, 96, 97
Ryan, Thomas Fortune, 127, 128

Sage, Russell, 133
Schiff, Jacob, 13, 14, 120, 122
Seitz, Don C., 150
Senate, U.S., 135, 244–245, and ch. 7, *passim*
    Foreign Relations Committee, 114, 220
Sewall, Arthur M., 59
Shaw, Albert, 114
Sherman, John, 50, 61, 85, 108, 129, 178, 219, 223
Sigsbee, Charles D., 182, 184
Silver issue, 60, 134
"Silver Republicans," 114
Smith, Charles E., 96
Smith, Joseph P., 48
Smith, William Alden, 225
Spain, 69, 105, 117
Spanish-American War
    antecedent factors, 117
    Beards' account, 1–2

causes of, 7, 8, 27, 246
Cannon Resolution, $50 million appropriation, 194, 195
exceptional character of, 247
newspapers, role of, chs. 5 and 6, *passim*
partisanship and, 108, 116, 117–118, 152, 154, 163, 171–172, 219, 221, 222, 224, 226, 231, 232–234, 241–242
pro-war advocates, 112
settlement of, 7, 111
war declared, 117
Spooner, John, 116, 230
Standard Oil Company, 13, 54–56, 123
Stanford, Leland, 10
Stewart, Alexander T., 11
Stillman, James, 13, 122
Storer, Bellamy and Maria, 49, 88, 89, 93–94
Straight, Michael, Willard D., and Dorothy, 97
Sweezy, Paul M., 98
Sugar, 107, 130–131

Taft, Charles P., 50, 53
Taft, William Howard, 89
Tariff
    McKinley, 51, 58, 61, 106
    Wilson-Gorman, 51, 58, 61, 106
Taylor, Hannis, 91
Technocratic assumption, 20–21, 96–97. *See also* Elitism
Teller, Henry, 114, 218–219
Teller amendment, 107, 110, 118, 135, 218–219
Textbook accounts, 164–165
Theories. *See* Class dominance, Elitism, Marxism, Mass society, and/or Pluralism
Thurston, John, 224–225
Torpedoes. *See* Mines, naval
Tower, Charlemagne, 91
Turpie, David, 117, 135, 162

United States
    early development, 10–11
    exports, export expansion, 134–135
Upper class, radicalism in, 97–98

Vanderbilt, Cornelius, 10
Vanderbilt, William H., 10, 12
Vest, George, 154, 214, 233
Villard, Henry, 10
Virginia, first families of, 9
Virgin Islands, 110

Walker, Robert L., 53–54, 93
Wall Street, 96, 227. *See also* Elites,
    business
Wall Street Journal, 128
Wanamaker, John, 11, 120
War, causes of, xi, 5–6
War powers
    in authoritarian regimes, xi
    in U.S. Constitution, xi–xii

Warwick, 1, 95, 248
Watson, Thomas, 59
Weld, S. M., 125
White, Andrew D., 91
White, William Allen, 83, 149, 164,
    252
Whitehead, Alfred North, 240
Whitney, William C., 17, 20, 128
Who rules?, 3–5
Williams, William Appleman, 129, 133
Wilson, James, 90, 92
Woodford, Stewart L., 91, 130

"Yellow press." *See* Newspapers,
    Hearst, and Pulitzer
Young, John Russell, 130